The Souls of Purgatory

SERIES ADVISORY EDITOR:
Lyman L. Johnson,University of North Carolina at Charlotte

Figure 1. Seventeenth-century portrait of Ursula de Jesús
by José de la Cruz. Photo by Daniel Giannoni.

The Souls
of Purgatory

THE SPIRITUAL DIARY
OF A SEVENTEENTH-CENTURY
AFRO-PERUVIAN MYSTIC,
URSULA DE JESÚS

URSULA DE JESÚS

*Translated, edited, and with
an introduction by*
NANCY E. VAN DEUSEN

University of New Mexico Press
Albuquerque

For Preston

© 2004 by Nancy E. van Deusen
All rights reserved. Published 2004
Printed and Bound in the United States of America

08 07 06 05 04   1 2 3 4 5

LIBRARY OF CONGRESS CATALOGING-IN-PUBLICATION DATA

Jesús, Ursula de, 1604–1666.
[Diary. English & Spanish. Selections]
The souls of purgatory : the spiritual diary of a seventeenth-century
Afro-Peruvian mystic, Ursula de Jesús / translated, edited, and
with an introduction by Nancy E. van Deusen.— 1st ed.
p. cm. — (Diálogos)
Includes bibliographical references and index.
ISBN 0-8263-2827-X (cloth : alk. paper) — ISBN 0-8263-2828-8 (pbk. : alk. paper)
1. Jesús, Ursula de, 1604-1666—Diaries. 2. Women mystics—Peru—Diaries.
3. Women, Black—Peru—Diaries. 4. Purgatory.
I. Van Deusen, Nancy E. II. Title. III. Diálogos (Albuquerque, N.M.)
BX4705.J47A3 2004
271'.97302—dc22
2004011779

The complete transcription of the Spanish text for
Ursula de Jesús's diary is available on-line at:

http://www.unmpress.com/Book.php?id=6588

DESIGN AND COMPOSITION: Mina Yamashita

Contents

ILLUSTRATIONS

Acknowledgments

Some years ago I stumbled on a biographical account of Ursula de Jesús while reading documents at the Franciscan archive in Lima. It was one of those archival epiphanies when something inside clicked, and I instantly became fascinated with this amazingly profound woman. I resolved then and there to translate the complete biographical account and write a scholarly introduction to the text.

However, as serendipity would have it, my life took another course. I have Ana María Vega to thank for leading me to the original diary, housed in the Convent of Santa Clara. The abbess, Sor Isabel Hernández, graciously allowed me to access the convent's private collection and to transcribe the original diary. I am forever grateful to her for this exceedingly rare privilege. I also wish to extend my thanks to the vicaress María Lourdes Rojas F., to the wonderfully spirited Camila de Santa Clara, and to the rest of the community of Santa Clara: all very special women who have devoted their lives to God. I have learned more from them than they will ever realize.

Several grants and awards enabled me to follow through on the various stages of conducting research and writing the book that now lies open before you. They include a nine-month grant from the American Council of Learned Societies (1999–2000), a Franklin Research Award from the American Philosophical Society (2000), a sabbatical leave from Western Washington University (2001–02), and a Summer Research Grant from the Bureau for Faculty Research (2001).

Translating this seemingly indecipherable text has been a labor of love. Although I accept full responsibility for the translation and transcription, the work would not be what it is without the assistance of two individuals. First, I would like to thank Javier Flores Espinoza for his advice and critique of my translation and for the many hours we spent seated, the four-volume *Diccionario de autoridades* close at hand, and totally engrossed in deep discussions about the nature of the text, purgatory, and the seventeenth century. In addition, the meticulous and knowledgeable editorial suggestions offered by Meredith Dodge (whom I have never had the pleasure to meet, but feel I know) helped enormously.

Colleagues from around the globe have been fascinated with this project since its inception. In particular, I thank Ken Andrien and Karen Powers for their continual encouragement. At Western Washington University I thank the previous chair of the History Department, George Mariz, for his support and for answering numerous questions about Catholic theology. I especially thank Alan Gallay for taking the time to critique the translation and introductory text. For references, comments, and conversations, I thank Jodi Bilinkoff, William Christian, Allan Greer, Kathleen Myers, and Ramón Mujica. At the University of New Mexico Press, I would like to thank David Holtby, Alex Giardino, and, in particular, Lyman Johnson for his careful reading of the manuscript and his faith in this project. At Western Washington University, I appreciate the editorial assistance offered by Heidi Small, Sarah Nelson, Megan Riddle, Corrine Winter, and Josh Hayes. In Peru, I especially thank Ilana Aragón Noriega for her archival forays and for reviewing the transcription. I thank Daniel Giannoni and Ana María Vega for their photographic expertise.

For years now, friends and family have been listening to my "Ursula" stories. In Bellingham, I would like to thank Cecilia Danysk, Dawne Y. Curry, Kathleen Kennedy, and the members of Dance Gallery, my second family. In Columbus, I thank my poet friend John Bennett for his creative spirit. In Lima, I would like to extend a very special thanks to Margarita Suárez and Rafael Varón for their gracious hospitality year after year, and for our many and varied conversations. I thank my much-loved parents, Nancy G. and Edwin H. van Deusen for reading parts of the book and for the special relationship we have. Finally, I would like to thank the sparkle in my eye, Preston L. Schiller, for being there from sunrise to moonlight. It is to you, Preston, that I dedicate this labor of love.

PART I

The World of Ursula de Jesús

Ursula's Life Story: Portraits and Portrayals

Until now, the life of the religious servant (*donada*) Ursula de Jesús (1604–66) has remained one of the best-kept secrets of colonial history. She could easily have remained in relative obscurity like the hundreds of women of color who lived devout Christian lives while serving as laborers or donadas in convents. Fortunately, a number of visual and written texts have recently emerged, and each furnishes distinct representations of a fascinating and unique early modern subject. One of her portraits (see Figure 1), which hangs in the vestibule of the Convent of Santa Clara in Lima (of the Order of the Poor Clares) shows a serious, thoughtful woman. Why did the artist depict her in this way? What story do the objects surrounding Ursula tell about her life? Three small crosses in the window allude to one of her many visions; they suggest mystic abilities. Numerous books, including the lives of Saints Francis, Clare, and Teresa of Avila (1515–82), denote literacy and Ursula's place within the Franciscan Order. The second painting, a posterior copy of the original (see Figure 2), distinguishes her features more clearly: the lovely, peaceful countenance, the clear, inwardly seeing eyes. Her left hand clutches a cane, a sign of advanced age, and her rosary, worn from constant fingering. A shoulder-length, pristine wimple—the length required for donadas—conceals and protects her throat and head. She is cloaked in a chestnut brown religious habit, the color worn by penitent Franciscans. In her other, right hand, Ursula holds a large cross, signifying her devotion to the Passion of Christ. A tome entitled *The Lives of the Saints* forms the backdrop, another essential component of Ursula's life. We see the window of her cell: the same three crosses.

Around 1686, her confessor (most likely, Francisco de Vargas Machuca) composed a biographical account of her life, based on a diary she had begun in 1650 under orders of one of her earlier confessors, with whom Ursula was required to consult.[1] This version of her life reports that she labored as a slave for forty-three of her sixty-two years. Born in Lima, Ursula was the legitimate daughter of Juan de Castilla and the slave, Isabel de los Rios.[2] She spent her formative years in the home of her mother's owner, Gerónima de los Rios, and then in 1612 at the age of seven or eight, for some unknown reason, she went to live with the *beata* (lay pious woman) and mystic, Luisa de Melgarejo Sotomayor (1578–1651). Ursula remained in Melgarejo's custody until 1617, when she entered the Convent of Santa Clara to work for Gerónima de los Rios's niece, the

Figure 2. Portrait of Ursula de Jesús, posterior of Figure 1.
by José de la Cruz. Photo by Ana María Vega.

sixteen-year-old novice, Inés del Pulgar.[3] Inside this cloistered setting, Ursula spent twenty-eight years as one of hundreds of slaves whose exhausting daily work regime afforded little spare time to contemplate religious matters. Each day she attended to the needs of her *ama* (owner) in her cell. She prepared her food and washed her clothing and linen, and once those tasks were complete, performed communal labor with the free servants in the kitchen and infirmary until late each evening.

Despite a grueling work regimen, Ursula maintained her own material interests. Her biographer claimed that like many female slaves in Lima, she was known for her frippery and desire to wear elegant clothing.[4] That said, he then recounted an event that occurred in 1642, which transformed Ursula's life and, as he claimed, permanently altered her reputation for vanity within the convent. Angry that she had loaned a skirt to someone who returned it soiled, she promptly washed and then hung it out to dry on a plank that covered the mouth of a deep well located in the center of the convent. While arranging the wet skirt, the platform she stood on collapsed, leaving Ursula suspended above the chasm trying to hold on—literally for her life. Unable to offer her any assistance, witnesses fervently prayed that Ursula would not suffer a painful death. Ursula maintained that her prayers to the Virgin of Carmen rescued her, and miraculously, she recovered her balance and gained enough leverage to reach safety.

Ursula's biographer sought to recount her transformative "awakening" in a way that matched the narrative structures of contemporary hagiographies. Such accounts often delineated distinct phases in the life cycles—from childhood to old age of devout and venerable women.[5] Often, holy women like Ursula might experience a calamity and subsequent miracle that propelled them in a radically different direction. As the story goes, Ursula nearly fell to her death, which led her to reject the material world and choose a path of intense spirituality. From this event she gained a sense of a larger purpose in life. Beseeching God and certain nuns to instruct her in "spiritual matters," Ursula dedicated any spare moment to prayer and now took pride in the exacting labor required of her. The nuns began referring to her as a "servant of God," as Ursula willingly subjected herself to even more humbling tasks.

Just as the miracle and conversion she experienced conformed to contemporary notions of female sanctity, so too did her developing sense of charity and need to sacrifice herself for others. Moreover, Ursula's mortification practices, which included fasting, self-flagellation, and wearing agonizing garments, showed her understanding of how the denial of the flesh resonated with the sufferings and Passion of Christ. For Ursula, her body only impeded her greater connection to Spirit.

Ursula's spiritual trajectory followed that of many contemporaries, with one important exception: she remained a slave. Misunderstandings between Ursula and her owner developed because, according to her biographer, she neglected her daily work regimen in order to attend to matters of the spirit. Feeling despondent and desperate, she requested permission to leave the convent to search for a new owner. Concerned that the convent might lose a gifted holy woman, one of the nuns promised to purchase Ursula's freedom.[6] Ursula appreciated the nun's generosity and was pleased when she was granted her freedom in 1645. Still, she decided not to become a donada for several reasons. Although becoming a religious servant would seem like the obvious next step for a recently freed women with deep spiritual values, the circumspect Ursula was not sure she wished to continue living in the convent. As a donada she would still be considered a servant, and Ursula did not wish to continue subjecting herself to someone else's will. Like other freedwoman, Ursula was proud to be her own master after forty-four years in bondage. She also wished to be "free" from the draining communal tasks to devote herself entirely to God's service. Although we do not know the specific detail of Ursula's letter of freedom (*carta de libertad*), others often specified that a freed slave should continue to serve her owner for a determined number of years.[7] We do know of one case in Santa Clara that occurred the year after Ursula's death. The mother of the *mulata* (woman of African and Spanish descent) donada Isabel María filed suit against one senior nun in the convent. She claimed that Isabel María had been manumitted with the stipulation that she profess in Santa Clara as a donada. Once she entered the convent, her new "proprietor," Marceliana de Carbajal (a well-known visionary in the convent) ignored the agreement and tried to sell Isabel.[8]

Even though fear of continued bondage may have influenced Ursula's decision to become a donada, her biographer interpreted her reticence as resentment toward the donadas of the convent, whom she considered to be pompous and vain.[9] The donadas probably considered the enslaved Ursula to be of a much lower status; thus, her animosity may have stemmed from class disparity among the ranks. Certainly, one can find instances of mistreatment of donadas toward their slaves: a practice not uncommon in convents. For example, María Malamba had served for decades as the slave of the donada Francisca de la Cruz in the Convent of Santa Clara. When Malamba died in 1656, Cruz sent someone to seize her paltry belongings, which had been transferred to her bereaved husband's home.[10] Ursula may have fallen prey to such intraclass conflict; nonetheless, she came to regret her vanity and tenaciousness. Even more convincing, however, was a "sign" she received from heaven on October 20, 1645 (vespers of Saint Ursula's feast day), when a chapel in the convent with a number of important religious objects burned (an event to which Ursula and her "voices" refer several times in her diary).[11] In addition, the quiet, but insistent encouragement she received from an angelic young black novice preparing to become a donada convinced Ursula to don the simple religious habit on December 18, 1645.[12]

During her novitiate year (required for all donadas), she gained a reputation for exceptional piety because she lived with "singular advancement of her spirit, continuous mortification of her senses, and served as a rare model of penitence, and repeated fasts."[13] Ursula prepared for her formal profession by spending her spare time on her knees in the choir. She wore a hair shirt (a garment of course haircloth, worn next to the skin as penance), a crown of thorns hidden beneath her hair, and straps laden with iron studs around her waist and arms. On her back, she carried a barbed cross, held against her body by a bodice made out of pigskin, the bristles turned inward to intensify the effect. Each day, she whipped herself before retiring to bed and again at four when she arose. Under the guidance of the Jesuit Miguel de Salazar she conducted what was called a general confession, which entailed an intense retrospection of all sins committed throughout her life.[14] Finally, after completing a year of study and preparation, Ursula professed on June 13, 1647, "the day of the Holy Trinity, with great devotion and humility."[15] She expressed a fervent desire to comply strictly with her vows of poverty, chastity, obedience, and enclosure and to obey the Rule of the Order of Saint Clare.

As her commitment to a religious life grew, Ursula began to experience visions and communicate more frequently with God. Dead souls eager to diminish their stay and alleviate punishment for their sins in purgatory also approached her. It was then that Ursula took on her role as intercessor by helping to extricate souls from purgatory, a punitive and redemptive domain located somewhere between heaven and hell. As a coredeemer working with Christ, Mary, and various saints, Ursula said prayers, dedicated her communion, or requested masses on behalf of beleaguered souls in purgatory. Generally, Ursula's efforts were believed to alleviate the suffering of some, and in a few cases, she claimed to witness their ascension into heaven. She related many of her uncanny experiences to her cellmates, who claimed that "although she was in no way ignorant, the visions proved too much for her."[16] Her biographer wrote that she was unaware of the need for secrecy, prudence, and discretion in such matters, and "in sincerity and simplicity she related them by saying, 'You won't guess how this imposter [the devil] tried to deceive me . . . with this, and this and this.'"[17] One concerned nun urged her to find a more sympathetic ear, someone who would be seriously attentive to her revelations.

Fortunately Ursula found several confessors who supported her endeavors.[18] Not only did her spiritual advisors have faith in her spiritual gifts, but many *clarisas* (nuns of Santa Clara) also held Ursula in high regard and took her visions seriously. Sometime in 1647, before she professed her formal vows, her confessor (probably Miguel Salazar) ordered her to record her visions, many of which replicated patterns of orthodox spirituality found in the spiritual diaries and hagiographies of medieval and contemporary mystics.[19] Her irregular diary entries thereafter covered the period from 1650 until 1661. Some entries do not follow a logical chronological sequence, indicating they may have been bound and numbered improperly by someone other than Ursula. More than half of the folios were dictated to one or more nuns designated as her scribes, a succession evidenced by clear distinctions in penmanship, the manner in which the entries were dated, and the narrative style.[20]

For a slave and servant of that time, Ursula lived an exceptionally long life.[21] After lying ill for more than three weeks, she died with her eyes open on February 23, 1666, as though she were in a state of ecstasy.[22] Witnesses claimed that she died a "good death," by preparing her will, disposing of her worldly possessions, confessing her sins, and receiving extreme unction. The nuns deeply mourned her passing, and a number of high ecclesiastical and secular authorities—including the *vicereine*, doña Ana de Silva y Manrique, the wife of Diego Benavides de la Cueva, Count of Santisteban (viceroy of Peru, 1661–66)—attended her funeral. Because of Ursula's lifelong devotion to Our Lady of Carmen (a Virgin who specializes in aiding souls in purgatory), Ursula was buried beneath the floor of her chapel in the Convent of Santa Clara.

Ursula never gained the recognition that Isabel Flores de Oliva, known as Saint Rose of Lima (1586–1617) achieved in the seventeenth century. Nevertheless, she served as a model of emulation for women of color in Lima, in small but significant ways. For instance, five months after her death, the *parda* (a woman of African descent) Francisca de la Cruz, who had served the convent for twenty years, petitioned the abbess to become a donada "following the example of the Mother, Ursula de Christo."[23] She also served as an example of religious piety for the nuns of Santa Clara, members of the Franciscan order, and the secular population of Lima. Subsequent to her death, the nuns commissioned a local artist to paint her portrait, which remained in the convent. In 1686, her diary was recopied and edited, and several seventeenth-century chronicles, including Francisco Echave y Assu's 1688 work, *La estrella de Lima*, mentioned her name in passing, thus confirming her importance.[24] Even today, the nuns of the Convent of Santa Clara recount tales of her miracles and acts of humility. Until recently, the inhabitants of the Barrios Alto neighborhood (where the convent is located) were permitted to enter the vestibule of the convent to kneel before her image and pray.

The two portraits found in the convent and several written portrayals from the seventeenth century are what remain of Ursula. But, do the painted images, and the highly stylized biographical narratives provide a clear sense of her many faces, of her multifaceted lives? In Ursula's spiritual diary, a deeper, huskier voice emerges. We "hear" and "see" suffering, joy, exhaustion, and humility in the fragmentary, sometimes abbreviated representations of this sensitive and sturdy religious servant. We sense the innuendos of convent life, the strained relations among the nuns, servants, and slaves, as well as the fellowship, the grinding daily work, and exacting spiritual regimen. We glimpse how racial constructions were given meaning "*in terms of* situations, the *political* process of giving, modifying, contesting, shading, and acquiescing in one or another label."[25] Above all, we gain a deeper appreciation of the distinct manifestations of baroque Catholic spirituality.

Part I, which serves as an introduction to the English translation in Part II, and Part III, which contains excerpts from the Spanish transcription of Ursula's diary provided in this book, are meant to situate Ursula within an early modern context. This effort includes an exploration of her ambiance: the context of the bustling metropolis, Lima; Ursula's early childhood years as a slave in a large household; her brief residence at the home Luisa Melgarejo, a beata at the epicenter of a blossoming spiritual culture in Lima; and the remaining decades of her life as a slave, and after 1645, as a freedwoman immersed in the spiritual, material, and social worlds of the Convent of Santa Clara. Because so many of Ursula's visions center on purgatorial intercession, Part I will then turn to a consideration of purgatory's quintessential role in medieval and early modern Catholicism. The book argues that redemptory efforts to "save" dead souls made by a spate of European medieval female apostles eventually became a common practice among sixteenth- and seventeenth-century female intercessors, both in Catholic Europe and in the urban centers of colonial Latin America. Lima's mystics were no exception, and the fertile spiritual climate provided ample opportunities for men and women of color to express their piety. On the one hand, Ursula's perceptions (and her authority) were firmly rooted in this largely feminine European tradition dating to the medieval period. On the other, unlike many seventeenth-century mystics sanctioned by religious communities and ecclesiastical authorities, Ursula was a black woman who had experienced the deep wounds of human bondage and inequality. Part I will then consider *how* Ursula's spiritual diary conformed to, and yet departed from, standard hagiographic genres evident in European and Latin American visionary texts. In order to understand how and why Ursula gained respect and authority in her own singular fashion, it is important to gain a sense for both the "worlds" she inhabited and the path she followed to become a venerated mystic.

A Walk Through Lima

In 1612, at the tender age of eight, Ursula witnessed dramatic changes in her native Lima.[26] The city was known as the "City of the Kings," but a more apt description might have been the "City of Kings and Popes," because this flourishing colonial metropolis integrated the secular and the sacred in a single spectacular corpus. In fact, visitors compared Lima with some of the finest European cities. Everywhere, in the buildings, the clothing, and the activities of Lima's inhabitants (known as *limeños*), Ursula witnessed expressions of Catholicism and the power of Spanish colonial authority. Lima was one of two vice-regal capitals, as well as the seat of the archdiocese, responsible for overseeing ten bishoprics (ecclesiastical jurisdictions, including Cuzco, Charcas, and Quito), which divided the viceroyalty. As a center of religious expression, Lima hosted a large number of regular orders (see Glossary), including the Dominicans, Franciscans, Augustinians, and the Society of Jesus (the Jesuits). Still, while more than 10 percent of Lima's population wore religious habits and cassocks, pious expression was not limited to nuns and priests. Catholic liturgy, expressed in public worship and ritual, regulated the pulse of the city. It divided time into religious functions, sermons, processions, and masses. Expressions of devotion to distinct advocations of Christ or Mary were apparent in the artwork, the architecture, and the ornate celebrations held throughout the city. Religion permeated the daily lives of humble migrants and established *vezinos* (citizens). Even secular authorities like guild, university, and city council members took vows to defend the mystery of the Immaculate Conception.[27]

By the beginning of the seventeenth century, Lima had evolved into a key center of ecclesiastical, commercial, and secular government activity. It boasted five convents for women, six monasteries, six hospitals, an Inquisition tribunal, a royal mint, and a university. Some twenty-five thousand people inhabited the four parishes situated on the banks of the Rímac River (see Map 1). Not only did Lima attract Spaniards, divided between *peninsulares* born in Spain and *criollos* born in America, but also native Andeans of various ethnicities who migrated from the coast and the highlands. Slaves were distinguished as *bozal* (a recently arrived unbaptized African) or criollo (Peruvian born and/or baptized).[28] Although Spaniards and Africans formed the majority of the population, the *castas*, or people of mixed ancestry, which included *mestizos* (native Andean and Spanish), *mulatos* (African and Spanish), or *zambos* (African and native Andean), showed signs of growth. Some of the castas were enslaved; many worked as shop owners or artisans; a few gained more lucrative posts.[29] Although Spaniards attained the highest secular governmental positions, mulatos and mestizos with talent and influential friends might also aspire to lower-ranking offices in the colonial bureaucracy.

In 1612, as Ursula began her walk around Lima, she would have noticed that the city's boundaries now extended beyond the four-parish limit. In fact, artisans had just finished constructing a bridge leading across the Rímac River to the newly established barrio of San Lázaro (See **W** on map). Native Andeans established modest dwellings, and recently disembarked West African slaves were housed there in rough, barracklike buildings. Authorities had chosen this location as a medical checkpoint for the many sickly slaves who had endured the ghastly conditions on the cramped vessels that crossed the Atlantic. It was thought that by "seasoning" the slaves at this location across the river, diseases would not spread to the more densely populated central areas. The segregation of slaves was also intended to curb the growing number of fugitives. Another sign of expansion could be seen on the eastern outskirts of Lima. Around 1590, colonial authorities built a walled district called El Cercado (**X**). This *reducción* (forced congregation) of native Andeans was meant to prevent them from integrating into the more Hispanized city of Lima. Yet, in spite of the efforts undertaken by authorities to segregate native Andeans in this neighborhood, many Indians continued to maintain shops and residences in Lima proper.

By 1612, Ursula had begun serving in the household of Luisa Melgarejo de Sotomayor in the thickly populated parish of Santa Ana. Her home was a stone's throw from one of the city's cultural meccas, the Colegio de San Pablo (College of Saint Paul, **A**). Operated by the Jesuits, this religious college (it also featured a church and a residence for the Jesuit professors) was famous for a number of reasons. For one, the school's educational standards rivaled those in Europe, and students admitted to study at the Jesuit Society's school were not only of Spanish ancestry but mestizo and mulato as well. The Jesuit professors of San Pablo were renowned scholars and teachers who also offered their services to the general public. For instance, secular limeños sought the professors' moral guidance and advice on Christian matters. The Jesuit teachers also offered their pedagogical services to others. As Ursula wandered by, she noticed a queue of slaves from Guinea-Bissau waiting to enter a door of San Pablo to receive their weekly religious instruction. The school also contained an ample and spacious library, which housed more than four thousand volumes of theological and secular works. At the main entrance to the Colegio, she saw a mule train outside. The pack animals laden with hundreds of books purchased by the Jesuits were destined for other more distant parts of the viceroyalty. Not only did the Jesuits promote education and spiritual literacy for different sectors of the Lima population, but they also attempted to diffuse that knowledge throughout Peru.

Some Jesuits specialized in medicine, and the Colegio maintained an elaborate pharmacy, complete with medical compounds recommended in the latest

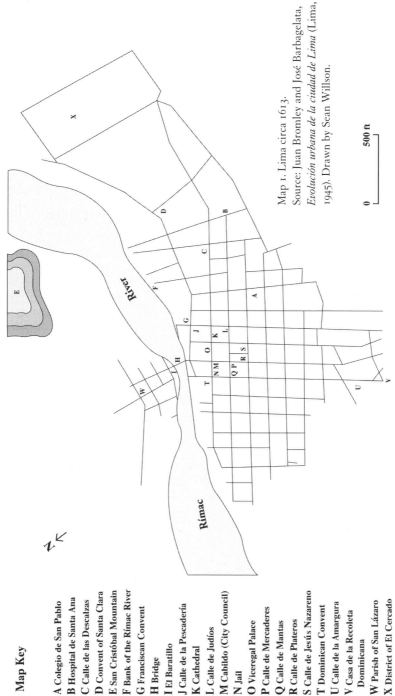

Map 1. Lima circa 1613.
Source: Juan Bromley and José Barbagelata, *Evolución urbana de la ciudad de Lima* (Lima, 1945). Drawn by Sean Willson.

0   500 ft

Map Key

A Colegio de San Pablo
B Hospital de Santa Ana
C Calle de las Descalzas
D Convent of Santa Clara
E San Cristóbal Mountain
F Bank of the Rímac River
G Franciscan Convent
H Bridge
I El Baratillo
J Calle de la Pescadería
K Cathedral
L Calle de Judíos
M Cabildo (City Council)
N Jail
O Viceregal Palace
P Calle de Mercaderes
Q Calle de Mantas
R Calle de Plateros
S Calle de Jesús Nazareno
T Dominican Convent
U Calle de la Amargura
V Casa de la Recoleta
  Dominicana
W Parish of San Lázaro
X District of El Cercado

French manuals. The college even operated a small infirmary for the slaves arriving from the Jesuit haciendas just outside of Lima. The Colegio de San Pablo maintained a well-equipped pharmacy, infirmary, and a voluminous library, but it also sponsored some of the finest religious festivities of the city. Just this year, like thousands of other limeños, Ursula had witnessed the fabulous annual Corpus Christi celebration (a Catholic feast to commemorate the Body of Christ) that originated and ended at San Pablo. The priests even ordered fireworks to be set off from the roof of the building. The religious sodalities organized by the college were also famous, as was the entertainment they offered. Accomplished Jesuit-trained African musicians played drums, flutes, guitars, lutes, clarinets, and even *chirimias*, described by historian Luis Martín as "the Spanish version of the Scottish bagpipe."[30] The public could enjoy a choir of native Andeans, singing in Quechua, Spanish, and Latin in the chapel at the college. Its comedies or *autos sacramentales* (dramatic works with religious content) performed by its students also attracted members of Lima's aristocracy eager for entertainment. As Ursula stood outside the building she remembered hearing that in 1607, the students had staged "The History of Joseph, the Ancient Patriarch" in honor of the arrival of the current viceroy, don Juan de Mendoza y Luna, the marquis of Montesclaros.[31]

This religious establishment held great prominence in the lives of many limeños, but San Pablo had another significance to the young slave Ursula. Whenever she went to fetch her mistress, Luisa de Melgarejo, who attended mass there on a regular basis, she noticed the ornate interior of the nave, the wondrous paintings and *retablos* (altar screens), and the pilasters and domes with ivylike ornamentation. Near the entrance to the sacristy she could gaze at an enormous painting of the Virgin of Candelaria holding the Christ child in her arms. Ursula felt proud to know that the altar of the Jesuit church housed a sliver from Christ's cross, considered a particularly precious relic. Inside the church, she had also witnessed Melgarejo and a number of other beatas, including, Saint Rose (canonized in 1671), gathered together, their heads bowed in prayer.

As Ursula left the vicinity of the college, she passed by the Hospital de Santa Ana (**B**), an infirmary that catered to the needs of native Andeans. It featured a chapel with an advocation to Saint Ann, where priests administered the sacraments both to the sick and to other Andeans who came to be baptized, to marry, or to confess. Nearby, on the street called Calle de Las Descalças (**C**) (named after the Monasterio de las Descalças de San José), she saw slaves fetch pails of drinking water from the Caja de Agua de la Caridad, from which potable water ran through three main irrigation canals throughout the city. As she turned and walked toward the river, she passed by yet another convent, Santa Clara (**D**), an enormous property that consumed four blocks of the city. Ursula had heard about the convent from doña Luisa Melgarejo, but little did the child realize that she would spend most of her adult life enclosed within those walls.

At this point, Ursula decided to turn southeast and walk toward the great Rímac River. From this vantage point, the great San Cristóbal Mountain (**E**) came into view. She stood in awe and gazed at a great cross, planted firmly at the summit of the large peak. Closer to the river, Ursula saw another, unseemly side of the great "City of the Kings." She noticed that small huts of native Andeans and freed slaves dotted the riverbank (**F**), an area considered dangerous because of the mudslides that occurred regularly during the rainy season. She walked along the river on one side, the wall of the Franciscan convent to her left (**G**). She was anxious to stand on the recently constructed bridge (**H**) leading to the parish of San Lázaro. There to the right she saw an area that would later be named El Baratillo (**I**). This sight troubled her, because it was in this forlorn place that elderly slaves, abandoned by their masters scrambled in the garbage dumps for scraps. Off to one side, Ursula noticed one decrepit man with two hideous brands on his face and arm. She knew well what that meant; he had changed owners more than once. She also noticed an Augustinian friar named Bartolomé Badillo, affectionately called *pico de oro* (golden tongue) preaching to other bedraggled slaves.

She then retraced her steps and passed the façade of the Franciscan church (**G**), where two years earlier she had witnessed the impressive funeral procession of Francisco Solano (1549–1610), a Franciscan missionary considered a saint by limeños (he would be beatified in 1675 and then canonized in 1726). She remembered the long line of spectators that had filed by his open coffin, some tearing off swatches of his religious garb, because it was believed to hold curative powers.

Just then, Ursula heard a church bell ring and realized that she still had a little time before she would be missed. She decided to walk down the Calle de la Pescadería (Fish Street, **J**), where she could buy fresh seafood. A freed black man, who operated a corner store that sold wax, came out to greet her as she passed by. As she turned and walked toward the main plaza, she was now in the parish called La Catedral. This was the true heart of the city, which featured the main plaza and the magnificent cathedral (**K**), currently undergoing reconstruction because an earthquake had damaged the elaborate structure the previous year. Still, the presbyterium (the area where the high altar stood) of the cathedral was breathtaking. Close by the main entrance, a high-ranking ecclesiastical official had just posted the *tablilla*, a broadsheet that listed those individuals excommunicated for sundry crimes. On a screen door off to one side of the church, Ursula noticed a painting that showed Jews praying, which inspired the street name, Calle de Judíos (**L**). As she looked around the perimeter of the main plaza, she surveyed the *cabildo* (municipal government, **M**), the city jail (complete with a chapel to administer mass to prisoners, **N**), the vice-regal palace (**O**), and the houses of the notaries. But there, inside the nucleus of the main plaza, she witnessed an enormous array of activity. All at the same time, a mulata sold cooked food to passersby, a priest lashed his lame slave for stealing bread, and a beggar requested alms for the patron saint of the hospital for lepers. In another quarter, a beata dressed in a drab brown robe with chains wrapped around her arms, preached to a captive audience. This, Ursula realized, was the beating pulse of the city.

As she headed northwest, away from the main plaza, she noticed a clustering of streets that corresponded to distinct artisan trades that gave this city its reputation for economic vitality. She passed by the shops of hat and glove makers and of well-known artisans such as Francisco de Madrid, a sword and belt maker, Alonso de Villa, a button maker, and Diego González Guerrero, a cap maker. The Calle de Mercaderes (**P**) was dedicated to merchants. On the street named Mantas (**Q**)

Indians owned tailor shops and workshops. Because of ordinances established by Viceroy Francisco de Toledo (viceroy, 1569–81), the gold- and silversmiths had congregated onto their own street called Plateros (**R**). Sweat-shops, called *obrajes*, packed in Indian women and children who wove the woolen saddle blankets and clothing sold in these shops.[32] Nearby, Ursula noticed a few free black cobblers and tailors standing outside their shops, enjoying the temperate air. Curious to see where some of the wealthy lived, she headed southeast toward the Calle de Jesús Nazareno (**S**), where one of the famous conquerors, Francisco de Ampüero, had once lived. In this area the principal families of Lima had built homes that resembled the architectural style of Seville. Many had one or two stories, with entrance-ways lined with painted tiles (*azulejos*) and wooden balconies featuring iron grillwork with Arabic accents. Interior patios led to elaborate gardens and fragrant orange trees. Interspersed were the *corrales* (also known as *callejón de cuartos*) or more modest residences. The main entrance of the corral led to an interior patio, surrounded by two- to three-story apartments that faced inward. Some were owned and managed by women who rented out single rooms.

Ursula then backtracked and walked northwest again. To her right she could see the Dominican convent (**T**). She stood on the Calle de la Amargura (Street of Bitterness, **U**), and gazed to her left, looking as far as she could in the distance. She had heard that on Thursday of Holy Week, the Dominicans held a procession, during which they carried an image of the Nazarene Christ, down the nine blocks of this street, to the Dominican House of Recollection (Casa de la Recoleta Dominicana, **V**). There they set up a replica of Calvary, complete with a dramatization of the crucifixion. Different penitents (*penitentes*), dressed in the mourning color of purple, carried heavy crosses on their shoulders, while scores of confraternity (*cofradia*), members each with their patron saint, filed solemnly along. Ornately designed and richly colored tapestries, cloth, and other adornments draped the balconies along the street, and crowds of spectators craned to get a glimpse of events as they unfolded.

By now the hour had passed, and Ursula had to scurry home. She felt content, because she had completed her errands and had seen a lot of exhilarating things. She felt grateful to be alive during such an exciting time and fortunate to work in the pious Melgarejo household. As she reflected on her short life, she remembered her mother's own fortune at having been purchased around the turn of the century to work as a domestic servant in the aristocratic household of Gerónima de los Rios.

Ursula's Early Childhood

Ursula's upbringing seems fairly typical for a female slave born and raised in a wealthy Spanish household in colonial Lima. Her owner, Gerónima de los Rios, came from Seville. Gerónima's husband, Juan Manuel de Anaya, served as a treasurer for the Real Audiencia (royal court) from around 1605 until his death in 1616.[33] Both familial connections and Anaya's occupational position put the couple in contact with a number of highly placed peninsular members of

Andalusian and Lima societies. Like other elite Spanish women, Gerónima actively engaged in business negotiations (usually giving power to a male figure to represent them), especially the buying and selling of slaves, some of whom were employed on lands in the Chicama Valley of northern Peru.[34]

Doña Gerónima had no children, but the large household consisted of other family members, including her niece Inés and a number of family dependents, slaves, female and male servants, and retainers (*criados*).[35] Considered an aristocratic family, Gerónima and her husband predictably employed a number of Spanish, mestiza, and black girls who worked as cooks, laundresses, maids, and gardeners.[36] Gerónima also garnered additional income by selling the embroidered handwork crafted by her free and slave female dependents.[37] Although Ursula's biography reports that doña Gerónima died in 1612, it is most likely that she passed on in late 1616 or early 1617, continuing her business negotiations up to six months before her death.

Because wealthy households demanded a steady supply of domestic and agricultural labor, Peru witnessed a boom in the importation of slaves beginning around 1580. Merchants rich from the silver bullion produced by the Potosí mines paid high prices to buy and bring slaves to Lima. In fact, the vice-regal capital became a distribution center for slaves sold throughout Ecuador, Chile, and the interior provinces of Peru.[38] As a result of the increased forced exodus of slaves from West Africa, and their insinuation into the urban environment, the African and Afro-Peruvian population reached 50 percent of the city's population in 1593 and 54 percent in 1636. Within this population group, the gender ratio favored women throughout the first half of the seventeenth century.[39] The majority of female slaves like Ursula and her mother worked as household servants. Then after laboring in their master's home, many were also hired out as day laborers (*jornaleros*), where they garnered extra wages for their masters and for themselves, by working as food vendors, nursemaids, wet nurses, or domestics.[40]

Thus, Ursula spent her formative years in a large household, filled with Africans, Spaniards, and native Andeans, who most likely shared and exchanged distinct aspects of their cultural traditions. Her early years replicated the circumstances facing many enslaved females who spent their lives working for others and whose family relations and destinies remained intricately linked to their patrons. But work formed only one aspect of her upbringing. Like many young girls living in a society where Catholic tenets often dictated cultural norms, Ursula developed a particular devotion to the Virgin of Carmen and prayed the rosary and fasted once a week.[41] Although many West African religious traditions traveled with the diaspora, modified Catholic devotional practices also flourished among African and American-born slaves who conserved relics, prayed silently for saints to intervene on their behalf, and gathered to commemorate feast days.[42] Like other Afro-Peruvians, Ursula was a devout Catholic who was also influenced by her mother's cultural heritage. But, she was unique in other respects.

For some unknown reason, Ursula went to live with the renowned holy woman, Luisa Melgarejo Sotomayor in 1612 and remained in her care until 1617. Although not related by blood, the connection between Gerónima de los Rios and the Sotomayor family may have developed through their husbands' business dealings and during a brief term when both served on the Real Audiencia in 1616.[43] Evidence points to a trusting, intimate relationship, because Luisa's husband, Juan de Soto, served as the testamentary executor of Gerónima's will.[44] Whatever the reason, Ursula was fortunate to enter yet another prosperous Lima home.[45] While living in the Melgarejo household, Ursula performed domestic chores usually assigned to young slave girls, but she also received an unconventional religious education that eventually expedited her change in status from a slave serving her master to a freedwoman working in God's service.

A Niche of Female Mysticism

In her diary, Ursula never mentioned her association with the Franciscan tertiary (a member of a third order of the regular clergy), Luisa Melgarejo, but this famous visionary influenced her tender soul in numerous ways. Melgarejo was considered one of the most influential and important lay spiritual figures in seventeenth-century Lima.[46] When her profound dedication to spiritual matters began is not clear, but by 1610, her public reputation for sanctity was already established. The Franciscan missionary, Francisco Solano served briefly as her confessor. After Solano's death in 1610, a beatification hearing was held, and ecclesiastical authorities asked Melgarejo to testify that his body remained incorrupt after death (a critical sign of sanctity).[47] Being asked to bear witness on such a matter was considered a great honor, and this event increased her credibility in the religious community. By 1612, Melgarejo's private and public mystical exercises had also become a subject of discussion. One friar reported seeing her in a state of ecstasy (*arrobamiento*) more than two hundred times.[48] Between 1612 and 1622, Melgarejo filled at least fifty-nine small notebooks with theological notions discussed and endorsed by beatas, nuns, and prominent ecclesiastical authorities throughout the vice-regal capital. However, these theological propositions eventually attracted Inquisitorial interest, and in 1623 she was accused of illuminism and her writings were confiscated. She managed to escape conviction (several prominent Jesuits protected her) and soon reestablished her reputation. By the time of her death in 1649, the Jesuit Antonio Ruíz de Montoya (1585–1652) claimed in his *Silex de divino amor* (1650) that she had reached the highest level of spiritual perfection, and the Franciscan Diego Córdova y Salinas dedicated a chapter of his masterful account of the Franciscan Order in Peru to her life.[49]

Like many early modern men and women, Ursula lived in a home replete with sacred objects and artifacts that rendered many aspects of baroque Catholicism tangible. Their iconographic presence allowed the viewer to link the image to specific actions such as contemplation, prayer, and meditation, or to the reading of religious texts. Images also helped internalize particular religious messages. Melgarejo closely followed the founder of the Jesuits, Ignatius of Loyola's (1491–1556) advice to position religious images in key areas and to focus the imagination on contemplative practices related to those images, such as the meanings and implications of suffering during Christ's Passion.[50] For instance, the door of Melgarejo's living area featured an altar screen of the Lord's descent from the cross, and her private chapel included—among other images—a large painting of the Holy Trinity. In addition, Melgarejo maintained an altar in her home complete with religious objects—chalices, chasubles, and other sacramental ornaments—supplied by her Jesuit confidantes.[51] We can only wonder how those images and objects influenced the impressionable slave girl, Ursula, who spent a great deal of time in such a stimulating environment. In one diary entry she later recalled, "When I was a child, I was always looking at the images of our Lady. I would say, 'Would that I could be the little black servant of the Mother of God.'"[52] When Ursula assembled with the members of the Soto household, she learned to concentrate on and interpret specific images relative to written and visual texts. These visualization techniques would serve her in later years when she recorded her lifelike experiences of Christ's birth, Passion, and resurrection in her diary.

In addition to the informal tutelage she received, the young and inquisitive Ursula was surrounded by books that either she learned to read, or heard being read.[53] Some medievalists suggest that by the late Middle Ages, inward piety was increasingly associated with reading, and that devoutly pious urban women were often enthusiastic readers. By 1600, the proliferation of the printed word in Europe meant that the lay population, which had previously received the majority of its spiritual education from iconography, sermons, and the confessional, now learned visually or aurally through books.[54] Female readers could gain knowledge from a number of recently translated hagiographies that recounted the virtues of medieval and early modern female saints and mystics.[55] In fact, many of these hagiographic and instructional works became more readily available for women in Lima to buy or borrow.[56] Luisa Melgarejo de Sotomayor owned a number of key spiritual texts, including the *Flos Sanctorum* and *El perfecto christiano*.[57] In addition, her proximity to the Colegio de San Pablo and her familiarity with some of the most important Jesuit intellectuals of the time gained her access to the society's four-thousand-volume library, considered the most extensive collection in Lima.[58]

Doña Luisa and other privileged women shared their literary knowledge with other women. For instance, the mulata tertiary Estephanía de San José (d. 1645) held sessions with the richest, most "principaled" women of Lima. Her biographer, Francisco de Ávila wrote:

> She knew what was suitable for that lady and her household to read. She entered the house saying, *blessed be Jesus Christ . . .* and wanted them to read the book she carried: and if the opportunity presented itself and it did not bother or annoy anyone, she took out her book and said . . ."read me a little," and then went to another part and said, "read a little of this," knowing that what she read or heard was important for that person. But, [she proceeded] carefully, and not in an obvious way that might raise suspicion.[59]

Ursula assimilated knowledge from written works, but her observations of Melgarejo taught her how the human body served as a means to render God's presence visible. Like her contemporaries, Melgarejo considered ecstatic trances, visions, mortification, and prophecies to be orthodox, acceptable, and accessible *public* practices. Witnesses provided extremely detailed, almost scientific descriptions of the position of the head, coloration, or other bodily movements. Men and women of the time employed terminology and applied an interpretive framework—dating to the thirteenth century—that "read" these external signs of spirituality expressed *by means of* the female body.[60] Such an elaborate, interpretive vocabulary argues that ecstatic trances were comprehensible and acceptable—perhaps even common—phenomena. Reportedly, Luisa Melgarejo once explained that entering such a trance "was no more than to relinquish and place oneself in God."[61] Various witnesses reported seeing her enter an altered state of consciousness at a Jesuit chapel and at home. Luisa's sister-in-law, Isabel de Soto, who became a member of the Melgarejo household when she was widowed at age fifty, witnessed Luisa's frequent mystical raptures. She described one vision that occurred in 1614:

> While [Luisa was] seated one night on a chair on the patio, she saw Our Lord seated in a chair, surrounded by a number of saints. While disciplining herself, she also told me she saw an area full of demons that frightened her, and soon thereafter she felt Our Lord so near, that she felt his hair touch her cheek, and then, she heard him say: "Daughter have no fear; I am with you."[62]

Priests, passersby, and other female visionaries reported that Luisa Melgarejo regularly fell into ecstatic trances at the Colegio de San Pablo, the Jesuit chapel she frequented in her neighborhood. Although we have no direct evidence, Ursula probably observed these or similar episodes. One even wonders if she was the slave who arrived each day to the college to tell the enraptured doña Luisa that the afternoon meal was ready or to inquire how she would like her eggs prepared.[63]

The five crucial years spent in Luisa Melgarejo's home brought Ursula in direct contact with a number of "living saints," or individuals recognized by the community as worthy of sanctification. Of these, Saint Rose was by far the most celebrated. In 1612, the same year Ursula entered the Melgarejo household, the thirty-four-year-old Luisa met Rose at the home of a mutual friend.[64] They quickly became friends and spiritual confidantes. Both frequented the chapel at the Colegio de San Pablo where they received communion and shared the same confessors. Reportedly, as their intimacy grew, Melgarejo showed her writings to Rose on bended knee as a sign of reverence and humility. Then, in 1617, as Rose lay dying, Melgarejo sat by her side singing and playing the guitar. Once she expired, doña Luisa entered a mystical trance, envisioning her friend's triumphant entry into heaven. Although Melgarejo's Inquisition hearing and acquittal (1623–25) temporarily tarnished her reputation, by 1630 she had regained her spiritual authority in Lima and was summoned by ecclesiastical authorities to testify at Rose's beatification hearing.[65]

Life in the Melgarejo household—whether focusing on religious images, reading hagiographic texts, or holding spiritual gatherings—formed a microcosm of the cultural and religious activities throughout the vice-regal capital. The young Ursula witnessed a spiritual renaissance, where mystical practices already condemned by Inquisition authorities in Spain, were reaching their zenith in colonial Lima. The Jesuits, one of the city's most influential religious groups, openly advocated mystical practices involving various forms of divine contemplation and mental prayer. The writings of Ignatius of Loyola deeply inspired Jesuit priests and their female protégés, including Luisa de Melgarejo.[66]

The racially and culturally diverse vice-regal capital served as a vinculum between liturgical Catholic rituals and the private veneration that occurred in homes, both humble and grand. The devout could listen to sermons, pray a *novena* (a nine-day devotion for a religious intention), or seek inspiration from any number of colorful religious icons scattered throughout the city. Peninsular and Creole (American-born) Spaniards, members of the huge mixed population, the castas, as well as Africans and native Andeans expressed their Catholic devotion in a variety of ways. In the ornate religious structures, as well as on the streets and plazas, Lima's inhabitants could participate in processions, or enjoy religious festivals filled with music, dance, and lively sermons. A church, monastery, or convent (many of which were constructed in the seventeenth century) graced nearly every city block, and the central plaza, located in the heart of the city, featured the architectural splendor of the magnificent cathedral. Because Lima was the seat of an archbishopric, limeños were the first to hear news brought from Rome or Seville. As home to the Holy Office of the Inquisition they also experienced the efficacy of clerical surveillance.

Not only was Lima a major entrepôt of Catholicism, but during the first half of the seventeenth century, the vice-regal capital witnessed both a spiritual renaissance and a "feminization of piety" characterized by mysticism, visionary experiences, contemplation, penitential asceticism, and suffering in imitation of Christ.[67] Women either took formal vows as members of a third order of the regular clergy, or lived informally as beatas. For instance, like many women of that era, Feliciana de Jesús (1600–64), feared that convent life would be too cloying. She emulated Saint Rose, became a tertiary, and supported herself, her mother, and her sister as a florist, gardener, and seamstress. By frequenting hospitals, schools, convents, and private homes, these tertiaries imparted their own sense of Christian benevolence to the Lima community.[68] However, some women went even further. A contemporary of Feliciana, the mestiza Isabel de Cano, expressed her notion of female Christian charity by sewing mattresses for the sick. She also crossed traditional gender boundaries of spirituality that claimed that Christian women should not preach and addressed spiritual matters in public. These women gave new meaning to feminine practices of piety—some of them considered traditionally male—in private and public settings.

Evidence suggests that Lima's rich spiritual climate created a receptive environment for women of color, albeit within certain parameters. Like Ursula, some slaves and servants who witnessed and participated in the delicate intimacies of their masters' sacred lives also received informal tutelage from them.[69] For instance, Mariana, the native Andean servant of Rose of Lima, came to understand the desire to "deny" the flesh when she saw the tunic of rough pigskin Rose wore beneath her Dominican habit. She learned that beauty and vanity were considered sinful, as she obeyed her master by placing lime on Rose's hands because someone

had told Rose they were pale and lovely. Not only did Mariana maintain an intimate knowledge of Rose's mortification rituals, but she also introduced the servant
of God to a famous pious *cacica* (native female administrator), Catalina Huanca.[70]
The mulata Luisa Mexía, a servant employed by one of Rose's spiritual sisters testified at the future saint's first beatification hearing how she had *observed* Rose's charity toward others.[71] In that sense, Luisa gained a nonliterate knowledge of feminine
expressions of charity, through the exemplum tutelage offered by Rose. The future
saint also trained a number of other protégés, some of whom she called her spiritual daughters, or *hijas espirituales*. Young girls sought Rose's spiritual counsel;
select beatas stayed in Rose's tiny cell, or aided Rose in dressing and adorning an
image of Catherine of Siena with flowers on her feast day.[72] In fact, some ten years
before her death, a number of young girls and widows began to gather regularly at
her home, and then later, under her direction, took their vows as Dominican
tertiaries.[73] One can only wonder what knowledge these faithful protégés and
servants would have offered to others once Rose died?[74]

The congenial spiritual ambiance present in early seventeenth-century Lima
also provided a locus for gifted lay and religious women of color to gain notori-
ety, independent from their female patrons. However, forms of "spiritual"
expression had their limits, especially for women of color who were targeted
more frequently by Inquisition authorities for untoward conduct. Although the
Panamanian-born *quarterona* (three-quarters Spanish, one-quarter African) and
Franciscan tertiary Ana de Castañeda was denounced first in 1592 and again in
1612 for sorcery, she maintained a wide-ranging clientele who trusted her
prophetic skills on marital predicaments, lost items, or fugitive slaves in the City
of the Kings.[75] Some years later, a number of casta beatas who frequented the
home of Luisa Melgarejo formed their own spiritual networks to discuss theological matters and predict the fate of souls in purgatory. Unfortunately, they too
were placed on trial for heresy by the Inquisition and convicted in 1625.[76] Still,
not all pious women of color were denounced. Some tertiaries escaped the
inquisitorial eye and were recognized for their singular spiritual gifts and contri-
butions. One seventeenth-century chronicle extolled the virtues of Estephanía de
San Joseph, who charmed the elite with her vibrant personality. She preached
daily sermons at Lima's plazas, tended to the sick and the poor in various hospitals, and collected alms for the nuns of Santa Clara.[77]

Tucked away in monasteries and convents, exemplary casta men and women
who generally occupied servile ranks as donados or donadas also expressed their
devotional practices.[78] Word traveled throughout Lima that Francisco de la
Concepción, a humble, African donado could miraculously appear in two places at
the same time and had the gift of prophecy.[79] Hundreds of rich and poor limeños
knew of the sensational curative abilities and charitable efforts of the Dominican
mulato donado Martín de Porras (1579–1639). Beggars and the needy formed long
lines outside his convent because they knew he would offer them as much assistance as possible.[80] He gained such fame as a humble barber and mystic, that after
his death most houses in Lima had "some canvas of his portrait or images, and dirt
from his tomb."[81] Such was the public devotion to Porras that twenty years after his
death, hearings were begun in an attempt to beatify him.[82] Other servants of God

followed in his footsteps. Near the end of Ursula's life, a donado named Juan, "always smiling, and with the word of God on his tongue" swept the floor of a church each day.[83] In 1663, Francisco de Santa Fé, a mulato donado in Santo Domingo, who spent at least ten years in close contact with Martín de Porras, received permission from his ecclesiastical superiors to enter the priesthood. Not only had he followed the exemplum of Porras, but he had learned basic tenets of Christianity from his mother, Augustina de Castro, a deeply pious free black who confessed and took communion regularly, helped the poor, and collected alms for the image of the Virgin del Rosario, housed in the Dominican church.[84]

Not only did casta men and women situate themselves within the pantheon of Lima's popular "saints," but the cult of the Señor de los Milagros (Our Lord of Miracles, an image of Christ) grew steadily during Ursula's lifetime and reached a fevered pitch among people of African descent following a major earthquake that struck the city in 1655 when the image survived intact. Other activities served to motivate the casta and black population. Numerous Afro-Peruvian religious brotherhoods in Lima catered to the needs of the faithful. Aside from providing funds for religious festivities and the burials of their members, these brotherhoods developed cults around particular saints whom they believed could send messages from the beyond.[85]

Efforts to proselytize by Jesuits and Augustinian friars also increased an awareness of basic Catholic doctrine. Realizing they could not ignore the substantial population of enslaved and free blacks and mulattos, numerous men of the cloth declared themselves the "slaves of slaves," because of their efforts to minister to recently arrived African slaves.[86] While Ursula washed the rags of the sick in the Convent of Santa Clara, the Jesuit Francisco del Castillo (1615–73), "the apostle of the blacks," searched for African slaves abandoned by their owners near the bridge leading toward a neighborhood called the Baratillo. There, as he preached and taught basic Catholic doctrine, he attracted a few African male and female disciples "anxious to achieve perfection," whom he trained as assistants in the sacristy.[87]

The deep spiritual piety evident in the homes, on the streets, and in the monastic settings of colonial Lima became accessible in various forms to men and women of color. In Ursula's case, the fertile religious climate afforded her an education that eventually served her years after she first entered the Convent of Santa Clara in 1617. Because of the permeable boundaries between street and convent, individuals continued to pass ideas from private homes to the *locutorios* (visitor parlors) of the various convents, and vice versa. Even servants and slaves like Ursula who entered Santa Clara as laborers, transported their own understandings of Catholic tenets, which were then transformed once these hard-working women insinuated themselves into the monastic setting.

Life in the Convent of Santa Clara

Social discourse among individuals on the street influenced perceptions held by the nuns and donadas of Santa Clara, but the monastic communal setting also encouraged fruitful exchanges. In fact, the culturally and intellectually rich climate within the world of walls fostered unique understandings of theological matters.[88] Most inhabitants adhered quietly to fairly mundane religious routines and rituals, but forms of spiritual expression did not always occur while gazing at the monstrance (a vessel in which the consecrated host is exposed), or reciting psalms at daybreak. The adolescent Ursula entered an environment where many clarisas saw the world in terms of supernatural signs; they exercised extreme physical mortification and experienced lengthy periods of ecstasy.[89] Some of the nuns wore hair shirts studded with iron, or wrapped long iron chains or leather straps around their limbs. Some subsisted only on bitter lettuce or seeds; others slept on an iron grill, or laid on the refectory floor for others to step on them. Five clarisa nuns, all Ursula's contemporaries, were known for their unique devotional practices. Catalina de Cristo, a baker in the convent, swore to the abbess that Saint Clare awakened her each morning by saying, "Let's go Catalina, and knead the dough." She also reported that she saw souls suffering in purgatory while attending requiem masses in the convent. The pious clarisa Augustina de San Francisco supervised the slaves and servants who worked in the refectory, including Ursula, with a firm, but kind hand.[90] Another nun, Juana de Christo, gave spiritual council to the convent's servants and attempted to imitate Christ's suffering on the cross by sleeping on a wooden plank in the choir. Gerónima de San Dionisio claimed that for decades she had dedicated herself to the wounds of Saint Francis and carried the cross of the Blessed Souls in a procession held each Monday.[91] Juana Gertrudís wore eleven iron hair shirts and, as the religious community slept, performed the Stations of the Cross, her weary back bearing a large crucifix. Yet another clarisa, Ana de la Cruz, wept bitterly and beat her face because Christ had endured the same abuse from his tormentors.[92]

Books, read or heard, the paintings and religious objects observed, or the spiritual matters discussed in the refectory, corridors, and cells served as the visual and aural aliments that nurtured the spiritual practices of clarisa visionaries. In many ways, the hagiographies, mystical tracts, and renderings of the lives of saints housed in many convent libraries "structured daily monastic life."[93] The library of Santa Clara was no exception: the clarisas maintained a modest, but still significant collection that featured a hagiography of Saint Lutgarde of Anwières (in modern-day Belgium, 1182–1246), the complete works of Spanish mystics Teresa of Avila and María de la Antigua (1566–1617), Alonso de Andrade's *Órden de vida para la eterna vida*, and Luis de Granada's *Guía de pecadores*.[94] These titles suggest the acceptance of mystical practices among the nuns of Santa Clara. Several works, including a biography of Ignatius of Loyola by noted theologian Juan Eusebio Nieremberg (1595–1658), indicate a strong Jesuit presence in this Franciscan nunnery.[95]

Works of art that graced the passageways and rooms of the convent also structured daily life. They provided iconographic venues to the symbolic mysteries of the past, or the beyond. For the nuns who gazed upon them, these visual narratives could capture an instant of eternity. One triptych in the convent depicted Saint Catherine of Siena with Jesus. In that image, Jesus offered Catherine a heart, while another heart palpitated against His chest.[96] Ursula could also gaze at a full-sized painting of Saint Rose, her cheeks flushed, her head graced with a crown of roses. Ursula could imagine Saint Francis receiving his stigmata, or reflect on some of the elements in a painting of a pathetic Christ figure, stooping and bearing a cross on his bloody shoulders, that also appeared in one of her visions. She could sustain her childhood devotion to the Virgin of Carmen by viewing a painting of this magnificent Lady standing on a half moon, cloaked in a brown habit, white cape, and donning a star-shaped scapular (a covering worn over the shoulders). In the distance, two angels hovered protectively, while in the lower section of the painting, two ghostly soul bodies stood engulfed by flames in purgatory.[97]

Ursula could also learn about the foundation "history" of the convent by observing a painting of its founder, Archbishop Toribio de Mogrovejo (1538–1606), standing with a clarisa before him on her knees, the other sisters in a queue behind her. Over the decades, Ursula probably heard different versions of the origin myth related in the refectory (the dining area of the convent) or in the sermons delivered at Sunday mass, and later eulogized in Córdoba y Salinas's 1651 Franciscan chronicle:

> Extremely eager to increase the number of virgins, the blessed archbishop, Don Toribio Alfonso Mogrobejo founded the convent. Without any doubt, God has multiplied them, because of the worthiness of such an illustrious prelate (the living image of the Apostles), and by filling him with His blessings and gifts. In less than fifty years, 260 professed nuns of the black veil have come to live there and serve their celestial husband. In addition to them, and the nuns of the white veil, novices, donadas, servants and slaves, more than 600 souls are enclosed within the walls.[98]

No doubt, Ursula knew the "straight story," but she also developed another understanding of what had happened to several of the "progenitors" of the convent through a vision she recorded in her diary:

> [A] throng of nuns came out from under the earth, and two by two they came by way of that deep place from the area near the kitchen. First, there was doña Teresa, looking very well, with her wimple beneath the habit very white. I recognized some of the nuns who had died more than twenty-four years ago. They all came with their veils covering their faces; only Teresa was unveiled. I recognized a Beatris, two Juanas, and another named Mensia. I was astonished that they had been in purgatory for such a long time. They said, "Does that frighten you? We have been there since the days of [one of the convent's founders, Francisco de] Saldaña."[99]

In fact, on August 10, 1605, four nuns and Archbishop Toribio de Mogrovejo's niece, Beatríz de Prado Quiñones, entered the newly constructed Convent of Santa Clara to establish their new lives. Mogrovejo himself barely lived to see his dream come true. Although he died the following year, part of the blessed founder's body became forever immortalized within the convent walls. His heart became an honored relic and occupied a special place next to the gospel on the main altar.[100]

From its inception in 1605, "God multiplied" his celestial wives and the convent quickly became a haven for elite women as well as a place of employment for hundreds of female laborers that replicated the social and religious hierarchies found in Franciscan convents throughout Latin America.[101] Called *urbanistas*, the nuns remained subject to the local bishop, not to provincial Franciscan authorities.[102] Santa Clara was one of five *conventos grandes* (large convents) that occupied several blocks in the southern section of the rapidly growing city.[103] Like many Poor Clare convents, the structure began modestly, and along with its older counterpart in Cuzco, expanded throughout the seventeenth century.[104] Immediately following a disastrous earthquake in 1644, the construction of a new church in the convent began. By midcentury, the convent featured a clear Arabic architectural influence, three medium-sized cloisters each with long walkways and spacious patios, seven ample communal living quarters, individual cells with windows facing the street, an infirmary, a large garden, an orchard, and animal coops.[105] The convent also boasted one altar dedicated to their patroness, Our Lady of the Rock of France, and an effigy of the Christ of Burgos, usually taken out in procession during Holy Week.[106] Chapels to Bethlehem, the Solitary Christ, María Santíssima de los Dolores, and Our Lady of Carmen graced other areas of the convent. In addition, multiple images of Christ and Mary provided the nuns with places to contemplate different aspects of their lives. Even in the infirmary, the use of a portable altar meant that the sick could hear mass on Sundays and other religious holidays.[107]

The magnificent structures and ample spaces helped cultivate a self-sufficient spiritual and economic domain. It also opened up the possibility for hierarchies of power and spatial distribution to develop among the women of the convent. Specific ranks included nuns of the black veil (*velo negro*, also called *madres*; senior or older nuns were also called *señoras*), who had paid a large dowry upon entry. They brought enough capital to purchase and furnish their own cells; they sang the canonical hours in the choir and voted on administrative matters during the conventual capitulary (called the *capitular* and defined in the constitution as a meeting where nuns were encouraged to confess their faults and make collective decisions). The second rank, nuns of the white veil (*velo blanco*, also called *hermanas*), paid half this dowry amount and did not necessarily own their cell. Pedigree, education (particularly their knowledge of Latin), financial means, and, in some instances, legitimacy or family status differentiated those who pertained to these two ranks.[108] Access to particular spaces also distinguished them. The nuns of the black veil symbolically sat closest to God above the others in the upper choir loft; nuns of the white veil, as well as novices, lay women (those who paid bed and board to reside in the convent, often with relatives), and servants occupied the lower choir. In the refectory, the abbess sat at the head of the table, followed by former abbesses, nuns of the black veil seated in the order they had taken their vows, and then the nuns of the white veil. When the nuns died they were buried in a crypt directly below the choirs according to rank. Below that crypt, the dank ossuary harbored the bones of commoners.

Both lay and religious women spent time in the common areas such as the chapel, gardens, the general work room (*sala de labores*), and the refectory.

Figure 3.
Exterior view of nuns' cells.
Photo by Ana María Vega.

Servants and slaves spent most of their time in or near the kitchen, public baths, laundry, and storage areas, or around the chicken coops, orchard, gardens, or infirmary.[109] The convent featured seven large dormitories that provided separate quarters for the nuns without cells, lay women, schoolgirls, novices, donadas, servants, and slaves. Although the revised *General Constitutions* (1639) advised nuns to sleep in the common dormitory with their servants and slaves, it proved difficult to relinquish the comforts of a private residence.[110] (See Figure 3.) The cells of the wealthiest nuns were lavish and well heeled. Many contained individual kitchens, chicken coops, and a small library and housed a large retinue of relatives, servants, donadas, and slaves. The most pious nuns established individual chapels.[111] Individual cells may have provided private domains for nuns eager to maintain aristocratic customs; however, the choir was considered the most important and reverent space in the convent. Divided into lower and upper sections, a variety of activities occurred there. Novices professed their vows, the religious community received communion, the nuns of the black veil sang, and many of those present quietly contemplated the life of Jesus, the saints, or their own defects. In the choir, visionaries, including Ursula, found a safe haven to commune directly with God.[112] (See Figure 4.)

Figure 4. Ruins of the church of Santa Clara. Note the choir on the left side.
Photo courtesy of the Franciscan Archive, Lima, Peru.

All community members conformed to a complex matrix of rules that regulated time, space, and comportment. Conventual routine meticulously regulated each hour of the day, in an attempt to maintain equilibrium between prayer, work, silence (the "key to the soul"), teaching, recreation, and different religious rituals.[113] Pealing bells also demarcated time and space, because "at any given hour of any given day the nun would be in the same place at the same time."[114] Daily activities centered on the liturgical calendar—in fact, many of Ursula's diary entries are defined chronologically by a saint's feast day. Praying the Divine Office (daily canonical hours of prayer) divided the day into clear components: beginning with lauds, followed by prime, terce, sext, nones, vespers, compline, and matins (at midnight, except in winter and summer when it was said at 8 AM). Mass, terce, and vespers were always sung; lauds, prime, and compline involved prayer. The nuns were prohibited from speaking from compline (said in the evening) until terce the following morning, and in certain spaces: including the chapel, dormitories, and refectory. While eating, discretionary conversation could occur.[115] Ritualistic gestures of submission were deemed important: all were expected to bow deferentially before superiors, enter the high choir with great dignity and composure, and sit in a completely upright posture until the Divine Office began. Weekly chapter meetings ensured that community members obeyed the rules and constitutions; any negligence was publicly reprimanded and privately punished with whippings.

To maintain a sense of harmony and order within, the nuns carefully regulated communication with outsiders: some guarded entrances and exits to the outside world (the *porteras*); others (the *celadoras*) ensured order by keeping watch in the common dormitories, the confessionals, the grille near the choir, or in the high choir. *Acompañadoras* chaperoned doctors, confessors, and other important male visitors to the convent, while the *escuchas* listened and reported informational exchanges to the abbess that occurred in the different parlors (the locutorios). They also patrolled the parlor where the abbess conducted business, the general work room for servants and secular women (*sala de las mujeres*), and stood near the revolving window akin to a "large, cylindrical lazy susan" (*torno*), where the nuns received goods, letters, or even abandoned infants![116] The position of messenger held great prestige in the convent, and only several senior, trustworthy servants were permitted to leave the convent and bring coveted news and goods from the outside world.[117]

Nuns were expected to uphold the four vows of obedience, poverty, chastity, and enclosure; fulfill their obligations to pray the Divine Office; heed the needs of the community and the sick; and maintain proper decorum. But, careful regulation of time and space also obligated them to face the quintessential task: exercising control of the internal self and one's vile nature. True spiritual conformity consisted of mastering the sins of arrogance, vanity, envy, or avarice. It also meant refraining from criticism or malicious gossiping (*murmuración*), disobedience, or fomenting sororial disputes.[118]

A rigorous monastic life required careful vigilance and discipline, but feeding and caring for the convent's inhabitants were also essential. In the seventeenth century, the Convent of Santa Clara required huge capital investments to support a population that had grown by nearly 20 percent between 1630 and 1650 and now consumed vast quantities of food and supplies. The convent spent hundreds of pesos on wheat flour, sugar, and corn to feed the 140 chickens eaten each month and raised in coops inside the cloister, and on cords of wood to stoke the ovens in the kitchen and in the organ.[119] The abbess also hired male day laborers on a temporary basis to transport heavy goods, build additions, and make repairs to the convent walls or irrigation canal that brought fresh water to the convent.[120] Still, the convent depended chiefly on female workers housed within to do the gardening and light carpentry work.

Each year, the abbess drew up a new job roster, which apportioned out and rotated different managerial tasks and positions to the nuns of the black and white veils, and more menial positions to the donadas. Because work was a central feature of convent life, and idleness was considered the soul's enemy, the abbess governed the entire religious community and appointed specific nuns of the black veil to the coveted supervisory positions.[121] The title of abbess (or *prelada*) was the highest post, and elections for this office occurred once every three years. Abbesses could (and did) serve multiple terms, and given the remarks in Ursula's diary, some elections were highly contentious.[122] Four *definidoras* or advisors (many had served previously as abbesses) accompanied the abbess on her duties and discussed internal administrative matters with her in council. Other posts reserved for nuns of the black veil included overseeing the purchase and distribution of goods (*provisoras*); operating the kitchen (*refitoleras*) or working in the infirmary (*enfermeras*); administering the various dormitories for novices, schoolgirls, secular women, and donadas and for the listeners, or escuchas. The delegation of these supervisory positions among the nuns of the black veil reinforced an internally differentiated class structure based on status and tenure.[123] Nuns of the white veil held notable, but less prestigious positions. They assisted the madres in charge of provisions for the convent or infirmary, served as *maestras* or teachers of the novices or schoolgirls, supervised the donadas, servants, and slaves working in the kitchen and performing other duties, and worked as celadoras, nurses, or *sacristanas* (female sextons).[124] Given the importance of regulating time in such a highly structured environment, a few nuns of the white veil were responsible for maintaining the clock in good working order. Others fashioned candles, tended the well, or assisted in the upkeep of the church, choir, or convent.[125]

The original constitution, written by the order's foundress, Clare of Assisi (1194–1253) encouraged all able sisters to perform manual labor and share in communal tasks. She hoped the nuns of her order would devote themselves to a life of poverty and independence in a self-sufficient environment.[126] However, medieval convents supported much smaller populations than during the early modern period. Even at its inception, the Convent of Santa Clara in Lima had a disproportionate ratio of servants or slaves to nuns. By Ursula's death in 1666, the number of nuns equaled the number of slaves and free servants.[127] (See Table 1.)

Table 1. Population and Social Categories in the Convent of Santa Clara, Lima, 1625–1669

Year	Black Veil	White Veil	White Veil Novices	Religious Servants (Donadas)	Servants (Criadas)	Slaves	Lay Persons (Seglares)	TOTAL
1625	126	16	—	21	—	—	—	163
1630	160	37	33	18	—	120	—	368
1633	157	22	—	62*	—	—	—	241
1637	201	26	27	39	147#	—	6	446
1651	261	21	10	—	175	98	46	611
1669	279	41	—	48	148	128	76	720

\# 147 servants and slaves; *includes 47 donadas, and 15 novices.
Sources: AGI, Lima 40; AGI, Lima 94; 1633, AAL, SC; Vargas Ugarte 1959, II:258; Tardieu 1997, II:202–3; Lavallé 1982, I:28bis; van Deusen 2001, 173–75.

In spite of Saint Clare's wishes, the Lima convent maintained a large servile population, in part because the majority of the nuns of the black and white veil disdained the more difficult and tedious manual labor. But economics also played a role. Many nuns of the black veil brought enough capital to pay the large dowries, purchase cells (or a portion), pay for living expenses, and buy and maintain slaves and servants: all of which could reach an estimated value of 12,000 pesos. For this reason, scholar Jean-Pierre Tardieu argues, slaves—a tremendously valuable commodity in colonial Lima—were hired out as day laborers, and their wages were used to defray the nun's living expenses.[128] This might involve preparing food or pastries for families who paid for their services and then fetched the goods at the torno on a specified day.

In order to circumvent ecclesiastical laws requiring a formal petition to the bishop to allow the entry of individual slaves (the Council of Trent prohibited an individual nun from owning property), a novice had to specify clearly that the slave would serve the community and, only in her spare time, her individual owner.[129] A benefactress interested in complying with monastic regulations and in procuring dependable labor for a daughter or relative in the convent might also stress the slave's piety and devotion toward the religious order or community in her petition. Donations often included provisions that stated that when the current slave owner died, ownership would then transfer to another nun specified in the will. This ensured that the female slave and her children would remain in the convent.

Between 1617 and 1645, Ursula was one of between 100 and 130 female African and criollo slaves who lived and worked in Santa Clara.[130] Like Ursula, many had entered with their owners, or formed part of a testamentary legacy. Some Creole slaves were born and raised in the convent and formed their own multigenerational family units. Still others came and went as day laborers, or stayed only until they married, or were sold. Often underestimated (or not included at all) in the convent censuses were the slave children who also resided and worked in the convent setting. Evidence for a later period shows that the very young—including four- and five-year-old boys and girls—came and went freely and performed small tasks such as running errands outside the convent. Others remained in the cloister to be raised by their masters.[131]

Enslavement meant legal bondage, but the social standing of a slave in Santa Clara depended on several complex, interrelated factors. For one, the status of the mistress, and whether the slave formed part of the novice's household before entering the convent, often determined the power and authority of the slave once she entered the cloister. Historian Luis Martín has found that the slaves of aristocratic nuns were considered senior to those slaves whose owners came from less affluent backgrounds. Privileged slaves lived in comfortable cells and were not subjected to the more menial and humiliating tasks such as cleaning the irrigation canals or carrying water.[132] Given the fact that clothing served as such an essential marker of identity in colonial society, many of these slaves dressed in expensive silks and were beautifully adorned. This also distinguished them from slaves considered to be of a lower class. Even Ursula, who on later reflection considered herself to be vain and frivolous, once wrote, "In the past, I went to the visitors' parlor beautifully adorned from head to toe. It is very true that if my stockings were not a certain rose-colored shade I would not enter."[133] Either her master, Inés del Pulgar, maintained sizeable assets and provided her with lavish clothing, or her extra work as a day laborer fed her frippery. On the other end of the spectrum were the "community" slaves without an individual owner, family member, or patron to look after them. They occupied the lowest rung on the social ladder and often performed the drudgery others avoided. The convent provided each with basic necessities such as a blanket, a dress made out of coarse grogram (a coarse, loosely woven fabric), and a few accessories. It also assumed minimum medical expenses—to see a healer or doctor and obtain medicine—and, at death, her burial fees, a mass on her behalf, and a dress to be buried in.[134]

If patron-client relations between master and slave were key in determining the status of the slave, so too were occupational skills, personality, marital status, productivity, and remunerative skills.[135] A slave's access to the outside world and the ability to garner additional income as a wet nurse or food peddler, also brought esteem; and, in a world of never-ending moil, physical strength had great value. Strong and obedient slaves were exalted; sickly or chronically ill slaves were asked to leave temporarily or were sold.[136] Personality also mattered. Most nuns were concerned about the reliability of such slaves and preferred to hire those considered docile, hard-working, and reliable. A lawsuit in 1635 between the clarisa doña Angela de Francia and a lay woman provides a glimpse into how doña Angela ascribed value to her slave, Catalina Moçambique, because of her cooking abilities, punctiliousness, and restraint:

> In two years, she did not flee. In the convent, she served me with great care and intimacy; she only left the convent to marry, as many slaves do, and gave advanced notice. She is well known as an excellent cook, and she always served me and her other owners punctually.[137]

The hundreds of African and Afro-Peruvian women who formed part of Ursula's world had somewhat different experiences, depending on their access to capital, who their patron was, and their qualifications. In spite of these differences, however, a buffer zone clearly demarcated those women and children in bondage and their "free" superiors: the *criadas* (servants) who comprised more than one-quarter of the convent population. Because clarisas followed the second-order rules that tolerated servants, hundreds of these women worked for individual nuns and performed the never-ending communal tasks.[138] Like the slaves, the criadas were differentiated by their skills, productivity, and patron-client relations with their employers, the nuns.[139] Many who entered with a novice remained for life.[140] Criadas were legally free, but some had once been slaves and had then gained their freedom. This distinguished them from the slaves; however, the murky realm between "free" and "freed" could be a sticky matter, particularly when the legal status of a worker remained in doubt. In one suit that occurred in 1663, the mulata "servant," Feliciana de Salinas, pressed charges against doña María Salinas, a black-veil nun who claimed to be her owner. She argued that, although her father, Don Juan de Salinas, had had "an illicit friendship" with her mother, he had purchased Feliciana's freedom. She claimed that he "publicly recognized me as his daughter, fed and raised me, and sent me to the convent under his sister's care." Unfortunately for her, the judge ruled that her freedom was contingent on doña María's death.[141]

Criadas might occupy the indistinct terrain between freedom and enslavement, but donadas often supplanted servants if the criadas' numbers surpassed the acceptable limit of one criada for every ten nuns, or a vigilant archbishop decided to conduct an ecclesiastical visit.[142] That may be why, in 1631, Archbishop Arias de Ugarte mandated that donadas perform communal labor in addition to individual service.[143] The abbess readily complied, because three years later, a report enumerated forty-seven professed donadas and sixteen novices. This represented a significant demographic surge relative to the rest of the female religious population (see Table 1, above).[144] Still, their numbers never rivaled the numbers of criadas present in the convent. In fact, the vast majority of the donadas had spent most of their lives in the convent working in the service of a nun as a criada. Some had even entered as abandoned infants on the rotating torno. Many were illegitimate or orphaned with few family bonds outside the convent. Nearly all donadas in Santa Clara were Indians, castas, or Afro-Peruvian. A few, like Ursula, had once been slaves.[145]

Procedurally, the candidate herself, a nun, or a family member requested formal admittance as a novice in the following manner:

> I, doña Josefa de Castilla Altamirano, nun of the black veil in this Convent of Santa Clara, have a girl named Josefa, a quarterona. She has lived here in my care since the age of two, and she has never left the convent. Presently, she is serving the community with great care and wishes to become a donada to better serve Our Lord. I am obligated to give 400 pesos for her dowry at the time of her profession. I request that the abbess propose that the nuns cast their vote for this to take effect.

A nun promoting a donada's candidacy to the community emphasized her occupational skills and any distinguishing virtues. Candidates generally specified spiritual motives, as well as their fear of living in the *siglo* (the secular domain) as their main concerns and reasons for wishing to become a donada. If the application received communal approval (subject to a vote), the abbess would then write to the archbishop:

> The information provided by this nun is correct and it is true that Josefa María is very virtuous and is serving the community well. This year she rings the bell. From a tender age she has always been obedient—I ask Your Honor to give the license . . . doña Beatríz de Aguilar, Abbess.[146]

After one year as a novice, a chaplain examined the girl, asking formulaic questions about her age, because donadas were required to be over sixteen.[147] Was she married, or had she consented to marry? Did she carry any contagious diseases? Had she voluntarily chosen her profession, or did she think that being a donada would guarantee more freedom from the harsh work regimen of the convent? After answering these questions and affirming her desire to spend her life in the cloister attending to the needs of the community, the novice recited her vows and donned a shoulder-length white wimple, distinct from those worn by the nuns.

Because donadas underwent a formally sanctioned procedure to become religious servants, they gained additional status and held more prestigious occupations than did the criadas or slaves.[148] For instance, once donadas had completed their assigned daily tasks, they could assist in the Divine Office.[149]

Although supervised by a nun of the white veil, some worked as sextons, cleaning religious objects and washing the linen for the altar. Each morning they prepared the chapel for mass: they lit candles and ensured that the flowers, incense, ornaments, and other religious objects were readied for the priest. Donadas who were not sextons performed other religious duties. A few rang the bell to specify the liturgical hours. Those with great strength carried the heavy cross during religious processions held within the convent. The nuns welcomed donadas who exhibited a particular artisanal flair in fashioning candles for processions, festivals, and special masses. They also recognized those donadas like Ursula for their remarkable expressions of piety, mortification, and humility.

Just as women of color outside of convents could express their spiritual fervor by tending to the ill in hospitals or convent infirmaries, by preaching in the streets, or by holding spiritual gatherings, Ursula represented a group of women in convents who sought to define themselves primarily as spiritual beings *in spite* of how other perceived them. The feelings of many donadas are probably echoed in the words of the mystic Juana Esperanza de San Alberto, a contemporary of Ursula and a slave in the Carmelite convent of Puebla, Mexico. At one point when she was asked to leave because the nuns wanted to live a more Spartan life with fewer material possessions and slaves, Juana resisted by saying, "Although I am black, I am beautiful, and the powerful King loved me and brought me to His Church to introduce me to this delightful House of Retirement."[150]

Although donadas performed tasks associated with religious rituals, Ursula often wondered in her diary whether the donadas had any significant religious value. Indeed, Saint Francis and the soul of a pious black women who had lived and died in the convent affirmed to Ursula in several visions that pious donadas were cherished by God. Perhaps Ursula felt that donadas were not well regarded by members of the Santa Clara community. Certainly, the questions put forth to candidates about to profess their vows—whether they had been asked to marry, had any infectious diseases, or wanted additional freedom–lacked any tangible concern for spiritual matters.[151] Moreover, descriptions of pious donadas by conventual chroniclers failed to mention the exacting communal tasks they performed repeatedly. Although Ursula took her vows as a donada in 1647, she continued to labor each day, either in the kitchen, sacristy, or infirmary until her death in 1666.[152] (See Figure 5.) Her tasks also changed from month to month and from year to year. In her journal she reported kneading the dough, cooking, tending the kitchen fire, serving food to the nuns in the refectory, and, at one point, working in the infirmary each Friday changing bed linens and bandages.[153] Although such tasks were tedious drudgery, they also afforded other opportunities. As Ursula cleaned soiled bandages in the infirmary she witnessed doctors (*medicos*) being escorted into the infirmary and nuns trained in medicine (*enfermeras*), bleeding and purging patients of their "impurities." She watched and learned from the *ensalmadoras* (those who cured the sick with psalms) as they assisted in the healing process.[154] She may also have applied skills learned decades before she entered the convent from the criollas and mulatas in Lima renowned for their curative powers.[155] The healing techniques she learned eventually enabled Ursula to exercise her own spiritual prowess and gain a reputation as a

Figure 5. View of the kitchen where Ursula and other slaves and servants spent much of their time. Photo by Ana María Vega.

healer in the convent. In her diary Ursula described using contemporary methods of bathing the ill frequently and supplying a plethora of remedies to cure various maladies. When other tonics failed, she placed her hands (like an ensalmadora, but without referring to herself as such) on the injured part of a body and invoked religious creeds, such as psalms.[156] Afterward, she would muse on the value of illness as "divine censure," or as a way to understand the propensity to sin. From her experiences, she came to view sickness as an opportunity to reflect on past transgressions.[157]

Like other donadas, Ursula changed the bandages of the sick and cleaned out irrigation ditches. But she tolerated the repulsive and menial tasks because she felt protected by spiritual beings, in particular, by the Holy Virgin Mother. After nearly falling to her death in the deep communal well, and after being saved by the scapular of the Virgin of Carmen (a specific apparition of the Virgin Mary), Ursula's life took a different course. This "signal" of divine favor earned respect from some nuns, who now saw her as a gifted, chosen child of God.[158] She also began having visions. The majority consisted of souls in purgatory communicating their woes to Ursula in the hope that she might convince Christ or Mary to have compassion and diminish the sentence of those souls trapped in this tortuous habitat. Over the decades, Ursula became familiar with the interior worlds of living and deceased nuns in Santa Clara. Ursula even received "visits" (apparitions) from priests revealing their sundry peccadilloes, including one who claimed to do his penance for his "useless diversions" at the grille near the choir.[159] The spirits of Afro-Peruvian servants or children appeared to recount the grave illnesses and excessive work they had endured. Over time, Ursula's redemptive skills garnered a tremendous amount of respect in the claustral community, in part, because by the seventeenth century, concern for, and awareness of the otherworldly realm of purgatory preponderated the early modern Catholic world.

"In the Grave I May Speak Through the Stones": Purgatory and Popular Perceptions of the Beyond

By the early modern period, the majority of Catholics believed that only the most unsullied souls ascended directly to paradise; most resigned themselves to spending some time in purgatory.[160] The idea of purgatory, which developed gradually during the medieval period, presupposed the acceptance of an afterlife. It also involved a temporal interlude, during which each soul would become involved in "judicial proceedings" that would then entail a specified type and amount of punishment and purification in a locale called "purgatory."[161] Each soul knew its stay was temporary and depending on the gravity and number of transgressions, "time" spent in purgatory varied from several hours to centuries.

Purgatory functioned as a parallel dimension of earthly "reality," because the notions of judgment and punishment corresponded directly to the ideas of free will and individual responsibility for conduct.[162] Once in purgatory, many awakened, as though their life had been a dream. They witnessed their wasted hours and acts of egregious folly squandered in games, useless chatter, or sinful indulgence. This realization formed an initial stage of their purgation, along with the knowledge that sins might have been expiated by prayer, contrition, and good works. As a result, some suffered emotional pain as a result of their separation—albeit temporary—from God (*pena de daño*). However, the vast majority of sinners achieved purity through a type of "soul body," by experiencing tremendous physical pain (*pena de sentido*) that varied proportionally to the type of sins committed.[163]

Theologians and female mystics who experienced visions of purgatory, often described the purgative process in alchemical terms.[164] As one spirit explained to Ursula, "in order to go to Heaven, souls had to be purified with fire: to become like the purest crystal—without a single imperfection—before entering into Glory."[165] Others described the soul's allegorical transformation into clear gold.[166] One of the most celebrated medieval saints, Birgitta of Sweden (1303–73) provided a graphic description of this chemical process. Above the darkness of hell

> is the greatest pain of Purgatory that souls may suffer. And beyond this place is another place where there is less pain, that is none other but the lack of firmness in strength.... The third place is above, where there is no other pain but the desire of coming to God . . . as if other metals were meddled with gold and burnt in a most hot fire and should so long be purged, that the other metals were refined away; and the gold stayed

pure and clean though the other metal was strong and thick, so that it should need the hotter fire, and the gold was like running water, and all burning. Then the master of the work puts the gold in another place, where it shall take its true form and shape by sight and by touch.[167]

Most theologians believed that the separated soul body could experience fire corporeally because it was considered the most common purifying element. Purification also involved torture, but the amount and degree varied considerably. Still, as church father Thomas Aquinas (1225–74) once said, the slightest pain in purgatory "surpasses the greatest pain one can endure in this world."[168] Visionaries recounted souls being subjected to horrible atrocities, including extreme temperatures: from flames licking ethereal bodies to being plunged into gelid waters.[169] Souls experienced pestilence, epidemics, or storms; some tore out their hair, gnashed their teeth; others were encased in chains or engulfed by darkness. Those in the lower levels could hear the screams of the condemned, while being tormented incessantly by demons.[170] Some experts thought that torture could be mollified and souls allowed periods of respite. Most agreed, however, that suffering diminished as the soul undergoing purification drew nearer to God.

Humans experienced the external world through the five senses of sight, hearing, touch, smell, and taste; sin involved abusing those senses in some way.[171] Theologians postulated that after death, worldly sensorial phenomena lost their "natural" functions and became instruments of torture in purgatory. That is why so many treatises exaggerated the senses. Accounts described soul bodies with large cavernous mouths. Horrible odors accosted them; nightmares impaired their vision; an unquenchable thirst or bitter taste affected the palate; they endured eternal hunger pangs; or flames discharged from their mouths.[172] Ursula once witnessed atrocities being waged on sinners' eyes:

> Then devils appeared with some iron meat hooks, pulling out their eyes, and then putting them back in place. I said, "I believe in the Most Holy Sacrament." The voices said, *Who do you think they are? In their lifetime, they did not shed a single tear for their sins. Those eyes that should have paid attention to God's mercy never mended their ways.*[173]

Some theologians took great pains to catalog sensorial torture methods. In Lima, an instructional manual written for Jesuit pupils at the Colegio de San Martín associated each sense with a distinct form of corporeal punishment:

> Vision is tormented by the presence of demons and other condemned ones.
> Hearing with continual curses and jibes from the tormentors.
> Touch with incredible fire and other forms of horrendous torture.
> Taste with an intolerable bitterness.
> Smell with the pestilential odor of the many who are there.[174]

Graphic descriptions of torture were equally matched by discussions of purgatory's location and its defining features both during the medieval and early modern periods. Numerous medieval texts and popular oral traditions focused on purgatorial prototypes. They spoke of pilgrimages, otherworldly journeys, and the apparitions of ghosts, or "wandering souls" near cemeteries.[175] Others insisted that purgatory consisted of the spot where the individual had sinned. The church fathers, from Augustine (354–430) to Saint Gregory (d. 385) and from Saint Bonaventure (1221–74) to Thomas Aquinas, pondered the location and size of a place where purgation might occur, as well as the nature of punishment after death.[176] According to Hildegard of Bingen (1098–1179), purgatory comprised three-fifths of earth; only a high mountain range separated the "stench of sins" from the abode of mortals.[177] Considered a "classic" visionary of purgatory, Dante Alghieri (1265–1321) created a fantastic "space" consisting of seven circles—one stacked above the other—representing each of the deadly sins.[178] As one approached the summit, the circumference diminished and the soul became more purified. Medieval renderings of Saint Patrick's purgatory presented a specific place to purge sins.[179] Saint Birgitta's *Book of Revelations* described what would eventually become the standardized conception of purgatory among theologians: levels ranging from the darkest regions closest to hell, to the apical reaches, where highly evolved souls no longer suffered physical pain but continued to be tormented by their longing to enter heaven.[180] Early modern accounts tended to situate purgatory next to hell in the center of the earth. Often descriptions alluded to bizarre flora and fauna, deep rivers and dank lakes filled with pestilence, or to strange beasts and mewling demons, and their wailing, braying, trumpeting, or uttering of guttural sounds.[181]

Throughout the medieval and early modern periods, some described different cavities (*senos*) that corresponded to a taxonomy of vices and occupations. For instance, the medieval Saxon mystic Hildegard of Bingen saw souls soaked in bitterness and "those who had chosen the gluttony of the belly" burning in fires of assorted colors. For the sin of envy:

> I [Hildegard] saw a large mountain with a cave filled with fire and boiling pitch. There were a lot of vipers crawling around the mountain and the cave had a narrow mouth through which souls entered and left. In addition, near this mountain there was a tremendous cloud of great horror that had a fiery cloud above it filled with scorpions. The souls of those who had sweat with the hatred of envy while they had been alive were twisted by these torments.[182]

In Lima, the seventeenth-century clarisa nun Marceliana de Carvajal witnessed the sufferings of avaricious merchants, lascivious couples, gluttonous nuns, and foul-mouthed individuals. Once, she envisioned a table in flames where gamblers sat, each with a devil at his side encouraging him to win, while knowing full well:

> They would lose their estate, and [then] suffer horrible torment, because [the devils] grabbed them by the mouth with tongs of fire, letting them know this was for swearing and the pledges they had made while gambling. The [gamblers'] swollen, black tongues hung from their mouths, while the devils who accompanied them during the playing session gave them strong blows on their teeth, causing them extremely intense pain.[183]

Ursula also beheld horrible atrocities, including demons shoveling pitch into the mouths of "vagabonds who spent their lives indulging in pleasure: the liars, gluttons, those who could not leave well enough alone, the vengeful and dishonest ones, and those who did not fear God."[184]

Although rare during the medieval period, apparitions of the dead after 1500 increased proportionally as beliefs in purgatory grew and the Catholic Church worked to exploit them.[185] By the sixteenth century, the fear of the devil, spurred the publication of "how-to" manuals that helped curious readers discern between helpful and diabolic ghosts.[186] For the living, the experience of communications with tortured prisoners in purgatory varied. Some souls could be heard making raucous, disruptive noises, while others actually appeared in a recognizable "earthly form." This notified the visionary of an unexpected "visitor" and reassured her that the dead soul was a friendly being. A renowned Spanish mystic, Francisca del Santíssima Sacramento (1561–1629), sought to explain how and why the dead appeared:

> Always, when souls appear, it is in a reserved and anticipated manner. First, they make noise, next they appear as shadows, then [they become] clearer, and finally all of them appear. That is so that those who will pray on their behalf, and [those] who see them, will no longer be fearful.[187]

To Ursula some souls maintained their human "form" and were recognizable by their countenance or by telltale garments. Others she only perceived audibly, or they were sheathed in shadowy darkness. When Ursula beheld such figures, especially when they looked as though they had been disinterred, she often suspected that the vision was inspired by the devil.[188]

Over the centuries, theologians spilt a great deal of ink trying to determine the distinct theological, geographical, and social dimensions of purgatory. They determined how to assist souls by granting indulgences, requesting masses, or giving alms. Yet, purgatory continued to be nebulous and imprecise; its lure created comprehensible, fantastic spaces and "events" that gripped mystics, lay persons, and church fathers for centuries.[189] Once session twenty-three of the Council of Trent (1545–63), formally reconfirmed its existence and the ability of the living to intervene on behalf of the dead, theologians throughout Europe began quoting and debating explanations found in medieval texts. As a result, treatises on the subject proliferated. Throughout Catholic Europe, a "golden age of purgatory" ensued, as the ideas printed in these fresh texts reached a lay audience long familiar with such discussions.[190] Such rich material became the manna of literary and theatrical works.[191] Graphic descriptions of the torments of hell and purgatory found in devotional manuals served as a favorite topic for preachers seeking to play on the human emotions of fear and morality.[192] Sermons also drew on myths of the popular Valencian saint Vincent Ferrer (1350–1419), known to have released his sister from her otherworldly entombment and considered God's messenger of penance to prepare for judgment; or extolled the virtues of the Italian saint Nicholas of Tolentino (1245–1305), known to help souls in purgatory.[193] Visual depictions of saints rescuing beleaguered spirits from purgatory became a more popular theme for the frescoes and altar paintings throughout Europe.[194]

The cult of the saints developed in tandem with the growing concern of mortals about to face judgment or concerned for their departed loved ones. After the Council of Trent, the living chose carefully from among the cadre of spiritual beings in heaven for extra assistance to save their own souls from the fires of purgatory or to diminish the stay of those already there. Apparitions of souls or ghosts that had long been common now served an additional purpose.[195] Angels assisted the living, as did certain saints.[196] Since the fourteenth century, when Saint Birgitta spoke of Mary the Queen of Heaven as an important intercessor, the Virgin had been seen as the most efficacious ambassadress on behalf of souls.[197] As an additional recourse, penitent individuals sought out gifted holy women to serve as celestials channels, because they could consult with them in the flesh and report back on events in the beyond.

This vital connection between the inhabitants of the spirit world and the living may seem odd, but in the medieval period, the dead formed an integral part of "life." They were considered an active "age group" that fomented a sense of social cohesion.[198] By the early modern period, death had become even less of a frontier between the living and the deceased, and the existence of purgatory meant that loved ones could "extend" the life of the dead and help intervene on their behalf.[199] Family members expressed concern, love, and support for those in the beyond through their prayers and requests for masses (provided for by the deceased in their wills); or by fasting, buying indulgences, participating in confraternities dedicated to such causes, or leaving bequests in their own wills.[200] Such acts served as a form of social "exchange" in the sense that the living believed their efforts could accomplish two goals: they might alleviate the suffering and diminish the length of time of their loved ones' stay in purgatory; and their charity might eventually assist their own case.[201]

Fear also played a decisive role. The idea of measuring a soul's worth encompassed the entire spectrum of human emotions: including, fear, hope, self-interest, altruism, punishment, and notions of sin and salvation.[202] Few enjoyed the prospect of entering into a state of passive subjection to God's judgment; thus, fear became the modus vivendi for many wishing to avoid being surrounded by devils in hell.[203] Such arguments certainly furnished intellectual weaponry for Catholic reformers attempting to stamp out sin, but there is no doubt that by the sixteenth century, preparation for a "good" death, which commonly involved paying large sums for indulgences, masses, chaplancies, or establishing wills, became a more popular practice.[204] The dissemination throughout the Spanish Empire of a Spanish translation of Ignatius of Loyola's *Spiritual Exercises* (1613) included meditations on death and the afterlife that had a tremendous impact worldwide.[205] For Loyola, the imagination served as both a deterrent against moral lassitude and the principle meditative tool to conjure up the flames, laments, odors, and emotional intensity of life in hell.

Preparedness for a "good death" also entailed drawing up a will specifying prayers and masses to be said for the deceased. People believed that proper burial rituals, including dressing the corpse with the religious habit of a particular order, surrounding it with lighted candles, incense, bread, and wine, and the practice of distributing alms to a charitable cause, ensured reaching paradise on the day of judgment.[206] By the seventeenth century, services offered on behalf of the dead had been regulated and systematized by the church. Of these services, masses became more differentiated and focused: they ranged from those for orphaned souls (*ánimas solas*), specific family members, or those suffering the most in purgatory.[207] Even on the Spanish imperial level the response was enthusiastic. In 1624 King Philip III wrote to Pope Urban VIII asking that priests and friars throughout his empire say three commemorative masses on the Day of the Dead.[208] Broadsheets explained how to leave bequests in wills, or how to request masses in the name of saints known to assist souls in purgatory.[209] Donations to pious and charitable works and institutions, thought to diminish time in purgatory, increased.[210] Papal indulgences proliferated, as did treatises trying to explain them.[211]

As the obsession with purgatory reached new heights in sixteenth-century Catholic Europe, it also traveled to the "new" world with the first colonizers. By the seventeenth century, it had reached a fevered pitch in the colonial vice-regal capital, Lima. Just as tolling bells throughout Catholic Europe indicated the passing of a soul from one realm to the next, each evening in Lima, bells chimed on behalf of dead souls (the *toque de ánimas*) while heads nodded in prayer. For a brief period, the timorous peals and murmured pleadings linked the living faithful with fleshless souls.[212] Lima's inhabitants also cared for their dead in other, more material ways. Evidence for Lima suggests corporate groups and individuals actively invested large amounts of capital in the afterlife, and that a growing number of confraternities—on the Metropolitan and parish levels— were dedicated to saving souls in purgatory.[213] For instance, the Chapel for the Souls of the Blessed Crucifix in the cathedral was obviously considered a "privileged altar," because it provided three thousand masses for souls in purgatory each year.[214] In 1616, the members of the Confraternity of the Blessed Souls of Purgatory asked the Pope for special indulgences for masses for the dead.[215] Even individual nuns of Santa Clara founded chaplaincies (*capellanías*) or funds that provided for masses to be said by a specific priest to benefit tortured souls. In 1644, the abbess of Santa Clara, María Magdalena Velez Roldán, established a chaplaincy to say eighty masses each year for souls in purgatory.[216] In addition, at least two brotherhoods for the dead existed in Santa Clara: the confraternity of Our Lady of Carmen (known for her redemptive skills), founded by Ursula, and the brotherhood of the Blessed Souls (of Purgatory).

"Apostoles of the Dead": Medieval Female Intercession

Although Saint Patrick and Dante Alghieri metaphorically traveled to purgatory, the work of intercession on behalf of the dead had long been considered a female responsibility.[217] It served as a natural extension of women caring for the corpse and of their weeping and mourning loved ones' absences.[218] Through birth, women brought life into the world; they also helped the dying make the transition to the next world. Medieval scholar Barbara Newman argues that women were the "midwives at the birth of purgatory" (which occurred long before the twelfth century), and that female notions of piety shaped conceptualizations of this fundamental redemptive and punitive domain.[219] Caroline Bynum Walker emphasizes *suffering* as the principle modus operandi of female mystics of the period, for whom "purgatory was not primarily a physical place somewhere, a logical complement to heaven and hell; it simply *was* suffering—redemptive suffering—which was simultaneously Christ's and the sinners."[220] Evidence of both arguments can be noted in the medieval Saxon mystic Hildegard of Bingen's work (written between 1158–63), which fused popular otherworldly vision narratives with an emphasis on formalized penitential practice. Among other remarkable talents, she contributed an original theology of penance, purgation, and suffrages (intercessory prayers).[221]

Over time, whether at the Saxon monastery at Helfta, or in the *beguinages* (lay pious houses) of the Low Countries, or along the Italian streets where Franciscan tertiaries walked, a momentum gathered that influenced mystics for centuries to come.[222] Some of the exceptional medieval female intercessors included the aforementioned Hildegard of Bingen (1098–1179), as well as Christina the Astonishing (Mirabilis) (1150–1224), Saints Lutgarde (1182–1246), Gertrude of Helfta (1256–c. 1302), Birgitta of Sweden (1303–73), Angela of Foligno (1248–1309), Liduvina (1380–1433), Catherine of Siena (1347–80), and Catherine of Genoa (1447–1510). Their theological understandings of purgatory, purgatorial piety, and intercession on behalf of souls had a significant impact on early modern understandings of the beyond.

These women engendered a feminization of purgatorial piety for a number of reasons. For one, most clerical authorities considered intercession a safe, contemplative experience that flowed naturally from the function of prayer. But, intercession involved more than prayer. In effect, it also meant gaining authority as spiritual almsgivers who patronized the "needy dead."[223] How then, did women gain that authority? Priests said requiem masses (considered the most effective form of helping souls in purgatory); female intercession served as a counterpoint to this form of almsgiving.[224] Women could liberate souls through prayer and by requesting indulgences or masses, but they found another way to ameliorate the purgative process. Because bodily suffering played such a central function in medieval Christianity, female mystics claimed to experience the sins of others in their own bodies. The "soul" body often resembled its earthly form, and medieval intercessors felt able to "connect" with it.[225] Thus, women cared for the soul "body," just as they tended the bodies of suckling infants, the infirm, and the dying. Presumably, such largesse attracted an eager "clientele" and brought about the release of thousands of tortured prisoners. The thirteenth-century laywoman, Christina the Astonishing is probably the most spectacular example of how the body could purge the sins of unknown souls. On behalf of tormented souls, she crept into fiery ovens, leaped into cauldrons, plunged herself into piercingly cold waters, always emerging unscathed.[226]

Lutgarde of Anwières, another principal medieval mystic, helped liberate beleaguered souls in purgatory by subsisting on bread and beer for seven years, and by means of her tender supplications to God.[227] Unwittingly, she empowered women by demonstrating that they had the ability to work alone or with celestial beings to free the dead from purgatory. With divine permission (and intervention), female mystics could gain the authority to assume a redemptive role.[228] For Lutgarde and others who believed in sacrificing their bodies, pain served as a form of spiritual currency that assimilated the Passion of Christ with purgatorial agony.[229] Gertrude of Helfta, another saint later popular among visionaries in seventeenth-century Lima, forged a link between eucharistic devotion and prayer because she believed she could liberate souls by concentrating on the Eucharist and praying to the five wounds of Christ to help fellow nuns escape purgatorial flames.[230] As a seer, she described to the living the alms, suffrages, and masses needed to offer solace to their loved ones in the beyond.[231] Her visions also led her to understand that certain sins evoked particular forms of punishment.[232]

Not only did these visionaries embrace the suffering of others and communicate the needs of the dead to the living, but their own "soul" bodies helped demarcate the topography of purgatory. In their astral travels they pondered purgatory's exact location, "viewed" its fiery cavities, witnessed the earth behave like a large cavernous mouth that engulfed sinful victims, "sensed" murky lakes and gorges, and beheld the most bizarre flora and fauna. Saint Liduvina, who was from Schiedam, Holland, reportedly traveled frequently in spirit with her guardian angel to purgatory where she saw numerous souls distributed in different areas according to their sins.[233] The medieval itinerant Swedish Saint Birgitta's simple and masterful *Revelations* contained images of judgment, purgatory, and various forms of castigation.

Profoundly influenced by Birgitta's spiritual and political missions, Catherine of Siena (1347–80) ordered her secretary to transcribe a two-volume manuscript copy of Birgitta's *Revelations* that remained in Italy.[234] Catherine, too, had a tremendous impact: her writings helped to further codify now longstanding practices of female intercession, and a number of hagiographies, including one by Spanish Cardinal Francisco Jiménez de Cisneros (1437–1517), helped promote her cult and saintly virtues throughout the Spanish kingdoms.[235] In addition, a biography written by Catherine's confessor, Raymond of Capua, circulated widely in colonial Lima; in fact, one seventeenth-century limeña nun compiled her own mystical visions based in part on what she had read.[236] Because of Catherine's devotion to souls in purgatory, Christ bestowed on her the ability to discern the state of souls through her corporeal senses and thus hasten their salvation.[237] Catherine's body became a vessel that absorbed others' suffering, just as Christ had suffered for all sinners. Hers was "the torch of the *imitatio Christi*" that lit the idea of the body as an instrument of transcendence for others' souls.[238] Another Italian tertiary, Catherine of Genoa (Caterina Fieschi Adorno), maintained a reputation for sainthood while living and composed a treatise on purgatory that focused on the positive effects of purgation. She argued that once fire, rays of light, and lightening consumed sins, souls could eventually discover the "divine ray."[239] Purgation brought about the "final consummation, the full actualization of the soul."[240]

These and other medieval mystics contributed an experiential, direct knowledge of purgatory that influenced theologians and female mystics for centuries, and that led to a renaissance in the seventeenth century, particularly in Lima.

They developed the idea that the body could substitute as an instrument for others' suffering; they equated purgatorial suffering with the temporary loss of God (*pena del daño*); they transformed into spirit and traveled to unknown and dangerous places; and acted as a channel between celestial beings and the living. Not only did female intercession help troubled souls, but these mystics also found a way to fuse their spirits with the sufferings of Christ, which provided them with a direct "divine" education and offered them an opportunity to gain a sense of power and authority that, under other circumstances, might evade them.[241] Saving souls in purgatory was seen as a social, selfless, beneficial enterprise, both for the living and the dead, and by itself was not viewed as a threat by increasingly scrupulous church authorities.

Early Modern European and Latin American Visionaries

In late-fifteenth-century medieval Castile, the "mothers of Saint Teresa (of Avila)" contributed their own renderings of purgatory, based in part on the knowledge they received from their northern European and Italian foremothers such as Birgitta of Sweden and Catherine of Siena.[242] These Spanish "mothers" recorded their visions, claimed that the voice of Christ spoke through them, and experienced unfettered visions and raptures during a tolerant and receptive era. After the 1520s, however, support for such practices began to wane.[243] By the time the Council of Trent had ended in 1563, authorities strived to develop clearer notions of orthodoxy and heterodoxy and reiterated the fundamentals of the Catholic faith. Theologians distinguished three different types of visions: intellectual, in which the presence of Christ is perceived but not "seen"; imaginary visions through the eyes of the soul; and corporeal visions, which occurred through the eyes of the body.[244] Ecclesiastical tribunals and theologians probed whether apparitions were well intentioned or steeped in diabolic discourse, while scientific treatises attempted to distinguish true from false prophecy.[245]

Alarmed at the increasing number of beatas and visionaries throughout the Spanish kingdoms who garnered respect and authority from paupers and princes alike, Inquisitors systematically began persecuting them from the 1520s onward.[246] Accused of false sanctity or heresy (a corruption of Catholic doctrine), they faced scrutiny for their claims to authority as conduits of the divine. Many visionaries conceived their "heretical" ideas out of ignorance or erroneous judgment, but others claimed to rely on their visions as their principal source of authority. Skeptical priests were most likely to censure a nun or beata if her writings bordered on heresy or a confessor had eulogized the intercessorial skills of a deceased protégé.[247] Perhaps, as scholar Clare Guilhem posits, inquisitorial persecution had less to do with rooting out heresy than devaluing "the feminine" and female practices of piety.[248] This may be true, because to some theologians, the female body, central to the visionary experiences of sixteenth-century mystics (as it had been for their medieval predecessors), functioned as a vessel of sin and corruption. It was considered to be humid and vaporous by nature, thus more receptive to "vehement passions."[249] Ultimately, it served as the "portal of the devil."[250]

In spite of such assertions, female intercessors in Spain actively contributed to a now longstanding tradition of intercessorial work on behalf of the living and the penitent dead. They did so in a climate radically different from their medieval counterparts but still drew on their knowledge of purgatory and the hereafter to help bolster their own authority. Spanish mystics also followed the lead of French, Italian, and Portuguese mystics who pursued a similarly cautious, more introspective course as redeemers of souls in purgatory.[251]

Undoubtedly the most influential Spanish mystic of the early modern period, Teresa of Avila once compared her trials as a nun with purgatorial suffering, adding that, in fact she only deserved hell.[252] Like other nuns, she prayed for the souls of purgatory and witnessed the fires of hell and dead companions in her visions.[253] She pleaded for the living to be penitent and vigilant: for then they might experience death as sweetness, rather than as travail.[254] To her, the horrendous bodily pain, which she experienced, signified the "tremendous work of the soul." Moreover, in her carefully crafted portrayal of the *moradas*, or levels of spiritual purification necessary to reach God, she claimed that the seventh required the cleansing of the soul: equivalent to the travail one faced in purgatory before reaching glory.[255] But, Teresa also duly noted the extreme difficulty in reaching this level when she wrote, "Oh, how we wish that the fire's flame would not have sufficient heat to burn us."[256]

Like her medieval sister, Catherine of Genoa, Teresa burned with the divine fire: the place near her heart, the color of saffron.[257] Juan del Castillo, a medical doctor and expert on mystical theology in seventeenth-century Lima, wrote a compendium on the ideas of Teresa of Avila, which influenced a number of holy women there. He explained what was called the *via purgativa* (purgative life) of Teresa in the following manner:

> One of the greatest gifts God can bestow upon souls of this world is that they can purge their sins on earth, and they are able to recognize and experience purgatorial suffering. Once they have experienced this, they understand what is meant by the purification and cleanliness of a soul. They are so pure, clean and noble that not a single trace of a defect remains. They now seem impeccable and in a god-like state: nothing bad can befall them.[258]

Still, Teresa's role as a brilliant saint deserving the emulation of others must be seen in light of the inquisitorial shadow, which cast fear into the hearts of visionaries. Unlike their medieval sisters, early modern visionaries, including Teresa, found it necessary to justify their visionary and corporeal experiences.[259] Claiming direct communication with God or Christ was still common, but that assertion could also lead to intense scrutiny and even the charge of heresy. As a result, women began emphasizing humility, charity, and obedience, three important characteristics of sanctity. As conduits of the divine will, they acted as submissive agents rather than as coredeemers and authorities.[260] They downplayed their role because acknowledgment of divine permission and assistance proved critical for holy women and for the male biographers or confessors who supported them. Stressing their humility and unworthiness to receive such a gift, they emphasized their obedience to God, to their confessor, or to other female or male religious authorities.[261] Many texts indicate that women still considered visions and intercessorial work on behalf of souls in purgatory to be safe if their visions occurred immediately after taking communion, and they avoided wild assertions and "contact" with diabolic forces.[262] They also knew not to be overbearing or arrogant. Those visionaries who emulated the medieval saints, such as Birgitta or Catherine of Siena, while claiming that their own redemptive and intercessorial roles had equivalent value, risked facing inquisitorial charges of false sanctity.

In spite of this shifting climate, and the precarious equilibrium between conformity and creativity, female intercessorial work still maintained a particular kind of openness. The resurgence of belief in the humanity of Christ and affective spirituality in sixteenth- and seventeenth-century Spain and Latin America left ample room for lay and religious women to explore the realms of the beyond.[263] In their work as apostles for the dead, they continued to rely on the tangible and ethereal, the spoken and the ineffable. The desire to control the unknown operated along a continuum where the boundaries between life and death, the quotidian and the esoteric, were not readily distinguishable. As the popularity of purgatory and the cult of the dead grew in the popular imagination, incantations and spiritual accounts written by or about nuns became increasingly laden with descriptions of purgatory and purgation. Just as apparitions of souls became more common, the number of lay and religious women claiming to predict their whereabouts also increased.[264] Some visions corroborated fairly standard descriptions of purgatory; other renderings stretched orthodox attitudes toward life, death, and the afterlife.[265]

In fact, many ecclesiastical authorities consulted and cited the testimonials of medieval female mystics on the beyond. For instance, José de Boneta y Laplana's *Gritos de purgatorio*, which went through thirty editions and translations into the major Western languages, cited the medieval revelations of Lutgarde, Birgitta, and Catherine of Siena as important authorities on purgatory.[266] Sixteenth- and seventeenth-century treatises brimmed with references to the meditative experiences of these and other medieval mystics.[267] For instance, an influential treatise on "authentic" forms of prophecy written by Juan de Horozco y Covarrubias in 1588 featured chapters on Saints Birgitta, Catherine of Siena, and the yet-to-be-canonized Teresa of Avila.[268] Leandro de Granada's work, *Luz de maravillas* (1607), examined the "truthful" nature of the corporeal, imaginary, and intellectual visions and cited Gertrude as a solid authority on purgatorial apparitions.[269] New editions and translations, including Angela of Foligno's work in Latin (1505) and Spanish (1510) prompted by Cardinal Jiménez de Cisneros, profoundly influenced Saint Teresa of Avila.[270] The translation and diffusion of these European accounts achieved two important goals. It helped continue the feminine "hagiographic tradition," because female visionaries in Latin America could more easily obtain verbal or written information about their medieval predecessors, and it fostered the transculturation of notions of purgatorial suffering and redemption to colonial Latin America.[271]

Given such a solid affirmation of the authenticity of medieval mystics and their incorporation into the theological canon, early modern Latin American mystics felt they had a firmer foothold to tread the murky realm of purgatory. They drew on popular lore and hagiographic literature to maintain a connection with female experts (which often met with the approval of male superiors). Thus inspired, they then fostered their own interpretations based on this theological bedrock. They called on Saints Gertrude, Birgitta, and Catherine of Siena for assistance or envisioned them while taking communion. More than any other mystic, however, Teresa of Avila served as the main source of inspiration among sixteenth- and seventeenth-century mystics in Spain and Latin America.[272] Even Ursula marveled at her teachings, which served as a blueprint for orthodox conduct.

In fact, contemporary biographies and autobiographies of holy women in the Americas reiterate many of the same patterns found in medieval and early modern Spanish, French, Portuguese, and Italian texts.[273] Like their European counterparts, visionaries (and their confessors writing posthumous works about their protégés) in the viceroyalties of New Spain and Peru considered visionary experiences of hell or purgatory a crucial component of their theological education, a type of "Purgatory 101."[274] Just as tales of purgatorial fires and pestilent waters served as a moral reminder for recalcitrant souls, an experiential knowledge of purgatory became integral to the curriculum vitae of Latin American mystics intent on demonstrating their charity, humility, and ability to suffer.[275] From their visions they understood how sins received particular punishments, and why it was so necessary for souls to gain assistance. As their spiritual knowledge deepened, they learned to "see" and "hear" the multitudes of needy souls.[276]

In Mexico, some biographers portrayed their female subjects with the attributes of compassion, clemency, and charity because of their efforts to free souls from their prison in the beyond.[277] They emphasized how their prayers, often said in the choir during mass (and more specifically during or after Communion), had the capacity to release them from the fiery depths of purgatory. In fact, many visionaries in convents maintained contact with nuns or family members in the beyond and procured their release from purgatory. Others claimed to witness hundreds of anonymous souls ascend to heaven.[278] In this sense, purgatorial intercession operated as a type of "life insurance" for family members and important authorities who could expect "rescue missions" from their loved ones after they died.[279] Scholar Kathleen Myers writes that when the Mexican mystic María de San José (1656–1709) entered the convent in Puebla, she relinquished physical contact with her family, but, "took on an even larger spiritual family, including human and supernatural members–among them, eventually, the souls of her own family members."[280] Latin American visionaries might view souls in the fiery depths of purgatory, or in the case of Catarina de San Juan (1609[?]–1688), known as the *china poblana*, from Puebla de los Angeles in Mexico, encounter them while walking down the street.[281]

Emphasis on living an ethical life and preparing for a good death complemented those visions that served as moral reminders, and even admonitions. Like the medieval mystic Lutgarde of Anwières who warned fellow nuns of their prospects of eternal damnation, Latin American nuns, in particular, emphasized the need for the living to pay heed. In fact, seventeenth-century accounts of purgatory maintained a more rigorous, moralistic tone. Nuns described saving their companions and, in the process, imparted a "moral" lesson to the members of their community. One nun in Puebla, Mexico, informed her sisters that their prayers could not alleviate the stay of one beleaguered nun in purgatory because she had talked during mass.[282]

Throughout the viceroyalty of Peru—in Quito, Tunja, Lima, and Arequipa—nuns and lay visionaries, all contemporaries of Ursula, were also busy saving souls.[283] In Arequipa, Peru, Ana de los Angeles Monteagudo (1602–86), a nun in the Convent of Santa Catalina, maintained a special devotion to Nicolas of Tolentino and followed his lead in assisting the souls of purgatory. Clearly intending to promote her beatification, the bishop of Arequipa, Antonio de León, wrote to the Council of Indies in 1679, describing the seventy-five-year-old nun as a sensitive creature who, "throughout the day is surrounded by the souls of purgatory whom God sends to her for assistance."[284] She was considered among the elite because the souls of King Philip IV, the viceroy, Pedro Fernández de Castro, the Count of Lemos (1667–72), a pope, and a legion of cardinals, archbishops, bishops, and other dignitaries had appeared in visions to Ana de los Angeles asking for suffrages.[285]

Ambassadresses to the Beyond in Seventeenth-Century Lima

Astonished at the spiritual gifts being bestowed on her, Ursula once wondered, "My Lord, am I Saint Catherine or Gertrude?" Certainly, as an intercessor, she was well aware of the paths her medieval predecessors had traveled.[286] Hagiographies, or the popular *Flos Sanctorum*, told Ursula and other pious women that the efficacious prayers of Saints Birgitta, Catherine of Siena and of Genoa, and Lutgarde had released thousands of souls from purgatory.[287] In convents and homes in seventeenth-century Lima, women heard tales of the intercessorial feats of Margaret of Cortona (1247–97), Angela of Foligno, and the "mothers of Saint Teresa."[288] They learned how Saint Lutgarde's efficacious prayers released the souls of prominent individuals from purgatory.[289] They imitated Saint Catherine of Siena by claiming to understand the "condition" of the dead through their senses and their souls.[290] They also learned from pictoral representations. For instance, the tertiary Feliciana de Jesús (a contemporary of Ursula's) gazed at a painting of Saint Gertrude for visionary "advice," to offer the important personages who consulted her.[291] Not only did seeing their images and hearing their stories "educate" a new generation of seventeenth-century limeña visionaries, but also they actualized a sense of timelessness and connection among females exercising purgatorial piety in the same mystic space.

The fact that women served as intercessors had just as much to do with popular patronage of these activities as with the venues they found to express their unearthly dialogues. Various documents, including beatification proceedings, Inquisition hearings, and idolatry records, show that the general populace, including influential authorities like the vicereine, frequently solicited spiritual advice on the whereabouts of dead or dying relatives from nuns, beatas, and lay women known for their esoteric skills.

In Lima, the "consumption" of purgatory was so pronounced that a diverse range of women crossing the porous markers of race and class worked as intercessors on behalf of the living and the dead to satisfy the "market demand."[292] Male clerics said masses, but consumers flocked to consult with healers and beatas; they "pulled at the sleeves" of nuns about matters of the beyond.[293] They even sought out those who specialized in "seeing" the "blackened" souls of the living.[294]

Women learned to become consultants to the beyond by apprenticing one another. They also developed and maintained tremendously diverse social networks.[295] Female intercessors did not necessarily know one another, but they shared a common discourse that enabled them to foster creative paradigms related to the beyond. They studied recondite secrets about purgatory in various settings: in the homes of other women, in the vestibule of a convent, or in the particular church they tended to frequent.[296] From sermons they understood how sins received particular punishments and why it was necessary for souls to gain assistance. From visions they learned to "see" and "hear" the multitudes of needy souls. In churches they "read" the narrative details of paintings depicting "naked souls" caught in flames and reaching for redemption.[297]

Women in seventeenth-century Lima, including Ursula's mentor, Luisa Melgarejo, attended wakes, requiem masses, and funerals, during which they paid close attention to the state of the body and soul.[298] One witness testified at the Inquisition hearing of one beata in 1622 that at the wake of Catalina Galván:

> [Ana María Pérez] had told [the witness] that the dead woman raised herself up from the coffin. Realizing that the friars and others were nearby, she waited until they were alone. Then the dead woman grabbed her by the wrist and said "forgive me, Ana María."[299]

Did this troubled soul wish to make amends in order to diminish her purgative travail? Given the common belief that apparitions and the dead could "speak" to the living, this particular witness must have been stunned.

In Lima Catholics of all walks of life believed that the earth near the sepulchre held magical, restorative powers. Among people of African descent, links between the living and the dead reinforced their devotion to the cult of the saints through the use of grave dirt and human relics for ritual purposes.[300] Indeed, concern and aid for the dead impregnated life, both in the secular and sacred realms of colonial Lima. For the nuns of Santa Clara, death was immediate and tangible. The catacombs underneath the main chapel served as a reminder that the bodies of the dead remained below the feet of the living, and that they too would soon become dust.[301] Religious literature offered guidance to help the nuns detect the visible signs of death's impending arrival.[302] When a clarisa died, each sister said fifty "Our Fathers" for the safe passage of her soul to the beyond, and the Constitutions of the Order of Saint Clare obliged the sisters to recite the special prayer for the dead and hold a general fast.[303] Nuns were intimately familiar with the process of dying; they could touch and observe the corpse and imagine the soul's trajectory from this world to the next. After the beloved Catalina de Cristo had died while on her knees in prayer in 1634, the clarisas kissed her feet, and touched the rosaries, religious metals and ribbons gracing the corpse during the three-day period before her burial. Some claimed that by touching her face they experienced a unique sense of pleasure and spiritual consolation. This signified to the community that her soul was at peace. On another occasion, when the nun Luciana de la Santíssima Trinidad expired, one nun saw three rays of light extend from her tomb up toward heaven.[304] Not only did they care for their own dead, but each Friday the community of clarisas participated in a procession around the main cloister for the redemption of souls trapped in purgatory.

Whether inside or outside convent walls, limeña intercessors on behalf of the dead expressed their concern in different ways. Some apostles for the dead wished to earn their daily bread, others, paradise. For other intercessors, their modus operandi involved imitating the humanity of Christ and his immense sacrifices for sinners. Still others acted as intercessors because they felt Christ had called on them to become coredeemers with Him. A fear of eternal purgation also inspired life-altering conversions to become apostles for the dead. The lovely, silk-laden mestiza visionary Isabel Cano experienced a transformative vision when her guardian angel appeared to show her purgatory and hell. She witnessed the horrible punishment lost souls endured, which contrasted with a vision of an Oz-like, heavenly city where she saw Saint Francis—brilliant like the sun—who informed her that she was unworthy of such a splendid place. Awakening in a "mortal sweat," she sold all her worldly possessions and, like Mary Magdalene, devoted herself utterly to a religious life.[305]

Sorceresses, beatas, and nuns in seventeenth-century Lima employed differ-ent *means* to alleviate suffering souls. They interceded using incantations, prayers, or self-flagellation. Continuing a medieval tradition, these apostles for the dead collected alms for requiem masses for "orphaned souls" or for a particular client, they dedicated their communion to a deceased soul, or entered a meditative state to locate a soul (in heaven, hell, or purgatory) or to predict the fate of the living.[306] Gerónima de San Francisco, a seventeenth-century nun of the discalced Convent of San Joseph, gained a reputation among limeños as an ambassadress to the beyond. Money in hand, lay persons flocked to her convent to solicit masses for the souls of their departed loved ones. However, she played another intercesso-rial role. Dead spirits appeared to complain when family members had not kept their promises or complied with specific bequests in their wills. Once, in a vision, a dead soul claimed that she, Gerónima, had been "negligent"! The spirit bitterly chastised the nun because she had failed to heed his request to quench the fires that consumed his ethereal soul. In her defense, Gerónima claimed that, although his will specified that two hundred pesos be paid to the convent, he was still remiss. Annoyed because of this, Gerónima had desisted in her efforts to help him. "Fearful of the cruelty with which she had treated that soul," she began feeling the effects of her negligence, and her nose bled uncontrollably. Nothing could allevi-ate her predicament until the two hundred pesos arrived, and the nun began to pray for his soul. When her nosebleed stopped, a humbled Gerónima recognized that she needed to serve as a channel of divine will, not her own.[307]

Several of Ursula's contemporaries in Santa Clara were renowned for requesting masses to help beleaguered souls. Gerónima de San Dionisio referred to herself as "Gerónima, slave of the blessed souls of purgatory." Not only did she collect alms to pay for masses (financing them out of pocket), but she kissed the feet of the dead, black or white, and claimed to have seen in visions more than three hundred souls dressed in habits and wimples.[308] Her dedication reached extremes. During the mass for the dead she imitated a corpse: "I placed myself as a dead person, with the shroud, four long candles, processional candlesticks and a cross from the altar; and the community sang a responsory for the dead for me."[309] Another clarisa, Marceliana de Carvajal (1607–99), proclaimed that she wanted to empty purgatory. During her lifetime, she requested more than eighty thousand masses for the souls in purgatory and wrote that while splashing holy water on the tombs, she heard voices clamoring, "Sprinkle some on me."[310]

Intercessors who envisioned souls in purgatory, often called upon a retinue of celestial beings to come to their aid. Some chose the assistance of guardian angels, the "Mother of mercy," the Virgin Mary, and a variety of saints.[311] Some invoked the spirit of Saint Martha, "the bad one," the lost soul, or the soul of a hanged man, all of which supposedly had the power to intervene on behalf of the dead. Many intercessors had learned these prayers from Spanish women who crossed the Atlantic to live in Peru. Their soft incantations went as follows:

> Lonely soul, lonely soul, lonely soul,
> The loneliest of all souls, the loneliest of all souls
> Come, soul
> I call out to you–I have some business for you
> I conjure you up, oh lonely soul.[312]

Of course words and objects (from Andean, African, and Spanish cultural traditions) used in seventeenth-century Lima to cast each spell varied.[313] Contemporaries of Ursula, including the beata Ana María Pérez, kneeled and gazed into a candle to detect whether souls would be lost or saved. She also reported seeing souls wandering in a narrow alley, which to her signified condemnation.[314] Ysabel Terranova de Angola, called a *çahori* (one who sees spirits), carried an image of Christ and of Saint Andrew in her mouth to determine whether a soul was in heaven, hell, or purgatory.[315]

A "career" as an intercessor also *garnered* a variety of results, whether income, the salvation of oneself or others, prestige and status, or divine favor. Some continued the medieval tradition of creating "life insurance" for family members by predicting the whereabouts of departed souls, or by witnessing the release of loved ones from their suffering. They knew that conjuring up dead spirits in purgatory could aid the living by fostering social exchanges between the dead and the living that also helped earn a living. Seers who did not charge money often claimed to have the ability to see loved ones being released from their suffering, or already enjoying the virtues of heaven.[316] Some tackled larger problems. Gerónima de San Francisco "negotiated" with God that "not one nun of this house be sent to hell."[317] Others saw important individuals, sometimes in compromising situations. Luisa Melgarejo saw the soul of her Jesuit confessor ascend to heaven and, much to the dismay of high-ranking ecclesiastical authorities, also espied the blessed and esteemed Archbishop Mogrovejo, who had died in 1606 suffering in purgatory. Ursula de Jesús herself once described seeing the queen of Spain, Isabel of Bourbon (1602–44):

> I saw thick walls, perhaps eleven feet high, in a big chasm. Below them, very large hands held iron ladles that spewed a lot of fire. In another area were sticks, like those used in a barbecue, on top of these walls. A lady of great authority stood above this. I wanted to know who she was, and they told me she was the queen of Spain. She sat with many books in front of her and did not seem to be suffering too much punishment in Purgatory.[318]

Others chose to save anonymous sufferers, sometimes by the hundreds.[319] Juana de Jesús de Guía, who professed as a nun of the black veil in the Convent of Santa Catalina in 1626, felt certain that tormented souls appeared to plead for her succor in gaining their release from purgatory. Her assistance often resulted in their ascension to heaven and, posthumously, the mention of her mystical abilities in a famous seventeenth-century Dominican chronicle.[320]

Purgatory's dominion over the lives of individuals became even more obvious in the visionaries who chose a lifelong path of suffering on behalf of others. Like the medieval saints Gertrude, Lutgarde, Christina the Astonishing, and Catherine of Siena, holy women in seventeenth-century Lima claimed that they felt the wracking pain of human suffering in their immaterial bodies, as well as in those of flesh and bone. The tertiary, Feliciana de Jesús, for example, suffered extreme temperature swings while purging the sins of others.[321] In her autobiography, the clarisa Marceliana de Caravajal claimed that suffering the torments of the souls of purgatory resulted in tremendous bodily pain and fatigue.[322] At her Inquisition hearing in 1623, where she was accused of false visions and miracles, one witness reported seeing the beata Isabel de Jesús:

> That night she went to a small alley to perform physical mortifications. There she heard the extremely loud sound of a trumpet and had a vision of four blacks making a huge racket. Holding a piece of paper, they declared all her sins in a loud voice. A boy, around nine years old came at them with a cutlass, saying "[Get] out of here, you bad guys, it is not so." Horrified and fearful, she fell to the ground where she remained for a long time. A neighbor who happened by took her to her room. Since then, she [has] reported suffering terrible pains and torment that have lasted over six years. She thought they were the afflictions of purgatory [*penas del purgatorio*], and she prayed to God to alleviate them.[323]

According to Isabel, her suffering only increased her desire to take formal vows as a nun in Santa Clara (which she never fulfilled).[324]

Although some apostles felt privileged because God had granted them the ability to alleviate the tortures of purgatory, very few dedicated their entire lives to saving souls, and even fewer sacrificed their bodies to save others.[325] Ursula did dedicate her life (because she felt chosen to do so) but did not directly experience the physical torment of souls in purgatory who asked her to commend them to God. Rather, she suffered because she feared that the content and authenticity of her visions might be questioned by her religious superiors. She worried constantly about the intentions of the spirits that prevailed upon her. Was that "big-footed monster" or trickster (both coded references to the devil) trying to fool her again, or were her visions divinely inspired? Why was she privileged to such information? In several of her visions, Ursula described Christ telling her that the lessons he taught, while she metaphorically sat at his feet, served as her book of knowledge. By "listening" to Christ's teachings, which came to her in visions both aural and visual, she could assimilate more doctrine than by reading a book. And by "witnessing" Christ's Passion (just as Angela of Foligno and Teresa of Avila had done)—and "feeling" his bruised and pierced flesh, she could comprehend the horrors of suffering and then apply that knowledge as she prayed for the release of tortured souls.[326] Like her medieval predecessor, Catherine of Genoa, Ursula emphasized the Christocentric nature of suffering. Her visions also reiterated the medieval sense of *suffering* as the principle modus operandi of purgation—in this life, or in the next. Above all, her diary revealed an honest bewilderment at the incomprehensible enormity of it all.

Ursula and other visionaries represented a group of ambassadresses in seventeenth-century Lima devoted—to one degree or another—to the beyond. However, of all Lima's holy women, the Dominican tertiary Rose of Lima had the supreme dedication to alleviating the suffering of the departed. Imitating the medieval Italian saint Catherine of Siena who helped souls escape "perpetual death," Rose offered to suffer in their stead. She also requested that, if possible, her body "would serve to attack the maws leading to hell, in order to prevent such large swarms from entering into [those] obscure dungeons in the future."[327] She felt wracking intestinal pains because of the "narrow path upon which so many miserable souls walked precipitously close to hell."[328] The interior fire experienced by Rose while she was living—and considered more refined than the more basic, elementary fire experienced in purgatory—"transubstantiated her natural faculties, burning, embracing and consuming her own sins."[329] Because of her profound sense of spirituality, Rose, like Teresa of Avila and Catherine of Genoa centuries before her, also experienced the *vida purgativa* (purgative life).[330] In fact, one of her devotees confirmed in Rose's second beatification hearing that the Dominican tertiary identified her suffering in life with purgatorial pain. For Rose, the ultimate sadness of not experiencing (or even minutely comprehending) the Allness of God's love, actualized a purgatory of "death while living."[331]

The Singularities of Ursula de Jesús

At a time when many frequently uttered the name of Rose of Lima in their prayers and supplications, some considered Ursula to be "an extremely humble plant, worthy of hanging in the lucid Choir of Virgins" of the Convent of Santa Clara. In other words, because of her mystical abilities, Ursula belonged with the nuns of the black veil who sat in the conventual choir. Among other accolades, her biographer also compared her to other noteworthy blacks: including the Queen of Saba (Sheba), the Greek sibyl, Cumana, and other illustrious religious

figures.[332] Religious authorities and missionaries Christianizing enslaved
Africans arriving at Peru could draw on a long tradition of black saints to
support their evangelizing efforts.[333] For instance, the Franciscan chronicler
Diego Córdova y Salinas praised the wonders of the black Italian saint, Benito of
Palermo (1526–89), and others eulogized the local "saints" of their respective
orders.[334] Elsewhere, local heroes dotted the historical landscape. Although tried
by the Valencian Inquisition in 1588, the black slave Catalina Muñoz attracted a
large following that admired her prophetic skills.[335] Far off in the Kingdom of
Kongo, doña Beatriz Kimpa Vita (1684–1706) claimed that not only was Christ
Kongolese, but that she was possessed by Saint Anthony.[336] Carmelite nuns in the
convent of Puebla, Mexico, were so enchanted with the black Juana Esperanza
de San Alberto's sense of *recogimiento* (internal recollection), they gave her
permission to take her vows as a nun of the white veil after sixty-seven years of
servitude in the convent.[337]

Unfortunately, Juana Esperanza and other casta women did not, or were not
permitted, to record their experiences. In fact, only a handful of biographical
accounts of women of color exist. The hagiography of the "china poblana,"
Catarina de San Juan, was based on the notebooks kept by her confessor of
fifteen years, Alonso Ramos.[338] At Kahnawake (New France), the abbreviated
life of the pious Iroquois, Katari Tekakwitha (1656–80) fascinated Jesuits who
later refashioned her into a "saint," in accordance with contemporary hagiographic traditions.[339] In Lima, authorities sanctioned the saintly activities of some
Afro-Peruvians and even recorded brief accounts of their lives.[340] Although
several seventeenth-century religious chroniclers mention the saintly mulato
Martín de Porras, we know more about him because of the collection of testimonies (1660) of limeños who fervently supported his nomination for beatification.[341] Therefore, Ursula de Jesús may be considered extraordinary because she
is the only known woman of color urged by her confessors to record her mystical experiences. Still, in spite of her singularity, it is important to consider how
Ursula fits within contemporary notions of female spirituality.

Early modern spiritual diaries and life writings (called *vidas*), of which
Ursula's is one, are quite numerous for the colonial period. The narrative structure is often similar, because female authors were required to follow certain
guidelines. For one, the "individual" female claimed that divinity spoke through
her, *and* she required a confessorial stamp of approval to write. Each author
found it necessary to avoid discussions of the devil and to conform to contemporary notions of humility, while obeying the will of both her confessor and God.
As scholar Kristin Ibsen observed, "A woman could not admit to writing on her
own initiative: from a strategic perspective, it was necessary to justify this act by
framing it as the will of God and her confessor."[342] Female autobiographers also
copied from other female writers. Many life writings of female religious figures
fit neat, formulaic literary and spiritual genres of the time, because they reproduced and altered the texts of celebrated mystics, including Gertrude, Catherine
of Genoa and of Siena, and María de la Antigua. This practice reproduced
orthodox thought, but it also fostered a sororial, hagiographic "genre" over the
centuries. Female mystics "continue[d] each other," to use a phrase coined by

twentieth-century novelist, Virginia Woolf.[343]

In order to communicate independent or critical notions, female visionaries had to develop "strategems of the strong" by using the literary techniques of ambivalence, ambiguity, and conformity.[344] They claimed that the divine spoke through them, but their own issues and concerns were also apparent. For instance, differences of gender, class, education, age, and period of time, "affect[ed] the choices a writer . . . [made] . . . in creating a literary text."[345] Not only did writers imbed a sense of themselves in their texts, but their daily interactions with others and their historical context also helped inform the content. Like other female mystics, Ursula faced an "autobiographical double-bind" because she needed to "develop a rhetorical strategy that allowed her to comply with the demands made by her audience, the need to follow orthodox Catholic mysticism, while at the same time communicating a sense of identity independent from the authority she represented."[346] That audience included her confessor, the community of nuns, and the servants and slaves working at Santa Clara.

Nevertheless, Ursula's singular experiences of being a black freedwoman *and* a donada also affected her narrative choices.[347] For one, her visions concerned racism and race relations because these formed an important and constant quandary in her life. Ursula's language reflected her struggle to find the range of her own voice while simultaneously wrestling with the tensions separating her own internally defined self-image with the racialized perceptions held by others of her. Given the complexities of race relations in colonial society, Ursula experienced the confluence of her mutable, multiple identities as an Afro-Peruvian woman, as a slave, as a freedwoman, and as a religious servant who lived in an enclosed community that upheld racist and hierarchical views. The discourse of her text demonstrates her painful familiarity with the racial slurs and actions of her oppressors, as well as her need to conform and to be obedient and humble. Her text revealed the braided ways in which enslaved and freed women expressed themselves, while being aware of their social location in the dominant society and the forms of oppression experienced in that domain.[348] Ursula once pointedly remarked:

> I would rather the nuns beat me than do me favors when I chance upon them. I would rather the earth swallow me than have them see or speak to me. Even if the queen were to call me, I would not go; it would mean less to me than piles of rubbish. I, the worst of all. If I wanted acclaim, I know how to position myself, how to gain it, and get what I want, but God's love for me meant that I left all that behind for Him. Now, everything in the world tortures me.[349]

Although here she portrayed herself as "the worst of all," it is also clear that her indomitable spirit shone through each utterance like a pregnable beacon.

Ursula wrestled constantly with the complexities of racial identity, while also attempting to imitate hagiographic models that emphasized humility, subjugation, charity, and self-sacrifice. But the contingencies she faced and the choices she made fostered a unique racialized relationship to her physical body, the social body of the convent, and the spiritual bodies in the beyond. For decades, Ursula observed and experienced corporeal forms of piety, and she was well aware (even from her youthful experiences in the Melgarejo household) that physical suffering, and particularly bodily mortification, formed acceptable and necessary manifestations of female submission and humility to God.[350] Physical experiences of agony, sorrow, or rhapsody remained key for women because these actions resonated with the Passion of Christ and, above all, with his humanity.

Thus, Ursula "denied" her flesh by wearing a hair shirt and fasting when her spirit guides told her to, even when she felt weak and frail. She knew that many female mystics began to torture their flesh at a tender age: one published description made of Mariana de Jesús (1618–45), known as the "Azucena de Quito" said "her youthful diversions consisted of bearing a cumbrous cross on her shoulders that caused her to fall."[351] So, like other mystics, Ursula subjected herself to demeaning and burdensome tasks. In the infirmary she cared for the most contagious and physically repulsive patients, volunteered to wash the infected clothing, and cleaned the sewer.[352] She was certainly aware that her contemporary, Rose of Lima, poured lime on her hands when someone admired their smooth beauty. She was also familiar with other acts of self-mutilation recounted in the *Flos Sanctorum* or undertaken by the nuns in her community. But such behavioral practices that were based on the assumption that the female body was corrupt, sinful, and weak did not fit with Ursula's notion of the female body and femaleness.[353] Unlike contemporary "privileged" white visionaries, Ursula did not actively seek to define herself as passive and fragile, because her notion of the female body (and womanhood) never subscribed fully to this dominant model.[354]

Above all, Ursula experienced her social position in a habitual and prosaic manner through her body, which bore the text of her life.[355] Like other slaves, Ursula began her working life as soon as she could stand up. Decade after decade she performed difficult physical tasks; her back, her legs, and her arms obeyed her masters' commands. This corporeal "identity" of the strong female laborer (whose body was not her own) contrasted with contemporary hagiographic "ideals" of spiritual femininity that sought to efface the beauty and sensuality of the physical. Ursula could abandon the worldly practice of adorning her body with silken garb, but she required her strength and vitality to survive. In her later years, as her use value diminished, she felt angry and "alienated" because her main asset–her body–could no longer carry out her material *and* spiritual obligations.[356] Her diary entries attest to her interminable weariness, aches, and pains and her pitifully thin body. As she once described herself, "My heart races and everything tires me out."

Not only were Ursula's notions of the body distinct, but her participation in the social body of the convent also differed from white female mystics. In their writings, privileged visionaries familiar with the Christian ideal of charity discussed how they spent their time sewing, laboring in the kitchen, or healing the sick in the infirmary. Many called themselves "slaves" as they dedicated their lives to the service of Christ or Mary. A few even handled the convent's rubbish or scrubbed floors.[357] Yet, many holy women could afford to perform humiliating tasks like sweeping floors or caring for the sick because they had servants and slaves who regularly attended to their other needs. For them, charitable or humble work was in fact a luxury.[358] Some visionaries claimed that they endured hardship *because* they had unreliable servants.[359] Most often, the munificent Ursula could not control the demands placed on her time and energy. She expressed frustration that she did not have enough time to devote to spiritual practices: as a donada and "free" woman of color, time was not *hers* to possess. Work formed a constant, banal aspect of her life, and while she resigned and sacrificed herself to the demands placed on her, her priority was to spend time alone with God. Service to others formed her most acute form of torture, because she did not believe it defined her essence as a spiritual being.[360]

Certainly, Ursula's position as a donada granted her more prestige than that experienced by the servants and slaves of Santa Clara. Ursula took her vows as a donada at the late age of forty-three, and in the remaining nineteen years of her life, she deeply lamented being called on to supervise the servants and slaves in the kitchen or the infirmary. At one point in her diary she asked which obligation took precedence: her commitment to worship God, or her communal duty to grind the wheat or knead the dough. Her celestial voices responded by immediately commanding her to work. Often, when she asked Christ why she had to labor excessively long hours, she was reminded of the excruciating suffering he endured during his Passion. One diary entry read:

> The following Saturday, I was up to my ears with cooking and other things, desiring only to be in the mountains where there are no people. I turned to God and said that were it not for Him, I would not do this. The voices responded that the Son of God was quite well off in paradise, but still He came and suffered for our sake.[361]

Known in the community for her extreme humility, Ursula never lifted her eyes; whenever she saw a nun she bowed so low, her mouth nearly touched the ground.[362] Still, she occupied the murky realm of freedwomen, where quotidian circumstances constantly reopened the ghostly wounds of human bondage. As a donada, Ursula experienced a kind of double bondage: she was legally "free" but was not quite the owner of her labor and her body. Acutely aware of the centrality of patron-client relations, and the necessary attributes of obsequiousness and humility for those in bondage, she never forgot her former position as a slave. Still, to Ursula, some nuns transgressed the opaque line that separated the slave and the free individual when they demanded that she prepare them food or cure their illnesses. One of her entries enforced this point:

> On Wednesday morning, doña Antonia de Serrantes sent her slave to ask me to cook for her. I told her black female slave, "Go with God, your owner only remembers me to give orders." But then, I called her back again to do what she asked me. During the siesta I went to pray, and the voices said, *If you have left the world behind why do you complain? Was it not better to accept that without becoming angry and do it out of compassion and love of God?*[363]

Her dilemma was how to suffer this unceasing racist behavior and wrongful subjugation, while remaining humble and submissive: both key words in a female religious vocabulary. She regretted the exacting communal labor required of her, but resentfully complained about the nuns who could not comprehend what "freedom" meant to her (and perhaps, to others). To Ursula, the nuns were like "poor dogs that won't wag their own tails" (a saying popular among enslaved Africans in the U.S. South) because of their indolence and dependency on others.[364] She tried compensating for her frustration by constantly restating her vow of servitude to a higher authority: God. Still, the issues of humility and submissiveness before her female religious superiors remained her most formidable struggle. Her entries were replete with complaints about the demands of pampered nuns, the onerous kitchen work, and being spat on and ridiculed.

Power relations that foster stratification and hierarchy often perpetuate inequality toward those of a lower station. At times Ursula found herself caught between her superior position as an acknowledged visionary and freed servant, and her need to "function as a point of consciousness of her people."[365] She was not the only one to face this dilemma. The mulato, donado Martín de Porras, who later became a saint, also dealt valiantly with the stark realities and incongruities of racism in colonial Lima. Some religious superiors taunted him with cruel words, but the Spanish and Creole community generally considered him to be superior to other mulatos because of his spiritual gifts. Despite his frustrations, he himself admonished slaves who disobeyed their masters.[366] Ursula understood that slaves and servants often suffered the cruelties of abuse, physical exhaustion, and unjust recrimination, but she also comprehended that they were property. This is particularly evident in how she recounted an incident that occurred during one Corpus Christi celebration. When a large ember from some fireworks lacerated the head of a slave, Ursula's concern rested, not with the slave, who suffered a deep, mortal gash, but with his master, a priest well known among the nuns, who was about to lose his valuable servant. When she begged Christ to have mercy on the poor and sick priest, a celestial voice immediately admonished her, saying that had the poor boy lived, he would have fallen irretrievably into mortal sin. Ursula realized that she had focused her attention on the interests of the owner, rather than on the boy, and that the events that led to the boy's death followed divine laws that valued each soul as precious and in need of saving.

Strains caused by the intense work regime, the necessary interdependence among nuns and servants, and the unwieldy labor hierarchies in the religious community also informed Ursula's narrative content. Sometimes she expressed anger or impatience toward the women of color she supervised:

> One night while serving dinner in the dining hall, they sent me a plate of salad, which I placed next to me. When I finished working, I could not find it. A young girl was there next to me, and because I suspected she had taken it, I said so. At that instant, the voices reprimanded me, Why *had I said that in malice? Even though it was a small affront, that girl had been hurt.*[367]

In her writings, she allowed her visceral, all-too-human "voice" to speak, but she framed her "truth-telling" in such a way that her experiences with racism, power struggles, and moral quandaries served as exemplum for others in the community. Her narrative content proclaimed the triumph of an individual soul who struggled to conquer her own demons of frustration and impotence.[368] In fact, many of her apparitions, dialogues with celestial guides, and daily experiences functioned as parables about spiritual growth: for herself, for her community (female and male religious, servants and slaves), and for those in the beyond.

Ursula resented the onerous, repetitive daily tasks required of her, but even more painful was the lack of credibility among some of the nuns who ridiculed her presumptuousness and made surly accusations that a "saint" resided in their midst. Obviously, some of the nuns felt uncomfortable and perhaps envious of the status of this black mystic, a term that for them was oxymoronic. To Ursula, their concerns only reiterated the contradictions of her social positioning. But this paradox formed part of a generalized phenomenon throughout colonial Latin America. The words of Juana de Jesús María, a white contemporary of the *morena* donada mystic, Juana Esperanza de San Alberto in Puebla, Mexico, reiterated the dilemma facing many white nuns in the midst of casta and black visionaries in convents throughout the Americas:

> It is certainly true that often I feel admiration to see this *morena*, so joyous and at peace, and without anyone else [here] of her color. Although it is true that all the nuns respect her, it sometimes seems natural to treat her like someone of her *calidad*.[369]

Not only were donadas considered glorified servants, but to some nuns, they could never be quite holy enough. Ursula frequently grappled with this issue and sought spiritual counsel from Saint Francis, who contradicted the dominant viewpoint:

> This time, she asked Saint Francis, "What is this? They say that the profession of donadas has no value?" The saint replied, *There is a difference because the nuns are white and of the Spanish nation, but with respect to the soul, all is one: Whoever does more, is worth more.*[370]

This celestial "truth" helped confirm Ursula's belief that nuns may have been of the Spanish nation and in positions of authority, but that did not make their souls more pristine. In the sight of God, moral and pious conduct held the most privileged rank.

In spite of the disaffected grumblings of some nuns, Ursula held a unique and unprecedented status as a mystic and writer in the Convent of Santa Clara. In fact, her authority could hold sway over the entire community. On one occasion, while in a trance, Christ explained to Ursula his disappointment with the lax morals of his wives, the nuns (a complaint not uncommon in early modern hagiographies). Through Ursula, He ordered that celestial decrees be posted in the choir that directed the nuns to center their thoughts on spiritual matters before, during, and after communion.[371] This was a tall order, because it required Ursula to criticize nuns who had been her superiors for decades. But both her confessor and the abbess took this directive given to Ursula seriously, and no one in the community doubted its veracity. After hearing from Ursula, the abbess called a general meeting and read out the reforms dictated to Ursula by Christ. These stated clearly that the nuns should take their obligations to receive the Holy Sacrament more seriously and should deliberate on how they had been remiss.[372]

Ursula's diary expressed a commonly held belief that male and female religious figures had a greater moral responsibility than lay inhabitants "in the world" (*en el siglo*). Her work conveyed a politically correct moralistic tone (that resonated with her Spanish and Latin American counterparts), in claiming that if the clarisas sinned by disobeying the convent's rules or the Ten Commandments, they would receive harsher punishment in the hereafter than if similar sins were committed by secular women or men. One deceased nun explained to Ursula in a vision that those "wives of Christ" who occupied their time in business negotiations instead of spiritual endeavors paid a high price for their cupidity. Clearly, the threat of purgatory served as a reminder that nuns, and even servants, would be judged before the eyes of God. As Christ once explained to Ursula: even the ashes of the most powerful viceroy could easily dissipate in water. As it turned out, Ursula's "reform" visions (and the threat of future purgation) were far more effective in changing behavior in the convent than any ecclesiastical visitation from the archbishop. Certainly for her biographer, the moralistic timbre and the larger implications of her revelations resounded with the need to reform some the "worldly" activities within the convent walls.

As a mystic and writer, Ursula also gained authority by transforming and framing her monotonous life experiences of racism with language and imagery that fashioned a unique textual self in relation to her body and to the community of Santa Clara. She served God and the nuns, but she also believed firmly in the equality of souls and the principle that "the meek shall inherit the earth." Her "other" community of relationships consisted of the servants and slaves she worked with on a daily basis. In spite of their grumblings and altercations, her world was inextricably bound up with theirs.[373] In her diary, she empowered some of the "little ones" of the convent by naming the servants and slaves and vesting them with an important status among those watching from the spiritual realm:

> The voices told me how much in particular the insignificant and humble ones in this house please God. Florensia Bravo and Antonia de Cristo are outcasts, and no one pays any attention to them. The first is a wretched mulata and the other a blind, black woman. Afterward, I felt pensive, fearful, and skeptical. [They] said, *Why are you skeptical? If you hear that so-and-so is a trustworthy, honorable man, you have no reason to fear. You have faith in what men say and you place your confidence in them and not in me. Do not think I would abandon those who place their trust in me.*[374]

Ursula maintained a position of authority and respect among the deceased slaves and servants who appeared asking her to intercede on their behalf to relieve their pain and suffering in purgatory. By recording fragments of the experiences of the "little ones" in her diary, she "embodied" the voices of the dead and reenacted a kind of racial memory of the complexities of servitude and interracial conflict.[375]

In her diary, Ursula created an inclusive space for some of the disenfranchised women of color living in the convent, but her efforts extended beyond the physical domain of the written page and the convent walls. In her visions, the dead came to Ursula with numerous and sundry concerns. One female slave appeared to Ursula in her "earthly" form in the hope that she would be recognized. She feared becoming one of the many lost and forgotten (*ánimas solas*) in purgatory, without anyone to care for her well-being. This was not an unusual concern coming from a woman whose "family" may have consisted of her owner and a few other slaves and servants in the convent. Ursula clearly understood this important Afro-Peruvian notion of extended "family," because many slaves were separated from their mothers at a tender age, or they were orphaned or illegitimate, maintaining only minimal contact with anyone outside the convent.

Like Christ, who appeared before Ursula to admonish the clarisas for their lax morals, dead servants and slaves appeared. One slave, however, admonished the abbess. One night, Ursula awoke with a horrible fright. There before her stood a dead slave who had died without receiving confession. She communicated to Ursula that late at night she was made to cook and bake, leading Ursula to believe that she had died from being overworked and that "the señora abbess could have corrected that problem."[376] However, most of the slaves and servants who appeared in her visions did not express anger or resentment, but rather a resignation to their condition and a need to answer to a higher authority, both in life and in death. Although the majority *seemed* to have accepted the harsh realities of human bondage, they considered their souls to be equal in value to others, because of the belief that God gave memory, understanding, and free will to each soul to choose its destiny.

Ursula's singularities also arose from her cultural placement within overlapping European and African spiritual traditions. Ursula's understanding of, and ability to communicate with, the dead came from a centuries-long Catholic practice. But, it also meshed with West African conceptualizations of a world inhabited by supernatural beings and wandering spirits. As the peoples of the Mina, Guinea, Angola, and Folupa nations were forced into slavery and transported to Peru, they brought with them beliefs in ancestor worship, a powerful reverence for the dead, and notions of "this world" and the "other world." Many West Africans also believed that those humans who received images and messages from otherworldly beings were meant "to interpret these revelations and act accordingly."[377] Mediums (called the *nganga ngombo*) could maintain contact with dead ancestors, souls, or the "saints" for advice or to divine information.[378] This practice harmonized with Christian forms of augury and conceptions of purgatory as an "otherworld." African seers passed on theological conceptions to Creole Afro-Peruvians like Ursula. In turn, she framed her own understanding of Catholicism within her maternal cultural tradition. No doubt, as Ursula kneaded the dough or stirred the stew in the convent's kitchen, she discussed and mulled over African notions of the spirit realm with her coworkers.

Ursula's ideas of self-responsibility and punishment in purgatory meted out to different "talents," "stations," and "occupations" also corresponded to accounts provided by European mystics ranging from Hildegard to Francisca del Santíssima Sacramento. However, her main contacts consisted of individuals with a particular sensitivity to divisions—not just of secular or religious status but to those of race and *calidad*. One servant she had "saved" described to Ursula how heaven differed for the different "stations" in life:

> [In heaven] great harmony prevailed; everyone had their place according to their position; nuns pertained to one part, male religious to another; and lay persons and priests all occupied their places in order and harmony. Indians, blacks, and other people were punished in accordance with their condition and the obligations of their class.[379]

Everyone had their place, their designated spot in purgatory. Although generally considered a punitive domain, some saw purgatory as a semi-utopic space where souls could expunge racial, class, and gender differences. The soul of María Bran, a slave of Santa Clara, appeared to Ursula dressed in an alb (an ecclesiastical garment worn by consecrated priests who performed the mass), which was fastened with an ornately embroidered cord. She also wore a crown of flowers generally associated in the seventeenth century with Saint Rose. María assured Ursula that blacks and donadas went to heaven, a concern that a white visionary would not have. The fact that a slave, dressed as a saint/priestess would occupy a space in the lofty heights of purgatory, shows how this domain could be perceived as a space where justice prevailed, especially from the point of view of a colonial mystic who fought against racism and brutality her entire life. Purgatory equalized differences, but it also functioned as a mirror of fears and hopes of people with different life experiences and expectations.

Ursula was a mystic who held a position of power and authority within her religious community. She imitated dominant feminine models of sanctity, while also identifying herself as a hard-working woman worn out from years of abuse. She was neither fragile, beautiful, nor indolent. As a freedwoman, she became increasingly intolerant of racism but continually prayed for more patience and resolve to suffer the continual demands placed on her body. As a mystic and donada, she experienced both the possibilities and limits of authority to empower the "little ones" and to express her visions in written form, while continuing to serve others for hours each day. In her diary, Ursula searched for meaningfulness in her interactions with living and deceased nuns, priests, servants, and slaves. She "read" the codes of everyday life and subjectivity through the prism of the life stories from the beyond. In doing so, she envisioned an egalitarian world where God privileged goodness, while still acknowledging the incongruities of a racialized existence in colonial society.

The Text

Fortunately, we have access to Ursula's words, which still resonate with us today. It is difficult to gauge whether Ursula actually wrote any sections of the diary herself. Given the distinct penmanship in certain sections (especially folios 29v to 41v), it is likely that one or more of her female companions (nuns) recorded

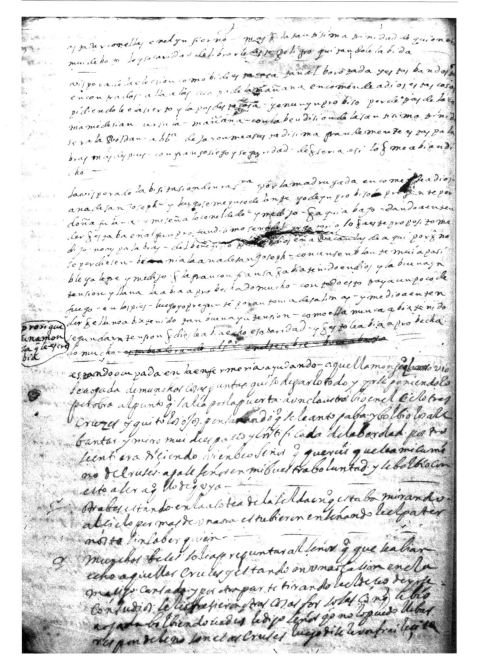

Figure 6. Folio 29v of Ursula's diary where the handwriting changed dramatically.
The margin reads "a nun carries on writing for her."
Photo by Nancy E. van Deusen.

Ursula's thoughts and visions. (See Figure 6.) In fact, Ursula specifically mentioned when one scribe began writing for her:

> . I asked Him if He wanted me to write, and He said, *Yes*. I asked if I should tell the nun who has been with me since the beginning, when these things started to occur. She had told me not to tell others because they might gossip; it was best to discuss such profound matters with someone who could truly understand. He said I should go to the one I was already working with and He named her. This sister is better read and is very afraid of these things.[380]

How closely Ursula was scrutinized for the veracity and orthodoxy of her supernatural visions is not clear. The diary was probably uncensored because it contains very few scratched out words or phrases and shows no evidence of editing. In fact, some of the content would have been considered heretical, which leads one to question how closely her confessor(s) monitored her writings. We know that all nuns took a vow of obedience to their superiors and were obligated to follow the directives of their confessors.[381] Might one assume that because Ursula was a donada, her confessors might not have taken her writings as seriously? Given the gravity of the Council of Trent's dictums that regulated and standardized confessorial guidance, why are her male advisors barely visible in her text?

After Ursula dictated or wrote her last entry, "I leave much unwritten because I can do no more. Fifty-seven folios are written," a nun Ursula had known in the convent wrote a short biographical account that was bound with the original diary. Then, around 1686, a friar composed a biographical account of her life, based on Ursula's uncensored diary and the accompanying introductory, biographical text. Two copies of her biography—one complete, another incomplete—were then kept in the Franciscan library. In 1777, Juan Francisco de Landa, the Franciscan Provincial, ordered that Ursula's biography be bound with numerous other hagiographical accounts.[382] Landa assigned Friar Fernando Rodríguez Tena (d. 1781), a Franciscan historian who also wrote a chronicle (still in manuscript form), primary responsibility for this task.[383] Both the partial and complete biographies of Ursula (in the same hand) can be found in that thickly bound volume.[384] The diary contains some of the information found in the biographical account. However, the narrative structure of the biography was radically altered, and specific dates and names were added. Most likely, her biographer depended on Ursula's cloistered contemporaries, still alive in the 1680s, for additional information.[385]

Ursula's text is not an "easy" read; it is sometimes difficult to follow or understand. With a few exceptions, Ursula (or her scribe) wrote in the first person. Like many texts of the time, the writing contains little punctuation (the section dictated to one nun contains some). Above all, Ursula's spiritual journal is unpolished; it clearly is a mixture of oral and written traditions. It is filled with repetition, imagery, and, above all, incredibly rich dialogues with celestial figures ranging from her guardian angel disguised as a friar, to Christ, Mary, and God. These voices weave in and out of each other: indicating a fusion of the spoken, written, and heard.[386] Her writing style (or that of her scribes) is inconsistent and telegraphic; many of the passages are extremely cryptic. She often switched tenses and confused direct objects associated with her multiple female or male voices. In addition, her sense of chronology frequently changed dramatically when she juxtaposed distinct "events." In a given paragraph she might jump from the life story of a dead soul pleading for assistance to an episode from Christ's Passion, then to her rendition of some upheaval in the convent.

In translating this text, with the essential editorial assistance of Javier Flores Espinoza and Meredith Dodge, I tried to remain as "true" to Ursula's voice and style as possible, while rendering her long, unpunctuated phrases into sentences of varying lengths that a contemporary reader could understand. To avoid further confusion, I translated most verbs into the past tense. Paragraph structure replicates the same structure of the transcription, some of which are only one or two sentences long. I added commas and quotation marks and capitalized references to God and Jesus (including He and Him), Mary, and other elements of Catholicism. Pronoun referents remained a thorny issue. The use of "they" could refer to "the voices," other celestial beings, including her guardian angel (dressed as a friar), or Christ and God. An exasperated Ursula once admitted that the "voices" did not identify themselves. Thus, Ursula regularly switched from plural to singular referents in the same sentence, which may be explained by her understanding that the Trinity consisted of three beings (God, Christ, Holy Spirit) in one, and vice versa. This is further complicated by the appearance of living and dead individuals, and the scribe who occasionally interjected her own voice. Whenever possible, I tried to identify the persons named in Ursula's diary. If they remain anonymous, it is because, as of yet, they remain silent in corresponding documents.

For Part III, I selected fifty pages of the original transcription (totaling 157 pages). Those entries focus on her purgatorial visions, explanations of seventeenth-century Catholic doctrines of sin, purgation, and purgatory, the Passion of Christ, Ursula's Marian devotion, and her understanding of the Trinity. The selections on purgatory refer to her contacts with a potpourri of dead nuns, priests, servants, and slaves. Other paragraphs depict convent life and social interactions among the different members of the community.

In the end, the original and translated texts must stand alone as a testimonial to Ursula and her world. I will be the first to admit that it is very difficult to scrutinize and analyze mystical texts such as these and to pass them like grist through the mill of our twenty-first-century minds. As scholar Mary Giles aptly put it, "No amount of conceptualizing will put God in a box."[387] And, no amount of speculating, analyzing, and probing will put Ursula in a box. She was, is, and will remain a wonderful spirit for young and old minds to ponder again and again. Let her text, like the images immortalizing Ursula, "speak" volumes to each reader in the days and years to come.

Notes

1. Her confessors included the famous Augustinian chronicler Antonio de la Calancha (1584–1654), Antonio Ruíz (Jesuit), Miguel Salazar (Jesuit), Francisco Rebelo (Franciscan), Pedro Urraca (Mercedarian), José García Serrano (Augustinian), Hernando de Valverde (Augustinian), and, in her last years, Francisco de Vargas Machuca (Mercedarian), with whom she made her last confession. Viceroy Francisco de Borja y Aragón, Principe de Esquilache (1615–21), considered Pedro de Urraca to be a saint (Vargas Ugarte, *Historia de la Iglesia*, 192). See also Lorente, *Historia*, 134; Eguiguren, *La universidad*, I:404. Valverde wrote a book entitled *Vida de Cristo*; see, Eguiguren, *La universidad*, I:403.

2. We know nothing about her father. Her mother may have arrived from Guinea to Lima in 1604 at the age of twenty. In 1604, Gerónima's brother-in-law, Pedro del Pulgar, sold María de Aguilar, Gerónima's mother, a slave named Isabel de Tierra Congo, AGNP, Francisco Ramiro Bote, 230, 1602–4, 1140v–41r.

3. Although her biography states that Ursula entered Santa Clara in 1617, her new owner, the young Inés del Pulgar, entered in December 1615 as a novice. Her aunt, Gerónima de los Rios, paid a fee of 156 pesos, 2 reales ("Autos seguidos," 1615/17, AAL, SC, I:156v [63v lists a lesser amount of 136 pesos]). That same year, Gerónima de los Rios also paid 28 pesos for the bed and board of María de Almoguera while she studied to take her vows as a nun of the white veil (56v). Ursula's owner, Inés, lived quite a long life in Santa Clara. She appears on "task lists" (*tablas de oficios*) as *portera* (portress) for the years 1653, 1656, 1657, and 1660.

4. Women in Lima had the reputation for dressing ostentatiously (Lewin, *Descripción*, 39).

5. Medieval female visionaries often experienced "awakenings" at middle age (Petroff, *Body*, 20).

6. In her diary, Ursula mentions that in the infirmary she cared for a nun who had saved money for her ("Ursula," ASCL, 29v).

7. Bowser, *African*, 276ff; van Deusen, "'Alienated,'" 10f.

8. "Autos que sigue Ana de Mora, negra libre," 1667, AAL, SC, XII:120, 1667.

9. "Vida," AFL, 586v.

10. "Autos . . . por Manuel Congo, marido que fue de Maria Malamba," 1656, AAL, Causas de Negros, XII:24.

11. "Ursula," ASCL, 3f. Folios 3r–6r contain a brief biography of Ursula, which is bound with her diary (8r–66r). It was probably written by a clarisa nun who was Ursula's contemporary. The anonymous nun wrote, "y quemose una capilla—del santo christo que estaba dentro del conbento donde a-/ bia un christo mui lindo—y todas las ynsignias de la pasion/ la que se ase la prosesion el biernes santo abia en esta capilla mu-/ chas ymajenes de christo y de la virjen y adornos."

12. "Ursula," ASCL, 3v; "Vida," AFL, 587r.

13. "Ursula," ASCL, 4r.

14. Miguel de Salazar (1585–1651) was born in Arequipa and attended the Colegio de San Martín in Lima. In 1617, he accompanied other friars, including Francisco de Ávila, on an extirpation-of-idolatries campaign to Huailas. He also formed part of a general ecclesiastical visit in 1626 (Vargas Ugarte, *Historia de la Iglesia*, II:313, 333). He later served as rector at the university (Vargas Ugarte, *Historia de la Compañía*, II:228; "Ursula," ASCL, 3v; "Vida," AFL, 587v).

15. This reference is given in her biography, "Vida," AFL, 589r. Other sources say that in 1647 the day of the Holy Trinity fell on June 8 and was celebrated on June 10 (Suardo, *Diario*, 134).

16. "Ursula," ASCL, 4r.

17. "Vida," AFL, 587v.

18. "Ursula," ASCL, 4r; "Vida," AFL, 587v.

19. "Ursula," ASCL, 6v.

20. For instance folio 19r refers to December 28, 1659, and folio 19v is dated 1650. The transition from 33v to 34r is not continuous. Ursula mentions one scribe in her diary ("Ursula," ASCL, 34v). Whether Ursula actually wrote any of the diary in her own hand is debatable.

21. European nuns tended to outlive their secular counterparts, which argues that convent life was propitious to longevity (see Brown, "Everyday Life").

22. "Ursula," ASCL, 5v.

23. "Autos de ingreso . . . Francisca de la Cruz," 1666, AAL, SC, XII:96. Ursula was referred to as Ursula de Jesús, Ursula de Christo, and Ursula de Jesucristo.

24. Echave y Assu, *La estrella*, 230. The Franciscan chronicle published by Diego Córdoba y Salinas in 1651 did not mention Ursula because she was still alive. However, he did write extensively about other noteworthy occupants of Santa Clara (Córdova y Salinas, *Crónica*, 899–906). Another Franciscan chronicle finished in 1773, and written by Fernando Rodríguez Tena (still in manuscript form), copied from Córdova y Salinas. Rodríguez Tena's work did not mention Ursula de Jesús. See "Origen," BNP, C1313, 157r–178v. Ursula is briefly mentioned in other chronicles, see, for example, Montalvo, *El sol*, 69.

25. Boyer, "Caste and Identity," 4; van Deusen, *Between*, 2–7, 192.

26. This "walk though Lima" is a fictionalized rendering of what Ursula might have seen at the time. I chose December of 1612, because by that time she was older and now residing with Luisa de Melgarejo Sotomayor in the parish of Santa Ana. A number of sources were quite useful for this reconstruction. See Bowser, *African*; Cobo, *Fundación*; Bromley and Barbagalata, *Evolución*; Durán, "Lima"; Suardo, *Diario*; Bernales Ballesteros, *Lima*. On the description of the Jesuit College of San Pablo, see Martín, *Intellectual*.

27. Martín, *Daughters*, 5.

28. Africans arriving from Guinea, or from the Xolofe or Mandinga nations, usually had not been baptized, while those from the Congo and Angola had "alguna manera de enseñanza" (see *Instrucción*).

29. Slaves were not necessarily *negro* (black), but could also be castas—including the racial categories of *mulato*, *moreno*, *sambo*, *pardo*, or *quarteron*.

30. Martín, *Intellectual*, 137.

31. Ibid., 46.

32. Durán, "Lima," 10.

33. AGNP, Protocolos, Francisco Ramiro Bote, 230, (1602–4), 1314v–15r. I would like to thank Ilana Aragón Noriega for locating this and other notorial sources that correspond to the life of Gerónima de los Rios.

34. Lockhart, *Spanish*, 159–60, discusses this practice among wealthy women.

35. Since the 1550s, encomendero's wives maintained large retinues of dependents, slaves, servants, and retainers (Lockhart, *Spanish*, 157). Lewin describes slaves carrying women in sedans to mass and other social events (*Descripción*, 39). Wealthy Spaniards frequently served as tutors and guardians of children brought from Spain, and the de los Rios household was no exception. Gerónima's husband raised the young Francisco de Esquivel, who received tribute revenue from an *encomienda* in the province of Yauyos (AGNP, Protocolos, Francisco Ramiro Bote, 230, [1602–4], 1391r–1411v). Honoring a promise made to raise an orphan from Seville, the seven-year-old Ana María de Anaya (she took her adopted father's name) helped Gerónima for twelve years with sewing and other tasks, was paid a small annual fee, and was given a dowry to marry at age eighteen (AGNP, Protocolos, Lopé de Valencia 1927, 1615, 634r–v). Gerónima's mother, María de Aguilar died in 1611.

36. Testimony of Joan Lorenço, 1617, AGNP, Real Audiencia, Causas Civiles, Leg. 42. It is difficult to ascertain how many slaves resided in the de los Rios household at a given time, but within a seven-year period (1603–7) they bought or sold at least five.

37. Testimony of Lorenço de Medina, AGNP, Real Audiencia, Causas Civiles, Leg. 42, 1617. On African domestic laborers in Lima, see Bowser, *African*, 101.

38. Bowser, *African*, 55.

39. Bowser, *African*, 339, 341. Estimates for 1593, blacks and mulatos (n=6,690); remainder of population (n=6,100); for 1636, blacks and mulatos (n=14,481); remainder of population (n=12,583). Bowser indicates 4,529 black men and 5,857 black women in the 1614 census; 6,135 men and 5,862 women in a 1619 ecclesiastical enumeration; and 6,544 men and 7,076 women in the 1636 ecclesiastical enumeration (*African*, 340–41).

40. Bowser, *African*, 103f.

41. Ursula's biographical account does not conform to hagiographic scripts that report childhood expressions of peculiar religious devotion, temptations, and fighting adversity, or resistance to the devil while on the path of spiritual development. However, scores of examples report pious young girls from elite families in Spain, Mexico, Ecuador, and Peru experiencing such turmoil. See Meléndez, *Tesoros*; on Rose of Lima, II:328–33; on the Dominican tertiary from Trujillo, Feliciana de Jesús (1600–64), III:750. For an example from eighteenth-century Mexico, see Valdes, *Vida admirable*.

42. Tardieu, *Los negros*, I:616–24.

43. Juan de Soto worked as a lawyer for native Andeans and served as *relator* for the Real Audiencia and rector of the Universidad de San Marcos in 1615.

44. AGNP, Real Audiencia, Causas Civiles, Leg. 42, Cuad. 158, 1617.

45. The *oidor* Blas Altamirano once commented about Soto-Melgarejo household, saying, "Doña Luisa provides the image, and Doctor [Juan de] Soto, the means to cultivate it" (Glave, *De Rosa*, 210).

46. Córdoba y Salinas inserted her biography just in time for the 1651 printing of the *Crónica*, 969. Recent studies include Glave, *De Rosa*; and Iwasaki, "Luisa."

47. AMAE, Santa Sede, Leg. 152, f. 231. Also cited in Iwasaki, "Luisa," 233. On the sanctity of Saint Francisco Solano, see also Gerónimo de Oré, *Relación*.

48. Testimony, Juan Muñoz, 1622, AHNM, Inquisición, Lima, Leg. 1647, exp. 5, 5r.

49. Ruíz de Montoya, *Silex*, 249; Mujica, "El ancla," 61, 115; Córdoba y Salinas, *Crónica*, 969–71. Apparently, Melgarejo told Ruíz de Montoya that he would go directly to heaven, but she died before him. Apparently, Ruíz de Montoya had a vision of her after she had died (Vargas Ugarte, *Historia de la Iglesia*, III:301–2).

50. Loreto López, "Familial Religiosity," 27, 33.

51. Iwasaki, "Luisa," 230, 242–43.

52. "Ursula," ASCL, 57v.

53. I am not totally convinced that Ursula learned to read, either as a child, or later as an adult in the convent. She does express a desire to read in her diary, and her paintings show her surrounded by books, which symbolized literacy. Nevertheless, her entries often refer to someone reading passages to her.

54. Spain produced hundreds of religious works; one library in Seville contained 697 hagiographies: 300 of them were written between 1600 and 1629 (Sánchez Lora, *Mujeres*, 375). Kathleen Myers writes that in Mexico (which had a printing press) "more than seventy percent of the books published in New Spain were devotional texts and hagiographies" (María de San José, *Wild*, 260).

55. Some included Saints Lutgarde (1182–1246), Gertrude (1256–c.1302), Birgitta (1303–73), Angela of Foligno (1248–1309), Hildegard of Bingen (1098–1179), Liduvina (1380–1433), Catherine of Siena (1347–80), and Catherine of Genoa (1447–1510); the works by Saint Gertrude, *Oraciones*, (1604); *Libro*, (1605); and her biography by Andrade, *Vida* (1663). On Catherine of Siena, see Capua, *La vida* (1511). Luisa Melgarejo cited the 1618 translation of Angela de Foligno's *Vida* (1618). See also Iwasaki, "Luisa," 221.

56. Eguiguren, *Diccionario histórico*, 695–722, includes an inventory of a bookstore from 1597 that contained the "Doctrina de mugeres," "Varia historia de ilustres y sanctas mugeres," "Dialogos de mujeres," "Vida de la Magdalena," "Guía de peccadores," and "Milagros de Santa Catalina." Josefina Muriel refers to the "classic" Spanish religious texts found in the homes of pious families in Mexico, *Cultura*, 20–21.

57. Testimony of Ynes de Velasco, 1623, AHNM, Inquisición, Lima, Leg. 1647, exp. 5, 12v.

58. Martín, *Intellectual*, 85. For a description of the Colegio de San Pablo see Cobo, *Obras*, II:422–25. Melgarejo's borrowing privileges were not unique. At the time, a few generous friars were known to share their books with talented female protégés. On Estephanía de San Joseph's access to Francisco de Avila's 3,108 volume library, see "Estephanía," AFL, Reg. 17, no. 43, 569v; and Hampe, "Universo," 119.

59. "Estephanía," AFL, Reg. 17, no. 43, 570r.

60. Bynum, "Female Body," 172; Simons, "Reading," 12ff.

61. Testimony of Ynes de Velasco, 1623, AHNM, Inquisición, Lima, 1647, exp. 5, 10v.

62. Testimony of Isabel de Soto, 1623, AHNM, Inquisición, Lima, 1647, exp. 5, 20v.

63. Testimony, Dr. Pedro Rodríguez Toro, 1623, AHNM, Inquisición, Lima, 1647, exp. 5, 19r; also cited in, Iwasaki, "Luisa," 223.

64. After 1612, Rose lived in the home of María de Uzástegui; they and Uzástegui's husband, Gonzalo de la Maza, maintained an exceptionally close relationship (Vargas Ugarte, *Vida de Santa Rosa*, 39, 69).

65. Diego Martínez, a Jesuit missionary in Tucumán and known as a "siervo de Dios," Juan de Villalobos (1575–1654), rector of the Noviciado in 1618, Antonio de Vega Loaiza, who arrived in 1613, and Diego de Peñalosa all communicated with Rose and either served as her spiritual directors or supported her mystical practices (Vargas Ugarte, *Vida de Santa Rosa*, 71–72; Torres Saldamando, *Los antiguos Jesuitas*, 373; Iwasaki, "Mujeres," 591, n. 28; Mujica, "El ancla," 61; Meléndez, *Tesoros*, II:311).

66. Juan Muñoz was a strict Ignatian who disowned the mystical trends that had developed among the Lima Jesuits. Diego Alvárez de la Paz (1549–1619) was a distinguished theologian, mystic, and influential teacher (he acted as prefect of advanced studies (*estudios mayores*) at the Colegio de San Pablo [1609–17]); he also served as Luisa de Melgarejo's first confessor (Torres Saldamando, *Los antiguos Jesuitas*, 349–53; Iwasaki, "Luisa," 227). Melgarejo was said to have predicted that he was destined to serve as a missionary in Paraguay (Vargas Ugarte, *Historia de la Compañía*, 103, 285). Doña Luisa also worked closely with the renowned Jesuit missionary Diego Martínez, who supervised her for at least eight years and encouraged her to write (see Testimony of Diego Martínez, 1623, AHNM, Inquisición, Lima, 1647, exp. 5, 32r–v; Iwasaki, "Mujeres," 594, n. 41). Mexican women also read Loyola's works (Muriel, "Lo que leían," 163).

67. Medieval scholar André Vauchez has discussed the "intermittent cycle" of lay piety that emerged in twelfth- and thirteenth-century Italy and again at the end of the fourteenth century at a time when the feminization of lay spirituality occurred (Vauchez, "Lay People's," 21, 24; Vauchez, *Sainthood*, 348–54, 369–86, 409; Weinstein and Bell, *Saints*, 220–23; Bynum, *Holy Feast*, 16–30). A similar growth in lay feminine spirituality occurred in early seventeenth-century Lima.

68. Meléndez, *Tesoros*, III:746–67; Vargas Ugarte, *Historia de la Iglesia*, (1960) III:438–40.

69. Testimony of Polonia de Beza, 1622, AHNM, Inquisición, Lima, 1030, 329v. See also, Iwasaki, "Mujeres," 606. On Mariana de Jesús, the Azuzena of Quito, see the discussion of her Indian servant, Catalina, who testified at her beatification hearing. She claimed to know her intimate habits and washed the blood off her back after Mariana begged her to whip her (Espinosa Polit, *Santa Mariana*, 176, 216–17).

70. Fernández, *Santa Rosa*, 39, 46, 63; Mujica, "El ancla," 195; Vargas Ugarte, *Vida de Santa Rosa*, 57–58.

71. González, *Rosa mística*, 46.

72. Deposition of Catalina de Santa María, 1618, Jiménez Salas, *Primer proceso*, 349.

73. Vargas Ugarte, *Vida de Santa Rosa*, 76–77.

74. Some of Rose's "sisters" and "spiritual daughters" included Luisa de Santa María, daughter of Juan Daza de Oliva and Juana de Valencia; Catalina, Lucía, Francisca, and Felipa de Montoya, all of whom, except Felipa who later married, became nuns in Santa Catalina; Bartola [Barbara?] López and Ana de los Reyes, daughters of Andrés López, the servant of Gonzalo de la Maza; María de Jesús, daughter of Simón de Sosa and María Flores; Leonor de Vitoria, a widow; and María Antonia, the widow of Juan Carrillo (Meléndez, *Tesoros*, 2:374, 401; Vargas Ugarte, *Vida de Santa Rosa*, 77–78). See also Fernández, *Santa Rosa*, 20.

75. AHNM, Inquisición, Lima, 1028, 231r–v.

76. For instance, Isabel de Ormaza (Jesús), a *quarterona de india*, and Ana María Pérez, a *quarterona de mulata*, were the constant companions of the Franciscan donada Catalina de Santa María, an *india*.

77. "Estephanía," AFL, Reg. 17, no. 43, 570r; Córdoba y Salinas, *Crónica*.

78. The conventual chronicles mention a number of them. Echave y Assu, *La estrella*, 240, discussed Fabiana, a mulata servant in the *Descalças de San José*, and a morena donada in *La Concepción*. Juan Meléndez, *Tesoros*, 72, mentioned the saintly donada mestiza, Isabel de la Cruz, who professed in *Santa Catalina* in 1627. On a native Andean donado in the Dominican convent, see Cussen, "Fray Martín," 53, n. 101. See also Ramos, "Death, Conversion," 363–65.

79. "Francisco de la Concepción," AFL, Reg. 17, no. 21.

80. Friar Fernando Aragonés, a witness for his beatification hearing in 1660, stated that "todo el día y toda la noche, exercitándose en ella, sirviendo de sangrar y curar a los enfermos, dando limosnas a españolas, indios, y negros, que a todos los quería y amaba y curaba con singular amor y caridad" (*Proceso*, 124).

81. Cussen, "Fray Martín," 218, n. 367. She says, "The images are normally hung over the bed of the devotee, his slave, or child." See also *Proceso*, 164, 176–77, that describes a very ill *negra criolla* named Tomasa praying to his portrait. Other examples include doña María Beltrán placing a piece of a sleeve of Porras's garment on her daughter's heavily pregnant belly to facilitate her labor (*Proceso*, 187, 190); doña Mariana de Villaroel using part of his tunic (given to her by a priest) to cure illnesses (*Proceso*, 201, 217); and a *lego* in a Dominican convent sending some earth said to have stuck to Porras's bones (when officials moved his tomb) to a sick priest who drank it with some water and cured his illness (*Proceso*, 378).

82. Martín de Porras was beatified in 1837 and canonized in 1962.

83. Castillo, *Un místico*, 16.

84. Tardieu, *Los negros*, II:879–85. For a fascinating study of an eighteenth-century black mystic from Minas Gerais, see Mott, *Rosa Egipcíaca*.

85. Evidence shows active collaboration and solidarity in Lima's urban confraternities and in the development of the Afro-Peruvian cults of Saints Eloy, Bartolomé, and Benito de Palermo (Tardieu, *Los negros*, I:509–63; Gómez Acuña, "Las cofradías," 28–39; Bowser, *African*, 249ff.).

86. These included Alonso de Sandoval in Colombia and Gabriel Perlín and Bartolomé Vadillo in Lima (van Deusen, "'Alienated,'" 17).

87. Castillo, *Un místico*, 15–16. He was said to have a frenzied preaching style (Lorente, *Historia*, 147–48).

88. Arenal, "Convent," 219.

89. The *Constituciones* ordered community mortification practices on Mondays, Wednesdays, and Fridays (67v). On supernatural "events" among clarisas in Quito, see Paniagua Pérez, "Las décadas," 140ff.

90. "Escritas . . . Soror Gerónima," 1652, AFL, Reg. 17, no. 35, 433v–36r. See also Mendiburu, *Diccionario*, (1935), Apéndice, II:415–16.

91. One of the miracles of Saint Francis of Assisi, the founder of the Franciscan Order, was that the same five wounds that Christ experienced appeared as stigmata on the body of St. Francis.

92. Many of the examples cited in this paragraph come from Córdoba y Salinas, *Crónica*, 899–904.

93. Muriel, *Cultura femenina*, 20; Ibsen, *Women's*, 9, 62.

94. Luis de Granada (1504–88) was one of Spain's greatest mystics of the sixteenth century.

95. I wish to express my profound gratitude to Ana María Vega, who conducted an inventory of Santa Clara's library and shared the list with me. The citations only indicate those seventeenth-century works still extant in the convent's collection; undoubtedly, other artworks existed. The works of María de la Antigua may have been acquired after Ursula's death. Nieremberg's works were also popular among families, in convents and schools in colonial Mexico (Muriel, "Lo que leían," 163).

96. This scene also reminded viewers of the sacred exchange of flesh between Saint Catherine and Jesus, as discussed in Raymond of Capua's 1505 biography (Capua, *La vida*, ch. 6).

97. Ana María Vega, "Catálogo" (unpublished document), AFL.

98. Córdoba y Salinas, *Crónica*, 899.

99. "Ursula," ASCL, 10r. The four were Justina de Guevara, Ana de Illescas, Barbola de la Vega, and Isabel de la Fuente. In one document I found, a nun of the black veil named Teresa de Meneses petitioned to have a special cell set apart for her as she recovered from an illness. She said she deserved this because she was one of the first foundresses ("Autos . . . Teresa de Meneses," 1641, AAL, SC, VI:24). Could she be the Teresa to whom Ursula refers? The Portuguese Francisco de Saldaña was one of the founders who donated between 12–14,000 pesos of his estate to finance the construction of the convent (Cobo, *Obras*, II:433).

100. Rodríguez Valencia, *Santo Toribio*, I:180–81; Portal, *Lima religiosa*, 144.

101. For the Viceroyalty of Peru, see Martín, *Daughters*, 171–200; on Cuzco, the excellent study by Burns, *Colonial*, 101–27; on Lima, van Deusen, *Between*, 66, 170–73, and Fernández

et al., *La mujer*, 413–72; on Tunja, McKnight, *Mystic*, 88–90.

102. They were called *urbanistas* because they followed the second-order rules developed by Pope Urban VI (1263). For an insightful overview of the history of the Convent of Santa Clara in Lima, see Fernández et al., *La mujer*, 413–74.

103. Martín, *Daughters*, 172ff.

104. Burns, *Colonial*, 106.

105. Bernales Ballesteros, *Lima*, 269–70.

106. Portal, *Lima religiosa*, 148.

107. "Visita . . . Santa Clara," s.f. AAL, Visitas, Leg. 25, 4r.

108. Several nuns of the white veil were orphans; "Autos de María Nuñez y Francisca de Guevara," 1632, AAL, SC, IV:25. Others had received a divorce sentence, "Autos de ingreso de doña Ana de Mendoza, divorciada, [nun of white veil]" 1643, SC, VII:14; "Autos de ingreso de doña Micaela Bravo, divorciada [nun of black veil]," IX:143. 1656. See also Fernández et al., *La mujer*, 448f; Martín, *Daughters*, 184f; on Cuzco, Burns, *Colonial*, 120–21.

109. For a comparison with Cuzco, see Burns, *Colonial*, 105–12.

110. "Visitas . . . Santa Clara," AAL, Visitas, Leg. 25, s.f.

111. Córdoba y Salinas, *Crónica*, 904. Francisca de Alfaro received permission from the prelate to establish a chapel dedicated to Christ. On the Wednesday of Holy Week a procession of crosses began from her cell, and on that Friday, the nuns performed Christ's Descent.

112. María de San José, *Wild*, 270.

113. *Constituciones*, 67v.

114. Ibsen, *Women's*, 97.

115. *Constituciones*, 55f, ch. 5.

116. Some were the illegitimate children of wealthy Spanish or Creole mothers whose families could not deal with the public humiliation. They knew their children would receive a decent upbringing in the convent. Others were the baby girls of women of color who could not afford to feed another hungry mouth (see Martín, *Daughters*, 80–83; María de San José, *Wild*, 269; Burns, *Colonial*, 102, 113).

117. "Los oficios," 1653, AAL, SC, IX:70. For a discussion of daily life and vocations in Mexican convents, see Loreto López, "Los espacios"; for Peru, see Martín, *Daughters*, 191; on Cuzco, see Burns, *Colonial*, 111–12; Ibsen, *Women's*, 97–98.

118. *Constituciones*, 62, ch. 8.

119. "Cuentas . . . 1626 hasta 1629," AAL, SC, III:23, 1r–2r.

120. Tardieu, *Los negros*, I:189.

121. *Constituciones*, ch. 7.

122. Several abbesses had longer tenures; doña Justina de Guevara maintained the office—almost without interruption—from the convent's inauguration until 1622 (Fernández et al., *La mujer*, 424). Magdalena Vélez Roldán (1645–50; she was chosen as interim president in 1650; 1656–58); Beatríz de Aguilar (1653–56; 1665–66); Ana Manrique (1660–62). The election of 1656 was particularly contentious and may be the one to which Ursula refers in her diary. Vélez Roldán was chosen and began her tenure the following year (1656, AAL, SC, IX:149). They began and ended their tenure on the twenty-seventh of June.

123. Kathleen Myers makes this point in her discussion about discontent among the nuns of the black veil in the Convent of La Soledad in Puebla (María de San José, *Wild*, 274f).

124. "Tabla de oficios," 1653 (for 1653), IX:52; 1653 (for 1654), IX:70; 1655 (for 1656), IX:134, AAL, SC. Fernández et al., *La mujer*, 448.

125. This list is based on the following "task designations" (*tablas de oficios*) for the years listed in parentheses: AAL, SC, IX:157 (1657); X:16 (1658); X:35 (1659); X:72 (1661).

126. Petroff, "Medieval Woman's," 66–79; Wood, *Women, Art*, 29.

127. AGI, Lima 94, 1606, no. 8, "Respondese a la cédula," listed the population at twenty-five nuns, seven donadas, and eight slaves.

128. Tardieu, *Los negros*, II:187.

129. A common request of a nun or novice read as follows, "Because I am alone, without a servant or a slave who can help with my necessities, my godfather, Manuel Baptista, donated a black slave named Esperança Bañol to this convent, [with the understanding] that after serving

the community, she could serve me in her spare time" (see "Autos . . . Antonia de Acosta," 1634, AAL, SC, V:2, 11; also cited in Tardieu, *Los negros*, I:146).

130. Native Andean slaves were rare. For one example, see "Autos . . . Luisa de Escobar," 1642, AAL, SC, VI:32.

131. "Testimonios," 1695, AAL, SC, XXI:10.

132. Martín, *Daughters*, 190f.

133. "Ursula," ASCL, 16r.

134. "Autos seguidos," 1626, AAL, SC, III:23.

135. Tardieu, *Los negros*, I:144–45, 190ff; Martín, *Daughters*, 190.

136. "Solicitud . . . Petronila de Castro," 1611, AAL, SC, I:33.

137. "Autos . . . Maria de Arevalo," 1635, AAL, SC, V :20. See also Bowser, *African*, 376, "moral defects."

138. *Constituciones*, chs. XII, XIII. McKnight discusses the second-order rules followed by the Clares in Tunja (*Mystic*, 84).

139. Martín, *Daughters*, 191.

140. See the example of "Doña Maria de la Peña," 1668, AAL, SC, XII:181.

141. "Autos que sigue Feliciana de Salinas," 1663, AAL, SC, XI:71.

142. *Constituciones*, 101. The Papal Bull of Gregory VIII (1583) stated that the convent should have no more than one criada for every ten nuns.

143. Those donadas who did not comply were punished and sent to a *panadería* (bakery), Tardieu, *Los negros*, I:400.

144. "Relación de religiosas y donadas," 1633, AAL, SC, IV:42.

145. Tardieu, *Los negros*, I:394. For examples, see "Autos de profesión . . . Pascuala del Pulgar, negra donada," 1642, AAL, SC, VI:35; "Autos de profesion . . . Maria Rodriguez, cuarterona donada," 1642, AAL, VI:37; "Autos de profesion de Gracia Maria de Jesus, negra," 1664, AAL, XII:27. Tardieu, *Los negros*, I:394.

146. "Autos . . . de Josefa María, cuarterona," 1666, AAL, SC, XII:99.

147. Most applicants were under twenty, but a few were in their forties. Occasionally, a donada owned a slave, which indicated some wealth or family connections. See "Autos que sigue doña Ana de Zarate," 1636, AAL, SC, V:42.

148. *Constituciones*, 99v.

149. Ibid., 100r.

150. Gómez de la Parra, *Fundación*, 310.

151. "Autos de . . . Pascuala del Pulgar," 1642, AAL, SC, VI:35.

152. She never appeared as "Ursula de Jesús," on the annual roster of *oficios* set forth each year by the abbess to rotate the various positions. Several "Ursulas," are listed, but all are nuns of the black veil (*madres*), with the exception of Ursula Barba, whose name only appeared once on the work roster for the year 1659 to assist the *provisora* ("Tabla de oficios," 1658, AAL, SC, X:35). Could she have been Ursula?

153. "Ursula," ASCL, 12r.

154. Iwasaki, "Fray Martín," 164–66. Quoting Pedro Ciruelo's *Reprobación de las supersticiones,* Spanish historian Sebastián Cirac Estopañán defined *ensalmadores* as those who "try to cure sores and wounds, and do other things that surgeons generally understand" (*Los procesos*, 99).

155. Forty percent of those women in Lima accused of *brujería* (witchcraft) between 1571 and 1702 were free mulatas (Tardieu, *Los negros*, I:572–80). The mulato donados Martín de Porras and Juan de la Cruz were both barbers and spiritual healers in Lima.

156. "Ursula," ASCL, 47v.

157. Iwasaki, "Fray Martín," 159–60, 64; Tardieu, *Los negros*, I:636–37, 644–45; Rio Hijas, "La sanidad," 574–77; "Ursula," ASCL, 28v.

158. Asunción Lavrin's wonderful article, "Indian Brides," 234f, discusses "signaling" as an important feature of seventeenth-century spirituality and as a venue for women of color.

159. "Ursula," ASCL, 16r.

160. John Donne, *Devotions on Emergent Occasions* (1623–24), cited in Greenblatt, *Hamlet*, 40.

161. On early modern conceptions of purgatory, see Díaz, *Tratado;* Andrade, *Órden*; Roa, *Estado*; Boneta y Laplana, *Gritos*. Jacques Le Goff claims that this concept had been consolidated

by the twelfth century (*Birth*, 3, 5). Whether the doctrine of purgatory—and particularly its "spatialization"—experienced a "deceptively neat evolution" is still the subject of debate. Many medievalists, including Barbara Newman, do not accept Jacques Le Goff's conclusions. See Newman, "Hildegard," 90; Edwards, "Purgatory," 634; McGuire, "Purgatory," 61–66; Bynum, *Holy Feast*, 399, n. 54. What occurred during life after death remained the subject of debate from the thirteenth century onward (Bynum, *Resurrection*, 279; Koslofsky, *Reformation*, 23–31; Schmitt, *Ghosts*, 89).

162. Martínez Arancón, *Geografía*, 68–69.

163. On "soul bodies," see Bynum, *Resurrection*, 281, 283; Martínez Arancón, *Geografía*, 78. Gregory the Great discussed the amount of time spent purging sins (see Atwell, "From Augustine," 178). See also Pérez de Montalván, *Vida y purgatorio*, 35; Moncada, *Declamación*, 18; on types of sins, see Santoro, *Discurso*, 48–51.

164. Alchemy was a medieval science and philosophy that had as its goal the transmutation of all base metals into gold.

165. "Vida," AFL, 589v.

166. Pérez de Montalván, *Vida*, 37; Catherine of Genoa, *Purgation*, 80.

167. Holloway, *Saint Bride*, 58–59.

168. From his *Supplement*, and quoted in Le Goff, *Birth*, 273. The Italian visionary María Magdalena Pazzi (1566–1607) found this suffering difficult to fathom (see Pazzi, "Breve relación," 301r). Louvet claims that of all the saints, Pazzi's visions of purgatory probably provide the most detail (*Le purgatoire*, 73, 118–19, 180, 210).

169. Martínez Arancón, *Geografía*, 76–77, 80, 82; Boneta, *Gritos*, 29ff; Roa, *Estado*, 10.

170. Pérez de Montalván, *Vida y purgatorio*, 34.

171. Sebastián, *Contrarreforma y barroco*, 30.

172. Martínez Arancón, *Geografía*, 69–70, 96–98.

173. "Ursula," ASCL, 38v.

174. Martínez Arancón, *Geografía*, 99, cites Arriaga, *Directorio espiritual,* 306. See also Loyola, *Ejercicios espirituales*, "Ejercicio del infierno."

175. Zaleski, *Otherworld*; Gardiner, *Visions*; Díaz y Díaz, *Visiones*; Goldey, "Good," 6.

176. Le Goff, *Birth*; Brown, "No Heaven," 447–56; Martínez Gil, *Muerte*, 503.

177. Newman, "Hildegard," 94.

178. On punishment in the place where one sinned, see Carrillo, *Explicación*, 49.

179. Atwell, "From Augustine"; Le Goff, *Birth*, 11, 107–8; Zaleski, *Otherworld*, 34–39, 66ff.

180. Bridget, *Saint Bride*, ch. XVII.

181. See Roa, *Estado*; Serpi, *Tratado*; Martínez Arancón, *Geografía*, 104–5. The astral travels of seventeenth-century Spanish mystic, María de Agreda (1602–65)—a nun who corresponded regularly with King Philip IV (1621–65)—detailed the precise dimensions of hell, purgatory, and limbo. On María de Agreda, see Agreda, "De la redondez," BNM, Ms. 9346, 7–8.

182. Hildegard, *Book*, 105, 107, 155.

183. "Marceliana," AFL, 360r.

184. "Ursula," ASCL, 42r.

185. Schmitt, *Ghosts*, 5f.

186. Martínez Gil, *Muerte*, 506–7; Horozco y Covarrubias, *Tratado*, 34.

187. Palafox y Mendoza, *Luz a los vivos*, 37f.

188. "Ursula," ASCL, 51r. Manescal distinguishes between those who speak and are "inquietos y temerosos" (possibly influenced by the devil), and voices that are "consolados and quietos" (and coming from God) (*Miscellanea*, 182).

189. Greenblatt, *Hamlet*, 33.

190. Nalle, *God*, 191. Individuals throughout medieval Spain narrated tales of journeys to the beyond (see Díaz y Díaz, *Visiones*).

191. For example, see the works of Calderón de la Barca. The publication of the *Vida y purgatorio del glorioso San Patricio* in 1628 by Juan Pérez de Montalbán gave rise to a popular play on the same subject by Lope de Vega (Martínez Gil, *Muerte*, 274).

192. Eire, *From Madrid*, 173. See, for example, Díaz, *Tratado*; Roa, *Estado*; Alejo Venegas, *Agonía*; Martínez Arancón, *Geografía*, 58–59.

193. "Peticion," BNM, Leg. 4467, no. 19. On Saint Nicholas of Tolentino, see Martínez Gil, *Muerte*, 275–76; "Memoria," BNM, ms. 18728, no. 9, 42r–44v. In one instance, a witness in the Inquisition trial of the beata Juana Bautista reported that her first husband had appeared to her a few days after dying, reproaching her because his request to have masses said to Saint Vincent Ferrer on his behalf had not been carried out (AHNM, Inquisición, Toledo, Leg. 114, exp. 9, 1636, "Juana Bautista," 27v). See also "Juana Bautista," BNM, ms. 18728, no. 9. On Vincent Ferrer, see also Louvet, *Le purgatoire*, 176; Martínez Gil, *Muerte*, 220–21.

194. On paintings of Nicolas of Tolentino, see *San Nicola*, 70: one early seventeenth-century painting by Ignoto Marchigiano; one at the altar of the Augustinian church at Matelica; and a painting by Ignoto (1680–90) of the Virgin of Carmen with Nicolas of Tolentino

195. Schmitt, *Ghosts*. See also Manescal, *Miscellanea*, 160ff. I would especially like to thank William Christian for this reference. See also Koslofsky, *Reformation*, 26; Carrillo, *Explicación*, 83, 88f.

196. Francisca del Santísima Sacramento sought the assistance of Saint Nicolás Tolentino (Arce Reynoso, *Francisca*, 113).

197. Holloway, *Saint Bride*, 42, 54; Saint Birgitta, *Book of Revelations*, ch. XVIII. See also Moncada, *Declamación*, 161.

198. Geary, *Living*, 78.

199. Le Goff, *Birth*, 233; Martínez Arancón, *Geografía*, 58.

200. Gómez Nieto, "Actitudes," 70; Barriga Calle, "La experiencia," 81–102.

201. Davis, "Ghosts"; García Fernández, *Los castellanos*, 90.

202. Protestants argued that deliberately inculcating the fear of purgatory into secular society merely increased pecuniary gain as a result of payment for masses, indulgences, and burial fees (Marshall, "Fear, Purgatory," 152–53).

203. Martínez Arancón, *Geografía*, 72.

204. García Carcel, "Cuerpo y enfermedad," 135–36; García Fernández, *Los castellanos*, 68–72. See also Ariès, *Hour*; Vovelle and Vovelle, *La mort*.

205. Loyola, *Exercicios espirituales* (1686), "Exercicio de la muerte," "Segunda parte del exercicio de la muerte," "Exercicio del juizio universal," and "Segunda parte del juizio universal." As early as 1549, Jesuit Manuel da Nóbrega held public "disciplines" in Bahia for mortal sinners and the souls in purgatory (Letter from Manuel da Nóbrega to P. Simão Rodrigues, Bahia, 9/VIII/1549, Leite, *Cartas dos primeiros Jesuítas do Brasil*. I:131) In Lima, the Jesuit preoccupation with "la buena muerte" was particularly strong, and Juan Alfonso Polanco's, *Regla*, circulated widely (Iwasaki, "Luisa," 230).

206. Díaz, *Tratado*; Ariès, *Hour*, 31. On alms to poor in Galicia, see Poska, "Matters," 99f. For death rituals in fifteenth- and sixteenth-century Castile, Segovia, and Madrid, see Gómez Nieto, "Actitudes," 62–70. On preparation for a good death in Castile, see García Fernández, *Los castellanos*, 68–72 (his study also covers the eighteenth century). On leaving food, wine, and wax at the gravesite on All Souls Day, see Rábade Obrado, "La religiosidad," 447. On dressing in a religious habit, see Martínez Gil, *Muerte*, 268; Poska, "Matters," 101. The practice of dressing the corpse in religious garb continued into the eighteenth century (García Fernández, *Los castellanos*, 218–19).

207. "Peticion," BNM, Leg. 4467, no, 19. See also Santoro, *Discurso*; Carrillo, *Explicación*; Moncada, *Declamación*; Pinelli, *Noticias*; Cruz, *Tesoro*; Roa, *Estado*. Michel Vovelle calls the seventeenth century in Europe the "great century" of purgatory (Vovelle and Vovelle, *La mort*, 308). For Portugal, see Abreu, "Purgatório"; Araujó, *A morte*.

208. Letter, King Philip III to Pope Urban VIII, 1624, AMAE, Santa Sede, (Culto), Leg. 151, no. 189.

209. Specifically, Saints Gregory, Vincent Ferrer, or Nicolas of Tolentino. See "Petición," 1622, AHNM, Inquisición, Leg. 4467, no. 19. Friar Pedro de Valdivía requested permission to reprint the *Memoria de misas* (printed in Zaragoça, Luis Sánchez, 1616) and take copies to Chile.

210. Gómez Nieto, "Actitudes," 70; García Fernández, *Los castellanos*, 295.

211. Moncada, *Declamación*, 198–203; Carrillo, *Explicación*, pt. 2; Cruz, *Tesoro*.

212. On Spain, Poska, "Matters," 96f; on Portugal, see Goldey, "Good," 4; on Lima, Barriga Calle, "La experiencia," 96.

213. Ramos, "Death, Conversion," 185.

214. Echave y Assu, *La estrella*, 72–75; Cobo, *Obras*, II :394, 455. Poska discusses "privileged altars" in Galicia where testators requested masses for souls in purgatory ("Matters," 107).

215. "Autos seguidos," 1616, AAL, Cofradías, Leg. XXXVI:6.

216. "Fundación de capellanía," 1645, AGNP, Protocolos, Sebastían Muñoz, 1643–45, (Feb.–March 45), no. 1192; "Vida," AFL, 594v. See also Boneta, *Gritos*, 187.

217. The term "Apostoles to the Dead" is taken from Newman, "On the Threshold," 109.

218. Bloch, "Death," 215, 226.

219. See Newman's two wonderful articles, "Hildegard," and "On the Threshold."

220. Bynum, *Holy Feast*, 120.

221. Newman, "Hildegard," 91–93; Dronke, *Women*, 179.

222. *Beguinages* housed *beguines* in northern France, the Low Countries, Switzerland, and the Rhineland. *Beguines* lived chaste, poor lives and dedicated themselves to charitable services, such as caring for the sick, needy, and uneducated. *Tertiaries* (in Spain they were called *beatas*) also lived in the world, yet were separate from it, associated themselves with a mendicant order (often, the Franciscans), and also lived austere, penitential, and charitable lives.

223. McNamara, "Need," 210–13.

224. Newman, "On the Threshold," 112.

225. Following the logic of Thomas Aquinas, Caroline Bynum states that the belief was that the soul accounts for the "whatness" of the body, and that any matter that exists at the end of time will be a "soul" body (Bynum, "Female Body," 192ff, 195f).

226. Petroff, "Medieval," 184ff.

227. Thomas of Cantimpré (1201–72), *Life*, 28–32. Newman says that Cantimpré, a Dominican professor of theology at Louvain, championed female visionaries who saved souls in purgatory particularly where Cistercian nunneries were located ("Hildegard," 95). The *beguines* then carried on this tradition.

228. Newman, "On the Threshold," 119.

229. Bynum, *Holy Feast*, 171.

230. Gertrude, *Oraciones*, book III, ch. 18, 237–38; Andrade, *Vida*, 234–37.

231. Newman, "On the Threshold," 118.

232. Andrade, *Vida*, 238.

233. Bynum, *Holy Feast*, 127, 353, n. 67.

234. Holloway, *Saint Bride*, 22.

235. Huerga, *Santa Catalina;* Jiménez de Cisneros, *Obra*.

236. Testimony of Inés de Ubitarte, 1629, AHNM, Inquisición, Lima, Libro 1030, fs. 395ff.

237. Capua, *La vida*.

238. Bynum, *Holy Feast*, 171; Petroff, *Body and Soul*, 164.

239. Catherine of Genoa, *El tratado*, no. 10.

240. Catherine of Genoa, *Purgation*, 72, 86. Angela of Foligno emphasized purgation while living and outlined the steps necessary for the "faithful follower of Christ" to cleanse the body of sins. She believed that, ultimately, a living soul could achieve illumination, or spiritual purity (Angela of Foligno, *Vida*, 112–17).

241. García Fernández, *Los castellanos*, 90.

242. The term "mothers of Santa Teresa" was coined by scholar Ronald Surtz. They were Teresa de Cartagena (1420[?]–[?]); María de Ajofrín, Juana de la Cruz (1481–1534), and María de Santo Domingo 1486[?]–[?]). See Surtz, *Writing Women*, 2, 11; Serrano y Sanz, *Apuntes*; Teresa de Cartagena, *Writings*, 1, n. 2.

243. In 1525, the Inquisitor General issued an edict of faith, containing forty-eight propositions against *alumbrados* (enlightened ones), who were viewed as heretics (see Hamilton, *Heresy*). On the effects of these changes on female visionary writers in Golden Century Spain, see Manero Sorolla, "Visionarias," 310ff.

244. Teresa of Avila, *Escritos*, *Libro de la vida*, 28:4.

245. Horozco y Covarruvias, *Tratado*, was approved and published in 1588 as a means to counter what was seen as an epidemic of false revelations, 5. If a dead soul wanted to gain something other than suffrages to leave purgatory, it was considered a false revelation, or the

work of the devil (Martínez Gil, *Muerte*, 506–7; Horozco y Covarrubias, *Tratado*, 34; Navarro, *Tribunal*, 38r–43r).

246. On the appeal of Sor María de Santo Domingo, see Giles, *Book*, 37f. In spite of persecution, beatas continued to flourish well into the seventeenth century (Pons Fuster, *Místicos*).

247. AHNM, Inquisición, Censuras, Leg. 4432, no. 19, Francisco de Cepeda, "Censura y juicio. Magdalena de la Trinidad monja en San Ildefonso de Ocaña, 1665"; Inquisición, Censuras, Leg. 4440, no. 18, "Censura del sermón," 1679.

248. Guilhem, "La Inquisición."

249. Giles, "Introduction," 12.

250. Navarro, *Tribunal*, 32r–35v.

251. The French mystic Susanne de Riants de Villarey (1639–1724) considered her visions of purgatory to be a great gift, and in her writings, she reconstructed conversations with deceased nuns, bishops, and missionaries who confessed their foibles and suggested what prayers or indulgences might alleviate their pain (Riants de Villarey, *Vinte e cinco*, 12–28). On the Portuguese Maria de San Joseph, Abbess of the Convent of Discalced Carmelites in Lisbon, see 2711, "Carta de Fray Félix . . . ," 28r. In Italy, María Crocifissa (1645–99), Cabibbo, *La santa*, 103. See also Valerio, *Domenica*, 138–43; Cecilia Ferrazzi (1609–84), *Autobiography*, 65.

252. Teresa de Ávila, *Escritos*, *Vida*, 8:6.

253. Teresa of Avila, *Escritos*, *Vida*, 32; 34; 38:26–32.

254. Teresa of Avila, *Escritos*, *Camino*, V, 40:9.

255. Teresa of Avila, *Escritos*, *Vida*, 30:5; *Las moradas, sextas*, 11.

256. Teresa of Avila, *Escritos*, *Las moradas, sextas*, 11.

257. Catherine of Genoa, *Purgation*, 136.

258. AHNM, Inquisición, Censuras, 4466, lib. 5, 5r–v.

259. Muñoz Fernández notes that early modern female saints drew on Italian medieval models but were more cautious in their undertakings (*Beatas y santas*). The same held true among post-Tridentine Italian mystics (Cabibbo, *La santa*, 100, 103).

260. Some included Isabel de Trillas, Marina de Escobar, Hipólita de Jesús, and Mariana de Jesús. This list is not exhaustive by any means.

261. Ibsen discusses this point in relation to autobiographical writings (*Women's*, 26).

262. For instance, see how the beata Francisca de los Apóstoles claimed authenticity in her visions, when she appeared before the Inquisition tribunal in 1575 (Ahlgren, "Francisca," 124f).

263. Affective spirituality was notable among the Franciscans. Catherine of Siena also emphasized the soul's affection toward Christ to promote spiritual union.

264. On Francisca de la Hara's curative powers, see Romero, "Exemplar primoroso." On Gerónima de Noriega, see "Doña Gerónima, beata del Carmen, vecina del Madrid," 1627, AHNM, Inquisición, Toledo, Leg. 115, exp. 1. She assisted at the death of a neighbor's mother, helped prepare the body, and then, at the funeral, the dead woman appeared in a widow's habit. Now in purgatory, the soul requested that a certain number of masses be said on her behalf. Leonor de Ahumada (Cordova, 1613–1661) knew when people would die, and her biographer reported that Christ said that He would apply her suffering toward souls in purgatory (Ahumada, *Libro*, 24, 43).

265. See the case of Manuela de Jesús, tried by the Inquisition, who confessed to communicating with souls in purgatory. She claimed that one could get pregnant from a fountain in Seville, and that while using her castañets, the angels from heaven would come dance with her (BNM, ms. 718, 406r–v). See also "Isabel Ortíz," 1564–65, AHNM, Inquisición, Toledo, Leg. 104, exp. 5.

266. Boneta, *Gritos*, 7, 11f, 29, 31, 47. His work also cites seventeenth-century Spanish mystics like Ana de San Bartolomé (1549–1626).

267. Roa, *Estado* (Gertrude) 20–22; Ortíz de Moncada, *Declamación*, 12 (Catherine of Siena), 33 (Birgitta), 455 (Lutgarde); Carrillo, *Explicación*, 49 (Gertrude); Cruz, *Tesoro*, 162–65 (Birgitta).

268. Horozco y Covarrubias, *Tratado*, 23.

269. Leandro de Granada, *Luz*, 205–17.

270. Foligno, *Complete*, 114. The works of Angela of Foligno and Catherine of Siena had a profound influence on María de Santo Domingo (Giles, *Book*, 88).

271. For instance, the sermons of Juana de la Cruz were copied by three nuns, and treatises

of Sor María de Santo Domingo were published in Zaragosa in 1520 (MacKay, "Mujeres," 497). It also meant that well into the seventeenth century, purgatorial intercessors like the Pamplona nun Francisca del Santíssima Sacramento received wide attention from theologians on both sides of the Atlantic (Martínez Gil, *Muerte*, 505; Louvet, *Le purgatoire*, 87–88). On European mystics' influence in Latin America, see Ibsen, *Women's*, chs. 3 and 5; Glantz, "El cuerpo monacal"; María de San José, *Wild*, 304–11. Female readers in Mexican homes, schools, and convents read the works of Gertrude, Birgitta, María de la Antigua, and the seventeenth-century Spanish mystic María de Jesús de Agreda (Muriel, "Lo que leían," 165). For instance, the female saints who "populated" the nun from Tunja (Colombia), Francisca de la Concepción de Castillo's (1671–1742) texts included Clara of Assisi, Elisabeth of Hungary, Catherine of Siena, Teresa of Avila, Mary Magdalene of Pazzis, and Saint Rose of Lima (McKnight, *Mystic of Tunja*, 64). On the notion of transculturation, see van Deusen, *Between*, 12–16.

272. Ibsen, *Women's*, 14–15; María de San José, *Wild*, 306f. See also Schlau, "Following," which discusses her centrality for Mexican holy women. Some, however, went too far in their imitation practices. Sclau cites the case of the Mexican *ilusa*, Teresa Romero Zapata, whose "attempted emulation of Saint Teresa ultimately failed," 307.

273. Muriel says that theological tracts and the writings of the Fathers of the Church could be found in many homes, and circulated widely in Mexico (*Cultura femenina*, 20). Individual nuns such as María Magdalena de Lorravaquio Muñoz (1576–1636) referred to the *Flos Santorum* in their writings. On Lorravaquio Muñoz, see María Magdalena, "Libro," BLAC, Ms. G94, 321.

274. See, for example, the chapter "Meditation on Hell," written by the Mexican Dominican tertiary Francisca de San Joseph (+1725), in Quiroga, *Compendio breve*, 126–30. See also Arenal and Schlau, "Leyendo," 214.

275. Medievalist Jo Ann McNamara says that for medieval mystics charity served as a powerful tool to criticize the wealthy. Early modern mystics may have done the same ("Need," 209).

276. For an example of "hearing" souls in hell, see Salmerón, *Vida . . . Isabel de la Encarnación*, 104v–5r.

277. On the Concepcionista nun, María de Jesús, from Puebla, Mexico, see Pardo, *Vida . . . María de Jesús*, 61v–66v; Félix de Jesús María, *Vida . . . María de Jesús*, 163–69. On Ana Guerra de Jesús (1639–173), see Síria, *Vida*.

278. Pardo, *Vida . . . María de Jesús*, 62r.

279. Newman, "On the Threshold," 114–19.

280. María de San José, *Wild*, 265; on her particular visions of family members in purgatory, 176–81.

281. She had said prayers on his behalf, and he appeared, translucent and cleansed before her (Castillo Grajeda, *Compendio de la vida*, 104).

282. Félix de Jesús María, *Vida*, 169.

283. On the purgatorial visions and spiritual aide rendered by Francisca de la Concepción de Castillo, see McKnight, *Mystic*, 155. See also Josefa de la Concepción de Castillo, *Obras completas*, II:198–200 (her *Afectos espirituales*, no. 86), which advises people to emulate Christ and care for the poor and the souls of purgatory. On the visions of the tertiary from Quito, Juana de Jesús (1652–1703), see Santa María, *Vida*, 329, 332.

284. Vargas Ugarte, *Historia de la Iglesia*, III:358, 427.

285. Montoya, *Vida*; Vargas, *Piadoso*, 19f; Morales, *La virgen*, 12f, 25–29; Carmen Passarell, *Vida*, 27–32.

286. "Vida," AFL, 588r.

287. Villegas, *Flos sanctorum*: Santa Lutgarde, vida 161. Inés de Ubitarte specifically mentioned having read her life (Testimony of Inés de Ubitarte, 1629, AHNM, Inquisición, Lima, Libro 1030, 396v–97r).

288. Villegas, *Flos Sanctorum*: Margarita de Hungria, Vida 174; Margarita de Cortona, Vida 180; Angela de Fulgino, Vida 183; Maria de Ajofrin, Vida 193; Juana de la Cruz, abadessa, Vida 206.

289. Villegas, *Flos sanctorum*: Santa Lutgarde, vida 161.

290. By way of the "sentidos de su ánima conozcan y alcancen las condiciones de las ánimas" and their salvation, Capua, *La vida*, f. xxxii.

291. Meléndez, *Tesoros*, III:752.

292. On Europe, see Scully, "Marriage"; for Guatemala, see Few, *Women*, ch. 5; on Mexico, see, Jaffary, "Virtue"; for Peru, Sánchez, "Mentalidad"; Flores Espinoza, "Hechicería"; and Estenssoro, "La construcción."

293. BNP, Rodríguez, 162v. Popular perceptions of the beyond were not limited to the sorceress on the street. The knowledge and practices associated with purgatory were much more fluid between secular and religious groups (see Estenssoro, "La construcción," 415).

294. Córdoba y Salinas, *Crónica*, 900.

295. Estenssoro traces the elaborate patron-client network of several sorceresses in Lima ("La construcción," 419, 424–26). For a discussion of the circuits of spiritual knowledge developed by women in seventeenth-century Lima, see van Deusen, "Circuits."

296. In the case of medicinal practices, Africans and Europeans healers and barbers carried their own "magical-religious" healing practices into the convents where they worked (Tardieu, "Genio y semblanza," 566, n. 32), which cites an article on the same subject by scholar Fernando Romero.

297. Vovelle, *Les âmes.*

298. Women often accompanied one another to funerals. One example is found in several women "acompañada de otras amigas," who went to the funeral of Martín de Porras in 1639, see testimonies of doña Ursula de Medina, *Proceso*, 141, and Juana de los Reyes, *Proceso*, 160.

299. Testimony of María Ramírez de los Reyes, 1622, AHNM, Inquisición, Lima, Libro 1030, 330r. See also the testimony of doña Ana de Carbajal who reported the same event and said that the soul asked Ana María for forgiveness for "enojos y pesadundres que avian tenido," 331v.

300. Cussen, "Fray Martín," 62–64; and Tardieu, *Los negros*, I:624. In West Africa, see Thornton, *Africa and Africans*, 244.

301. Ibsen, *Women's*, 97.

302. Juan Eusebio Nieremberg's *De la diferencia entre lo temporal y lo eterno*, housed in the Convent of Santa Clara, contained a graphic physical description of the dying process (cited in Milhou-Roudie, "Un transito espantoso," 12).

303. *Constituciones*, 65v.

304. Córdoba y Salinas, *Crónica*, 901, 903.

305. Ibid., 954.

306. Testimony of Francisco de la Madrid, 1619, AHNM, Inquisición, Lima, Libro 1030, 247r. He said that after she took communion, Inés requested that it serve as an indulgence to help one particular troubled soul. Trial of Leonor Berdugo, 1621, AHNM, Inquisición, Libro 1030, 296r; Beatríz de Trejo y Pariaga, 455r.

307. "Gerónima de San Francisco," AFL, Reg. 17, no. 38, 473v. See also, van Deusen, "Gerónima."

308. "Escritas . . . Gerónima de San Dionisio," AFL, Reg. 17, no. 35, 433v.

309. "Escritas . . . Gerónima de San Dionisio," AFL, Reg. 17, no. 35, 433r.

310. "Marceliana de Carvajal," AFL, Reg. 17, 359v. See also Rodríguez, "Origen" (book manuscript), BNP, ch. III, 162v. The seventeenth-century Spanish mystic Francisca del Santíssima Sacramento believed that holy water cooled off souls burning in purgatory (Arce Reynoso, *Francisca*, 121).

311. Testimony of Inés Ynojosa, 1624, AHNM, Inquisición, Lima, Libro 1030, 308v.

312. Cirac Estopañán, *Los procesos*, 131–33. Estenssoro cites the testimony of Francisca de Espinoza who explained her understanding of the lonely soul ("La construcción," 430). Five of the Afro-Peruvian women accused of witchcraft between 1571 and 1702 claimed they used the invocation to Saint Martha (Tardieu, *Los negros*, I:581).

313. For examples of spells invoking the lost soul, see Trial of Ana Vallejo, 1655, AHNM, Inquisición, 1031, 388r; Trial of Josefa Tineo de Guzmán, 1665, 518r.

314. Testimony of doña Francisca de Villaroel, 1622, AHNM, Inquisición, Libro 1030, 327v; Testimony of Alonso Mesia, 325r–v.

315. Bigamy trial of Ysabel, negra de casta Terranova, 1619, AHNM, Inquisición, Libro 1030, 213v.

316. On Ana María Pérez, Testimonies given in trial of Ana María Pérez, 1622, AHNM, Inquisición 1030, 308v; Alonso Mesia, 325r–v, and Ana de Carvajal, 330v, doña Francisca de Villaroel, 327r–v. On the visions of María de Santa Domingo, see her deposition, 1624, AHNM, Inquisición 1030, 308v; on Inés de Ubitarte, see the declaration of doña María de la Torre, 1629, another nun in La Encarnación to whom Inés dictated her visions, 399r.

317. "Gerónima de San Francisco," AFL, Reg. 17, no. 38, 468r.

318. "Ursula," ASCL, 35r.

319. The beata Inés Velasco saw "some above, and others below. Some souls suffered more torment than others" (Testimony of Francisco de Madrid, 1619, AHNM, Inquisición, Lima, Libro 1030, 347r). For the efforts made by the clarisa nun, Marceliana de Caravajal, to save anonymous souls, see "Marceliana," AFL, 360v.

320. Juana de Jesús de Guía professed in 1626 (Meléndez, *Tesoros*, III:71).

321. Meléndez, *Tesoros*, III:763.

322. "Marceliana," AFL, Reg. 17, 360v.

323. Testimony of Juana Salazar, Lima, 1623, AHNM, Inquisición 1030, exp. 5, 315v.

324. She explained that at the same time she began to suffer the torments of dead souls she also began going barefoot and meeting with some of the nuns of the convent (Testimony of Isabel de Ormaza (Jesús), 1623, AHNM, Inquisición, Lima, Libro 1030, 319r–v).

325. Testimony of Inés de Ynojosa, 1624, AHNM, Inquisición, Libro 1030, 308r–v; Meléndez, *Tesoros*, vol II:71.

326. On Hipólita de Jesús's education of the Passion, and the celestial spheres, see Lorea, *La venerable madre*, 47, 50, 128; on Marina de Escobar, Puente, *Vida maravillosa*, 461–65; on Isabel de Jesús, *Vida*, 225, through visions, Christ taught her to "guardar su rebaño de los lobos infernales." Teresa de Jesús María talked about "trabajos interiores" to develop oneself (Teresa de Jesús María, "Tratado"). On Angela of Foligno, see Petroff, *Medieval Women's*, 212.

327. Hansen, *Vida admirable*, 246. See also Capua, *La vida*, pt. 2a, ch. 4, f. xxxi, ch. 7, f. xlviii; Gama, *Astro*, 60–61; Mujica, "El ancla," 110–11.

328. Hanson, *Vida*, 246; González, *Rosa mística*, 75–93.

329. Mujica, "El ancla," 134; *Rosa limensis*, 191–96, 191–94. See also "Calificación del libro," AHNM, Inquisición 4466, exp. 5, 1625. In the initial letter from the calificador, Fray Francisco de Agustín, 17/III/1625 described Dr. Juan del Castillo's idea of the "via purgativa," 5r.

330. Dr. Juan del Castillo, a medical doctor and well-known mystic, spoke about *oración de unión* with Rose (Vargas Ugarte, *Vida de Santa Rosa*, 83f, 107; Mendiburu, *Diccionario*, 1932, IV:97). He compared her to the level described by Santa Teresa in her *Moradas Sextas* and wrote about Rose's mystical experiences in a tract entitled "De la contemplación y grados della en que Nuestro Señor a puesto a un alma." See also Mujica, *Rosa limensis*, 191–96.

331. Mujica, *Rosa limensis*, 191ff.

332. "Vida," AFL, 585r–v.

333. On the discussions among secular and ecclesiastical authorities over whether to reform and systematize Christianization efforts because of the growing population, see Bowser, *African*, 238–41.

334. Córdova y Salinas, *Crónica*, 679. On Juan de la Cruz, a mulato slave in the Augustinian convent of Lima, see Tardieu, *Los negros*, I:636–42; on Benito de Palermo, I:655–56; the Jesuits boasted about Miguel de Guinea, the slave of Francisco del Castillo, I:656; the Franciscans supported Francisco de la Concepción, de casta Bran, AFL, Reg. 17, no. 21. Tardieu refers to Meléndez's chronicle, and an unpublished one by the Augustinian Juan Theodoro Vázquez. Benito de Palermo was born in Sicily of African parents and later became a Franciscan lay brother in Palermo, where he became renowned for his humility and mystical gifts.

335. Ehlers, "La esclava," 102f.

336. Thornton, *Kongolese*.

337. Gómez de la Parra, *Fundación*, 62.

338. See Myers, "Mystic Triad," 509–24; Myers, "Testimony"; Morgan, *Spanish*, ch. 6.

339. Greer, "Savage/Saint"; Shoemaker, "Kateri."

340. See notes 78 and 79, above.

341. See del Busto Duthurburu, *San Martín*; and Cussen, "La fe."

342. Ibsen, *Women's*, 22.

343. María de San José, *Wild*, 306ff, discusses how Latin American mystics looked to their European sisters as models for their writings. See also Ibsen, *Women's*, 64. I am indebted to the pathbreaking works of Kathleen Myers, Kristine Ibsen, and Alison Weber, which have deeply informed my own understandings of Ursula as an author.

344. Arenal and Schlau, "Strategems"; Weber, *Teresa*.

345. Petroff, *Medieval Women's*, 3–4.

346. Weber, "Paradoxes of Humility," 211. See also María de San José, *Wild*, 302. Ibsen, *Women's*, 26–30.

347. Petroff, *Medieval Women's*, 3–4. Some elements of her narrative style seem to adumbrate the issues addressed in the autobiographical accounts of nineteenth-century religious African-American women in the United States committed to "religious faith, human rights, and women's struggles" (Braxton, *Black*, 73–75).

348. A growing literature on race relations in colonial Latin America attempts to identify the paradigms and perplexities of nonelite racial constructions (Cope, *Limits;* Johnson and Lipsett-Rivera, *Faces*). African-American feminist scholarship has also deeply influenced my thinking. For example, see Collins, *Black Feminist*. Collins, a sociologist, uses feminist standpoint theory to privilege the epistemologies (standpoints) of marginalized peoples as a way of understanding dominant groups, or the privileged "center." I refer to "identity" as a category of practice, and as a product of "multiple and competing discourses" that highlight the nature of a fragmented self (Brubaker and Cooper, "Beyond 'Identity,'" 8).

349. "Ursula," ASCL, 25v–26r.

350. Ibsen, *Women's*, 73f.

351. Espinosa Polit, *Santa Mariana.*

352. "Ursula," ASCL, 12r.

353. Collins, *Black Feminist*, 11, 14–15, particularly her reference to Sojourner Truth, who cried out in her mid-1800 speech, "Ain't I a woman?" On Saint Rose's extreme bodily sacrifices, see Graziano, "Santa Rosa."

354. Doriani, "Black Womanhood," 203–6.

355. St. Jean and Feagin, *Double Burden.*

356. Patterson, *Slavery*, 5ff.

357. Some nuns took on additional labor, or difficult tasks. María de San José (1656–1719) chose to stitch rough cloth (María de San José, *Wild*, 85). In Spain, María de la Antigua (1571–1617), a donada from the village of Marchena in Andalucia, described how she worked in the kitchen for one week (*Desengaño*, 18; "Vida de la Venerable Madre Sor Jacobela Maria de la Cruz," BNM, Mss. no. 23, ff. 117–53, Sor Jacobela "worked ceaselessly in the enfermería," 126). The Spanish tertiary Juana de la Cruz, considered the horrible smells from the infirmary to be a test of the devil; she also washed pots and plates. While doing so, she "received many favors and particular gifts from God and his Blessed Mother" (Daza, *Historia*, 34f).

358. Ibsen, *Women's*, 71.

359. See the example of the Colombian nun Gerónima del Espíritu Santo discussed in Ibsen, *Women's*, 7–8.

360. Sharon Harley argues that black women during the Progressive era often did not believe that their occupation "was an accurate reflection of who they were" (Harley, "When Your Work," 25–37). I argue that Ursula did not view her work (which she did for hours each day) as central to her definition as a spiritual being.

361. "Ursula," ASCL, 21v.

362. "Ursula," ASCL, 4r.

363. "Ursula," ASCL, 17r.

364. Collins, *Black Feminist*, 50.

365. Braxton, *Black Women*, 5.

366. Tardieu, "Genio y semblanza," 572.

367. "Ursula," ASCL, 15r. For other examples, see 14r, 17v.

368. Greenspan, "Autohagiographical," 165. On the problem of "truth-telling" in autobiographies, see Smith, "Construing."

369. Gómez de la Parra, *Fundación*, 312; also cited in Ramos Medina, *Místicas y descalzas*, 207.

370. "Ursula," ASCL, 32r.

371. "Vida," AFL, 603v.

372. See "Vida," AFL, 589v, 593r. On ecclesiastical reforms and claims of moral laxity in Lima's convents, see van Deusen, *Between*, 134.

373. Maclay Doriani, "Black Womanhood," 203.

374. "Ursula," ASCL, 15v.

375. Homans, "'Racial Composition,'" 88–89.

376. "Ursula," ASCL, 13v.

377. Thornton, *Africa and Africans*, 236.

378. Ibid., 243–46.

379. "Vida," AFL, 591v.

380. "Ursula," ASCL, 34v. Although the handwriting of the last twenty folios more closely resembles the first twenty-nine, Ursula mentions "she who writes this" several times in those pages, "Ursula," ASCL, 43r, 46r, 53r.

381. On confessorial scrutiny, see Weber, "Paradoxes"; María de San José, *Wild*, 316–24; Bilinkoff, "Confessors"; Ibsen, *Women's*, 19–22.

382. Diego Córdoba y Salinas commissioned several biographies in 1637, *Crónica*, xxi.

383. Heras, "El. P. Fernando Rodríguez Tena," 584.

384. AFL, no. 25, "Ursula," 339v–56v contains an incomplete version (dated 1686) that ends abruptly. The second, complete version (no. 45, 585r–607r) says at the bottom of folio 585r, "Disponê la vida, segun lo que hallarâs copiado de buenos originales en el trasumpto siguiente."

385. This was not uncommon. For information on Santa Clara, Córdoba y Salinas questioned Abbess doña Magdalena Vélez Roldán and three others, and included eight other signatures of principal nuns in the convent. He sent a first completed draft to Madrid in 1640, made some additions in 1642, and completed final revisions in 1648 (*Crónica*, xxxvi, 903).

386. Vitz, "From the Oral."

387. Giles, *Book*, 108.

PART II
Translation of Ursula's Diary

(8r) In the name of the Holy Trinity, I do not know if this is something that comes from that trickster. Since the New Year, which was last Friday, and until now, vespers of the Epiphany, each time I go to pray, a Franciscan friar appears to me. I never knew him, but he is the one who threw himself off the wall. God only knows if it is true. The friar appears and asks that I commend his spirit to God. He is suffering terribly, and on his behalf he wants me to offer to the eternal Father the terrible torments that our Lord Jesus Christ suffered those three hours that He hung from the cross, until He died. I asked myself, "Did God experience so much agony?" He replied that as a man He experienced terrible agony, but did not need to, He only did it for our salvation. When He commended Himself into the hands of the Father, He also did it to teach us and serve as an example. He did not need to do this, because He is God. Among other things, he said that many friars and nuns of their orders behaved like statues: with only their bodies participating in their religious practice. If they observed the Divine Office it was without regard, devotion, or mindfulness, and during mass, they were distracted and unprepared. I do not know how to say what happened then. Finally, the friar said that because of these misdeeds they suffered terribly. From the moment he fell, which he had done without evil intent, he had performed many acts of contrition, and he now suffered the very same torment that exists in hell. He showed me a small wall the height of my chest and said that only that wall stood between him and hell. In spite of the wall, the flames there tormented him. I said to God, that if this came from Him, I would do everything, everything possible for the friar, including all the stations of the cross and earning all the indulgences possible. Today, on the vespers of the Epiphany, the friar returned to thank me and tell me that God would reward me and would give me the respite I had given him. I asked if God had received that little bit, and he said, yes, that God took heed of what was done for the living and the dead. I should continue to commend his spirit and earn indulgences for him because he still suffered from head to toe: especially around the crown of his head, where he experienced particular torment because he did not wear the tonsure ordered by our father, Saint Francis. I only remember all this in bits and pieces. But I do remember that he said that the time it takes to say the creed is equivalent to years of suffering in purgatory.[1] Because I am not sure these things are real, I do not speak of them as soon as they happen to me. But for ten days that friar persisted, pursuing me each time I entered a state of recollection.[2] I have always seen him standing, his hands folded and covered in flames from head to foot. Because he continually insisted, I said to him, "Who am I, what worth do I have to do such a thing?" He answered that God could place His special gifts in anyone. Many kings and monarchs, emperors and powerful leaders were in hell: priests and nuns as well. He would be there too, were it not for the great mercy of God, and other things along those lines that I have forgotten.

On the day of the Epiphany,[3] I was in a state of recollection after having taken communion. I do not know whether these are tricks of the big-footed one,[4] or from my head, but I recalled María Bran, a slave of the convent who had died suddenly some fourteen years ago: one of the things most forgotten for me in this world. At the same time, I saw her in a priest's alb,[5] the whitest of whites, beautifully embellished and gathered together with a short cord with elegant tassels. She also wore a crown of flowers on her head. The celestial beings arranged for me to see her from the back, although I could still see her face and she was quite lovely, and her face a resplendent black. I said, "How is it that such a good black woman, who had been neither a thief nor liar, had spent so much time in purgatory?" She said she had gone there because of her character, and because she slept and ate at the improper time. Although she had been there a long time, her punishment had been mild. She was very thankful to God, who with His divine providence had taken her from her land and brought her down such difficult and rugged roads in order to become a Christian and be saved. I asked whether black women went to heaven and she said if they were thankful (8v) and heeded His beneficence, and thanked Him for it. They were saved because of His great mercy. When I ask these questions I do not do so because I want to but, just as I soon as I see them, they speak to me without my wishing it to happen, and they make me speak without wanting to. I need for them to commend me to God because all this torments me. She also told me that I should thank God for the gifts He had given her, and although I thought she went to heaven, I could not be certain.

I am burdened by a terrible temptation. When I run into the nuns, I want to bury myself so that they do not see me. On my way to the choir, I encountered a circle of nuns standing there, and so-and-so among them.[6] As I passed by, she said, "Is there anyone in this house who performs miracles?" I felt like dropping dead on the spot. Distraught, I went to God, as He knows. "Why did you allow this to happen, my Lord—what is it in me that they say such things?" I was so bereft that my heart would not stop pounding in my chest. *Pay no attention to this, leave it to me. They called me a trickster and imposter, and they did not believe me, even when I was afflicted. And there, at the end when I was dying, they said it again. What you now ask is more difficult than if two hundred men wished to move a mountain from one place to another by their own might, without it being my will.* Later, I had the opportunity to climb up to a lofty cell and from there I saw a mountain. What the voices had said to me, here inside myself, now happened. *Even if they were one thousand, or even more.* I looked again at the other side, and there I saw the San Cristóbal Mountain.[7] Within myself, the voices explained that even if they were many, without the will of God, they could do nothing. I forgot to mention that Christ told me not to fear this deceiver; he had no more power than that which they wished to give him.

Thursday, one day after the Epiphany, while with the Lord, there was an earthquake. I was so frightened, I did not know what to do with myself, and while running from there, I forgot about God.[8] I returned later and then did what the Lord taught me to do. I made an offering to God, in the name of what His Divine Majesty did for us and, in particular, on behalf of those of us in this house living in mortal sin. I asked Him to forgive me for having left Him without even remembering my sins. The voices explained that asking for forgiveness takes time, because when trouble comes, nothing can be done. They told me it happened so that I would praise God. I thanked God that we had not perished during that earthquake. They explained that the blood of Christ clamored to His eternal Father on behalf of the offenses committed against Him. Had I not seen when they insulted the one Son, to such a degree that His Father wished to vindicate that offense, and to such a degree that the Father wished to end everything until the Son returned to placate His Father? They commit many sins of all kinds: some covertly; others without the slightest shame or fear. And they offend Him even more in religious houses, where they should only love and serve Him. Hell is full of those who live their life in an uproar and in diversions. The sinners say, "What is this all about? God is good." They refuse to pay any mind, nor do they ask forgiveness for their sins. They do not even remember that there is a God who should be feared. How many tears did our Lord Jesus Christ shed in Jerusalem for those sins? How much did He suffer in order to save us? His blessed mother wept her entire life from the moment her Son became flesh. Although during that one moment she experienced joy, the rest was bitterness and tears. I do not know how to put into words what happened there, nor do I understand what it was like then, although at the time it was presented to me I understood it very well. God knows, (9r) and I tell Him that He knows I only seek to please Him.

The following Friday, some nuns took communion and among them, one arrived, and they said if they were to take away all those things it would be better. More about all that.

In the choir I saw a lot of smoke billowing and asked what it was. The voices explained that mortal sins caused that.

Sunday, on the last day of Epiphany, I felt terrible anguish. Wishing to enter a state of recollection, I had forgotten that hell exists, but then I saw a depth so foul-smelling, and even deeper than many wells. It seemed to me that its depth is comparable to the distance from here to heaven. There I saw a great multitude of people who resembled ants, and they said, "Oh poor me, here forever." I said, "Jesus be with me. There are many people here." The voices told me, *Every day, as many as you see there fall in. As you can see, they come from all parts of the world: infidels, Moors and Jews, and of many nations.*[9] *Of the Christians, few were saved because of their carelessness; nor were the ungrateful ones, who were inclined to follow their vices.* The voices said that the blood of God would remedy things. I said, "I believe in God the almighty, creator of heaven and earth, and in Jesus Christ." They said, *Those poor, unfortunate ones who do not believe in Jesus Christ.* The flames rose up above their heads, and above them, there was something like a mesh, where the flames reached through. They said, *What is above the netting is purgatory and although the punishments there were also terrible, they were nothing compared to the affliction of not being able to see God.* It also seemed to me that I saw some nuns there. I felt such terrible distress about this and asked God to free me from such visions. The voices responded that it was very beneficial to learn about hell. I do not know how to explain, nor do I understand what happened there. May God be with me and give me His light, and may He keep me in His hand. The voices also said that God had His hands lowered and that when He raised them it was to punish and cast them out, and that He was as just as He was merciful.

Monday, as soon as I had gone to the choir and prostrated myself before the Lord, I saw two black women below the earth. In an instant, they were beside me. One of them said to me, "I am Lusia, the one who served Ana de San Joseph, and I have been in purgatory for this long, only because the great merciful God showed compassion toward me.[10] No one remembers me." Very slowly, she spoke of God's goodness, power, and mercy, and how we should love and serve Him. Lusia had served this community in good faith, but sometimes they had accused her of certain things, and at times she suffered her penance where she tended to cook. For the love of God, would Ursula please commend her spirit to God. Before Lusia died, she had endured awful hardships, and because of them they had discounted much of the punishment. This is all mixed up, as I remember it. She spoke at length, and her appearance corresponded to the way she looked while living. I did not know who the other dead black woman was. On another day, in the morning, Lusia returned with the same demand and requested the same for doña Polonia de Moya.[11] She said doña Polonia had endured terrible suffering and had no one who would remember her, and I thought I saw her there. I said to God that if He sent the suffering, I would commend them to Him and offer whatever I could for them and for that friar, who almost always appears before me. On one of these days, the friar told me that what a community (9v) did together for a soul was great and worth more than when it was done for many souls, because then, only a little went for each one. I see that the flames do not come out of the top of her head as they did before, now they only reach to the middle of her forehead. I do not know whether this is the chicanery of that trickster.[12]

Another time, the *morena* [black woman] Lusia returned with the nun, doña Polonia, saying that I should ask the Father in the name of the Incarnation of his Son on their behalf: I said, "In the name of the Incarnation?" and the Angolan woman said, "Yes, in the name of the Incarnation." She explained, "Had He not become flesh, been born, suffered, and died for our redemption?" I saw the nun with that peculiar eye that looked as though it would burst.

Thursday, at times I would like to know how the nun, doña Mariana Machuca, is.[13] While having this temptation, I asked my Lord Jesus to guide me so that I would no longer have it and would do only what He wished. Today, while I was where I usually am, a desire swept over me. I resisted it as much as possible, because I do not know whether these are contrivances of that one [the devil]. I saw her in purgatory, in the same way as she was here: seated on her chair with her cane held close to her. I wondered, "In purgatory? How can such a saintly person be there?" The voices said that she was there, purging herself, and that *it is worthwhile for the living to mortify themselves in many ways, although they live as though they had not done that. They see and hear as though they cannot hear or see, and in this manner, many things are not the way they really are.* The voices said, *that in order not to sin they avoided certain things, so as not to be punished when they deserved it, or they let obligatory matters slide. All these were the devil's tricks. No matter what, one should never stop fulfilling one's duties. God's creatures will not be left without receiving the proper discipline, because that might be the cause of their perdition. They are redeemed with the blood of our Lord, Jesus Christ.* I do not know how to describe what happened there. The punishment doña Mariana experienced was minimal, and that children also pass through the fire, and that on the day of the Incarnation she will go to heaven. This is written the way I remember it, in bits and pieces. God only knows what it is; I pay no heed.

Friday, I have the nerve to say, "My Lord Jesus, and there, have they heeded this?" Because I said this, the voices repeated what they had said before, saying *My good Jesus.* I said, "I should say, 'My Lord, Jesus Christ.'" They said it is important for a child to treat his parent with love and reverence. Later, near the end, I see her[14] on her deathbed, with large candles, and all the other things they place on the dead. This must be a trick of that devil.

Later, in the evening, while in my bed and praying to God with my eyes closed, Cecilia appeared in front of me. I was so terribly frightened that I began shaking like someone poisoned by mercury. Wherever I turned she appeared before me, in the same way and dressed in the same manner as when she was alive. She was an Indian donada who had died some years ago.

Saturday afternoon, on the day of San Marcelo,[15] I was praying the entire rosary, and the voices told me to meditate on when they took my Lord down from the cross and the intolerable pain and agony He suffered there. I should consider that the Lord had suffered all He had suffered from the moment He entered this world solely for our salvation and redemption, and He had done it all because of His eternal Father's (10r) will. If His Father willed Him to be born, He said, "Thy will be done"; if He willed Him to suffer, "Thy will be done"; if He willed Him to die, "Thy will be done," all in such a way that He followed the will of God in everything. I said I did not wish to see or hear anything. I want to get up now and leave here. My Lord Jesus was our teacher from whom we should learn obedience, humility, and all the other virtues. I should recognize that I am nothing, a worm, and deserved only hell. Only because of God's goodness and love did I receive His beneficence. I should be extremely grateful for these gifts and worship my Lord with the same reverence and love with which the angels adored Him in the manger, on the cross, and in the tomb. I should also ponder how, because of God's will, He had moved that tremendous slab away from the tomb. At that moment, within myself I had the desire to understand how they had carried my Lord to the sepulchre. They explained that it happened in the same way that I see them carry the most Holy Body in the procession on the Friday of Holy Week, and in the same manner that the venerable men, accompanied by angels, went along singing. I do not know how to describe what happened there. Afterward, I offered three decades of my rosary for each soul,[16] most of them clerics and friars outside the convent. In a chastising tone, the voices said, that with so many in the house for whom I could plead or offer prayers, why did I look for those outside, naming so-and-so, whom I had named in my prayers. While saying this, a throng of nuns came out from under the earth, and two by two they came by way of that deep place from the area near the kitchen. First, there was doña Teresa, looking very well, with her wimple beneath the habit very white. I recognized some of the nuns who had died more than twenty-four years ago. They all came with their veils covering their faces; only Teresa was unveiled. I recognized a Beatris, two Juanas, and another named Mensia. I was astonished that they had been in purgatory for such a long time. They said, "Does that frighten you? We have been there since the days of Saldaña."[17] I asked after a few nuns, particularly doña Ana Delgado.[18] The voices told me that she was in heaven. I asked after another whom I won't name, and they responded that from the moment she died, terribly burdened, she had descended into hell. They awaited her there, with terrible cauldrons, where she will remain forever. They named the sins she had committed that condemned her and for which she had never asked forgiveness. Although she was always taking pleasure from her vices, she suffered from some of them. If, as she lay dying, she had asked for forgiveness, God, in His goodness would have pardoned her. She did not do that, though, and I should see the harm caused by living carelessly and allowing oneself to be carried away by the appetite. This taught me a lot about the importance of spiritual exercises and that in this house the one sin that displeases God, our father Saint Francis, and our mother Saint Clare greatly are the friendships. What happened there I am unable to say, but I was dumbstruck by it all, and for having asked after the one who is so far beyond my (10v) recall. They make me ask against my will, and I do not even know who speaks to me, and I afraid that someone undesirable will respond. If it were up to me, I would ask after other, very different dead souls. In that same procession I also saw a black woman named Lusia off to one side. I asked if black women also went there, and they responded, *Yes, they remain separated to one side, and everything there occurs in great concord.* On Sunday, while in a meditative trance pondering what had happened, I saw doña Teresa in a very well lit place. She looked happy, and her face was well covered with a pristine wimple; her veil was very long. It seemed that she only suffered now because she could not see God. I asked myself, "Does purgatory have cavities?" The voices said, *Yes, and that specific sins brought specific punishments. Those punished in the cavities received the same torture as those in hell. That well where I saw Alfonsa was where they went when they had committed a mortal sin. Although they asked for forgiveness, confessed their sins, and were forgiven, they still went there to be purged. In order to go to heaven they had to be purer than one thousand crystals. Those wishing to please God were fearful and careful not to offend Him and asked forgiveness. Those are the ones who are like doña Teresa. If they are miserable, wretched, and fall into mortal sin, they should ask God for forgiveness, if they are truly remorseful for having offended Him. They can then be certain that this is what the blood of our Lord Jesus Christ is for and offer it to the eternal Father for all He suffered.* This was an important lesson. I do not know how to describe what happened there. May God be with me and free me from all evil. Everything torments me.

On Tuesday while doing my spiritual exercises, I saw that wretched one they told me about the other day, a thousand depths below. She was in that wretched place, lying flat on her back on something like a barbecue, surrounded by many demons who tormented her. Flames came out her mouth, eyes, and ears, just as when flames burst from a firework that is not allowed to leave the ground. She had that noise in her head, and they touched her head, using a thousand different methods of torture. Others came and placed horrible pieces of iron around her feet. The voices said, *See, this is how the indulgent and lazy ones live. They turn their backs on everything and pay attention to nothing. They do not fear God, but only feed their appetites, spending their time jeering and causing a ruckus. God offers them the help they need.* In speaking of the woman who was standing there, God said that He had provided her with memory, understanding, and will so that she could make the appropriate choice. She had chosen that life, in spite of the confessors, preachers, the inspirations, and books. Our Lord Jesus Christ said, *Be vigilant and pray in order to avoid temptation. She had made that choice and fallen into temptation.* Everything goes to bits and pieces as I recall it. It is amazing how everything there is said harmoniously, (11r) and in such an orderly manner. When I leave that place I feel so confused, wondering why they come to me with such things, me, a poor little woman who means nothing, what use am I? Sometimes I want to get up and run from there. I already told God that He knows very well I want nothing more than to please Him. I do not come here because I want them to speak to me, and the same with the visions. The voices also told me that when I see someone in that way, I should counsel her gently for her good.

On Wednesday, the feast day of Saints Fabian and Sebastian,[19] after I had received communion, the voices told me that, when, at one time I wanted to learn to read, it was so I could be saved. They gave me such weighty lessons for that purpose, and when I went about saying to the Lord God, "When will this come to an end?" and thinking it was all in my head, it turned out that everything was divine inspiration. The celestial beings placed five terrible things of mine in front of me, saying, *Who but God would have gotten you out of those messes? All the good inspirations we receive come from His hand. When we do not act on them, we run into trouble. Sins create other sins, and vices cause other vices, and when one asks God for forgiveness, absolution occurs instantaneously. If someone confesses and receives communion, though, and then repeats the same sins they just confessed, they lose God's grace. Sinners did not realize that by living tranquilly in pleasure, and eating and sleeping, they angered God. Out of weakness, they might fall into mortal sin, like committing robbery or other types of mortal sins. They should first make peace and firmly resolve not to offend God again. This means making a good confession and trying to rid ourselves of our vices. Count them one by one, and if among them there is the vice of garrulousness, we should do our best to perform continual acts of contrition.* This all comes out, not in the order it was presented, but in little bits and pieces. What I do remember very well is that when the voices talked about paradise, they said that the blessed ones see in God everything that happens here.

Wednesday, the voices told me about when my Lord Jesus took his apostles to the Last Supper[20] and the compassion with which He washed His apostles' feet and then dried them with a towel. This was because the apostles were about to take communion, and washing and drying their feet signified confession and the cleansing and purification of their sins. Although my Lord Jesus was aware that Judas planned to betray Him, He treated him the same as the others. If one of us knew what Judas was about to do, we would become angry and say, "I cannot look at this one," but my Lord Jesus pretended not to know. He did not wish to scandalize the others. When he went to give Him the kiss of peace in the garden He could easily have made Judas die, but pretended not to notice, just as He does with us now. He waits, one year, then another, then many, and still, we continue to offend Him. The three Divine Persons love us so much that they held a divine council to address the issue of our salvation. They are all the same being, with the same power, wisdom, goodness, and love. The Father gave us his Son, as did the Holy Spirit, and the Son gave Himself for our salvation, but it came at such a terrible cost: spilling His blood and giving His life for those who are ungrateful. I said, "Jesus be with me, who comes to me with such things? I believe in the Holy Trinity, and everything the Holy Roman Church (11v) says. I do not come here so that they can disturb me, but to praise my Lord Jesus, whom the Virgin bore and who died on the cross." The voices said, *Why are you so afraid of that big-footed one?* I replied, "Because he loves to deceive." They said that God is greater than millions of them, and if they have power to deceive or tempt, it is because God allows it, and to thank God. We should go to Him in faith and confidence. In the midst of all these things, such thoughts come to me in waves.

Thursday, I do not know why they come to me with such stories. The voices tell me that my Lord Jesus brought His apostles to the Last Supper, washed their feet with such loving compassion, and did not refuse to do the same with Judas, though He knew what he had plotted. Washing their feet and drying them with that towel symbolized confession, and that when He gave them communion, He did the same with Judas in order not to scandalize the others. If we found out we were being betrayed, we would say, "I am enraged, I cannot stand the sight of him." When they apprehended Him and Judas arrived to give Him a kiss of peace, He could have killed him then and there, but He pretended not to know, just as He does now with us. He always waits for us, and here we always offend Him. I am in such a quandary with so many things coming all at once. I have no head or memory for such things. One other thing: we owe the Lord so much. He did so much for us, and still we turn our backs on Him. Instead, we serve the one who beats us with an iron rod.

In the afternoon, while praying a while, I remembered that a nun had urgently requested me to commend her friend's spirit to God. The friend was seriously ill, and the nun did not wish to see her die. I told the Lord the same thing the nun had told me, though it was not my intention to say anything on this occasion because I never wish to speak or ask while I am praying. Finally, I explained to the Lord, repeating the words she had spoken, that she, who was His creature, had implored me to ask after that sick one. The voices responded by saying, *Who helped Him when He was on the cross? His Father abandoned Him in the moment of His Passion.* He asked, *What matters most to the sick woman? If He wanted to free her from impediments and make her a saint, why not say, "Thy will be done?"* A while later, I saw an old priest coming toward me. I cannot recall ever having seen him before in my life, but as he came toward me he said, "I am Joseph Niño. I was the sexton of this monastery for a while." I asked what he wanted and he responded, "The Lord of heaven and earth sent me to you." Because I hesitated, he said, "I ask that you commend my spirit in the name of the Lord of heaven and earth." I said to the Lord that if Niño came from Him, I would do what I could for him. He was wearing a surplice and said that when he was sexton, certain things occurred while he was in the church, and that he went to purgatory mainly because he was a hypocrite when he was there.

On Friday I went to the confessionals to hide from the nuns. There was a cross inside the confessional, and when I saw it I said, "Jesus be with me, I do not wish to be here in order to see so-and-so in heaven. I have to go." I turned my thoughts toward heaven, and there in the distance I saw a very large Christ with great streams of blood pouring from His wounds. The voices told me, *That sea never runs dry. When* (12r) *a drop falls onto the heart of a sinner, he has the wind to his back until he safely reaches his Lord.* I covered my ears, but it did not matter because they are not the ears that hear such things.

This morning I was cleaning out the drainage ditch of the infirmary from beginning to end, and from time to time I got spattered and soiled. The nuns there were saying to me, "You get so dirty, and yet you keep doing it. Why do you do this?" I said, "Why do you stick your nose in somebody else's business? If I dirty myself, I am the worse for it," and many other things. They just wear me out, so I leave them. In the afternoon, I went to the choir and the voices began saying to me, [deteriorated (det)] Did I realize the solace I would find in the end because of these things done for God?, mentioning what had occurred that morning. *At that time,* the voice said, *You did such dangerous and extremely diffi-cult tasks, all for God. It will be seen then how good it is for us, and how grateful He is. He rewards everything, whatever it may be. Let us say, that if a king or any man gave him a present of one million, he would always be thankful to this man, and each year he would grant him a favor and* [det] . . . *he would owe him whatever he asked for. This is how God treats his servants.*

Another evening, I went to the choir. I was so tired I could not help but fall asleep. I said to my Lord, "I am going to go now because I cannot go on." It must have been divine providence, because I chanced on a very sick woman who called me and asked me to light a candle and the charcoal and do a few other things and to summon a nun to help cure her, which is something the sister usually did. The nun responded to me very disagreeably, saying she was too tired, that the sick woman was too much trouble, and that she had already fulfilled her duties. I returned to the sick woman saying I had already called the sister. She took so long in coming that the sick woman asked me to summon her again, but once again the nun told me she did not wish to go. I told the sick woman that she was not going to come and that she should order me to do what I could. For better or worse, I would take care of her needs as best I could. When it was very late, and the night nearly over, the sister said, "I have been unable to sleep all night out of guilt because I did not help the sick woman." I went to the choir, and I don't know who it was who started speaking about how she was enjoying Christ's glory and how He left it for us and He came and suffered terribly throughout His life to redeem us and set a good example. For all that, we never failed to for-get His kindness, and that He raised and redeemed us with such great effort. In this way she referred to the favors He had done and continues to do. Afterward, the voices told me to say, "I thank you, my Lord, because you made me a Christian. I thank you a thousand times over for bringing me to your house, one hundred million times for the blessed sacraments you sent for our benefit, one

hundred million times because you wanted us to receive them today." In this way
they referred to the many favors and how we should give thanks for them. They
told me how often for each of them and how much evil they have saved me from,
how much I deserved to be in hell, and how I should give thanks to God for this.

(12v) Another time, after I had taken communion the voices told me to
commend the spirit of a black woman to God. She had been in the convent and
had been taken out to be cured because she was gravely ill but died a few days
later. This had happened more than thirty years ago, and I had forgotten about
her as if she had never existed. I was frightened and thought to myself, "So long
in purgatory?" The voices responded, *For the things she did.* Here, the voices led
me to understand that she had illicitly loved a nun and the entire convent knew
about it, but that my father, Saint Francis, and my mother, Saint Clare, had
gotten down on their knees and prayed to our Lady to secure the salvation of that
soul from her Son. That is because she had served His house in good faith. Later,
almost in front of me, I saw a crown of large thorns being lowered from heaven,
suspended by a ribbon. I could not tell how many there were, maybe sixty or so.
Within two days, I saw the morena again in that same corner, somewhat distant,
like the first time I had seen her there. Then the voices told me that she did her
penance in the old dormitory, and I now saw her in her human form, wearing a
green skirt and a head scarf. The morena explained that she was there because of
the tremendous mercy God had shown her and that our father, Saint Francis, and
our mother, Saint Clare, had gotten down on their knees on her behalf. I asked
her, not because I wanted to, but because they made me. Within myself, I asked,
"How, and why so much time in purgatory?" She told me that God loves His
wives[21] so much that when He sees them fail to carry out their duties, He feels it
deeply, just as husbands do when their wives are unfaithful. God, who raised and
redeemed us, is so beneficent. So much happened there that is incomprehensible.

When we are fatigued, overworked, and exhausted, they say that my Lord
Jesus Christ left paradise to struggle for our redemption and the solace we shall
experience in the end. One day, he was saying this, he who speaks, and I do not
know who he is. He was hovering over me for a moment. Then he said, *Blessed
Incarnation of the Son of God, or purest Virgin Mary, Mother of God, virgin before
the birth, virgin during the birth, and virgin after the birth, daughter of God the
Father, Mother of God the Son, and wife of the Holy Spirit.*[22] Later, he began to
recount his favors, how we should give thanks to Him, how we should prepare
ourselves to receive the sacrament, the purity and humility with which the
Virgin carried Him within her, and imitating her, speaking to her within
ourselves and giving Him thanks for so many gifts and other teachings. God only
knows what happens there.

A nun's mother was dying, and she asked the members of this community,
and her friends in particular, to commend her mother's spirit to God. She also
asked them to find a confessor who could teach and help her. They asked me to
do it. Later, another temptation came. Two nuns came, and each asked after a
family member of theirs, who in the past month had experienced a misfortune
and was now indisposed. I then felt great pity to see doña so-and-so in such a bad
state because her mother, sister, and black female slave (13r) had died. So I went

to God with all these things in mind, and the voices responded, *What would become of us if we suffered no affliction? He suffered from the moment He came into this world and lived in exieto throughout His life, until He died on the cross with such terrible struggle, agony, and pain.* Then they described the lashes, thorns, and all the rest that had occurred during His life. *He never forgot even the poorest of the poor, and it had cost Him all that. We were written in His wounds and that is so very forgotten. He sends us a test, and then another, and we still do not wish to understand that this is how He sends messages.* Then He described the benefits and referred to the sacraments He established for our redemption—baptism, confirmation, all these—and that He had remained in the Most Holy Sacrament. We forget all this. Who can say what happened here? Then the voices asked me to tell the woman who was dying that she should remember when she had so many things to do that she neglected and abandoned her daughter. Because she wholeheartedly wanted God's forgiveness for this offense, she should confess it.

On Palm Sunday, while preparing for communion, I said to the Lord that I would like to be the stool His Majesty stood upon in order to mount the mule that carried Him into Jerusalem. Later that same day, he responded, *You should receive Him in a humble, obliging, and thankful manner: that is how Saint Teresa of Jesús did it* . . . [det] . . . many fruitful things, but because I am so busy I cannot remember them all.

Later, I was in the choir in a state of recollection, and asked God to give me the grace to receive Him, I saw there in the ciborium, a large, crystalline window beyond compare. Behind it, I saw a spectacular, very white Nazarene dressed in a deep-red tunic with his hair falling to his shoulders and his arms open like the Savior. I began to call out to God that I could only believe in Him, and only for Him did I come to worship. I do not want to have visions or have the voices speak to me. After this happened I said to the Lord, "What do I need these visions for? What use are the visions to me?" The voices said that for those who love one another, the more they communicate, the more their love grows. By seeing what He did and how He suffered for us, we can be grateful and thankful and understand that sins are punished. I do not know how to explain what happened there. These are only bits and pieces. At that time, I heard about the curse of the fig tree. Just as He cursed the tree, He cursed rebellious, stubborn sinners. In spite of all the warnings sinners receive and the benefits He gives them, He continues to wait for them, year after year. The sinners say, "God is great and merciful," and they do not wish to mend their ways. When He realizes that the sinners do not wish to change their behavior, He curses them. Who can say what happens here? He also said that *just as souls are united with their bodies, so too are they united with the earth. Could I not see the agonies and travail experienced by those who were about to die? When bodies are uprooted from the earth, they suffer the same torment as when the soul is wrested from the body.* They told me many, many things and explained them very well. It is just that I do not know how to say it so well. The book also came out. This was what I wanted to know . . . in the book. . . . The book had to teach me what they were teaching me there.

Another day, just as I placed myself before God, they began speaking to me, which always happens. I said, "Jesus be with me, who is speaking to me?" They said, hurriedly, *Your guardian angel speaks to you. It was given to you from the moment you were born* (13v) *to watch over you. They also gave you another angel who is evil. The good one helps on the right side, the bad one on the left. The good one liberates you from evil; the bad one gets you into trouble.* [crossed out: the mother of one of the nuns was dying and they sent someone to ask] *Have you forgotten when he got you out of that mess?* He said one thing to me, but even if I had spent a year digging around I could not have remembered. When I turned away from something else, which I knew to be true, he mentioned three things, and some others in this way and that one ugly angel would have made me fall: entirely true. So many things passed by in a rush. I said to myself, "Are these lies coming from that one,[23] or is it my head?" They said, *Who could boast about himself? No matter how hard you try and break your head, you could not express concisely what they have told you here.* After this happened, they told me to look at that Lord who had suffered so much for us then. I said, "I believe in God the Father." [det] And then he made me see Him there, with His hands tied, in terrible anguish, sweating. They said I should consider what that Lord must have felt, to have taken on all the sins of the world. I said that mine were sufficient to put Him in that condition. I began to feel such terrible anguish [det] I should be confident that whoever wished to please and love Him and laid themselves at His feet had no reason to fear the devil's illusions. A few days before this happened, when I felt this same fear, the voices told me that if I had two people in front of me and loved one and hated the other, if I spoke with the person I loved, would I pay any attention to the one I hated even if he constantly mocked me? As such, I should go directly to God. Although this enemy would try again and again, I should not pay him any mind. I said to myself that I did not have anyone to help me determine if he were good or bad. They replied that God is the true teacher. What can the priest or books teach me that would do me as much good as what they teach me there? Whoever it is, it does me good.

On Holy Wednesday, I awakened before dawn at three with such a terrible fright that the bed and I both shook uncontrollably. God was very merciful toward me so that my screams did not knock down that room. I had begun feeling the same fear the day before because of a black woman from the convent who had died without receiving confession. Because she was sick they had taken her to a farm to see whether she might recover in a different climate, but as I said, she died. She told me that at that time of night she had so much to do because when she was a cook and baker she was made to work very hard, and the señora abbess could have corrected that problem. Later, I went to the choir during the hour when everyone went to the kitchen. When I prostrated myself I saw a crucified Christ. From the wound on His side a stream of the purest blood poured out, which then merged with the blood from the wounds on His feet. A thicker, more powerful stream was created from them. When some arrived, the blood fell on them, and when they left, others appeared. The voices explained that *This was a sea that would never run dry and it would last until the end of the world. Consider this: If everyone in the world took water from the sea would it run dry? In the same way, this sea would never run dry.* Who can say what happened there? I was in a state of shock, crossing myself again and again.

(14r) On Thursday of Holy Week, I had spent the entire night in front of the holy altar without being able to do anything but sleep. At dawn, I said to the Lord, "Hello. I have been lazy all night long." The voices said that I would see what I could do and a weak nature needs to rest. The entire night before I had prepared the food for this day in the convent. The voices said, *Why does that cooking matter to you? What matters is that you should look toward God. What matters is whether He looks or does not look at us. Look at what you accomplished during the night.* Then the celestial being repeated, *If I had a friend and I saw him working* [det] *and in danger of dying and then he recovered, I could leave him, but if he did not and I left, the friend would have reason to complain for the rest of his life.* I have forgotten much of what happened because a long time has passed and I am not going to write it down. I am not being conscientious.

On the second day of Easter, while pondering the wounds of my Lord, I told Him to take away these illusions. I asked the Father, and the voices told me that I should confide in Him and to ponder the glory of His resurrection and that all that He as God had done to enter paradise. What was it for? He did not need it, save to teach others what they should do to enjoy His Father's paradise. What would become of us if He had not suffered? Something came over me, and it felt like my heart would burst in my body. They taught me so many beneficial things, and I said to myself, "Would the enemy say such good things to me?" Then I turned back to God and said, "How can I believe it is you speaking to me, Lord? My God, I am nothing, of no use, do not allow me to have illusions from the devil. I come directly to you with the desire to please and love you. I have no other father, god, or teacher." Here he told me—after other things I do not recall—*Have you heard it said, when people affirm something, "By the Royal Crown"? So He says, "By His wounds."* I do not know how to recount what happened there. In the afternoon I left the kitchen for a short time. When I returned, I chanced on a companion who was angry that another cook, whom they assigned to work for a month, ate too much. I simply said to her, "One pot of food at midday and another in the evening." Still, she remained angry. Each time I see her do it I have to stop her. In the evening, I went to the choir and just as I prostrated myself before the Lord, the voices said, "Why had I said that about so-and-so, mentioning her by name. Would I want them to say that about me?" I said to myself, "The nuns were saying it," but the voices said, *Let them say it, but you confirm it by repeating it. This came from the devil because it was gossip. You know that you must speak to her in a kind manner and use words that do not anger her.* (14v) *If she does not correct her behavior, do not torture yourself, leave it to me. For my part, when I was in the world they said many things to me, and I remained silent.* I was frightened. These are just bits.

On the third day of Easter a mulata entered the kitchen. She was upset because each time her owner's mother came she mistreated and chastised her, lying to her daughter about her. On the contrary, she felt she did all she could to please them. During the siesta, I went to the choir and said to my Lord God, "Are you not God, the Father of mercy? Why do you not alleviate the suffering of this poor, disconsolate woman?" The voices said to me, *I am pleased when some suffer from what others do to them.* With this response, I desisted. A little while later, I said, "Lord, was I not careless there? Without being aware of this or having it pass through my thoughts, you brought it to my attention." By your order, that priest came and he never has time for me. *Do not belabor yourself, for I am also a priest, and Father of mercy, and as you say, a good teacher*, He replied. Among the many teachings [det] one should have confidence in Him. God told me, Could I not see how He had gotten me out of trouble when that priest took that desk? Others have suffered a lot. I do not know how to explain what happened there, although they explained it to me clearly. I said to myself, "If you are God why do you pay attention to this piece of trash, to this washrag that stays dirty, the more you clean it?" He said, *You are?* I repeated the same. They said, W*hen I was in Jerusalem during the time of my Passion, all the questions they asked made no sense.* He began by saying what He had done for us, and the sacraments He had ordered for our redemption. The Jews had killed Him there. He related the rest, how they had denied Him, but now, although men no longer deny Him, they still whip, crown, and crucify Him with their sins. I do not know how to explain what He referred to: the gifts He created for mankind, even the irrational animals He nurtured for the good of mankind. I was shrinking into myself and thinking, "Who am I that they tell me such things?" They tell me that because of my devotion toward our Lady and because of what I have always requested of her, they always received me. My desire to learn to read and understand the mysteries of His life and Passion is what they teach me now. Even if I read many books, I would learn nothing of what they teach me here. I walk about full of fear. I do not want these to be the falsehoods of the devil. These days, it seems that God is always talking to me about so many things, so correct, so orderly, so well stated and yet the desires and fears still remain. I do not understand; God alone knows. My only wish is to please, love, and serve Him. The members of the religious community say to me, "Why are you so thin?" The members of the community do not know the anguish and agony that lie in my heart. Commend me to God, for I very much need it. On the evening of Friday of Holy Week, I accompanied our saint [Clare] to Monserrate and began to speak nonsense, saying that she seemed more beautiful and lovelier than the sun (15r), moon, and the stars. The voices hurriedly said, *If you could only see what she really looks like.* Later, when I entered a state of recollection, that worker for the church who died more than a year ago appeared. He asked me to commend him to God, but I was very afraid of what he might bring with him, especially if they were tricks of the big-footed one.

In the morning, I went to the choir, and there, the worker asked again for the same favor. During the siesta, I saw him there, coming out of the depths, dressed in the same way and asking the same thing, for the love of God. I said to God that if this came from His Majesty I would offer everything I did all these days, including the first communion of the day for that soul.

On Easter, I told my angel to go to God the Father and give Him my joyous best wishes for the resurrection of my Lord Jesus Christ, His Son. The angel said Christ was not rising from the dead then, but that God wants us to remember what happened each and every year. I wondered to myself, "Does this angel deliver the messages I send?" The angel told me that the messages he delivers are most certainly the ones I give him, just as it is certain that Christ rose from the dead. If I could hold in my memory what occurred there, I would never finish. I do not tell everything, just bits and pieces, and it is all upside down. If I am working there they speak to me; if I go from here to there, they speak to me and teach me what I should think or how to mortify myself. If I become a little bit distracted, oh the reprehension, the instruction. One night while serving dinner in the dining hall, they sent me a plate of salad, which I placed next to me. When I finished working, I could not find it. A young girl was there next to me, and because I suspected she had taken it, I said so. At that instant, the voices reprimanded me, *Why had I said that in malice? Even though it was a small affront, that girl had been hurt. Would I not be hurt if they said that to me, or if María de Pineda had been the one who hid the plate in the place they indicated?* The Wednesday after Easter, I was in a very deep state, not paying much attention because I was thinking about what happened in that empty space where the altar used to be,[24] and about how many times they had cele-brated the mystery of the mass there. The voices said to me, *How many times so-and-so celebrated mass there without being worthy. God is so good that He lowered His hands for that priest, who died not long ago.* So I commended his spirit to God with all the earnestness I could muster, saying he was His priest and His minister, and the voices responded, *How easily one like him can lose his way.* I repeated, "He was God's priest and His minister." They repeated the same thing. I do not know what this is about; I take great care in commending him to God. The same day in the afternoon, I went to the main receiving room to see my mother,[25] whom I had not seen in many days although she had been coming. By God's mercy, I have left everything to her, but I have two concerns. First, I thought she would be poorly clothed, but I found her dressed, for which I gave God infinite thanks that I was now freed from this responsibility. The other is that sometimes (15v) I want her to make a general confession. I realized she had a deep desire to do so, and she did confess with a Jesuit priest, but he was in such a hurry he did a poor job. I told her I would find a priest who would do it with great care and to her satisfaction, and I named the one I was thinking about asking to take her confession that night. That night I prayed and asked God to put her in a state of mind to make a true and thor-ough confession in order to remain in His favor and asked God which priest should minister the confession. The voices responded, *The one I already mentioned would do what I wanted quite willingly.*[26] I should tell her to think about her sins at different ages, stages, and years when she had been in mortal sin. Other things happened that I do not recall. Thursday during the siesta they told me to meditate on what happened for men when Christ hung on the cross. Did He lift up His head, did [det] the thorns dig in further if He moved about, did the thorns move in any particular way, were the thorns still there if He moved? In the vision I saw Him just as He was in the painting, totally falling to pieces.[27] [See Figure 7.] The voices explained that when they were about to die,[28] they suffered terrible anguish and pain and would have wanted to do the impossible in the service of God. Any illness or sickness makes people plan to change their lives. Because God is eternal wisdom, He knew whether they would change their ways. He recognized those who would take advantage of the opportunity to change and gave them health. He made some of the others healthy as well. Though because they did not follow through with their intentions, they contracted another illness from which they died. *Do all that you can during that hour.* After this happened and other things as well, the voices told me how much in particular the insignificant and humble ones of this house please God. Florensia Bravo and Antonia de Cristo are outcasts, and no one pays any attention to them. The first is a wretched mulata and the other a blind, black woman. Afterward, I felt pensive, fearful, and skeptical. They said, *Why are you skeptical? If you hear that so-and-so is a trustworthy, honorable man, you have no reason to fear. You have faith in what men say and you place your confidence in them and not in me. Do not think I would abandon those who place their trust in me.* I forgot to mention that when I left the visitors' parlor after being with my mother, I then went into the kitchen thinking about God's mercy and how He helps me at every turn. I thanked Him because they say that, like my mother, they were given to me to help me. I should be grateful for His benevolence toward me now that my disposition has changed. In the past, I went to the visitors' parlor beautifully adorned from head to toe. It is very true that if my stockings were not a certain rose-colored shade I would not enter. Later in the choir, (16r) when they explained how my mother should confess, the voices repeated, *Was it not beneficial to enter the community dressed appropriately?* It is true. In order to show off, I used to wear fancy clothes and parade about the choir. The voices said, *You spent all your time dressing up to please yourself.* Now I wear that tight girdle[29] for the time I dressed for pleasure, and to please Him. I do not know what this is all about.

On the vespers of holy Sunday, while I was in a contemplative state the voices asked, *Do you believe I went to the Last Supper and washed the feet of my disciples? That I instituted the Most Holy Sacrament, took communion for the first time, and then gave communion to the others?* Later, I went to pray in the garden and lowered my head [det] . . . about the meaning of the sacrament. I was astonished and knew it was all true. Later the voices said, *Why do you not believe?* and I replied, "Because I am terribly afraid that beast might trick me." Christ said, *When it is His will, you should not fear, but now, you should be afraid.* Then, I saw Him there and our Lady too, although I could only see the base of her pedestal. He said, *You have nothing to fear, for I stand in his way. He always comes with faith and hope.* For a little while, He gave me His blessed counsel and asked me what faith I have when I speak with the friar. I responded, "That which the church teaches." With this He was silent. I asked Him if I could address these matters with a member of a religious order. Christ replied that He would discuss it with God, and that she could do nothing without His will. If I did not know the "Our Father" I should ask that nun, whom they had also told. The voices also said, *You always say you do not want visions, you do not want these things to happen, and our Lord should take them away.* Our Lady advised me to approach our eternal Father often, with great humility and confidence, and that I should ask for her Son's merits. I should calm down and fear only God, because He alone is powerful. The enemy does not give us a peaceful heart, such as our Lady had. Later the voices told me that each of my three prayers should go for the souls of purgatory, those in mortal sin, and for the welfare of the church.

Saturday after Easter: I do not know what this is, whether they are tricks of the enemy. God only knows. May He be with me. I do not know how to free myself from these things. During the siesta, I entered the confessionals. When I reached the arch where the church or the grille is, I felt a sudden wave of immense fear. Feeling more confident in God, though, I overcame my fear and

Figure 7. Deteriorated seventeenth-century painting "Cristo Caído,"
which influenced Ursula's visions. Photo by Ana María Vega.

carried on. When I placed myself in front of the Lord in a meditative state, it seemed to me that I felt the spirit pass by where I had just been and then move toward the grille where it tended to be. Because I knew it was a spirit, I wanted to flee from there, but it was impossible. Then that priest the community had commemorated began speaking to me. He said that no words could describe the horror of the torment he suffered there and that he was destined to experience travail for years to come. The intercession of the blessed Mary had helped save him from hell, and he now did his penance near the grille, because he had spent a lot of time there involved in useless diversions. When members of the community went to the refectory, he came to chatter, and when people came (16v) he hid in the sacristy. It seemed that the priest told me he always hid, especially during the evening vespers, and that she was a nun.[30] A minister of God should not have behaved this way because he had other, very different obligations. The voices told me I should commend his spirit to God. I see him standing there in the same place, beside the grille, in his human form and with that circumspect face, his hair gray, and his priestly mantle gathered underneath his left arm, the way he used to stand. I am only telling a small bit of what he told me. I never heard anyone say such things about this cleric, which is why I am so frightened. Has that trickster come to play tricks? I believe only in God. Mercy. I ardently commended him to God, but I feel such anguish. Such matters make me want to bury myself below the earth, dress in a hide, and not see, hear, or speak with anyone. I do not know what he wants me to do. God will take care of it.

On Low Sunday,[31] I made a great effort to pray the entire rosary, for him, the one in the kitchen. I told the Lord I would pray the crown,[32] which was not as difficult, in order to do it better. They told me to say the rosary 150 times and to lift the heart up to our Lady.

Another Tuesday, the voices told me that the Lord enjoys it more when a sinner is converted or is brought to Him than when people here on earth get jobs they really wanted. They also told me to counsel the young girl who came in the other day. I have forgotten much of what they told me, but I will tell what I can recall. They say that when an apprentice begins to work with a piece of stone, he is not as capable as a skilled craftsman. I should tell her what benefits her, and what does not. Living in a religious community is not for one's amusement. Those who have a true heart and desire should help and encourage her. The young girl was with me this morning saying that the nuns have caused her to worry because they gossiped and said she wanted to dance. I told her that the nuns had annoyed me in the same way when I took the habit and that it is necessary to suffer. If she paid attention to these matters, she would not get anything done. She should make herself pay attention and suffer everything for God. With that they will lose interest and leave her alone. Even if she did dance, she should not forget to pray, if they tell her one thing or another. I would not want that one to come with his lies, God help me. Later, they asked why I always doubt so much. If things are going well, or not and they deceive me, I should come back and try again. Why waste time worrying about such things? If I go directly to God and my intention is only to please Him, why distrust He who will not fail me? I should not fall short and I should be extremely diligent in obeying the Ten Commandments of His law, and all that the church requires. With this, I have nothing to fear. (17r) I should be very humble, spurn the egotistical ones, avoid becoming puffed up, and persist in prayer. Christ was the first to pray to His Father, and I should imitate Him. Everything goes to pieces.

On Wednesday morning, doña Antonia de Serrantes sent her slave to ask me to cook for her. I told her black female slave, "Go with God, your owner only remembers me to give orders." But then, I called her back again to do what she asked me. During the siesta I went to pray, and the voices said, *If you have left the world behind why do you complain? Was it not better to accept that without becoming angry and do it out of compassion and love of God?,* and other things of this sort.

Thursday, some days my heart races, and everything tires me out. I went before God to ask Him for His grace. There I saw a stairway extending from earth to heaven, with one path leading off to my right and another to my left. The voices explained that the stairway was the path of those who carry the cross. The right path is for those going to purgatory, and the left one for the condemned, and those who do not fear God and disobey His holy Commandments. The latter fall into this tremendous place and drop down precipitous cliffs. I saw extreme darkness there. Moreover, they said that although these two paths came together, and those in purgatory suffered the same torture as those in hell, still they have hope because it is not forever and they are consoled. Those who climb the stairway carry the cross that our Lord Jesus Christ carried first. Only those who follow Him can take this path. I do not know how to describe what happened there. On Saturday, I was preparing to take communion, and the voices told me that bodies are the monstrance of His sacrament. There in front, they showed us His great love, what He had done in His incarnation, life, death, and Passion, and the sacraments He left for us, identifying them one by one. He suffered and cared for us for such a long time. Many things of this sort happened there. Then the voices said that I should give an account of the good He has done, and they told me a number of things I should give an account of. A few days ago, they told me that those in the world paid a great deal of attention to kings and viceroys, but they were like bits of earth. He was the universal Lord of heaven and earth, and everything that has been made passed by His hand. He takes care of each and every one of us and is the judge of all. Here in my head they enumerated so many that the list seemed infinite. I do not know how to say what happened there. If I knew how to write and had the priest's approval, it would be admirable, but I forget everything. When I am working or in a state of recollection I remember things or things come to me. Everything happens so quickly that there is no time to tell it all. On one of these days, I was in the confessional, tired and being lazy. I began speaking to God and wondered whether He could hear what I said. The voices responded, *I hear everything, see everything, and I thank the poor pitiful ones for what they do for me, as it should be.* I do not know what word He said, and I do not know if it was the Trinity. (17v) It was something like when I entered a state of recollection facing the back of my Lord. As it happened, I saw His back covered with wounds and felt moved to compassion. I began feeling terribly distressed, and the voices said to me, *What can we do? It all comes from His hand*, and that I should see if I could do anything on my own. When does He not give? Three days have passed, and although I have wanted to leave this place, I cannot. I forgot to say, that in that same place, when they said that bodies are the monstrances of the Blessed Sacrament, he said that no one deserves to receive Him, not even the Blessed Virgin, who is so pure and holy. When she carried Him in her womb she always feared and greatly revered Him. She continually maintained an internal dialogue with Him, and that is what I should do. At times I quarrel with the multitude of young girls here, with all the work to do in the kitchen, and the other things they add on. I went into the narrow passageway of the kitchen and said to God, "I am the one worth nothing, what else can I offer?" They responded, *What I do for Him,* and it pays to look Him over from head to toe to see what He has done for me. Because I do not truly see Him, I shall never finish mending my ways.

Monday, 27 April, the nun in charge of provisions awakened at dawn feeling very ill, and for this reason, she could not go. The little time I do have to see my Lord is during the siesta. With all this happening, I hurriedly asked Him for His blessing, although I know very well I did not deserve it. I deserve to go to hell. Out of the blue, I can see more deeply, and they showed me a place deep down filled with fire and flames with many people there. They led me to understand just how much more I deserved to be there than they did. They did not speak to me in the usual manner. They also forced me to look within myself more closely and recognize some of them, but I resisted more than I thought I could. God give me spirit. Oh, how much I need it. I was on my way to the choir from the small clois- ter when I was seized by a terrible fear. The clergyman who died the other day seemed to be standing in the doorway to the confessional. I was afraid to walk by there until others going to the choir had passed by. Only then was I able to. I was wondering whether the trickster had come to hinder me, because that cleric had no business being there. The voices told me, as though it were he, *Are not the revolving door [torno], where I said such foolish things, or the grille, where I also said trivial things, or the benches where I sat, keeping watch, all there?* God only knows what this is all about. Tuesday, there was so much distress. Some came, asking me to run errands, others, to cook this or that for them; and then, the request from the convent, which, in itself is enough to stay busy all the time. I am always eager to go where the Lord is, and these things take away the little time I do have. It was a day of excessive work, but as it happened, after I served the food in the refectory, and without eating myself, I found a little time to prostrate myself before the Lord. While going there (18r) I asked the Lord, "Did you cause this to happen? If I knew it were not your will, I would not do more than what they order me to. So I come here to pros- trate myself before you." The voices said, *In the thirty-three years I spent in this world, I endured a tremendous amount of work and oppression. When I left this world they placed me on a piece of wood, as though I were a vile slave and thief.* These words alle- viated the distress and tiredness I felt, and I returned feeling happy, thanks be to God, because on some days I just want a chance to catch my breath. On Wednesday, I had to deal with the same cooking situation and oppression. I went to the Lord and I said that if that cleric were His, I would offer everything I did for him. I also commended that nun with whom I had quarreled. They told me that when I was in her house, I freed her from many dangers, and I understood that if she did not mend her ways, she would be punished. Thursday, a nun sent some meat for me to roast for her. I refused because I knew that if I did it for her this one time, she would always want me to do it. Afterward I felt remorse and sent her a little porringer of broth. The feast day of Felipe and Santiago:[33] ever since last night, I wanted to prepare to take communion and meditate on what it was I was about to do, but I could not think of anything else. After taking communion, the same thing happened. After eating, I went to the choir and chanced on a clarion[34] and drum brought by the one who helps with the Holy Sacrament. I commended her to God. The voices told me that one celebrates and enjoys God within the heart. The other was vanity and I should say so to doña so-and-so (whom they named). Later the same day, he asked, *Why had I not roasted that meat the nun requested? Was that not about being nice to your neighbor? Do you not say, 'Oh Lord, bring crosses, place heavy crosses on these shoulders, and then when it starts to get heavy, I take them off. He did not turn away from hard work. What did it mean to love, if not to endure hardship for Him?* There were a lot of cinders burning when they had finished eating, and I noticed that so-and-so was hanging around there. I told the cooks to put the fire out, but they did not do it quickly enough, so I took water and put it out myself. The voices asked me, *Were my intentions good? Would I like it if someone did that to me when I wanted to cook?* The devil made me do it. It is true that I did it in a complaining manner, which I did not realize until they pointed it out during the reprimands they made that day. I don't know how to explain this, except in these bits. On one of these past days, a compañera burned her foot while taking a boiling pot off the fire. She fell to the ground complaining a lot about the pain. I felt very sorry for her and took a little bit of water, then placed it on her in the name of the Father, the Son, and the Holy Spirit, and she stopped complaining. She is now working regularly, although she has a dark spot where the skin burned. Still, it did not blister. He and the others tell me today that with all those other people around, I did not pay attention to His gifts and that is why I did not give thanks. Now sir, am I to think she was healed because of me? So, when I awakened they began by saying I should think about the terrible pains the Blessed Virgin suffered when she saw her saintly Son hanging on those three hooks on the cross and how He suffered from that incomparable torment.

Sunday, at dawn, the voices told me to take communion for the sake of those in mortal sin, those at sea, the poor in hospitals–because this is His love–and for those in the throes of death. (18v) During the siesta, I went to the confessionals. I do not know whether this is temptation, I do not take it seriously. I placed myself there but was tired and kept nodding off. When they began speaking to me, I woke up. A while later, while in a state of recollection, I did not wish to pay attention to what they were telling me. They were very persistent, however, and it turns out, it was that cleric I mentioned before. The voices said I should commend his spirit to God. They told me about those nuns to whom he owed an apology, and why he does. I said to myself, "How did I get myself involved in this?" The cleric said, "Do it for the love of God." I said, "No, how can I say that?" He said, "Go to Licenciate Refolio, who can write it in his own hand, and then in secret you can place it on the wall of the choir.[35] No one would see you do it, and there they would read it." "Why can I not see who speaks to me?" "If you saw me you would die." I am feeling extremely anxious about all this. I already said that if it came from Him and that priest needed help, I would make an offering on his behalf, if it would do any good, and, when I took communion I would offer the first communion for him. On the other hand [det], I deeply desire to love God. On one of these days, I said to my angel, "What can I do to please God?" He told me to be very humble and please others as much as possible, and observe true poverty, cast everything aside, and always communicate with God internally. It is all in pieces. Monday, in the morning, the voices tell me to enumerate all the bad things He has saved me from. They all appeared in front of me. I recognize that they are all true and know that when they address this matter, it comes directly from God. When these visions come with other types of visions, they can, as they say, be illusions. I always feel fatigued. During the siesta, I went to the confessionals and saw a dog there gnawing a bone so persistently that blood came out of its mouth. I stood watching, fascinated, and the voices told me that sinners must work until they bleed to rid themselves of their sins. Then they talked about the poor souls who die before they are converted. This is a little of what happened there. In the afternoon, I passed by the door where I saw many nuns. There had been such a ruckus that the vicar general had come. I was commending so-and-so to God. They hurriedly told me that some people had arrived. *I, the Father, allowed that to happen because I do not want turmoil in my house. I wanted to discipline them and provide an example for the others.* In this way, He gave such a long and accurate litany, I realized everything He said was reasonable. I felt admiration and made this gesture to God. After this happened, I said to myself that I had a great desire to love God. They told me to ask the Holy Spirit, who is the true teacher.

(19r) On the Day of the Innocents, 28 December 1659, while in a state of recollection in front of the Lord, I saw a great, luminous light. Within this light, I saw a glass window clearer than any crystal and within it, my father fray Pedro Urraca, filled with this same light.[36] This vision lasted more than one-quarter of an hour. I said to myself, "Why does my father, José Garsia Serrano,[37] not have this same light, but a dimmer one, like moonlight?" The voices explained that one had worked harder than the other. Before seeing this light, and on other occasions when I entered a state of recollection, I saw Christ, our crucified Lord with two people at His side. I could not distinguish faces or bodies, but I could clearly see that they were there. Within myself, I thought it was the Holy Trinity. This crucified Lord told me, *Whoever adores me also adores my Father and the Holy Spirit.* He said this when I was feeling confused and fearful. [det] I do not want to see anything, only follow the will of God. Since I saw this light, I cannot erase it from my mind. Always, well, almost always, when I recollect I am in the presence of this great Lord, who performs these great acts of mercy toward this poor little woman who is worth nothing.

One day while in a state of recollection I saw a large cavity, there, in the center of the earth, and within, many enemies awaiting the souls who fell. They tore them to pieces and caused a terrible commotion,[38] just as a dog does when it tears apart a piece of meat or tears up an old rag and drags it about. This tormented me greatly, and I said to the Lord, "Why did I see this, when I did not want to see anything? I only want to succeed in loving and serving you." The voices tell me that after all, I had relinquished my will, my faculties, and my senses to the Lord. He governed me, so He should be served. The enemies who tormented and tore these souls to pieces called out their vices and the sins for which they were being tormented. God knows all. May His Divine Majesty take me by the hand and liberate me from evil.

During this month of March, a black woman was about to die.[39] I went to see her and made her perform an act of contrition. She did so in earnest while shedding many tears and beating herself repeatedly on the chest. I felt consoled seeing her commend her spirit to God. Then, I saw a holy Christ and this morena, wrapped in a shroud, was at His feet. This meant her death was certain and that she would be saved by God's mercy. I gave Him many thanks. I do not know whether it is my head, God only knows. I ask Him to take me by the hand. One nun, now dead, who was so contrite at the hour of her death and so confident in God, continually appears before me in the form of a newborn girl, leading me to understand that she is a soul of the Lord.

(19v) On 15 May 1650, the fourth Sunday after Easter, after I had taken

communion, I wished to lie at the feet of this blessed Lord. Such was the pres-
sure I bore to be with the crucified Lord that no matter how much I tried to carry
on with what I had to do, it was impossible. This often happens. Sometimes I
cannot help but be swept away because I can no longer help it. Later they said,
*Was it not true that He had suffered in order to release us from the devil's captivity, to
which we were condemned for our sins? Because of His great compassion for us, He
descended from heaven, left paradise, and took on human form, which is how He
suffered.* They recounted from the moment He was conceived, to His time on the
cross, and [det] all He endured for us. *He is greatly pleased when we take stock of
this; we should thank Him for that and see how to proceed quickly and diligently
toward our redemption. How lazy, how slothful we are. At the very least, we might
proceed in this way and offer to Him what He offered to us.* They used a parable to
explain it better to me. *If a man continually offered his king one million, what fame
would he have in the palace, how would he be received, what, what else would he
want of the king? What could he not gain from the king? It is the same with those who
take stock of what He did for us each day. It gave Him great pleasure, and was
extremely useful for us.* What happened there, I cannot say. After this, I saw a
lord[40] dressed in a bright red tunic, seated on a chair as beautiful as the sun. Saint
Michael was off to one side with his scale, weighing and turning the weight over
in a narrow, very deep, dark pit. They said, *What would it feel like if he heard,
"This one does not obey the Ten Commandments, and this other one does," or "This
one had this obligation but did not carry it out, and this one did"?* They repeated
many things in this manner. Those who had not complied felt complete chaos in
that pit. I asked, "What can we do to liberate ourselves from that?" They said,
*They can be saved by a miracle, by crying, by taking time to take stock of our sins, by
asking forgiveness at the feet of our Lord, and by not leaving penance until the hour
of our death, which is extremely dangerous. As soon as we feel an inkling of any vice,
we should resist. If we give it power and allow it to root, it then becomes extremely
difficult to pull out. Then the devil can take over the soul.* There is no way to explain
these things, and how they happen. It is all in bits and pieces and upside down.
Because we do not deny ourselves trivial pleasures, we go from day to day saying,
"Tomorrow," "Tomorrow." Thus, the years go by and death comes. What would
we feel if we saw ourselves enter there forever? Because of His compassion for
us, He suffered to free us, and without any exceptions, as terrible as they might
be. We are so defective and fail Him so much. Commend me to God.

I am so fearful when I place myself before God because of the answers I get.
I do not know what I prayed or what to do. It is because (20r) I see so much hardship and fear that what is happening elsewhere with these earthquakes will happen here. While asking God to free us, the voices responded, among the many
things I cannot remember, *that sinners feared and did not let opportunities to sin slip
by. The sinners were so attracted to them—like wolves to meat—that they forgot all He
did for us, by leaving paradise, becoming human, and enduring so much hardship for
us. Some men do not recall any of this throughout the year, not because they do not
know about it, but because they are so wrapped up in their earthly concerns they do
not remember what really matters. They do not strive to remedy this either. All religious orders plead with God to free us. They named the patron saints, Francis and*

Dominic and others, and the priests, nuns, and their patrons who ask God on their behalf. When God raises His hand, He can exonerate or destroy the four parts of the world.

On the feast day of Saints Philip and James,[41] after I had taken communion, they told me to make my heart into a monstrance[42] for this great Lord. I should worship and communicate with Him there just as the Virgin Mary did when she carried Him in her womb. I just hope that great beast is not coming around with his tricks. I said, "I do not come for anyone to say anything to me, only to adore and praise God, who came to save us, and worship the holy host." The voices asked me why I so feared the religious instruction He gives me. *God is loyal and available for those who seek Him with a true heart.* I said, "Because of that trickster," and they answered, *Because he knows how to seduce and bring vainglory.* They said, *Who are you? You cannot do such things. If any of that were mine, I would take a little ash and place it where there is a breeze to see if anything remained. I am just like that ash. Pay no heed to those bodies, only to the souls that will endure.* These days they tell me to commend fray Gregorio to God and gain some indulgences on his behalf. Things are better with him now. I should commend the spirit of Miguel Rodríguez as well and gain indulgences for the Passion of my Lord Jesus Christ. They showed me what he accomplished in this church and then made it so I could see him as he had been while living, wearing his priestly garments. I asked God whether it was real and said I would do what they asked. For many days [the members of the religious community?] have been talking about who the next abbess will be, as if I cared about that. For this reason, I answer, "Leave me be; whomever God chooses." Even if it were the least important person in the house, I would obey her willingly. The voices told me—*so and so—and she has the blessing of the Father, Son, and Holy Ghost.* These things come to me, when I can least recall them, those tricks of that hoofed creature.

(20v) I pay no attention and just let these things pass by; if I did not, they would be endless. Because there are so many and they happen every day, it is impossible to list them all. I write only a smidgen of what happens there. God be with me and give me His light. I need to be commended to God. Please do so, your grace.

On Sunday I saw a cross, so tall that it reached the sky and at the top, an absolutely perfect Christ. He looked down from there at the four parts of the world. Astonished, I said the creed and asked God to free me from that swindler. Then the voices talked about the Passion of our Lord Jesus Christ, who had suffered terrible torment in this world on that cross to redeem us. On this same subject they said—I do not know how to explain it correctly, and because I was unsure whether it came from God—*God sees everything and can do everything. He is almighty and incomprehensible.*

On the day of the Holy Cross,[43] I saw a cross, enameled from top to bottom with droplets of blood. They were the size of a thick pinhead, very close together and coagulated. The voices asked me, *Why is the cross respected so much?* I said, "Because my Lord Jesus Christ died on it." The voices responded, as though Christ Himself were speaking, *Try and comprehend that Jesus Christ suffered the most incomparable pain on that cross.* When I look at my hands, I often wonder what my Lord must have felt when they drove those nails through His hands.

They tell me that no matter how much I try to understand this, I can never fully comprehend the least bit of what happened there. I am so moved by His pain that it reached my heart. I do not know how to explain how much He emphasized it. I watched what happened there and focused intently on those droplets of blood on the cross. He said it was the enamel of all souls. Just as here crosses are adorned with pearls, diamonds, and rubies, there they are adorned with His blood. It is so powerful that even if one sinner committed all the sins of the world, one tiny droplet of that blood would be enough to save him and the entire world. If the most abominable, worthless sinner took sticks and made a cross, and then took great pains to adore it, wishing to please and feeling remorse for having offended Him, asking Him for forgiveness in the name of that (21r) cross, Christ would go immediately to see His Father and say, "That poor soul remembered what happened. Forgive him," and he would then be forgiven. He then said He had endured terrible hardship and incomparable pain for humanity and it had done no good. He had always enjoyed what belonged to Him. I explain this as I under-stand it, not the way they told me there. The voices also said that sin had never stained the purity of the immaculate Virgin, who was totally pure. With this and all the rest, a lot happened and in great order. I explain it as I recall it and in a choppy manner. God knows if it is His. It all torments me.

The following Tuesday, when I placed myself in front of the Lord, a young girl appeared who had died some years ago. She asked me to commend her to God. I do not know if this is some trick coming from the father of lies. I was so frightened I was unable to do anything. Later in the afternoon, I fervently commended to God someone who seems somewhat distracted. The voices asked me, *Why did I water the streets of Jerusalem, if not so that sinners could come to me to redeem their blunders and sins? They get so carried away by temptation, and yet, I gave them memory, understanding, and will for them to better themselves and do what is good for them. They do not wish to change.* I thought about when they watered the streets of Jerusalem and Christ said that when He carried the cross on His back, blood dripped in His eyes and ears and on His head. The thorns pierced Him deeply, and blood poured from around His knees and those other parts of His body. Is this not what the watering of the streets is really about? I forget so much. Later, when alone, many things come back to me. I let them pass by like things in the air. God, give me your light and free me from that hoofed trickster.

Thursday, on Saint John's Day,[44] as I prepared to take communion before the Latin door, I thought about those nuns who have decided to alter their habits.[45] I commended them to God, so that He would keep them in a state of grace until they reached glory.[46] The voices said, *Pray to God that it will turn out for the best. Saints Francis and Clare were always extremely humble. They saw them-selves as the least important people in the world. All the people they saw, whether common or great, seemed better than they.* The voices talked about the nuns' responsibilities and the need for patience and silence. They showed me a skull and said, *We should always keep that skull in mind.* They mentioned the cords they now make with buttons at the waist and explained that whoever wears or makes them would be punished.[47] After this, they came to me with something illusory. Because of God's great mercy, I disregard such things. I thought, "Who tells me these things?" They seemed to say within me, *Jesus Christ, our Lord*. I said, "Jesus Christ?" *No, your angel, look*. "Your grace, I have already asked God to free me from these things. Why would I want them?" (21v) I forgot to mention that when they were talking about the nuns' obligations, they said they should always try to imitate our Lord Jesus Christ. He could easily have tied the hands of those who were going to take Him prisoner, but because He was God almighty, He refused to in order to set an example for us.

The following Saturday, I was up to my ears with cooking and other things, desiring only to be in the mountains where there are no people. I turned to God and said that were it not for Him, I would not do this. The voices responded that the Son of God was quite well off in paradise, but still He came and suffered for our sake. The apostles felt very content in Christ's company, but He had to go to heaven so they could work, preach, and call together those around them.

When I began praying to God on Sunday, I felt the presence of a dead soul next to me. This one had died nearly a year ago, and he asked me to commend his spirit, although I could not see him. Later, during the siesta, I saw a horrible hole filled with insects and enemies. I have seen this place before, and the first time I saw it, they explained that it was a cavity in hell. The voices told me that were it not for God's mercy, we would be there because of our sins—and to free us. Then, I saw a crucified Christ, and they explained that because of God's mercy, He suffered what He suffered to free us from that place.

A dying nun was very distressed because she could not resign herself to God's will. She felt great anxiety and desperation and asked us to commend her spirit to God. I felt great pity toward her and commended her spirit to God. They told me that because God loves us so much He gives each of us what we need. In time He would give her relief, but for now this ordeal would do her good. Suffering helps to purify the spirit. It all comes in bits and pieces. I cannot explain what happened there. I go to our Lord and ask Him to give me patience, teach me how to suffer for others, and grant me peace of mind so that I do not criticize another in my heart. I am such a bad black woman. Sometimes I feel—I do not know what—toward my companion,[48] with all her scolding I do not know how to get along with her. If I ask her, bad, if I do not ask her, worse. Nothing seems to suit her. Sometimes she says, "Why don't you take your bag[49] and go beg for alms for the infirm?" Other times, "Why don't you heal them?," and other things of this nature that make me laugh. God only knows how. They tell me to suffer all that happens without complaint or criticism, not letting anyone know how I really feel, as though I were a stone. Do I not see it? What happens when they step on the side of a brick that does not move and then on those bricks that are loosely placed?

(22r) One day they told me that whoever does not imitate the virtues of our Lord Jesus Christ—humility, meekness, patience, obedience, and poverty—could not be His child or disciple.

One day, while in a state of recollection, I see within myself a Christ figure tied to a column and in a pitiful state. He told me that our sins kept Him bound to that column and crown of thorns and on that cross. What He suffered and what we caused Him to suffer would save us. He tried to inspire us. He awaited us, giving us many opportunities. We needed to commend ourselves to Him and ask His forgiveness. When we were defiant and refused to mend our ways, He also bound us.[50] The Jews acted out of ignorance, but because we know better, we offend Him. It is impossible to explain what happened there, it is all in pieces, only a segment.

Throughout this nine-week period before Christmas, I have been in such a state that even Jesus could not say. I was in the crèche, looking at that child and thinking about that mystery. I complained to the Lord and said, "What is this about, Lord? I spend all my time sleeping and being lazy." They said it was my lot and to see whether I could do something on my own. I started to say, "Virgin and Mother of God," because they told me to say it like that, just as here we say "king." There the greatest honor one can bestow upon our Lady is to call her "Virgin and Mother of God." After that, I saw a representation of what had happened during the Most Holy Sacrament, as real and authentic as in heaven. Because of His love for us, He remained in the host and was transubstantiated. This is all in bits and pieces. For us, He spent nine months in the Virgin's womb, and here a great number of benefits occurred. I said, "Virgin and Mother of God, Virgin before giving birth, during the birth, and after giving birth." The voices explained, *This is the Catholic faith, which the Jews deny.*" I cannot recall it all; it is impossible to say what happened there. It all happens in a disorderly manner, upside down. They also mentioned that God's breath formed the Son and Holy Spirit. I said, "Jesus be with me, I do not want breath or faith, only to be taught the Catholic faith. I want to leave here, now." He said, *This is untrue,* and repeated each part of the creed.

On the day of the Innocents,[51] while commending myself to God, the voices told me to thank Him for the love He showed when He came down from heaven to earth, became a man in the Virgin's womb, and suffered such travail for our redemption. One by one, they repeated each. Neither the exile, garden, whippings, nor thorns remained, but the cross did and He remained in the host. They talked about the preparation needed (22v) to receive the knowledge of God and the gratitude we should have for such a great gift. After receiving Him, we should throw ourselves at His feet, thank Him, tell Him our needs, and ask for a remedy and mercy. They led me to understand that for those who do not prepare properly, it is better not to receive communion. I do not know how to explain what happened there.

The following day, they told me to give thanks for the benefits we receive from the Incarnation and for all He suffered for us, recounting each step, until His death on the cross, in case I were to do the stations of the cross. In the afternoon, I thought about my crucified Lord, commended this house to Him, and asked Him to have mercy on me and all the nuns. There, deep within myself, the voices said, *The Lord is just, and He carried a staff of justice.* I saw a staff, somewhat smaller than what the *alcaldes* [town magistrates] carry, standing up by itself. I felt very frightened and asked, "Is God not merciful?" They said, *Yes, merciful and just with that staff.* I write what I remember because I understand only a fraction of what happened there. They asked, *Have I not seen those born with the ability to speak who then lose that ability? Others lose their health to various illnesses; others, their eyes; others, their feet or arms? Others who are rich become poor? Others lose their fathers and mothers; others experience things that seem horrible? He does this out of mercy and justice. Because He is merciful, He does not mete out the justice they deserve; He does not want to foster arrogance. He presents these trials for them to realize their folly and mend their ways. His mercy and justice serve this purpose.* There was a lot about this, but it is impossible to explain because they are just bits, all upside down.

This happened around election time.[52] A great disturbance occurred Thursday when some nuns lost respect for the señora abbess. While facing God I said, "Why did you let drop from your hand those who wished to please you?" The voices said, *They do not wish to please me. Even if they want to, it is not done with genuine affection. They are full of their own designs. I never refused or turned away from the cross.* The abbess[53] ordered us to come inside, but I said I did not want to. Christ said, *Those souls who refuse to humiliate themselves fall to hell, and there enemies tempt and encourage them to do what they did last night. How do you think I feel about this? When a woman is married, she does nothing at home except what her lord wishes. When they seized me and slapped my face, I could easily have fooled them and sent them to hell. I tolerated them pushing me to set an example for humanity. On the cross I prayed for those who* (23r) *put me there and blasphemed me. I endured tremendous hardship all my life for your redemption and to set an example. What did I do in the desert? I asked my Father to assist and teach you to follow His will. That is why so much time has passed with so little progress, only pride and will-fulness. When someone humiliates himself, prostrating himself at everyone's feet, and he does it with a genuine heart and resignation, he improves and makes progress. When someone places herself in front of me, and I later reveal myself to her, it is because she needs it. If I did not reveal myself, she would not return. If she perseveres for a long time and I do not reveal myself, that is what is best for her. I give each person what is best for him or her. All must bear their own cross.* He also said that He wanted she who now governs to bear her own cross. All this comes back in fragments, lacking any order, and as I recall it.

One day while I was praying, the voices told me to think about the compassion He had when He extended His arms to be nailed to the cross. With His arms spread, He was like an eagle. Just as the eagle had its wings extended, so He would extend His, and would extend them, inviting and watching over us, until the end of the world. He wants us to be grateful for His gifts, and He counted them one by one. He left paradise and came to suffer such great travail to free us from hell and take us to paradise. He always thanked His Father. At the end of His life, He again thanked God because His ordeal was over. We forget about His help and fail to thank Him. We do so little for Him, and it is very insufficient. He is very grateful to the eternal Father, and we should offer to Him what Christ suffered for us. Because of His suffering, we should ask for His favor and the redemption of our ills and vices. One day he said, *If we do what God did, if we exercise care and are thankful that He suffered for us, we too shall inherit the kingdom of heaven.* It is impossible to describe what happened there, what it is. The voices continually preach love and fear of God and that we should perform many genuine acts of contrition in order not to lose Him. They said a lot about this, but mainly to commend this house to God because of the election. They told me that God was very offended when He saw those extremely burdened nuns, and the rebellious ones.

On the vespers of Saints Fabian and Sebastian[54] I was in a state of recollection and do not know whether it was the big-footed creature, but they told me that so-

and-so, a cleric, had condemned himself to hell because he had persisted in his sin.[55] I will not tell anybody who he is. I said, "I do not know who makes me speak; I do not want any more of this. Is God not merciful?" They answered, *Merciful and just. That cleric never wished to stop sinning. Each day he said mass and took God in His hands. That is why he was condemned.* I said, "The blood of my Lord Jesus Christ spilled for Him." They explained that the same blood that saves those who wish to benefit from it also condemns those who continue sinning. I asked, "Why did they tell me that, why do I want to know, what for?" They replied that when I see something like this, (23v) I should commend him to God to help remove him from that evil state. Later in the afternoon, just in case it was the devil's trick, I prayed the stations of the cross for the cleric. They said, *There is no need to, nothing will help him.* Many other things happened that are incomprehensible.

On All Saints' Day,[56] and just in case it was the enemy's invention, I offered my communion for the cleric. If it could not help him, I designated someone else. The voices explained that it was not the devil's ruse, but most certainly true. He was condemned, nothing could be done for him, and it would do him no good. Fourteen years ago the demons accused him of rebelliousness before God. I asked whether devils can speak to God. The voices said, *They presented their accusations to God twice each day. Is it not true that when we pray we speak to God but do not see Him? That is the way it is.* Then I saw him in a vast and horrid place, dressed in mourning and saying, "Oh, wretched me. Forever in this hell. But, it is worse not being able to see God, and all else pales in comparison." Then they explained how dangerous it is to leave one's conversion until the end and that very few actually achieve contrition to save themselves. They said people should pay attention to their actions, allow time to become worthy, do penance, set themselves straight with God, and free themselves from grave danger.

Another day, I spent three-quarters of an hour praying, until I could no longer stand it. I said to our Lord that if it were at all beneficial, I would offer one half hour for the cleric. The voices told me not to tire myself out because he had already condemned himself for his sins. *He spent his nights behaving as though he were married, and his days tending to his house and job.*[57] *He had no time to work at the task of searching for God.* Many of the things they said about this are difficult to understand. If God wished, He could easily save us without any effort on our part. This was why He gave us memory, understanding, and will in order to work and see what is best. He also gives us inspiration and everything necessary to be saved. If we become lost, it is our own fault.

On Saint Ildefonso's Day,[58] after having taken communion and while in a state of recollection, I unexpectedly thought I saw Licenciate Colonia. They told me to commend him to God by the love with which Jesus Christ came from heaven to earth. I should ask for that same love, and that He have mercy on him. Colonia spoke very earnestly about the terrible hardship there, and that it seemed like he had been there for a thousand years. He suffered terribly because of Francisca, his slave whom he had continually mistreated badly, without considering what she needed. I asked him (and I do not know who makes me ask these questions, which I do unwillingly), I finally asked after that priest. He told me he was already lost and he had condemned himself for that sin they had already told me about, referring again to how he spent his days and nights. I asked him how he knew, and he said that in God, they see everything. I asked him if those who are in purgatory see God, and he said that because they were souls in His grace and were not going to return here, they know these things in God. He also said that the intercession of our Lady and Saint Rose had helped him. They had prayed a lot for him, and it also helped when he said mass in this house, because he did it with particular devotion and attention. When he said the creed, (24r) he paid particular attention, especially when he said the words *quin a tres es de maria birjine* [the Virgin Mary is of the Trinity].[59] He enjoyed saying those words tremendously, and they helped him reaffirm his faith, as did the rest of the creed. When I remembered to commend others to God, I thought of him as well. It is true that for some time I had forgotten to commend him to God, but I had remembered others. He pointed this out to me. I asked our Lord whether this was true, and from Him, and I asked God for what the priest had requested, for the love with which Christ had come from heaven to earth, and to have mercy on him and free him from his suffering. I also said I would offer my communion and all that I might do that day for him. I also asked our Lady in the name of the steps she took when she looked for her Son, when she lost Him. All this is in crumbs, face down. First, something I had completely forgotten, which was that I saw a little animal pass by once and then once again. It was like a small dog, without skin, full of the most horrible leprosy, and all shrunken up. "What a bad thing," I thought to myself. "What is that?" The voices told me, *That is what sinners look like before God.* I said, "How do you get rid of that?" They answered, *With the blood of our Lord Jesus Christ, by crying for our sins, by prostrating ourselves at His feet, and by asking Him for forgiveness.*

Saturday, on the day of Saint Pedro Nolasco, or rather vespers,[60] something happened that I had totally forgotten about, as though it had never occurred. While in a state of recollection, something appeared, God only knows what it was, maybe it was the big-footed one who loves to deceive, and it says, "I am Marucha, Juana de Escobar's sister. For the love of God I beseech you to commend me to God. Although I was raised in this house no one remembers me." This saddened me, and I thought, "Why do such things happen to me?" I asked God if this were true, and from Him and to have mercy on her. On the saint's day, I took communion on her behalf and on behalf of other dead souls and other necessities. Later in the afternoon, I went to attend the ill in the infirmary and while seated there, began to meditate. Then I thought I could see Marucha, her face resplendent. She told me her faith in God's mercy had saved her. She had been in mortal sin until she became fatally ill. Because she knew she was dying, she regained her composure and placed herself at the feet of our Lord Jesus Christ, asking Him for mercy, certain He would save her. I asked after her owner, Alfonsa. She said she was in purgatory and had suffered a lot. There in purgatory all had their place and received punishment according to their social position. Nuns were in one part, male religious in another; and lay persons, priests, Indians, blacks, and all other generations were punished according to their conditions and distinct responsibilities. By God's mercy, Marucha had not been a liar, rebel, or thief; she only had that one weakness. Would Ursula commend her to God? Ursula said, "Who am I, but such a poor woman, why do such things come to me?" She told her to give many thanks to God for that knowledge He gave her, and in spite of the nobody she was, she should always ask God to give it to her. It pleased His Divine Majesty and it had helped shorten her stay in purgatory. This is just a tiny piece of what happened there, but it causes me anguish. Sometimes I am tempted not to go, or (24v) pray, because it might come from the enemy. I tell God how well He knows my internal desire to do His will, praise and love Him, without all these other things happening. If He wants me to suffer such things, "Thy will be done," and in the name of His love.

On Friday, 4 July, infraoctave[61] of Corpus, a grand festival was held. Among the many contraptions, they had fireworks. Throughout the day, they celebrated: applauding and showing great appreciation for everything. During the last procession, they set off fireworks to close the Most Holy Sacrament. A huge piece exploded and landed on the head of a little black boy, the slave of Dr. Retes. It blew away a piece of his skull and part of his brains. I grieved so because of the loss of that boy to his owner. I turned to God, asking Him to have mercy on that poor, infirm priest. The voices responded that if they had to take away the servant for the owner's well-being, then the loss was better for him than if the servant had lived, for this would open his eyes to the world. Here we sleep. In heaven all are vigilant, looking to see what is best for each of us to be saved. We cost Him so much, and He began referring to the whippings, the crown, the thorns, and the cross and all He did from the moment He became man. He could easily give a blow to so-and-so and so-and-so, or to those who were there, but for the moment, it was best for that boy to die. I should pay attention to how the festivals in this world have lost their meaning. Among the many things that happened, these are what I remember and what My Lord Jesus Christ did. The black boy lived until ten the next night. When I found out the next morning, on Saturday, I began commending his spirit to God. The voices told me to focus on how much his devotion to the Virgin helped, though his service to her was brief. Still, she was very grateful and a good benefactress, and she favors and helps those who are devoted and commend themselves to her. I should tell all of the Lady's devotion. He was a virgin, but was beginning to move his eyes toward his damnation, thus it was suitable to cut his life short. May God be blessed forever.

Vespers of the ascension of our Lady,[62] before dawn, there in the hall where they place the sacrament, I saw an old man dressed in black on his knees. I said to myself, "What could this be?" The voices told me, *This is so-and-so.* I was appalled that he had been there so long, in fact, since the loss of that ship that fought with the Dutch.[63] I said, "Well, did he not die defending God's cause?" The voices responded, *Yes, but he was in mortal sin. Much love was shown to him by forgiving him. He was engaged in hand-to-hand combat when he fell into the sea. Commend his soul,* (25r) *take communion for him, and tell others to commend him to God.* I said, "My confessor has ordered me not to say such things." The voices said forcefully, *You must tell who it is: Do not say it, just give a little paper to one of the nuns' priests, asking him to commend him to God.* I said to God that if he were His, I would take charge of commending him. When the time came to receive communion, I said forcefully, "For so-and-so, for so-and-so." For many days afterward if I went to pray, it was for so-and-so, if I took communion, the same. I need for many to be commended to God. A long time passed without writing anything.

A day of making amends. I looked at that blessed Christ and said to myself, "God closed His eyes for me, God died for me." Hurriedly, the voices tell me, *He died as a man.* I said, "Jesus, be with me, can I not come before God without them speaking to me?" The voices said, *Is it evil to talk about the Son of God's incarnation and think about that benefit? Is it wrong–God willing, we should always be thinking about it–to think about what He suffered to save the world? Is thinking about the benefits wrong? Or thinking about death and judgment or the Virgin's purity and the protection she gives us? Thinking about His help in extricating you from this, that, and the other thing?* I know everything they said is true. I should give many thanks to God because many carry on for years, and are not given even a tiny drop of the handful they give to me, not because I deserve it, but because God wishes to bestow His love on me, just as when you give to someone passing by on the street.

Sometimes they fib. One day, the voices said, *May God be with you, as your friends here are. When a friend is loyal, they find out his secrets.*

They commended that a nun read the *calenda*.[64] She said she did not see during the day, but at night. They asked her again, but she excused herself. They told me this offended God because it set a bad example for the community. In the afternoon, I was in the choir when there was a procession. They told me to consider whether I had seen what I now saw there on another occasion. I looked again and saw some nuns speaking whom I never see there. Another time, the nun who watched over the Holy Sacrament had been there, speaking with the others. They asked, *Was it not better to be thinking than chattering? This offended God, rather than serving Him.*

I saw an extremely pale, dead man in a sepulchre. I said, "Jesus be with me, I do not wish to see God dead, He, who is in heaven." They told me that this only represented what He suffered. *He died as a man for us, and what died was the flesh He took from you humans.*[65]

Often they charge me to watch over my heart and continually turn it toward God with different feelings of love, praise, thanks, and suffering, and in this way, follow the Virgin Mary. One day they told me that this had more value and merit than vexing myself . . .

(25v) when I commended this house to God, asking Him to give the nuns peace and make them conform to His will.[66] The reply I received was that just as He must keep His word and His truth, the abbess would remain. They led me to understand that everything would calm down. She remained as *presidenta*.[67]

While I commended the spirit of a dead morena—among other things that I do not recall now—they responded that we do not take our duties seriously here. Jews obey their law better than Christians do theirs.

One day they spoke to me deep inside myself. As God sees Himself with souls, so I saw, deep inside, our Lord Jesus Christ and a soul prostrate at His feet. He said, *Those who followed and those who say they will follow His will, should thank Him for what they received, consider how to receive Him tomorrow, and try not to offend Him. They were within Him, and He within them.* A multitude of things of this sort occurred that I do not remember.

One day a señora nun[68] came to the infirmary. She sat on a bed and began talking about acclaim and how people were praising the hair-brained[69] ones or saints. She spoke in such a way that I knew some of what she said was directed toward me. I kept my face lowered and carried on with the work I was doing. I am bad. It does not seem right that people of God should entertain themselves with insignificant things. As for the criticism she hurled at me: Am I so different from what they think? If they put mountains of gold in front of me, or all the treasure in the world, I would not pay the least attention because of God's great love. I do not even look at what is beneath my feet. I go directly to God and tell Him that I have worse things, and here I am judging someone else. Take away everything within me that displeases your divine eyes. Do not let go of my hand. Give me the grace to overlook my neighbors' faults and focus on my own. I commended this nun to God. The voices responded, *This is the way the world is. On the one hand, they say, thy will be done, and on the other, they complain. When Christ used to preach, they would say, "What does that imposter, liar, and conniver want here with us?" and other ignominies.* I would rather the nuns beat me than do me favors when I chance upon them. I would rather the earth swallow me than have them see or speak to me. Even if the queen were to call me, I would not go; it would mean less to me than piles of rubbish. I, the worst of all. If I wanted acclaim, I know how to position myself, how to gain it, and get what I want, but God's love for me meant that I left all that behind for Him. Now, everything in the world (26r) tortures me. All this is in bits and pieces, face down. When I sit down, somewhere, I remember some things, but then I forget again.

On the day of these saints, I went into a confessional after taking communion. I had been there awhile when a friar entered the church. The voices said, *Get up, little one, and go to the chapel because mass is going to be said there. Go, it will not be said here.* I said, "Leave me alone. I am here with God who gave me the will to commend certain individuals to Him." I asked God to give certain people His blessing to help remove them from sin. He spilled His blood for them. The voices tell me many things, and because I do not know how to explain them, they will all go to bits. They said, *We think we can do whatever we want and so get carried away by our appetites and our choices. We say that God is good, merciful, and He spilled His blood, but they offend Him, unhampered and without restraint. His mercy and His blood are for those who fear Him and for those sinners who wish to stop sinning, are diligent in their efforts, and avoid temptation. For them, God bestows His mercy upon them. He has done so much and endured so much hardship for our redemption. We know He loves us, we know the faith He had when He left His glory and came to suffer such horrible travail to do what was good for us. It was not necessary for Him to do this. Even though it is important, we do not persevere. Each day we become more inattentive, lazier, and more distracted, such that if we get lost, we can only blame ourselves.* A great deal was said about this. At the end, the voice said, *When you relate this, do not tell it all. His mercy is for those who prepare to receive communion, knowing what they will receive, and then, prepare again for tomorrow. Those who receive Him are His monstrance and caretaker. The blessed host is placed on the tongue, which afterward should remain silent, unless it is to please, praise, or thank Him.*

Your grace[70] already knows what happened in the infirmary and about the grumblings of so-and-so and others. In the name of God's great love, I willingly tolerate them. I lose my temper at times, but do not show it. I shall give a brief account of this. Fearful the evil one might come along with his pranks, I asked God not to let the devil come with his tricks, to free me from them and give me His light. The voices replied that *I should look within and see how I tolerate my neighbor. If you are deceived it is your own fault. When your neighbors cause something to happen, I should tolerate it patiently and not say a word that might incite them. I should do this from my heart, and if later, I feel pride or some vice, I should talk with my spiritual father, my confessor, and apprise God of what happened there.*

On the vespers of San Martín,[71] I do not know whether these illusions came from my head or from that father of lies. I lay prostrate before the Lord, and after a short while, the voices told me to commend the spirit of Bernarda to God. I asked whether she needed it. They responded, *Yes.* I said, "A women so devoutly religious, so simple?" The voices said, *She would be simple if she were alive or dead, but because she became caught up in transitory things, she was vain. Without dying in this life, there is still much work in the next, but those who mortify themselves have an easy journey.* I cannot explain what happened there.

(26v) On the day of San Diego,[72] as soon as I placed myself before God, the voices said to me, *Why did I not take communion?* I replied, "Because I took it yesterday." He said, *Today is the saint's day of the religious order.* Then, a friar appeared in front of me. I said to God, "What is being placed in front of me?" They say it was fray Gregorio, but I do not know whether it is he or the big-footed monster made to look like him. The friar said that for the love of our Lord Jesus Christ, I should commend him to God. He repeated this two or three times. Last week he appeared with the same request and explained that he had also been saved because of the great reverence and fear with which he held God in his hands and because he saw himself as totally unworthy to receive Him. He was trembling when he left the sacristy to say mass.

I ask God to teach me and give me patience. They responded that Job was a friend of God because he followed God's will in everything he did. In good times and bad, he said, "Thy will be done."

I commended Felisiana to God and asked Him to give her patience to deal with such misfortune and pain. They told me that *God had such love for her, because her suffering was for her good. He did not make people suffer more than they could bear. Because of their travail and pain they remembered Him, calling out to Him by saying, "My God, please do not forsake me." In our travail we invoke His passion, His death, and other things, asking for forgiveness for offending Him. Our nature is such that were it not for this path, we would not remember what is beneficial for us. When we want to make sure that something is secure, we either tie it down or put it in irons. He does the same with His infinite love. This love brought Him from heaven to earth to suffer such great hardship for our redemption, but we pay no attention to what really matters. This is why He makes them sick and puts them in those beds, so they can learn what is beneficial and attain self-knowledge.* Such a lesson occurred then, along with everything else. It is impossible to perceive so much; it is in little pieces. One other thing: when they fall into bed, they only care about pampering themselves, maintaining good health, and indulging their vices with no fear of God. They should fear Him though, in order not to lose Him. When they get better, as I have said, they become lost because of their behavior, as far as I have seen. I cannot say to God there should not be as many lies. I already asked God to free me from all that is not His and all that I do not understand, but then, another lie. Those who fear God, obey His blessed commandments, worship Him, thank Him, and recognize what He suffered for us, dwell in front of the holy Trinity.

On 19 November, just as I prostrated myself before the Lord, the voices snatched me away. Then I remembered doña Joana de Ynojosa, and though I cannot see her, she speaks. Someone I do not know comes, pretending to be her, but I recognize her voice. She asked for the love of God to commend her spirit to His Divine Majesty and to tell her mother, Catalina Ximenes, to have four masses said for her: one to Saint John the Baptist, another to Saint John the Evangelist, another to Saint Joseph, and another to our Lady of the Incarnation. I said I should not become involved in this because my confessor had ordered me not to. (27r) They told me, "Do it for the Virgin of Carmen, for doña Joana is in great need." I asked her if those masses would get her out of purgatory. She said they would not, but they would help her a lot. I asked her if people from this house were there, and she said, "Many." She had already been there for six whole years and was now in her seventh. She paid for every little thing: neglecting her religious obligations, as if it meant nothing to chatter and laugh in the choir; being careless about paying respects and other formalities; wearing a habit that did conform to the rule; breaking the silence that had been ordered; and after visiting hours were over, getting up and wandering from one place to another, speaking, gossiping, and breaking the silence with vain laughter and showing excessive love toward the young ones. She said so much my head cannot contain it all. No effort, no words, can describe what happens when the soul is wrested from the body. Despite the terrible torment, those in purgatory would never wish to return here, even as lords of the land— because of the danger of losing God. This is all there is to fear. Doña Joana said how important it is for the devout to have saints, and how lonely those souls who go there without their support are. She made a comparison: if a man here gave a king one million, he would then get everything he asked for. That is how the saints get what they ask for from God. Three times she requested masses in the name of the Virgin of Carmen. She would commend me to God and ask Him for the patience I continually sought. I am dazed by what happened there. She also said that the eternal Father granted what they asked Him, with faith in His Son's incarnation, and in the love with which the Virgin Mary gave Him to us for our redemption from her very womb. His love also allows adverse things to happen for our own benefit, and for this, we owe Him continual thanks. The Virgin Mary's requests to God are always granted because of the great pleasure she felt when the Word became flesh in her womb. All this goes from top to bottom in bits.

On the day of Saint Catherine the Martyr,[73] after I had received our Lord, I prostrated myself and spent a long time without saying "Jesus." Then, they finally said to me, *We are crosses for someone else.* María Flores tries my patience, and Marisa Angeles does the same to Felisiana. Fairly often, even from her bed, she starts saying "Fo fo," and all around there is so much spit it is horrifying. In my head I told her that with all the cleaning I have, she should be more tolerant of others. We all have others who tolerate us. She was upset by this and asked why I had said that to her. I was speechless and wondered whether I had let something slip from my mouth. Earlier, to reconcile myself, I had gone over in my mind whether I had spoken in an angry tone. So, I took communion, and they told me if it happened again, to do nothing except yield to God's will. If I did this or that to myself, I would feel hurt. It does not benefit me. Consider the saints' lives. They adapted totally to divine will. I should say, "Thy will be done," to everything because this prayer pleased Him greatly.

The following Saturday, I thought I saw a large hall filled with people, all in great order and representing different eras. At the end of the hall (27v) I saw father so-and-so, dressed in his cassock with his hands folded in prayer. Far below, in a deep place, I saw a lot of big flames, and although the priest was higher up, the flames reached him. The voices said that *he had been a good priest, very chaste and devoted, particularly toward our Lady, who spoke on his behalf to receive a favorable judgment when he died. When he said mass at the altar of our Lady of the Rock, he did so with particular devotion, and he feared God.*[74] I then said, "Poor me, and with all that, he is in such a state?" The voices responded, *To enjoy God for all eternity it is necessary to become purified. When he was ill, this priest had time to dispose of his worldly possessions. They had given him the opportunity, but because he thought he would not die, he did nothing.* I looked again at those flames, and they explained that it was a pit in hell and most of the souls who went to purgatory were first trapped in those pits. He asked me to commend him to God and for them to say a mass to our Lady on his behalf. I said, "If this comes from God I shall take communion on his behalf tomorrow."

On the first Sunday of Advent, immediately after taking communion I went to the infirmary. I deeply desired to remain there for a while to help cure that girl who was in such a bad state, even though someone else had taken charge of her. I decided to stay and keep her company and began to meditate. The voices told me my decision had pleased God because I had denied my own will and I should give many thanks to God because He had helped me understand that I had done what was best.

The following Monday: the sick girl is so ill that it is necessary to clean her frequently. My hands do this, but because the flesh is weak it is important to offer my task to God. Before sunrise, the voices told me that *I should bear in mind God's benevolence and love for the world when He brought His Son from heaven to earth. I should thank Him for giving Christ and for the love with which He now tolerates and waits for us. He did this for all of us, without exception.* Because I doubted this part, he repeated it again: *for everyone.*

On Saint Andrés' Day[75] the señora abbess performed the ritual ablution ceremony when they wash the feet, and I was not sure whether I should kiss her hand. I did not understand what I should do. The voices told me to be dutiful and disregard what people said. After communion, I recollected for a little while. They tell me so many fables; I do not understand what they are. I think I see a huge river. The longer I looked at it, the bigger it seemed. It was so clear that the stones were visible. On the shoreline, I saw innumerable monkeys with very long tails, hands with long nails, and faces like lions, jumping about in an exaggerated manner. A crucified Christ was on one side of river. I made the sign of the cross and said *Gloria Patri*. If the river seemed big, the oven next to it discharging horrible flames was even bigger. The voices said that there they punished those apathetic in their service toward God. From the ice they went into the oven, which seemed to provide relief, and from the oven into the river. They said that *God's love liberated us from this and that His beneficence wakes up sinners, punishing them and making them confess, so they begin to leave their vices behind. This love brought Him from heaven to earth (28r), where He suffered so much travail and torment, but then He remained in the Most Holy Sacrament in the altar. His love calls and inspires us, and His mercy moves Him to do this. What need does He have of us? Were it not for His love, what need does He have of anything we might offer? He appreciates it when we take time to ponder His wounds and what He has done for us. Just as the Virgin received Him, He enters those who receive the Most Holy Sacrament. His benevolence does all this. Had I not seen when they showed me how the sinners were bathed in His blood?* That happened a long time ago, though, when I saw a Christ figure with five rivulets of blood pouring from His wounds and falling into a wine press.[76] Many people surrounded Him, and two angels stood at His right side. From time to time the angels took some of those nearby and pushed them close to His wounds so they could drink. They reminded me of this, not in any particular order, but in bits and pieces. *When they baptized them, they also bathed them in the blood of our Lord Jesus Christ. We should give Him many thanks for so many benefits, and we should count them one by one to the eternal Father who gave us His only begotten Son. When they told the Virgin that the Holy Spirit had entered her, she received it with great humility and gratitude and was always appreciative, showing great care and devotion for the one she carried within her. Within herself, she always worshipped her Son. This is how we should imitate this lady when we receive His mercy.* This was an important lesson. *When we are given opportunities to sin, we should be mindful not to offend God. Who does this, if not His mercy? When we plead with God–Lord get me out of this or that, do not abandon me, do not let me offend you—who does this but God's mercy? When we say, "God, forgive my sins, make me more humble, make me more virtuous," who does this but His mercy?* I forgot to say that the two people I saw in hell were not in the river or the oven, but in that place where I have seen them on other occasions. The one woman was seated as if she were on a little stool—I could not see what else was there—and she was held up high in the middle of horrible flames that totally enveloped her. Even though she was there, I could clearly distinguish her features and how she was dressed. She wore a greenish skirt and an elaborately decorated white blouse and her flesh showed. She sat with one foot over the opposite knee, her right hand on her cheek, and had such a sorrowful semblance. She cursed herself, saying, "Bad," and "My sins," and "Why did I lose such an infinite good for so little?" This is how she lamented. Sometimes I want to leave all this behind because these things only confuse me. I ask God to take them away because when I go to praise Him these disquieting things start happening. When I go about my duties, they tell me what is happening here and here. What do I want this for? They told me something else regarding God's mercy. *I should consider all the things God has saved me from and compare that life* then with the one I lead now. Was it not a great act of mercy, because I deserve to be in hell, much more than many of those already there? Many are there for just one sin. I have already said that I deserve new hells, and although I am not who I should be, I recognize that He has saved me from much depravity. May He be blessed (28v) forever and may He grant me the grace so I will know how to give thanks and serve Him in everything and praise Him throughout all the centuries of centuries. Amen.

The second Sunday of Advent, after I had received communion they exhorted me to love God deeply. I asked, "How should I love Him?" The voices said, *By obeying His Commandments and all the obligations of the Order. Love Him with love, and fear, and filial love, not out of fear of punishment or the desire to be rewarded. When you comply with these obligations God is very grateful and gives great rewards. When you do not, He will punish you.* This is a small bit.

Later, in the afternoon, I saw some nuns who were all very troubled because of all this business of the election. I turned to God and said that He should have mercy on this house and give them His peace. The voices said, *Many would be at peace if they would follow my will. Even if they turned the world upside down, the abbess would remain in her place. I am responsible for everything, even the ants. They would not have what they needed if I did not provide them with it.*

On the third Sunday of Advent, after receiving communion I commended so-and-so, who is dead, to God. My head begins creating fantasies—that when the dead woman had gone to pray she stood in the middle of the crowd coming and going from the choir. She stood there watching and listening to what happened. Here, if someone wishes to speak with a respectable person about important matters, they go elsewhere to be alone. To be with Him, it was the same. During the Divine Office, the dead woman did not pay attention, but spoke and interrupted the priest. All must account for themselves according to their capacities, the donado like a donado, the black like a black, and whether they have upheld the Ten Commandments. The religious are judged more harshly because they have greater obligations. Along these same lines, one day the voices told me that *for the simple or ignorant there were sermons, spiritual counsel, and books.* They gave me to understand that *if they did not wish to mend their ways they would pay a price. He loves us deeply, but we forget about Him and His gifts and what He suffered for us, so He sends illness so we will attain self-knowledge, and call out to Him. Do I not see them when they are worn out and how they cry out, "My God, my God"? He sends illness so that we ask Him for mercy and forgiveness for our sins.*

When I found myself before God, I asked Him to enlighten her for what she wanted to do in His service. The voices responded disapprovingly, *What for? Her intention was caught up with her desire to have a name in Spain and recover her reputation there, because she used to have a good name. Who knows whether things will go the way she wants? How many have gone and not returned? What a good cross to bear, losing the responsibilities she once had of taking care of her family. To leave this is the same as a prelate, who in the name of God's service abandons the subjects he was obligated to govern to do other things.* This sister asked me if it were true, that it would be necessary to bring along other Christians?[77] I said that I thought so, but why did she ask? Ursula says a lot of this happened there, and I do not know how to explain or make sense of it.[78] Ursula also said that whoever wishes to perform similar activities in God's service should not cover themselves in silver, but only dress in His grace.

(29r) Our Lord is deeply offended by the forgetfulness we show toward His Divine Majesty. We walk about in His presence unconsciously and take little care with the things of His service, particularly our lack of preparedness and consideration toward what we receive, before and after taking communion. This is the cause of our total destruction and why the worst sins are committed. He wants us to show deep appreciation for His kindness and particularly for His Passion. This should not be combined with other cares. We should know that just as we remember God, He remembers us. When we place our efforts in the temporal world, we take away from the eternal one. We should fear this great God because we do not know whether He has dropped the whip from His hands. May His Divine Majesty give us His love. This is our obligation.

I was feeling quite ill and some nuns came to see me. They told me they were trying to make a sanctuary and were going to take me there.[79] I told them I was dying and was worth nothing. After they left I drew the curtain around my bed and began speaking with God, saying, "Here within my heart, you, Lord, are my sanctuary." Then a crucified Christ appeared before me and said that one [det] was enough for some, but these were only a few. He gave an example. *Have you not seen when they carry a pannier full of stones? When they turn it over, the entire pannier is emptied. That is how the chosen ones are. They should be very thankful that everything comes from God's hand. Nothing is ours. We cannot even say "Jesus" without His help. Many others still have a great deal of work to do. Have I not seen that some who go down the street turn to look behind them? Let them go to the sanctuary if they think that by doing so the crucified Christ will then appear to them.* I cannot explain what happened to me there. Then, an army of Jesuits appeared. Saint Francis Xavier was the one who first approached me. I have a special devotion to him. Saint Francis said, *Ursula, when you die, I, and all of those you see today, will come for you.* Many came wearing ornate dalmatics[80] with numerous tassels, some with blood falling from their heads and others bleeding from many parts. I realized these wounds were how they had been martyred. I do not know what this is. All this happens without thinking about it; I do not know where these things come from. Later, I experienced some internal darkness and so much affliction that I could not even say, "Jesus." From time to time they say, *Your head does not deceive you. Do not say it is all in your head.*

A few days later, before sunrise while in a state of recollection and preparing to receive communion, I noticed many Franciscans taking communion. They passed in front of me, their heads covered with what looked like pots filled with lovely flowers. Some did not carry flowers. I said, "How . . . ?" The voices responded, *They had not received communion in the same way as the others.* I said, "Poor me, how will I receive communion?" They said, *Go now, receive communion reverently and lovingly.* On Saturday, the Franciscans carried out their election. One of the friars had died suddenly that very night.[81] I commended his spirit to God, and then the dead friar appeared, kneeling, with his hands positioned like someone asking for mercy. Each time I commend him to God he appears like this. This went on for four days. The following Sunday, I received communion for him, and the voices explained that *If he had voted, he would have condemned himself, because these elections engendered ill will, the worm that eats the soul* (29v) *until they fall to hell. However, he was very devoted to the most holy Trinity, which loved him enough to free him from this danger by taking away his life.*

On the vespers of the election in Santa Clara, the entire house was in an uproar and the factions in strife. Because of this, at four in the morning, I commended these matters to God and asked Him for prudence and peace in this house. Unexpectedly, behind the bed, the voices said, *Ursula, tomorrow with the blessing of the most holy Trinity, Roldán will become abbess.*[82] These words left me feeling very frightened, but later, now calm and confident, I knew that what they had told me was certain.

On the vespers of the Visitation of our Lady,[83] at daybreak, I commended the spirit of Ana de San Joseph to God. She then suddenly appeared in front of me, and I asked after doña so-and-so. She pointed her finger and said, "Here below," which led me to understand that she was in some very deep cavity in purgatory. What she said was, "Words cannot explain the good God does by wrenching them from earth so they will not become lost." Ana de San Joseph looked peaceful and had a joyful semblance. She said she had benefited enormously from the great confidence she had had in God and because of her open and good intentions. Still, a few flames licked her feet. Then I asked after Antonia de Salinas, and she told me her intentions were not as good. But, because she herself had never been deceitful, God had loved her, and she had benefited greatly.

[A nun carries on writing for her.][84]

While in the infirmary helping that nun who had purchased her freedom, she felt worn out from so many things coming at once.[85] She wanted to leave everything and go, and the moment she reached the door leading to a cloister, she saw three crosses in the sky. She looked away, thinking it was an illusion, but then hesitantly looked up again and realized it was real.[86] She prostrated herself on the ground and said, "Lord, I know you want my path to be laden with crosses. Lord, do your will with me." Then she returned to what she had been doing.

Another time, while on the roof of the cell, Ursula looked at the sky for more than an hour. They were there, teaching her the "Our Father," though she did not know who they were.

She often asked the Lord what had become of those crosses. Once, while she was kneading bread, tired and only wanting to be with the Lord, other disturbing things appeared, and she felt vexed. She said to God, "I cannot carry on," and He responded, *Are these not crosses?* Later, someone she calls the little friar said, (30r) "See how many leaves fall from an olive tree? Not one falls without His divine providence."[87]

She says that at first this friar appeared after the evening meal, when she went to her cell. He remained until the hour of contemplation arrived and then said to her, "What are you doing, wasting your time? Why don't you go to the choir and commend yourself to God? You are not going to die."

On the vespers of the Incarnation, they carried an image of our Lady of

Carmen into the choir. Ursula was deeply devoted to her. They had decorated it for the procession the following day. That night Ursula stayed with the Virgin in the choir and began speaking to her. She said, "Oh Lady, as you know, this morning I received communion. With permission from our Lord and you, I will do the same this morning in spirit." This said, she prostrated herself a while and then saw a great procession of angels, all holding lights in their hands, in great harmony in their choirs. In the center, stood the Archangel Saint Michael with an elaborate monstrance in his hands. When they reached our Lady, they took a host and gave it to her. Ursula marveled at what she had just seen and said, "How is this so, Lady? I did not want this."

Another time, she saw our Lady, our father Saint Francis, and our mother Saint Clare come and stand at the Lord's side holding lit candles in their hands. Our Lady placed a scapular on our Lord. Another time, our father Saint Francis showed her the habit she would wear.[88] She saw Saint Michael the Archangel holding a beautiful towel and paten in his hands. He went to where some of the nuns had just received communion. A few of them placed the host they had just received on the paten, and he left with it.

Another time, she saw a huge, ferocious dragon's mouth and many souls there, rising and then sinking, as when a pot boils. When they went down, it was with a tremendous force, and they were enveloped in flames. They explained that that punishment was for those who received communion without proper preparation.

Another time, while all the nuns received communion, angels appeared at their side, but some had sad faces.

(30v) On 28 July, after receiving communion, she entered a state of recollection, and the voices told her, *Here comes the Prince.* They then arranged a seat and a beautiful pillow, and He sat on it with great dignity, placing His feet on the pillow. Christ asked her, *Who do you believe in?*" She answered, "In Jesus Christ, Son of the living God." He continued, *Do you believe I was born of the Blessed Virgin Mary, who remained a virgin throughout?*" She responded, "Yes." *Do you believe I suffered and died to save humankind? Do you believe that I rose to heaven triumphant and was given power over all things, including all the articles of faith?* Finally He said, *Do you believe I have a place below the earth called hell, designed to punish sinners?* "Yes," I believe," she said. *Well, if you believe that, you should know that the devil cannot cleanse anyone's sins. Nor have I allowed him to perceive what is internal. He can tempt, as he did with me in the desert. In order to deceive, he takes on my appearance and my mother's. He does nothing properly and cannot even deceive with his tricks.* In this regard, He said many things that can be found in the gospels. By his deeds you will know him. Christ also said the devil works with those whose heart is impure. Ursula said He wore a short white tunic, with rounded, embroidered sleeves. She said something else: He wore something red and white on His shoulders, similar to what the Indians wear on their heads, and His shoulder-length hair was parted in the middle. She looked carefully at how He was dressed, and He said, *Is it like your habit?* Furthermore, Christ said, *Men serve this enemy and abandon me, despite receiving so many benefits. I am forgotten.* This happened to Ursula three times in the same day, whenever she tried to pray. On this occasion and others she said, Who could help her with her vices? What if it were the devil? He counted the benefits He had given her one by one and said to her, *Did you not wish to be free? I complied and carried through for you.* A nun had told her she would be very pleased to know His will in two things that she had indicated, and Ursula received the answers. She says that, two days before, a young black woman entered her bed[89] and destroyed everything. When Ursula returned she said to herself, "It is one of your tricks. You came at a good time because on another occasion you would have caught me and I would have fought with you." (31r) Later, while she prayed, the Lord said, *You recognized the good I did for you but did not thank me.*

While praying, Christ, our crucified Lord, appeared to her. He ordered me to put a nail in her right hand, having ordered her many days before to place one on her left foot.[90] In her humility Ursula resisted, but the Lord insisted that she pass it through her right hand and watch closely and carefully, thinking about the torment and pain that nail would cause. In spite of all the terrible torment all the martyrs suffered, it did not gain them much advantage. Three times He told her she should watch and consider this. She should try pricking her hand with a pin to see what pain she would feel. Furthermore, He said that what offended Him most in this house was the improper preparation for communion and what they were about to receive. They did not recollect themselves carefully about what they had to do, either before or after. All they did was consume the gift and then leave. I have a comparison: if someone had to marry, she would think about it over and over.[91]

We are like the traveler who arrives at an inn in a hurry, asks to eat, and then leaves. As such, the traveler would not meet the innkeeper, and the innkeeper would not meet him. That is how they treat Christ's majesty. If someone received a gift, would they not wish to show gratitude by reciprocating in some way? He was the same. Moreover, He said a lot of people lived in the convent, and of the four parts, only one did its duty. In this regard, He wanted two papers posted, one on the choir door, and the other in the cloister. I misunderstood what He said about the ring. He says that when one has a ring with a valuable stone, one should examine it, recognize its value, and give it away, but not so with God.

The following day she got up at four in the morning to go to the choir. Because the doors were shut, she prostrated herself at the door of the Bethlehem chapel.[92] The voices said, *Why did you leave without asking? You found the doors shut.* Because of this, Ursula was extremely fearful about taking communion. She said to the Lord, "I would like to receive you, but I do not dare. What do you wish me to do?" After asking the Virgin to help her—because the Virgin always tells Ursula to come to her, and that she will treat her black woman favorably—she asked again, "Lord what should I do?" He said, *Go, receive communion.* After she had done this He said, *Do you think anyone* (31v) *deserves to receive my sacrament?* She replied, "No," and He repeated, *Not even my mother deserved it, but I granted it because of my kindness and mercy.* I forgot to mention that He talked about His mother being so blessed that she never had an impure thought, which was why she was the Mother of God. With this, He prepared her by telling her she would experience great travail and humiliation. When Ursula found herself in the midst of this, she should say, "For my Lord." That is how the Virgin endured them. *Remember how they brought me before the judges, all beaten up.*

Returning to her prayers, Ursula implored our Lord three times to pardon this house. He replied that *When a mother mistreats her child she says, "For nine months I carried you in my womb." She would let them kill her in defense of the child, and the child would do the same for her mother. For thirty-three years, I carried you on my shoulder, and now they do not wish to recognize me, save when they see the whip in my hands. Year after year, I watch over them, giving them many signs, but when I see they cannot mend their ways, I tell my Father, "This one is no use, cut it off," just as He did in Chile.*[93] *For quite some time now the same should have been done here.* He added, *Who would not die if they realized this?* After a while Ursula said, "Lord, what is this? Who speaks so much to me? I so wish that this did not happen to me; bring me someone who can understand." He responded, *You have nothing to fear, go, be humble. I am teaching you now; you do not need anything else. The devil cannot teach anything good.*

Another day, after one and a half hours in prayer, she felt like a piece of wood, without any sensation left in her body. When she stood up after praying, the voices said, *Does this come from your head?* She often feels bewildered by what they tell her. She responded, "Yes, I think this is from my head." Three nights ago she had stayed in the choir. After working in the refectory, the voices told her, *You have not gone to the choir for three nights, and from the cloister you did the reverence, asking for forgiveness. Would it not have been better to go inside?*

Another day, on the vespers of the Porciuncula,[94] a nun was very ill and at risk of dying. They reminded Ursula and told her to commend the sick woman's spirit to God. She said that the sick woman was a saint, and they replied that even saints were in danger of condemnation during this delicate hour.

Later, while many nuns were gathered together, the abbess entered (32r) and scolded them. Some were very annoyed, and Ursula said to herself, "What is going on with these nuns?" Our father Saint Francis responded, *If they read the book of rules, they would not behave in such a manner, or if they thought about this,* taking out a skull. Ursula was hoping to prepare to receive communion, and her father Saint Francis said to her, *Prostrate yourself at the feet of the eternal Father, make yourself into the smallest vermin of the earth, and ask Him in the name of the great merits, Passion, and blood of His only begotten Son to forgive you and place you in His grace to receive the Holy Sacrament honorably.* Ursula said that so much happens there, and they say so much, that when she tries to explain it she cannot remember, and therefore I, the scribe, only write a fraction[95] of what she tells me. This time, she asked Saint Francis, "What is this? They say that the profession of donadas has no value?" The saint replied, *There is a difference because the nuns are white and of the Spanish nation, but with respect to the soul, all is one: Whoever does more, is worth more.*

On the vespers of Santo Domingo[96] the voices told her, *Do you believe He went to the Last Supper, and there I washed the feet of my disciples and then instituted the Most Holy Sacrament? I received communion first and then gave it to my disciples.*[97] *Afterward, I went to pray in the garden.* Ursula lowered her head. She was dumbfounded, because He told her so much about sacramental matters and she knew it was all true. He said, *Why do you not believe?* She responded, "I am afraid the beast will deceive me." The Lord responded, *When you follow God's will, you have nothing to fear. Now, if I showed you an image of our Lady where you could only see her pedestal, you need not fear, because I am behind this. Always have faith and hope.* He stayed with her a while, giving her His blessed advice. He asked her what faith she had when she spoke with that friar.[98] She responded, "With the same faith the blessed church teaches us to have," and here she fell silent. The friar is the one mentioned earlier. She wondered whether it was important to bring the matter up with a Jesuit with whom she had confessed. Christ told her to deal directly with God, because without His will, she could do nothing. If she did not know the "Our Father," she should ask that nun whom they had mentioned. The voices also told her that she was always saying, 'I do not want visions, I do not want these things, our Lord should stop them.' The Virgin counseled her to go (32v) often to the eternal Father very humbly, but very confidently, to ask Him in the name of her Son's merits to calm her spirit. She should fear only God, who is almighty. The enemy could not leave a tranquil heart, such as she now had. They also told her that the three times she prayed, the first should be for the souls of purgatory, the second for those in mortal sin, and the last for the three necessities of the church.

She professed on the day of the Holy Trinity[99] and that same night saw a very beautiful angel kneeling before our Lady, the Virgin. At that moment, a beautiful and very resplendent dove placed its beak in the mouth of the Virgin and instantly she saw an infant within her. He was very lovely and resplendent and held the world in His right hand. There they spoke to her about diverse matters and, in particular, about the Last Judgment. She asked what would happen to those who would be living then. He said, *I will send them such hardship that with that and the flood, those who must be saved will be purified.*

The following day, the voices told her that just as she had offered herself to God during the mass, *I now want you to entreat my Father in the name of my minister, who is in purgatory. He is a cleric, who some years ago argued with so-and-so, another clergyman, at the main entrance to the convent. Do you not remember?* She said, "Is he in purgatory for that?" *This shocks you? Many condemned souls will remain there until the Last Judgment.* Then He added, *Look at him and ask my Father in the name of my merits.* She looked at him, and he was wretched, as though he had been exhumed for one thousand years, his hat falling off, everything faded and shrunken, in silence.

On the day of Santiago,[100] while Ursula was preparing to receive communion, the head baker entered, calling everyone to knead the dough. She said to the Lord, "What should I do?" He responded, *After you have fulfilled your obligation. Did you not promise to do this?* Instantly, she obeyed. The same thing happened another time, when they called for help to prepare the wheat. She wanted to go hear mass first. The Lord said, *Your duties come first.* When she returned after kneading the dough, I, the scribe, noticed she was not dressed for communion (33r) and said, "Why did you wish to leave it that day?" Ursula replied, "Because it was late and I was not properly prepared." I helped her resolve her problems and reconcile herself.[101] In the end, Ursula received communion, entered a state of recollection, and prostrated herself in her usual manner. After a while, the Lord said, *Today you have received me as they do in heaven and in the Most Holy Sacrament.* The voices said that when He washed His disciples' feet, He used a towel to eliminate the slightest speck of sin. He wanted those who were about to receive Him to prepare in the same way. Christ explained many things about the mystery of the mass, about His Passion, and about how easily people forget about the good He does. He constantly complains about this. He also told her that when they read the gospel she should see Him there and focus on the insults He experienced while facing the judges, and on His crucifixion, when they nailed Him to the cross, which lasted no longer than the time it takes to say [det] a prayer. When they tried to lift Him onto the cross they made Him fall three times. Consider how much pain He suffered when they tore open His wounds. What if He showed her how torn His right hand was and how the thorns pierced His head? He complained then about the forgetfulness and lack of respect we have for this. He taught the "Our Father" to the apostles so they would know how to pray and teach it to others. I have forgotten so many things; this always happens. Whoever experiences this forgets a lot.

On Saint Ann's Day,[102] she saw her leaning against a beautifully ornate canopy while the Most Holy Trinity crowned her. The Virgin was there dressed in white with a blue cape, and within her, the baby Jesus held the world in His right hand. And they told Ursula, [det], and to look at the lady Saint Ann, and Ursula asked where she should look. They responded, *In the widows' choir*, and there she saw an infinite number of angels all in great harmony, looking at that multitude. They told her to look at the choir of the martyrs, and she saw an army, with everyone dressed in white and colored ecclesiastical garments,[103] like the friars wear.

On another occasion, she saw our Lady with the moon at her feet. It was so large it seemed to cover half the world. She often sees our Lady, and usually when she is wearing a blue cape and white gown. She has spoken with her many times, but only twice has she seen her wearing the Carmelite habit.

When they brought the news about the desolation of Chile she began to lament, and among other things she asked, "Lord, how can this be?"[104] He seemed very offended and said that men paid Him no heed. *They fear the viceroy as though he were important because he can kill them,* (33v) *but do you not realize who the viceroy really is? Throw a little bit of dirt in water and then see whether they can pick up any bits. This is exactly what the viceroy is. Forgetfulness so great, a sin without restraint.* She said, "Lord, even the mountains?" And He said, *Even the mountains. Neither a king nor anyone can do what happens there. Do you not say in the creed, 'I believe in God, the Father almighty?' This is what it is all about, and yet, men do not fear me. Did I not do it for them? Have they not cost me a lot? From the moment of the creation, they have cost me a lot of work. I formed the clay with my own hands. I took great pains to shape it all and infuse the soul with one breath from my mouth. I gave everything else to humans. I only had to say it, and it was done. I am always doing good things for man, but he does not appreciate them. So much forgetfulness, and always sinning and more sinning without remorse or fear. What did I not go through for them? From the moment I was born Herod persecuted me, wanting to kill me. What I endured in Egypt, in the desert, and during the rest of my life.* Here there were many heartfelt complaints about the ingratitude. At the beginning of all this, a paper was read out in the choir that referred to what happened in Chile. All that and far more had already been explained to me. I said to the Lord, "Why at night?" God answered, *At night I exact my punishment. Did you not see when the chapel burned with my images? I wanted to destroy everything, but refrained because of the pleas of my mother, the Virgin of the Immaculate Conception, and Saints Francis and Clare. Still, because it was mandated, I exacted the punishment on my own images. Did you not see when the Virgin turned black and cried?* She said, "I did not see it—today." She also said, "Although I did not go to where the image was because I was in the choir, I still saw everything that happened there and the multitude of people who came in, but no, I did not see her image." He said, *Did you not see how, after burning the chapel, the fire did not advance any further, though the cells were very close by?*[105] *If He had carried out that punishment, who would have escaped, with everyone sleeping?* He led her to understand that if they did not mend their ways, the same would occur.

One of the following days He returned to complain about the same matters: the little attention they paid to His Divine Majesty; forgetting His gifts; and sinning without any remorse or restraint, as though no other life existed or without realizing what they do in this one. I asked, "Would they see the Last Judgment, Lord?" He said, *Those who truly died saw it. The others were terrified.* He led her to understand that only a few had been saved. In His hands He held a whip made of two leather straps as thick as two slim fingers. It hung down by His side.

(34r) In the name of His Son's merits, she insistently and tenderly implored God to forgive sinners, particularly the nuns. With great affection He responded, *I love them, but they do not love me; they follow their own will, so I let them.*

The complaints lasted a few days: the forgetfulness, the little fear men have of His Divine Majesty, the lack of appreciation for the good He does, and particularly for His life and Passion. He said that the nuns were even more decadent and forgetful. Most of the sins committed in this house occurred because of the faulty communions, received without heeding what they were about to receive, either before or afterward. As soon as they received communion and left the choir, their thoughts roamed elsewhere. There were many people in this house, and three-quarters of them were not prepared. All should receive communion; this is His will. He wanted two decrees posted, one in the choir, the other in the cloister. She who writes this took it upon herself to speak secretly with the abbess, and they ordered me, Ursula, to write up the two decrees. This occurred during the Porciuncula. The previous Sunday, after I had received our Lord, I prostrated myself at His feet, asking Him if it were His will, to please show me how to compose the two papers. There I was given words that resonated with His propositions, and different from others I had thought about. She went to ask [det] the blessed abbess, and Ursula spoke with great efficacy, asking the nuns to consider the responsibility and care with which they should prepare to receive this Holy Sacrament and the faults with which they did it. The abbess had the paper read out, saying that it came from God, who was very angry. With great affection, she told them many things along these lines. They should know that any little word often causes grumbling and a thousand opinions about who said what and where the lie came from, but in this case, no one spoke a word about this. All that happened was that after a few days, a nun who had read the paper told her she wanted to take a copy with her. Since this occurred, the nuns take communion more frequently and seem to do so with greater care. They are making general confessions and continue to do so, thanks be to God. This comes from the secretary, the scribe. Returning (34v) to our account, I, Ursula, told the Lord that they gave me the desire to go on my knees to receive Him, but feared what they would say.[106] He responded, *Nothing is yours, child,* and ordered me to leave the corner where I was and place myself in the middle of the hall where the nuns receive visitors. I resisted at first because even in the corner I die of shame. He insisted so much that I had to go. The voices said, *What I give you, I do not give to you alone. I want you to bring me sinners.* I did not know what to do. I asked Him if He wanted me to write, and He said, *Yes.* I asked if I should tell the nun who has been with me since the beginning, when these things started to occur. She had told me not to tell others because they might gossip; it was best to discuss such profound matters with someone who could truly understand. He said I should go to the one I was already working with and He named her. This sister is better read and is very afraid of these things. She said, "Does our Lord discuss these matters with vermin?"

Another day, while praising the Lord, I saw the crucified Jesus Christ within the ciborium. He looked alive and as large as life. His breasts looked like they would overflow with milk, and He said, *This is for the humble, penitent sinners.* His aspect was beautiful and white.

More than twelve years ago a young black woman died, around eight at night while I was alone in our dormitory. She had barely expired when I saw a white form. I began to feel tremendous fear, which caused me to feel a pain I usually get. I was in bed and from there commended her to God. They told me that the members of God's consistory had commanded that she should die, for if she continued to live she could not be saved. While praising God and commending myself to Saint Michael, the Archangel, they told me the Archangel was the great prince of heaven and God loved him deeply. He was Christ's standard-bearer and administrator of souls. They told me again about the Incarnation and many other things. What I remember is that as soon as the angel came and the Virgin had given her consent, the Word became flesh. At that moment the Virgin conceived and carried within her the very beautiful Son holding the world in His hands. I was unable to perceive all that occurred there. Then He spoke of the Passion, and at that moment, there below the earth, I saw a sepulchre with a sun. Within it was a very large body all covered with bruises, with drops of blood falling from the head onto (35r) a pillow. He said that while His Son was suffering, He sent many angels to collect the droplets of blood. At the head of the sepulchre stood Saint Michael, the Archangel, holding his white standard, and a crowd of people rising and falling. Then I saw our Lord resurrected, with a crown of rays of light on His head.[107] The voices asked me, *Did you not believe He had risen to heaven and been given power over all things?* Later they taught me about the Last Judgment. I said, "What worth do I have for such things?" *It is not because you or anyone deserves this. I choose whom I want. I could easily go to the powerful, to kings, like those I have in hell. Those kings who conform to my law and treat their subjects with love, rendering justice mercifully, go to my purgatory when they die, just as I now have the queen of Spain there*. I thought to myself, "What do they call her?" They said, *doña Isabel*.[108] I am unable to explain what happened that day. I was dumbfounded but commended the queen to God and received communion on her behalf.

Two days later I saw thick walls, perhaps eleven feet high, in a big chasm. Below them, very large hands held iron ladles that spewed a lot of fire. In another area were sticks, like those used in a barbecue, on top of these walls. A lady of great authority stood above this. I wanted to know who she was, and they told me she was the queen of Spain. She sat with many books in front of her and did not seem to be suffering too much punishment in purgatory.

Saturday morning they told me that little friar who had appeared had asked me to commend my godmother, Ana. It turned out that her guardian angel had prayed to my guardian angel because she was in great need, and the angels in heaven communicated with one other. It had been more than a year and a half since that little friar asked me to commend my *madrina*,[109] who suffered a lot of hardship. Still, I could not recall her. Later the thought occurred to me, "Which madrina is she?" They said, *Ana*. Until I received this message, I did not know she had died. I asked someone, and they confirmed it.

(35v) Later in the afternoon, I told the Lord I really did not want to think about any part of His Passion because I would then have visions. I did not want that one to trick me. I only wished to please and thank Him, for He knew my will very well. Within a half hour I saw the Lord within the monstrance, praying in a tomb, His body quite large and discharging blood from His head and feet. The rest of Him was covered with a holy shroud. After half an hour they told me I should look at His wounds, because I had not done so for many days. Then I saw the resurrected Lord, with a large white cross on His shoulder. He held a large white standard in His other hand. They explained that He had been resurrected in great glory. I have forgotten what He told me about limbo. After the Salve, I saw the one who wrote this among the other nuns and told her what had just happened. She explained that that soul had gone to limbo. I said, "I would have been pleased if you had said something about that because it would help me to understand the visions that occurred a lot." Sometimes, I did not understand very well when they spoke to me, or I forgot and asked them to repeat it, which they did. I left there with a sick woman experiencing great need. Because she was very ill she had not eaten. I made her eat and then returned to the choir. While in a state of recollection, I asked the Lord about that particular doubt. He said, *Have you not heard that the blessed fathers awaited His blessed arrival? He went down, left His body in the tomb, took those blessed fathers, and on the third day He rose from the dead. Do they not say He rose from the dead and for forty days remained on earth?* I did not capture this. I said, "Were not the forty days in the desert?" He explained to her that after His resurrection, He remained forty days until he went to heaven on the day of His ascension. I had forgotten that when I saw Him resurrected, the shroud remained in the tomb. I asked what had happened to it, and whether He took it to heaven. He said it remained there in the blessed house.

On Sunday, I took communion and thanked my Father for such a tremendous gift, even though I had offended Him. After a while they presented a multitude of

in the (37v) corner of the choir with my eyes closed it becomes possible for these things to come to me?" The voices replied that if I thought they were my invention I should go to my corral or any other place and see whether they occurred there. I should concentrate on the good He had done me and particularly the most recent one, when He placed me among His chosen. I should be very thankful. If I disobeyed His Ten Commandments, I would have something to fear.

I was in the choir, near the upper end because it was more concealed. From there I saw many nuns come in to perform a certain devotion. I wanted to die from shame and get up and leave, but the voices said they would force me to stay every time I tried to leave and that I should give thanks.

On the vespers of the ascension of our Lady,[114] while adoring the Most Holy Sacrament, I saw a crucified Christ dressed in white with His Father and the Holy Spirit at His side. They explained that the Father is always on the right side. The voices said, *Have you not seen how a hen gathers her chicks? The Lord Jesus Christ opens His arms to receive.* I paid a great deal of attention to this, but on the left side they were saying, *You come with such confidence, even though you are filled with sin.* Then I felt terrible anguish because I knew it was the enemy who seemed to be hindering me. While doing this, I fell asleep for an instant and then remembered to thank God for bringing me here. They told me *to give many thanks to the eternal Father because the entire inferno could not have brought me here.* These three persons were inside the ciborium. On this same occasion, they asked why I had not worn the hair shirt on Wednesday.

On the day of the ascension,[115] I felt terrible affliction three different times when I experienced great temptation and the enemy tested my resolve. With God's grace, I resisted as best I could, but then they said, *Neither good nor bad. Were they not insulting me when they spit hard on me?* After I received communion, I saw a child within my heart. Fearing it was some invention of the enemy, I went directly to the ciborium, and He said, *The enemy cannot (38r) enter souls, only bodies, and then only when I allow him to enter through the mouth. He tells many lies and plays many tricks to grab souls, but he does not have power over them. When they die, he receives the condemned ones, and in another time, but not those saved by my grace.* I said, "What can I do Lord, to be one of these? He said, *Obey the Ten Commandments, all that the holy church ordains, and your four vows.* Later, during the siesta, I entered a state of recollection and began considering how different I am now and thanked God for that. When I asked after a nun, He said, *Those who persecuted me were later converted and were saved.* Some days ago, they told me to wear the hair shirt on Mondays, Wednesdays, and Fridays. Saturdays were voluntary. I said I had not worn it on the Virgin's day because I had been ill. He answered, *Why did you not wear it Wednesday, the vespers of the ascension?*

On the feast day of San Jacinto,[116] some nuns claimed that all they did was pray, pray, pray. I left what I was doing and said, "Blessed be God, there is another way." They said, *That is nothing. The external eyes see nothing. While not in a state of recollection could I truly understand anything? God is found within, and sins, obligations, and the good He does are recognized. Nothing could be understood without mental prayer. When one loves another, the more they communicate, the more they love each other. When people are about to die, they wish they had spent their whole lives loving and serving me. Just look at how poorly they wasted their time and even now they do not wish to put things in order. I had no need of prayers or temptation. It was only to teach you. Temptation and fear will always exist. Give thanks to the eternal Father for His generosity.* I thanked him because He brought that departed nun whom I had commended. He told me that He always loves those who wish to withdraw from the world. *Yesterday, you thanked me because you recognized that the serenity you experienced in your heart was something I had provided. How different from when you were caught up in your diversions. If you did not enter a state of recollection and mental prayer, who could teach you that such prayer teaches us everything? Without it, what man has within is very hollow. The use of the bodily senses only serves as an impediment to necessary tasks. True prayer is when the heart is absorbed in God and in thanking him. After fulfilling your obligations, spend your extra time doing this, because this is what* (38v) *pleases me most. With prayer and the intercession of the Virgin one can achieve grace.* He spent a long time speaking about this. I cannot perceive what happens there, nor can I remember it. Everything I say is only a fraction of all the great teaching. He also said that those dying in agony and pain should look within themselves, for it would benefit them.

Still San Jacinto's Day, while going to pray, I told the Lord I wanted to contemplate hell while at His feet. He told me to think of all the sins I had committed, for many were there for only one sin. They showed me a dark place where two bodies were lying on their backs, surrounded by four devils holding tubes more than a foot long that were throwing off blue sulfur fire. When they tried escaping, the fire sprayed them, while the devils said, "Forever, forever." Just as they take fish from the sea, a thousand vermin appeared and began gnawing on those unfortunate ones. Then devils appeared with some iron meat hooks, pulling out their eyes, and then putting them back in place. I said, "I believe in the Most Holy Sacrament." The voices said, *Who do you think they are? In their lifetime, they did not shed a single tear for their sins. Those eyes that should have paid attention to God's mercy never mended their ways. I cut the thread of their lives. My mercy is for those sinners who fall, but then pick themselves up, repent, and confess. Even if they fall again because of their weakness, they rise anew. Give many thanks to the eternal Father who liberated them from such a place, for they greatly deserved it.*

The following day, while I lay prostrate before the Lord, the voices asked, *"So you know before whom you lie?* "Yes, before Jesus Christ, Son of the living God." *Do you know that at this very moment He could cast you to hell?* I replied, "Yes." I was thanking Him for His generosity toward me when some black women entered, in tears because another black woman had died. I said, "All this is vanity. What matters is to learn how to die." I implored Him on behalf of deceased women, and He said that Francis and Clare had gotten down on their knees for them. I felt great satisfaction that she had been saved. He said so many things that some just pass me by. He said that *just as He had created heaven for the good ones, He had also created hell for the bad ones. He would pay those who followed the one called the Prince* (39r) *of Darkness. He gave them memory, understanding, will, and what was needed to save themselves. He gave them free will, but they went their own ways, and He let them.* He also said, pointing to His feet, *This is the book from which you must learn.*

On this same day, I prayed our Lady's rosary while prostrate at her feet. The truth is, she seemed to be there with me. They explained that when the Son of God became flesh, the Holy Spirit appeared in the form of a dove, carrying a ray from the Father's bosom, and placed it in the Virgin's mouth. The conception occurred immediately, for she had already given her consent, and this sacred Lady remained a Virgin and mother. She was in a trancelike state when she gave birth, and no one on earth realized it was the glory of heaven. When she awoke from that state, she found him in front of her. I said I do not want to hear about the Incarnation; I do not want these things. Another time, they taught it to me in another way. This is how it happened in the new version, and this is the Catholic faith. *God is greatly pleased that you contemplated this mystery around one and one half years ago on Christmas Day.* Then, I saw the Virgin's womb open, and He was there, like a crystal, and emerged from there. An infinite number of angels, kings, doctors, and martyrs and the entire court of heaven were present. All adored that child, and they allowed me to kiss His tiny foot that He Himself lifted. Now they tell me the story in another way. I fear these are tricks of the enemy. I said, "My God, I do not want this. I only wish to know you and myself, and to serve you, without such things occurring. You know my intention is only to adore you. I do not know what head this is. Is it mine? These things appear when I close my eyes. This is not for me, for I am just a poor little wretch." I said I did not know what to do, because I always feared he might come with his tricks. The voices tell me, *No, the enemy does not do good things.*

Later I returned and said to my Lord, "You are my God, my Father, my Creator, my Redeemer, and my Savior. Teach me what to recollect upon and do not let me fall from your hand." The voices responded: *Think now about the sepulcrer, tomorrow about the Resurrection, and in the afternoon, as you usually do, about the coronation of the Virgin.* I am going to the upper choir to visit the Virgin and see her coronation. (39v) I stayed there until after matins, when they left. I had a terrible fright and had to pull myself free from the visions. I saw a sepulchre there below the earth and a large body covered with a shroud. It was very pitiful, particularly the head, which looked as though it had been punctured all over and was bleeding everywhere. The voices said, *Have you seen a father or mother who would suffer this for their children?* I said to myself, "Although it is below the earth and covered over, I still see it so clearly." They said, *Nothing is difficult for me.*

Sunday, after I received communion, I saw a resuscitated Christ within myself, here, above my heart. I saw Him again when I went to the ciborium, but they said nothing. I spent some time praising and giving thanks to the Lord. Then they said, *You benefited when I saved you from falling down the well. The devil wished to carry you away, and it was beneficial to know that if you fell, you would go to hell for the sins you had committed. I freed you because you commended yourself to the Virgin. God gives one hundred for every one.* I continued praising the Lord, and the voices said, *Do you believe in God, the Father Almighty?* "Yes, I do." *Do you believe in Jesus Christ, His only begotten Son? Do you believe He was conceived by the Holy Spirit?* "Yes." *Because you doubted the Incarnation, though, only now do you realize this.*

In the afternoon, I saw three people joined together, although the one in the middle was naked with a crimson sash. Our Lady stood in front of that person. She was dressed in white, with a silk cord around her waist, and her long, flowing blond hair reached her knees. All the people gathered together held their hands behind them, and they crowned her with a crown of gold, beautiful pearls, and gems of all colors. It was an imperial crown. I could not see the two people clearly, only their hands. They said that for the thirty-three years since the angel had first given her the message, the Virgin had cried because she knew what would happen. Within herself, she continually spoke and lamented Him, knowing what would happen. About to give birth, she wandered from house to house, unable to find a place. When she nursed Him, He cried, and she took His tiny hands and feet in her own hands. She cried bitterly and kissed those little feet with great tenderness, while realizing (40r) what would happen to them and that they would go to the cross. She spoke to her Son, and because He was eternal wisdom, He understood how Herod would persecute Him, wishing to kill Him, the flight to Egypt, and what happened there. She was always weeping, and here they listed the travails, one by one, and why she always had something to cry about. For this, they said, she well deserved the crown. Had I not heard about the mortal kings here who are crowned after achieving a great victory? They did the same with the Virgin. The day she ascended to heaven was the greatest triumph ever because the eternal Word and the Three Persons came for her. I asked myself, "Who was it?" The voices explained, *The Son of the living God, Jesus Christ, along with the nine choirs of angels with innumerable and various instruments*. They carried her in a litter to the throne of the Father, and there, in great triumph and glory, they crowned her. No one can understand what they told me there. They made her the Queen of Heaven and the advocate of sinners. What I say here and elsewhere are just specks of what happens there. I said to God, "Lord, what do you wish with this maggot?" It all causes such distress.

On Monday, I asked the Lord what I should do that day. He said, *Think about the Most Holy Sacrament of the altar and the tremendous benefit I gave in leaving it when I instituted it and took communion myself. Had I not done this, you would be like the dogs or other beasts. I just gave them instincts, but I gave you a rational soul with three powers*. As I got up to go grind the wheat, the voices said, *Have you not seen dead animals? That is how you would be.*

When I returned they repeated that man had cost Him a great deal ever since He had created him. It took great effort to make the clay and shape it, and we owe Him more than the angels do. After He formed us He gave us souls with just one breath from His mouth. *Had I not heard that when people die, they say, "Into your hands, oh Lord, I commend my spirit." This is exactly it. I created the angels and all other things just by saying, "So be it." I created the angels (40v) to serve mankind. Consider how many nations there have been, are, and will be. There are angels for everyone, and the angels have served them all. They will serve mankind, so humankind owes me more. Even my own mother was formed from this same clay. All the good from the Incarnation, the Redemption: I endured such travail to provide this sacrament for you. If I had not provided communion for you, what would have become of you? How would you communicate, if not by means of my sacraments? All those already in heaven, and all those who will arrive, go by this means. No other way exists. Have you not heard that when unbaptized children die, they go to limbo?* They spoke a lot about His generosity [det]. I cannot explain it all. The way I remember, it is upside down.

Later I said, "Remember me, Lord? I am the little slave of my mother, Saint Clare." The voices said, *The more you lower your head, the higher you can ascend.*[117]

It was already late when I was in the choir, and I felt uneasy because I thought they were watching me. At times I wanted to leave, but the voices said, *You always say "Thy will be done," but when something insignificant happens, you say, "You do not want this or that," because they will look at you.*

Lately, when I go to recollect, they tell me to lay myself out as though I were dead, with a cross held against my chest and my hands folded, and to meditate on death. Were it not for God's mercy, which keeps me here, I would be dead.

On the morning of Saint Bernard's day,[118] after I had received communion, they told me what I should contemplate that today, and that I should give many thanks to the eternal Father for having given me His Son in this sacrament. They occupied my thoughts with this, and so it was thus.

In the afternoon, a nun called me to listen to her read. Later, after prayers, the voices asked, *What did you learn from that reading?* I felt like a dolt. They said, *What is within is yours.* With great uneasiness, I persisted in my prayers for one hour and a half. It seemed that as many fleas as there are in the dung heap were jumping on me. On my left side the voices said, *Perhaps you think you have received communion the way Judas did. He did not really take communion. It was only the host (bread), and Jesus,* (41r) *the teacher, was not inside. They gave it to him because he was in front of the others. That is the way you have received communion. You want to act as though you are dressed in homespun wool in front of the others so they can see you.* They talked a lot about this, until the hour passed. Then, they said, *Tomorrow is Wednesday. Wear your hair shirt for one hour and then come to the choir with your hands tied. Then, think about when they did the same to me and what I felt with those cords cutting my wrists. Spend another hour in the infirmary, as you used to, because you have stopped going and do what you used to on Fridays.* I said I stopped going because a certain nun went. *But she is gone now*, they said. The secretary asked Ursula what she used to do. Although she refused to say, I, the secretary, insisted, and she told me that on Fridays she served beans in heaven and she ate them. On Wednesdays, she went to the infirmary, saying to herself, "And the nun who was with her?"[119] Ursula said, "I come to make the bed of my Lady, the Virgin Mary." Although there were many beds, this was for the servants. At each one she said, "This is the bed of my Lady." When she turned over the mattress, "This is my Lady's. This sheet or blanket is my Lady's. On Saturdays, I come to sweep the home of my Lady, the Virgin Mary." Finally, she explained that she said this because she saw something frightening. One day, while she held some bedding in her hands, she was unable to move. They all said to her, "What is wrong?" but she left and never did that again. I insisted that she tell me what she had seen. She said, "I saw our Lady come out from between the beds, dressed in white, her hair long and flowing and reaching her knees." Fearing it was a trick of the enemy, she left.

Wednesday, at daybreak, I, Ursula offered myself to the Lord, the way I always do, telling Him I was there for Him and would do what He wanted.[120]

In that instant, they told me to think about the ecce homo. I turned my thoughts toward heaven, and there I saw Him wearing a crown of thorns pressing into Him. He was holding a reed in His left hand and wearing something like a colored cape, held by a knot at the shoulder, the way they paint Him while seated, very pathetically wounded. I saw two people by His side but could not determine exactly who they were. The judge took Him to the window of his house to show Him to the people: ecce homo, "Behold the man." I said, "What is this? Why is this happening? I hope they are not trying to trick me with all this Latin. What do I understand of this?" I repeated the same: "Ecce homo, behold the man." Christ said, *There they taunted me a thousand times. They adored me while ridiculing me, like a sham king. They came right up to my face and repeatedly insulted me. I never opened my mouth to defend myself. I could have, but it was my Father's will.* (41v) *Though I gave them support, they came and reproached me, calling me an imposter, a sorcerer, and other ignominious names.* The señora vicaress[121] entered and said a few words about the virtue of restraint.[122] I did not say a word to her, yet twice I repeated what had happened. He said, *When they called Him to the column, did He say a word? Or, when they carried Him to the cross?* These things should neither be mentioned nor remembered, but only brought up when it is time to say, "Thy will be done." I was very busy all day, and I did not have a chance to make the beds in the infirmary, though I would have liked to. Evening came before I realized it. I told the Lord, "Even if it is only one, I need to do it." He said, *Not now, your desire is sufficient. You will do it when you can.*

Thursday, I was very busy and I realized that my duties made me forget about God. I also had a row with a black woman. I said to the Lord, "What is this about, Lord? I receive so much good from you, but fall so low, I am heedless." He said, *These difficulties result from being so busy, and they make you forget and lose your good will. Have you received?* I said, "Lord, today I was unable to go to mass." He said, *There is no excuse for not going on Sundays and feast days, which is what the church mandates. You can leave the other days for God. While praising Him, with all the things you have to do, you can still go at your specified time. Never stop going when they call you to work. I never had a moment's rest. Be careful to let yourself go.* A lot of things along these lines occurred. Later, I saw within myself something new that was guarding a small piece of flesh. I do not know how to describe it. It moved about and palpitated. I then realized it was a heart and two large, wide-open eyes were next to it. I was afraid and wanted to leave there. The voices said, *These are the interior eyes, and with these one knows God and can detect the light of truth.*[123] Finally they told me all that those eyes can do and that the exterior eyes have no value. While those are opened, the others are closed, and vice versa. How unhappy are those who die without having opened those interior eyes. I said to the Lord, "Give me the grace to see only with those eyes." Then they showed me a deep place with iron grilles and an unfortunate one lying there face down. He was surrounded by demons stoking that terrible fire, close by (42r) in a big tub.[124] The demons hurriedly removed its lid and took something out that resembled pitch and placed it in his mouth. They said to me, *Who do you think these are? They are the ones who, while living, opened their external eyes. They are the vagabonds who spent their lives indulging in pleasure: the liars,*

certainty that His Father is on the right side and the Holy Spirit on the left. They who speak to me said, *Look at Him in purple.*[129] I said, "Enough of purple. How do I know it is purple?" After this happened, I complained to our Lord that He had banished me to where I could not see Him. *Am I not in the kitchen or in Bethlehem or in Ballanos?*[130] He said, listing all the parts of the convent. *You can find me anywhere and everywhere.* She who writes this down[131] requested that I ask our Lord a question about a temptation that came to her every now and again. I asked three times but never received an answer until the last time. I forgot to give it to her, and she did not ask about it until now. She asked me what it was about. I replied without thinking and then felt confused because I have many qualms about saying one thing instead of another. Since (43v) it happens all the time, she forgets, and I can only say one atom of what happened there. No matter how hard she questioned me, I would not tell it any differently. So, I told the Lord I had said it without thinking. They told me, *Nothing is yours.*

On the day of Saint Augustine,[132] I barely had a little time to myself to recollect for a while. They repeated how he was a great saint who had achieved levels of glory. Although I would never be more than I am, we had to strive every day of our lives to see the Most Holy Trinity. I should rid myself of all the things of this world.

When I asked the Lord if it was His will that they should make amends when they started, He answered by asking whether His apostles had made little effort to reach heaven. *I fell seven times while carrying the cross. I spent forty days and nights in the desert fasting. Throughout my life, I never rested. Have you not heard them say, "The labors of Christ?" Those who are dedicated to me, what work do they have? It is well known that Lent is dedicated to me, so they can contemplate my suffering.* I said, "Lord why do some find it so repugnant?" He said, *Because they are the daughters of Adam.* During the canonical hours, they went to the choir to chatter, as though the day does not have twelve hours, and because they were lazy and inconsiderate. *Had Judas not thought he would make a profit from that money, he would not have sold me. If he had then considered that I was God and asked for my forgiveness, I would not have taken that into account. That is what they do here. Praying and sincerely reflecting on one's sins is the gift of the Holy Spirit, and the entire Most Holy Trinity knows what those sins are. What were they doubting? Were they doubting the three little times each year? What about those? They did not have to be satisfied with nine days, but they were, with what they did during those nine days.* Christ's Majesty endured it all with tremendous struggle, even when they dragged Him with the cross. He said, *Have you not seen when they drag a dead animal by a rope? Well, they dragged me the same way because my human strength had failed me. They made me walk by pulling the rope, giving me blows, shoving and beating me with clubs.* It seemed to me that the question had been insulting and I asked Him to forgive me. Because they had begged me, I had done it. He said, *As you are with a lord and a father, always be humble and obedient. As long as you obey my* (44r) *commandments, all is well, and you have nothing to fear.* Later He appeared as a shepherd, with His sheep on His shoulders. He taught me so much I cannot comprehend it all. He said He had been a shepherd in the world and was even one now. He was always tending and caring for His flock. I said, "Lord, why is it that when I see you, I cannot see those two people who accompany you?" *You see me as I was when I was made flesh in the world, but you will not see me as I was when I rose to heaven. Those who live in the world do not see God unless they are totally dead to the things of the world. They go to pray willingly and then know I am worthy of all praise. The Holy Spirit confirms them in its grace.* I said, "The Holy Spirit? How?" *No, it is the Most Holy Trinity. Yes, the Father is the Son and the Holy Spirit. It is all one essence and Three Persons. If they find prayer difficult, they should persevere before me, thinking of their sins and asking forgiveness. This is penance.* I said, "Prayer is penance?" He said, *One Hail Mary said with conviction is penance.* I said, "Lord I do not dare ask you to confirm me in this grace." He said, *Strive now and follow my will in everything. Have you not heard the Angolan slave say, "My owner orders it"? Do everything in the same way: with the desire to follow my will.*

Friday, I was in a hurry with many things to do, and I agonized all morning long. At midday, so many people were thronged around me to collect the food that in a rage I said, "Get away from me." Then I realized what I had said and asked the Lord to forgive me. Instantly, He said, *You could very well have told them to go away without getting angry. When it happens that way, there is no ulterior motive, and no bad feelings remain in the heart. Let it go.* Then I said, "Who is speaking to me in such a hurry? Can it be God?" He said, *Did you not ask for forgiveness?* I said, "Lord, every day I get worse." Another time, I was in the kitchen and very anxious to go to the choir. When I began walking there I broke down in tears. Now I feel so indifferent, miserable, impatient, and cannot remember anything. Any little task causes me to forget about God. He said, *This is your inconstancy. You are never of one mind.* I said, "Lord, get me out of the bad state I am in." He said, *What do you offer in return if I take it away?* I had said that morning that whenever possible, I would steal away for a short time to the small door near the kitchen that leads to the choir. Before I went to bed that night, I went to the choir, and He said, *Why did you not come through the small door?*

These days, I have so much to do I barely have any spare time at all. For this reason, my soul is in great anguish. When I took some time to go to mass to recollect for a bit, I did not recognize myself (44v) and was unable to do so. *Nothing is yours,* they said. Then they said if I felt bad, I could not take communion as I had before. I said, "Yes, my duties have me tied up. What should I do?" He said, *Receive communion spiritually. Prostrate yourself at the feet of the eternal Father and confess to Him. That is how you can do it. You always complain, I do not want this, I do want that, get rid of this, and you get upset because you miss this and that.*

Another time, I spent more than a half hour without being able to do anything. I could not even find any torment[133] to place myself into. He said, *Nothing you have is yours. Look, and see whether it is your head.*

Another time, while I was in the kitchen, they suddenly said, *The Father is the Son and the Holy Spirit. All Three Persons are one essence.* While I was there another time, the little friar came. I had not seen him in many days and was so glad to see him I almost laughed. He said, *You do not wish to think about this, about death.* I said I felt terribly frightened when I thought about that because of the things they teach me. He said, *It does not matter, go ahead.*

I was finding it difficult to pray, so I decided to renew the vows I had taken when I professed, but I could not remember how they went. I said, "Lord, I promise you everything I promised you when I professed." He said, *How could you do this without thinking?*

On my way to the choir, I found a ribbon with buttons made of gold and pearls. I looked for its owner. Then I thanked the Lord that I had not stolen that ribbon. They told me, *Nothing is yours.*

Wednesday I found a little extra time. As soon as I placed myself in God's presence He began saying to me, *You are so ungrateful. How many benefits have I given you, and yet you always doubt these gifts? What about when you wanted to leave the convent because you could not obtain your freedom and you spoke to me about the matter in the cloister? Then you gained your freedom; it was a gift. When you wanted to leave later and I appeared to you with my mother; it was a gift.* I saw this in an almost dreamlike state, and now they tell me it was a Lord, very large, dressed in scarlet robes reaching to the calf, very white and colorful. When I got closer, He turned His back to me, and the Virgin stood alone. I put my hands together and made a courteous gesture toward her. They did not speak to me then, but I understood that it was because of what I had decided. I promised Him I would not leave the convent. He said, *Was it not a benefit to have gotten you out of all that impudence you were so full of? Was it not beneficial to call to mind* (45r) *all your sins, without it costing you work, what you did during Lent, and granting what you asked of me?* What happened was that He had gotten me out of trouble and did so by His mercy. He says it now because I pleaded to the Virgin, my father Saint Francis and my mother Saint Clare and commended myself to them with all my heart. He made me recall other things that were all true: that I said I was afraid the enemy would deceive me; whether he could pull me out of my sins and vices, which I used to get myself into; why do I not believe. I said I did not want to hear or see these things, but He said the time would come when I would want it but could not attain it. He said, *The question you asked this morning came from Him.* It happened that I asked a sister worker whether she had seen one of the *provisoras*[134] do that. He said, [det] . . . *leave behind things that do not concern you, gossip with no one, and be vigilant over your heart and mouth.* I said, "How is it that I am here, where so much is offered?" *Let the nuns do what they want, but you should not get involved in anything.* Some years ago a nun loaned me twenty *patacones.*[135] She died but let it be known what she wanted done with the money. I repaid twelve of them and eight were for the Savior, which she said were to be given to a nun in charge of His feast day.[136] Although I wanted to give them, I have been unable to. I told the Lord I wanted to work to pay it off. He said, *Do not pay it, it is mine. I forgive the debt.* "So I do not have to pay it?" He said, *If this were promised to a nun, then you should pay it, but it was meant for me, and I forgive it. You do not have to work for that. If you ask some of my female ministers, they will say the same.*

Later, close to prayer time, I placed myself in front of an image of the Descent, which is in one of the cloisters. From there I saw the Three Divine Persons on a throne at a very great height. Although I could not see them clearly, I saw the Virgin, who was closer and descending from there, very clearly. They told me to look at the nine choirs of angels and all the other choirs. They said that when all those in heaven pray, they prostrate themselves. Our Lady pays her respects to them by lowering her head. Then they sit down again. I said, "They sit on chairs in front of God!" *Yes,* they told me. *God favors them in this way because they worked and earned it.*

This same day, they told me, *Was the donada's habit that you refused so fiercely not a benefit? Did you want a sign to convince you to take it? Well, you got your sign when my chapel burned. I refused to let you receive the habit before that because you would not make good use of it. Has your perseverance not been a benefit? It has been* (45v) *seven years since you came to me. Can the devil do this? As many troubles as there are, yes, you will get yourself mixed up in them.*

The following Thursday I asked the Lord whether it was a sin not to wear a head scarf that reached the shoulders as the Rule commanded. He said, *No, but follow each precept the Rule orders very carefully, no matter how insignificant it might seem, as well as my Ten Commandments and the rules of the church.*[137]

Later during siesta, I went to the choir. A great fear assailed me there. Although I could see nothing clearly, I realized it was a señora nun who had died some time ago. I left immediately and returned during the prayer hour. I saw her at once in a very deep hole where I have seen her before, but this time [det] I clearly saw her seated, with one foot over the other, as she customarily sat. She had a small piece of her wimple on her head, and her face was very dark. I have always seen her there. I was offering up my day's labor when she called me by name and said, "How can you forget me and help some but not others?" I said, "I always commend you to God." She replied, "Yes, but not with the affection that my necessity demands. Although you may have offered up your day, you can also make an offer for me because God is not a thief. For the love of God, I beseech you to remember me with great care and affection. Were we not raised together? Apply five days of work on my behalf and offer them in the name of the five wounds. See how much I suffer? Only because of God's mercy will I be saved. I was in great danger and about to condemn myself. I never fulfilled my duties, and although I had that long illness, I did not understand that I was dying. Thus caring only about my illness and the desire to be well, I did not perform acts of contrition until the very end." At this moment, the communal discipline began in the convent, and she bared her shoulders and whipped herself along with us. I was impressed by what I saw, and she said, "What? Do I not owe this?" Later, I saw her again in the kitchen, where I always see her, in that same deep place I mentioned. Every time I have seen her, she is there. She also said, "How poorly Gracia and I got along." Gracia, the slave of one of her sister's, had died a few weeks ago. Later, the Lord told me to look carefully at her right arm, for this meditation would make my work (46r) much easier. I only saw the arm and hand with the severe wound, and that the entire arm was very wounded.

Friday was a very busy day, but I escaped when I could and went to the choir. I had just started when I heard the abbess's voice. I got up and went to the confessional, and they reprimanded me there because I had gotten up after I had begun speaking with Him. *Why had I not said I wanted to move?* I said, "I left because then they call me names." He said, *Can you really offer anything? Nothing is yours.* Then the one who appeared yesterday came to thank me for what I did for her. She was most grateful. I told her to pay me when she was in God's presence. "Very gladly," she said. What she could do for me now, though, was to tell me that everything in this world is less than a little [det] . . . than loving and serving this Lord. "It is very honorable to say 'Loved, Served, and Venerated One,' and we should serve Him a lot. Even if one knows nothing else, this is very important. You should please God, and I would have done this from the time I gained the use of reason. Look, be persistent in this, and you will find yourself before God without getting into the same mess I did." She was no longer in the hole, nor as dark. From where I was, I saw the upper half of her body in its human form. While I was busy in the kitchen later, something came into my head, and I thought I would die. I remained in this state for a while and then gradually returned to my senses. During the evening when they were at matins, I reached the small door near the upper end of the choir and said, "Lord, how are you? I am very sad because I have not seen you today." He placed Himself in His monstrance, just as when they take it out for communion, in great splendor. He said, *Was I not with you when you had that ailment, and did I not take it away?* Then He said, *Will she sing the song about the holy altar cloth?* At that instant the aforementioned dead one said, "That is for me and the others." She said, "Each one applies it to whomever she wants." I asked the nun for whom she had said that prayer, and she answered, "For her, the one who writes this." The scribe had received communion that day for her and had done all she could to gain indulgences for her. The year before on the octave of Corpus they had decorated the altar where the most holy host would go with a large, but old, altarpiece of the Divine Trinity. I saw Saint Joseph very clearly, but in his place was a nun with her veil covering her. I thought it was just a silly notion, or my eyes playing tricks, so I wiped them and rubbed myself. I put myself at the different spaces of the grille, but the more I looked the better I saw her. (46v) This happened a number of times. I never understood what it was, and now they explain that it was so I would commend to God this nun, who was then dying. I had heard she was not dealing well with death and did not wish to hear about it. I took responsibility for her and asked others to help.

Saturday, on the vespers of the birth of our Lady,[138] I wanted to fast on bread and water, but because my character was so weak, and I did not wish to fail in my discipline, or have the nuns look for someone to replace me, I asked our Lady what to do. She said that praying for half an hour meant more than many fasts. I said, "Are these fasts of no value?" *I do not know if they are, but prayer is better and pleases God more.*

I asked my father Saint Francis to obtain God's grace in order for me to serve Him better. He responded as I saw him, *Do you not realize that when one digs a well, one does not stop until water is reached? That is how we must seek God: with perseverance, humility, and penitence. Had I never seen an unbroken donkey, jumping about and resistant? When they used the rein and loaded the donkey, they could do what they wanted with it.* He asked me, *Who was better, earth or I?* I said, "Earth," and he said, *Yes, because what is essential comes from it, and things are built from it, but it is only good for worms. The senses and faculties that do not focus on God are miserable.* "What can I do to please God?" *Suffer a lot, be humble like the earth, and have faith in God, who does not neglect His own.*

Tuesday I gave thanks because I awakened opportunely without having to work. The voices told me, *Then you will see that I worked doubly hard.* Later, after they had come in, I saw the Lord tied to a column, about four feet high in the ciborium. He was beautifully shaped and well crafted from head to foot. His hair reached His shoulders. I saw Him everywhere. They did not speak to me.

Thursday, intraoctave of the Birth of our Lady, at dawn, since I barely have any other time, I earnestly commended a nun to God. I had done so all these days, so they told me, *Stop this. Did they not take away all those fanciful cogitations you had? It is likely you are experiencing temptation.* Since this was something I was particularly careful of, I stopped thinking about it and then felt still and calm.

(47r) Later, during the siesta, while I was in the choir, four souls dressed in white appeared to me. I recognized one of them; she was the one we mentioned recently. She thanked me deeply and said that God would pay me for everything I had done. May our Lord Jesus Christ be with me in everything I lay my hands on. Many thanks and blessings. They remained with me the entire time I was in the choir. Not much else occurred, but I felt they would have stayed longer had I done so. I asked after doña Rafaela, and they explained she was not there.[139] Some days later, I asked again after her and they explained that since I had seen her dressed in white, she had gone. That was the day of our Lady of the O.[140]

Friday at dawn, just as everyone gets up with the desire to please their masters, so I wish to please my master, who is my Lord Jesus Christ. Something came upon me while I was in front of the others, which made me feel like rolling around on the floor. I said, "Lord, please do not shame me, because then they say, 'Holy inventions! No one can make a saint.'" The voices said, *If they say so, be thankful to God.* I said, "Lord, I feel like squeezing myself into a corner where no one can see me." He said, *No, you must be in the choir.* I said, "But they are making a fuss about it." He said, *Let them do so. Do not meddle and mind your affairs.* I said, "When will I go without speaking a word the entire day?" He said, *Will you not be in the choir until midday? Then take care not to speak until I order you to return to the choir and then, do not speak with anyone except my mother and me. In that way, you will spend the day without speaking.*

Within myself, I saw some eyes that greatly frightened me because I had seen them once before. The voices said, *You now know about these eyes. They are the ones that see.*

Saturday, just as I entered the cloister that leads to the choir, I felt absolutely certain that the Father and the Holy Spirit were present on both sides of the Most Holy Sacrament. Feeling no doubt at all, I prostrated myself and adored this great Lord, saying, "Here is this stone, this brick, this black woman of the house of my father Saint Francis." He said, *Here she is.* I was tired. I thought, "How can I sit down in front of you when I think of how you were standing up?" He said, *I spent most of my Passion on my feet, and just like a servant, I remained standing during everything else they put me through.*

On Sunday, among other things, they told me, *I want nothing from you except your gratitude.* About three months ago a nun summoned me. (47v) She had suffered from arthritic gout for a long time. She had been given various remedies and had taken arum two or three times, but nothing improved her condition. This sick nun who always mocks me, called for me. I thought this must be happening for a reason, and although I had refused, I knew I had to go. She asked me for the love of God to say some creeds over the sick part, but I told her I did not know how. I said I would bring a nun who knew how to do it, but I said this just to excuse myself. She doggedly persisted for several days, and I continued to excuse myself, but because she asked me for the love of God I could not refuse. I made the sign of the cross in the name of the Most Holy Trinity, and I do not remember whether I said a Hail Mary or an Our Father. I did not pay any more attention to this, because the devil may have been tempting the nun or me. [det] They said to me, *Was it not beneficial that she was healed?* So many other remedies had done no good. This nun, whom they called by her name, had told her relatives. One of them was seriously ill, and what did she do but call for me, but because I understood what it was for, I refused to go. One of the sisters of the nun I just mentioned came through the door and said, "Heal[141] me here where it hurts." I said I did not know how to do that and left. Later I forgot all about this, but when I went to pray, they brought it up. He also said that had it not been for this, I would now be lying asleep like the others. I forgot to say at the beginning that as soon as I began to recollect, the voices seized me with such force that I was unable to resist, and they carried me to another place.

After a while, I do not know what came over me, but I caused a little disturbance in the choir. Hurriedly, I said to the Lord, "Do not let the choir notice this. Do not humiliate me." He said, *There you will see, when you come to the choir.* I still have one week left in the kitchen, which means I have little free time. I even eat in a hurry, standing up. I do not know who it was who told me, "Eat slowly. If you do not, it will do you no good and will only make you ill." I said, "Mind your own business. For good or bad, it will be as God wishes." Other times, she [he?] says, "You used to get up at nine, and now you are an early bird at four. You will die." What does it matter if I die? There is nothing to it.

Monday, vespers of the wounds of our father Saint Francis, I noticed that many stayed in the choir to make amends. I asked the Lord whether He would stay with me that night. He said, *Do not stay. Go and rest.* I made myself believe that (48r) my head made this up out of laziness. I asked again whether I should stay, and He said, *No, go and rest and bundle yourself up well. Get up at four and meditate on the love with which I imprinted the wounds on my servant, Saint Francis. In my immense grandeur, I came down to do this, because he was so humble.*

Tuesday, on the day of the wounds of our father Saint Francis,[142] they told me our Father could easily have given him the wounds, without even coming down because of His infinite grandeur and power. Because Saint Francis was so humble He had impressed His own wounds upon him. He had never stopped being [det] . . . of His royal standard. I asked what a royal standard was. He answered, *My cross was always in* [det] . . . *most loyal servant,* and other things I have forgotten. Then they told me that the brother of a nun had died, and I should commend his spirit to God [det]. . . . I could, and I offered part of the communion for him, and he said when [det] . . . to convert, nor correct themselves, He sent them troubles and illness. *With this and the pain they suffer, they remember me and call out.* They led me to understand that the nun's brother had been saved. Later, while serving the food at midday, one of the nuns who serves food in the refectory entered to bring in some plates of food that another nun sent for me to eat. She angrily gave them to me and said two insulting words, such that I kept turning what happened over in my mind. He asked me, *How long are you going to hold onto this inside? The instant it happens you should stop thinking about it. Think instead about what those knaves put me through during my Passion, insulting me, taking me to and fro. With this, everything will be easily ventured.* During the siesta, I went to the choir, and He told me to think about already being there and to consider how many were buried in that choir and that I had not realized the full extent of His benefits. A while later, He said that all follow their paths, each his own, and there were many, but He carried me down a level and true path, without doubts, ravines, or the need to stumble. I asked whether He wanted me to do what the nuns did when they wished to make amends. He said, *How can you think of doing anything without permission? Are you your own?* He had done nothing that was not His Father's will. I said I already had general permission. He said no, I should mortify myself. My father Saint Francis was very obedient and humble, and the more gifts he received the humbler he became. I said, "Who could be like my father Saint Francis?" He said, *He was not of the flesh.*

    Thursday, I spent a little time in the confessional. Because I was so tired I sat in the corner facing front with my back to the wall. Then I saw the Lord in front of me. I said, "How can this be if He is behind me?" This happened internally, as do all my questions and answers. He told me, and I do not know who it was, *Only God sees in this way, because He is here, in Potosí, and in Spain. I brought life to everyone, but in the end they are in purgatory and hell.* I kept trying to see what was happening on the other side of the wall, although people were there.

    (48v) Friday, at midday, when it was my turn to hand out food to the poor, a girl arrived to collect some food.[143] When she took her pot, she must have spilled the contents. She said I had burned her and insulted me as she pleased. By the grace of God, I did not say a word, except that I had done nothing and would not think of doing such a thing, even to a cat. She left, and her mother came and complained, which caused a big hubbub. I responded to her the same way I had to the daughter. After this battle was over, I turned to God and said, "Lord, you know well that it was not my intention to harm anyone." He said to me, *They stepped on my clothing, my feet and my head, and I said nothing. If you keep my Passion in mind, it all* [det] *be easy, and you would not be in such straits.* So many of them were together there stepping on me and dripping the stew on me. I was getting into a huff . . . [det] "Or it all happens in front of me." *Think of the charity with which our father Saint Francis or our mother Saint Clare served everyone. I very* [det] *see how you are with your brothers and my children.* I said to myself, "Where do I see it, on the roof?" He said, *Am I not everywhere? Did you not see me the day before yesterday with four faces? Look here, there, and everywhere. There is nothing too small or hidden for me to see.* In the afternoon, He appeared before me, carrying a cross and dressed in purple. I said, "We do not need to see a cross to carry out your will. Give me light to know it and the grace and strength to carry through." Here, He said no more. He had previously said it was necessary to be armed with great fortitude for any eventuality.

Saturday, I promised that everything I did that day would be for the crown of thorns,[144] so all went well, although at times I got very upset. Still, I found the patience and equanimity the Lord wanted me to have. They said, *You are so ungrateful. You do not recognize the benefits, for you have not had to give thanks for the knowledge they gave you.* When I went to the choir and got near to it, I became infused with the clearest and most certain knowledge that the Father was on the right side of the Most Holy Sacrament and the Holy Spirit on the left. After this, I said that because I was in such a hurry I had not put on my hair shirt. He said, *The hair shirt is*—I am not certain how He said it—*the fortress of patience. It truly helps one to be patient.*

At night I went to the choir and said to God, "Lord, now I am finished in the kitchen. What would you like me to do now, for I am yours?" He said, *You should give many thanks (49r) to the eternal Father because He has brought you here every day, all month long, without missing a day. No one could have come here like you, what with all the trouble you have, if you were not brought here.* I said, "I am straw living amongst other straw, not among the princes, because they do not want me to."[145] I was so burdened and crying so much because I am so evil. I neither recognize the benefits given me nor love God. He said, *Many go for years without getting even a tiny crumb of what they give you in abundance.* He said, *Pray my mother's rosary again, as you used to.* Lately I have been so busy I neglected it. He said, *This rosary pleases her. I pray it while lying prostrate and kiss the floor at each mystery.*

I passed by a window and a nun shouted out to me, "Madwoman in a rush."[146] I said to the Lord, "See, this is why I hide. Why should I hide when they are nothing but ash? I have nothing to hide. God alone creates saints." *As much as they say you are one, praise my Father and thank Him. . . .* [det] . . . want to fly away. I have no reason to fear being seen [det] . . . and deny them like me." Whenever I am in the choir I would pay no heed to whether they look at me or speak about me." None of this mattered: to obey [det] . . . could I not see it, that I am not mine, and to ask permission to stay in the choir these nights. I said, "If you send me to the señora abbess, then they will begin calling me names and looking at each other." He asked whether I knew I had no will and whether I knew I had offered myself to Him twice: once when His chapel burned and then when I professed. He demands obedience. He said, *Is the habit you have yours?* I said, "No." He asked what I would do for His love. I said that if He asked for my arm I would let them cut it off. He said, *Yes, go work!* A while later they told me to look on that piteous Lord and ponder how those falls hurt Him, what blows those were, and how the thorns pressed further into His head while He was on the cross and even more later. I should consider what pain that must have been. They told me this while the first host was being raised. They told me to consider how the nails were driven in deeper when He fell, how the nails had frightened Him while being crucified, and how the blows ripped open His wounds. What suffering that must have been. I saw Him crucified and those nails starting to come through, as though they had been hammered in from behind. They explained how those falls had frightened Him. Then the Lord said that should I be in the choir and see them talking about me or thanking God for seeing me, as soon as the thanks were given, I should also thank God with all the choirs of angels. Why did they say that? While I was in the cloister two nuns passed by. One said to the other that the light of God was very gentle. See how it goes hand in hand with His good wishes? I said to the Lord, "This hinders her. Saying that God's law is very gentle, yes, it is very gentle, but it is necessary to work hard at it."

(49v) While in bed Monday morning, I felt ill. Next to me I saw a Christ more than a foot and a quarter high. I said, "Oh Lord, what is this? Why do I always see a crucified Christ? Is this temptation?" *No*, He said, *This is not temptation. This is how I want to be seen because I want all to see what He went through for us.* He wants me to be humbler than the earth and very willing and resigned to all that comes to me from His hands. I said, "Yes." Later, I went to the choir and commended myself to God, saying, "Here is that poor little woman who does not know you." I see the Lord tied to a column, more than four feet tall, so ... [det] ... the ropes tied so tightly you could see His bones. One time I felt such terrible pains all over my body I could hardly stand it. I asked Him, in the name of the pain He suffered [det], to take away from me anything that did not please Him. He said, *Because ... what you would feel is very different from what I experienced when they finally took me off the column. What you have is merely a scratch.* I saw a lot of spilled blood at the foot of the column. Two angels gathered it up with both hands, placed it in a chalice, and climbed up a very high stairway, crystal clear like the sun from top to bottom. Those angels went up carrying towels with the chalice and then returned to the column again, gathered up the blood, and did the same again. They told me that although His blood had spilled, not a drop had been lost because it had all been taken to heaven. He said that this was what He had taught me before. Then they showed me something resembling a well and our Lord standing at the railing atop the well. From His five wounds, five streams of blood poured into that thing that looked like a well. Two angels stood to one side, and many people surrounded the well. From time to time those angels took one of them by the arms and dipped him into that blood. They picked people out of the crowd and placed them there. When they went among the people, they got down on their knees with their hands folded in prayer. *That Lord*, they told me, *He was the reason for this.*[147] Well, now they tell me that what I saw today is what they had shown me long ago. Those who went in there became purified, and those fountains would last and never stop running, so long as the world lasted and so long as God was God. I should offer all that happened to the Father and offer that blood for those poor sinners who knew not what they did to themselves by sinning. I should kiss the earth seven times for the seven times He fell while carrying the cross and offer those falls to His eternal Father to pardon my sins. Then He said that whoever imitates Him must experience internal and external sorrow. He also said I should not look after myself but let Him care for me and leave everything in His hands.

On Tuesday when I awakened at four, they told me to say how kind the Lord is. *Although you have offended Him so much, He still wants you to receive Him. Look: if you had offended a moral man that way, you would never return to his grace. If you have drunk His blood you know this to be true.* It was God who said this. I thanked Him and told Him I wanted to receive Him today, even though I could not be as prepared as I wanted because I had work to do. He said, *You can be with me from now until nine, which will be five hours.* After I received communion, I then gave thanks to God. After this, the Lord told me that those who leave the world behind were worthier than the martyrs, because on those occasions when they found themselves with the strength given by His grace (50r), they let go their lives and then suffered those torments. The martyrs willingly surrendered so they would have no will of their own, and then fought against hell, the world, and the flesh all at the same time. Then He told them the glory of the Father was theirs. Many had been chosen, and many would still be chosen. I told Him I dared not ask to be one of those chosen. He said He had spilled His blood for everyone. All that there was in the world meant nothing. I asked Him to give me His grace, so that I could be at His feet. He said His feet would be my repose, my bed, and my book. One time, this sister wanted them to read her the book of Saint Teresa. Since then, they sometimes tell her that her book must be the feet of My Lord Jesus Christ.

When I was about to eat I said to my Lord, "When your servants served you in another way and mortified themselves, they sustained themselves with herbs. I am in such comfort here because you sent it to me." He said, *Their strengths were different.*

While climbing a stairway [det] . . . thrown there that belonged to a nun who had died more than a year ago. Because [det] I remembered her and was moved to pity, thinking of the nothing we are. He says in the . . . [det] head.

During siesta, and while in the choir I had [det]. . . . While in the middle of the choir, I sensed that they commanded me not to receive communion. When . . . [det], I should do nothing but obey without showing any emotion. I said, "Yes, I only wanted to do His will." He said, *If they tell you to sweep the kitchen, go willingly wherever they tell you to go.* I said "Yes." He said, *Even if some servant orders you, do it willingly.* I said, "Thy will be done."

In the afternoon I prayed for one and a half hours. I always tell the Lord that half an hour is for my father Saint Francis, and it seems that I can see him there. I said I would fervently commend my spirit to God so that He, God would give me His light and make me good. He said, *You should go as you began, for now all is going well.* I told Him to give me a sign. While kneeling in front of the Most Holy Sacrament, He told me to adore it and then confess to it. He told me I should know that the devil cannot receive the most holy host in his mouth and that whenever I hear something said about me, I was not to speak a word, but act as though I were dead, and that today's reply had been a good one. What happened was that I was in a cell where some nuns were talking about rebozos,[148] and what did I think about that? I said, "What did I know about that?" As though I were someone who really mattered. That was a good one. I then said, "How do you know?" He said, *From heaven the blessed ones see everything good or bad,* and to praise God for everything. I should be very humble and long-suffering, and that He and our mother were very annoyed in this world. I should not visit anyone, and only speak with great care when I run into anyone. I should be very diligent in fulfilling my obligations. I said I still did not feel very good about it, and He said, *Let the donkey[149] rest, because it can do no good.*

Wednesday, when I awakened they told me to think about the glory of the blessed ones. Later, while in the choir I saw a great many carrying palms. They told me to look at the choirs of angels, and there I saw the Three Divine Persons on a very high throne. I could not see them very well, but off in the distance, I saw the Virgin very near, wearing a veil lowered over her eyes. They told me that she lived that way in the world, with her blue shawl, and the tips of her feet showing. I saw all this very clearly and close to me. I said, "Today is Wednesday, the day of our Lady, and I will be here at the feet of my Lady." After a long time pondering what had just happened, they told me to think about hell for one hour. I said, one hour now and another one later. Then, though, I did what they told me although it is a type of meditation that causes me such tremendous fear (50v) that my very nature fears it. He said, *Do it with the Holy Spirit*. As soon as I prostrated myself before the Lord they took me to a very dark place where there were a large number of condemned individuals in chains, with their sinful pride. They explained that they were there for just one sin. They sealed the mouths of others with branding irons and said the same thing. Others were in horrible skillets being fried and dipped in there. Some went down and others came up, and they repeated that the comfortable ones . . . [det]. Others, very far below, looked as though they were aflame on some beds.[150] They explained that those were the friends of the bed.[151] Others had long, very thick chains, all tangled up in complete chaos. There is no way to describe what was there. They explained that each form of torture was for a certain sin that had been committed, and that many were there for just one sin. [det] and that I had committed them all. *Mind what you owe God and give Him more*. [det] They told me to look at all those who were there and that I deserved . . . [det] . . . you refuse to ask permission. When I left there I saw something [det] and I recognized a person who is still alive. They told me that already . . . [det] with her crafty ways and I understood that I would end up like that. [det] When I awakened, I saw them hastily carrying the viaticum to a sick woman . . . [det] They told me, *It is not fatal*.

As soon as I prostrated myself I gave thanks for the love with which He instituted the Sacrament, for those who received Him were in His grace. I had the tremendous knowledge that this Lord was the true God. Thursday, after attending the mass of the Most Holy Sacrament, I saw the Three Divine Persons in the ciborium, below the curtains. A short time later I saw the feet of my Lord Jesus Christ and threw myself at them. His clothing was white, and nothing could be seen, save what was uncovered. Then, He pushed away the clothes covering His heart, and I saw all of myself there on my knees. I said, "Lord, how can it be that I see myself there?" *This is what it means to be benevolent, even after I have been offended*. I asked if a small ant could be there. This ant spent one and a half hours there, looking at myself. He said that when the little ant lets go of its will, it would be there. I told Him that if I had everyone's will I would place it at His feet. I thanked Him and said, "You are God." He said, *Yes, when friends receive any courtesy, they call Him "Lord." Whoever eats and sleeps in a bed should be there*. He said that did not matter. What matters is that the spirit is willing. These are necessary acts. He said, *When you were about to fall into the well, you knew if you did, you would go to hell. Who helped you? You slept in mortal sin, and the Virgin pleaded to me for the poor little woman. Your father Saint Francis and your mother Saint Clare asked on your behalf.* After this, He told me that on Mondays I should lift up the mattress for the tortured souls, on Wednesday for those in mortal sin, and Fridays for the benefit of the holy church, the extirpation of heresies, peace among kings, all the sick and imprisoned, and all other necessities.

So when I prostrated myself, I said, "Here is the spittle of them all."[152] In the afternoon, I saw myself again in that heart. I said, "Lord, you are God, I do not know what to say, other than to thank you for the tremendous gift, but I experience great awe upon seeing (51r) something like this." He reminded me of something I had seen more than a year and a half ago. While prostrate in the small choir, I saw the little black friar, very lovely, very beautiful, wearing our habit, near the little dais in front of the lectern. Next to the oven, was another abominable one, whose habit looked as if it had been disinterred. He was telling me this so I would remember. He said the beautiful and resplendent one I saw represented those in grace, the observant ones who obeyed the rules and did what the community mandated. The other one represented those who were in the order for their own comfort, who did not want to follow orders, serve the community, purify themselves, but just do what they wished. I said to the Lord, "Order me to do what you wish; purify me as you will. I want nothing [det] your will. You had forgotten. When I left to perform a discipline, I returned feeling so distracted that I could not recollect again, and it seemed that all of hell had risen up [det] me. After a long time, I said, "What is this? It is all so different?" [det] I am thinking that all that happened is just a lie of my imagination. They told me, *In your . . .* [det], *you cannot always live in this manner. That is only for the blessed ones . . .* [det].

Friday, while receiving communion, it is still . . . [det] firewood.[153] I thanked the Lord. After a while, I saw within myself [det] a child, about two years old, with a band and a small flag. Nothing else happened, even though I stayed there giving thanks until twelve. Two or three days later they placed that queen[154] in front of me, the one they had once shown me, and asked me to commend her to God. I rejected this as temptation. I said, "Leave me be. Queen? What do I have to do with queens or kings?" He said, *All come to my feet; to me, they are all the same.* I have heard it said that what the donada professes has no value. I asked Him about this, and He said that it has value if it comes from the heart. Everything else is deception.

Sunday I was praising the Lord and told Him He was my Father, my shepherd, my consolation, and my refuge. I told my angel to go to my Lord and tell Him I was there to do His will. He should teach me how to please Him. He should tell the Lord that I did not want them to speak to me because then I was too weary. They told me to give thanks to God. *Was it not better to be weary than sinful and have a guilty conscience and have to spend time with the priests?* "Yes," I said. "No," I said. *Was it not better to have an untroubled conscience?* They told me that the angels were always annoyed when we did not want to get up. They complained among themselves, saying, *What will I do with this soul that God has given to me to care for? He does not wish to mend his ways, in spite of all the efforts made on his behalf.* They told me that the weariness I experience does not grieve them, but sins do. I asked my angel what I had done that troubled him so much. They said that here we slept, but angels do not sleep during the day or at night.

They told me that the angels said, *What account of that soul would they give God?* They told me that we should allow ourselves to be burned alive and have our flesh torn away, rather than sin.

I felt a desire to hear a book on the imitation of Christ read. They said, *Why occupy yourself with books and let them get in your way? Imitation meant considering how He descended from heaven, leaving behind His infinite greatness to become so very humble and poor that He only had a few rags, always walked barefoot, and left His head uncovered. (51v) Consider His meekness and how, when they went to apprehend Him, He could easily have burned them all. If someone struck a viceroy, would he get out alive? Being such a terrible sinner, you wanted Him to receive you. Look at what He suffered with so much meekness and humility and the patience with which He obeyed His Father. This is the true imitation of Christ. Consider Him in the desert, the need, poverty, and discomfort He experienced there, and yet, He continually prayed to His Father. This is imitation. Thank Him for not putting you in hell, for raising you with such care, for what He has suffered because of you, and for what He has saved you from. Be thankful for all the other benefits, counting them [det] one by one.* They told me that even if a person had a thousand lives to live [det] all in thankfulness, he still could neither pay for, nor satisfy, even with many advantages.. . . Give [det] thanks that God gives such benefits, not because there is merit, [det] . . . really make himself available, and who for His love leaves behind all the things that grieve him to . . . [det] they are always warned. Those who leave it for the hour of their death [det] . . . and agony, thinking about how they have offended God and being unable to [det] sins and so much anguish occurring all at once. It all seemed so garbled. Seeing death approach and feeling distressed about the reckoning that is drawing near, no matter how much they turn around, they still forget to ask forgiveness for their sins. God only knows where they would go later. What matters to Him is to have it all ready. Just as they cause me such great affliction, I cannot remember the last time I had an hour of consolation without a thousand fears about whether it came from God or I was being deceived. It seems the voices are telling me here, though, that these cannot be the devil's teachings, and that he cannot take away vices and sin, but only get us into them. The voices said, What labors do I have compared to those? What better consolation than to have an untroubled conscience? I should thank Him for the many good things and the perseverance He gives me. I should always come to where He is and fear Him, because it is right to be feared. Then I offered the Lord the hour and a half I had been there. I always tell Him that half goes to my father Saint Francis, and I said that if He willed it so, the half hour that usually goes to my Father—if it was worth anything—could go for that cleric. They said, *Can you not understand what it is worth?* They also said my book was to be at the feet of our Lord Jesus Christ. There I would learn. There was no reason to look for other books. When I wanted to know something, I should ask my guardian angel, and I understood that it was he who was speaking to me.

Monday evening after praying for a while, I recalled someone I had seen the devil pestering for many days. I commended her spirit to God. After a long while they told me that during the Passion, when those scribes and Pharisees wanted Him to perform miracles, He did not want to because it would not do them any good. The same happens here. He knows in His wisdom that nothing can do them any good. The cleric leaves them.

(52r) Tuesday, on Saint Bridget's Day,[155] I had no sooner placed myself in front of the Lord than they told me to thank Him for all the gifts there are. Being nothing, I said, "Yes, I already knew I was a tick."[156] He repeated, *Thank Him for being benevolent, meek and merciful. He is Father, friend, purifier, and Savior. He is tractable, and nothing is needed, save to approach Him. He is always prepared and casts no one aside, nor does He only heed those who conform to His will. If you went to the palace and spoke to the viceroy, would they not laugh at you and ask you to say what you wanted? Besides, they would not let you speak with him. Then there is God, the universal Lord of heaven and earth, so benevolent to all who wish to approach Him. All that is needed is the desire to reach out and approach His Divine Majesty.* Then He placed [det] in the ciborium, like the ecce homo, His hands tied, wearing a great crown of thorns [det] in an extremely piteous state, His bones falling apart. They told me to look closely at Him. He said what . . . [det] to save mankind. I should look at those thorns. They gave Him such terrible pain [det] . . . they pulled out the nails of His hands and feet, that terrible pain, and the pain [det] His heart. Those thorns pierced His temples and brain [det]. Consider how cruelly and angrily they had done [det] all their strength. When I think of my self-love and with my . . . [det] the image in front of me disappears. Then they told me to communicate frequently with my angel and ask him. I should always have God present in all that I do, and wherever I may be, I should consider God there. Wednesday, while outside the choir, I disciplined myself on my own, outside the community. While I went to the choir the voices said, *Why did you not ask for permission to perform that discipline? Are you your own?* I said to myself, "He must know everything, from the hair shirt to fasting. I would not fast today without asking permission. I should mortify myself. Let Him love whoever deserves it most."[157] They could flay me, but His Divine Majesty had not willed it. I have denied His will in everything. When I professed, did I did not say my will was no longer mine? When the donadas take their vows, some feel that they can leave the convent, but this does not apply to those who do so willingly.[158] Although He raised us as different nations, the will of blacks and whites is the same. In memory, understanding, and will, they are all one. Had He not created them all in His image and likeness and redeemed them with His blood? Should I become like a small child who does not know whether they placed him here or there? When a child is growing up, he already has free will. I must be like a child who has his hands tied. I should let myself be rolled along where I am told to go. I should do nothing, no matter how insignificant it might seem, without first asking permission. This is the true imitation of Christ. I deserve to be in hell for refusing to ask permission, and I should give thanks that I was not there. I felt the desire to know whether the donados of my father Saint Francis slept in their habits. He said, *The chosen ones do. They take great pains to comply punctually with everything that their Rule dictates. You should not add or take anything away, but do everything with permission. When you ask for it, think of yourself as dead, and think, "Tomorrow I will be dead, foul-smelling, and full of worms." This would make every-thing easier.* While praying the rosary there in my corral,[159] I felt someone speaking to me. I resisted, saying to myself, "What is this? Who speaks to me? Can it just be temptation?" Later, (52v) after this happened there, they told me three times that when I said, "Hail Mary, full of grace," I should see how I said, "full of grace," because she is filled with God. "The Lord is with thee." See how she is always with the Lord? "Blessed art thou among all women." Look, is there anyone like her in heaven? "And, blessed is the fruit of thy womb, Jesus." What fruit is like this? "Hail Mary, Virgin and Mother of God." Who is a virgin like this Lady, Virgin and Mother? "Pray for us sinners." See, she prays for us all. She placates God so that He forgives us at the hour of our death. She intercedes on behalf of all those who ask her favor.

After I had eaten, I thanked God [det] many gifts He gave me. I told Him He was my father and mother and that [det] giving to me, even what I would eat. They told me that His word could not [det]. . . . What have I done to deserve so many benefits? It was only because He is God . . . [det] . . . and I said to Him that if I held in my hand the wills of everyone in the world [det] . . . I would place them at His feet. Among other things, they told me that those feet had . . . [det] . . . that there I would learn. I do not know how they said it. When they say "Glory . . . [det] *utera yn prinsitio et yn secula seculorun*," that He was without beginning . . . [det] . . . Then they brought me many benefits, and among them, what they had done when I . . . [det] . . . in the choir, when I decided to take this habit.

Thursday evening, they made me spend the day cooking. Very late, when I was able, I went to the choir to give thanks because I had received Him, even though I am nothing. They talked to me for more than half an hour. For some days now, I have been having some problems. Wherever I go, day or night, when I awaken or whenever I close my eyes, I see a Christ figure more than a foot tall holding a cross about the same size very close to me. I am afraid of Him. As they say that the devil is so wily and old that he knows very well how to deceive, every once in a while I ask Him whether He is God because why should He be with someone who is such a sinner? I went to adore the Lord and I said, "What is it that I am always seeing?" After about half an hour, they asked me whether I believed He received communion when He instituted the Holy Sacrament? At the same time, I do not know, He mentioned the lamb. I said I did not wish to know anything and did not understand. I simply came to praise God. They said, *Do you not know that after He received communion He gave communion to His apostles?* How did I know it had been like that? I conceded that He had received communion to go and suffer. Did I believe that when they lifted the host on Holy Friday that He was in it and would remain there forever? Because I know the host remains consecrated, I said, "Yes." It was none other than Christ accompanying me. Did I know He could do anything He wanted, and could accompany His friends? I said, "Jesus, be with me, blessed be the Most Holy Sacrament." I got up from there and left. The previous afternoon they had asked why I had not asked permission to cook. In the future, I should do so.

(53r) Saturday afternoon I confessed. I forgot to do my penance, but did not realize it. When I awakened on Sunday before dawn, they said, *You did not say your penance*, and then I remembered that was true. I have been very slow-moving, these days, so sleepy, I cannot help myself. They said, *Is that not laziness?*

That and the flesh–reject it for it comes from the enemy.

Tuesday, I asked my angel if it would be good to receive communion and then go perform my duties. He said, *Go, do your tasks after receiving communion and think about what He bore and thank Him.* After I finished kneading the dough, I went to the hen yard, and while somewhat anxious, I was thinking about how I could order my life so that I would not do evil. The voices said, *Because of the health of your body, do you want to lose that of your soul?* For forty years He has accompanied me. That Christ I see so [det] is God. He always wants me to see what He did and suffered for us, and He [det] . . . and for this reason He is always crucified. When I receive the . . . [det] for half an hour I was able to adore Him within myself, and later, there, where [det]. . . . What they speak about within me, whether it is good or bad, fearing it . . . [det] enchanted, I went to the choir and was there an hour and a half [det] . . . the thing. I said that the half-hour I always give to my father Saint Francis should go to . . . [det] . . . finished the hour and a half. I did nothing the entire time but give thanks for having received Him. They gave me to understand afterward that try as I might, I could not conceive or invent what happens here within me. It is not mine, but only when God wishes does it come upon me. I usually think, well, sometimes, my head invents these things, but I now realize that if it does not come from the hand of God, I cannot even recollect. I wanted to know how old I was. From what he told me, it seemed that my angel spoke to me, saying he had been with me for forty years. When I asked this time, they answered that I was forty. When I made my own reckoning, it seemed so.

Wednesday while in a state of recollection, I told my guardian angel that I was sorry and deeply embarrassed to tell this to anyone, because they would take me for someone I am not. He said that when I tell it to the one writing this, I should say that I say this for the honor and glory of God. I should give many thanks to God and place my mouth on the ground.

I say this for the honor and glory of God. This afternoon I went to the choir and saw the Christ figure I usually see, beside me. I said I adored Him in the name of my Lord Jesus Christ. He told me that yes, He had come for the sinners and was always calling out, "Come to me," because He could not forget about them. In those wounds He held all those who came to Him with a clear heart and no ulterior motive. Finding God should not be done with other things in mind or be feigned. The angel said that when God permitted them to sin it was because of His secret judgment. I should give many thanks to God for the peace and quietude in my soul.

While I was prostrate and adoring God, who was before me, they turned my gaze toward one side of the choir where I saw a nun seated on a bench. She had died more than fifteen years ago. So much time had gone by that I was shocked, and asked, "What was that?" They said that death had caught her before she could do penance, and it had caught her in her distractions. In order to go to heaven, one had to be purified like gold, and the soul should be like a crystal. (53v) Here, if they order them to stop this or that, they do not, in this way, say there are many failings present in this community. For each one, they said, "What is this?" and still did nothing to mend their ways. They did not obey, they did not finish the point lace or the beds . . . [det] . . . or anything. They listed them one by one. Lay persons did not have as much to do. This dead woman sat on a bench next to the door of the choir with a small light glowing in front of her. She had the face she had had while living, and her veil was lowered over her face, just as they do for those who are buried. Her eyes were lowered; her hands, like death, just bones; her habit, as though disinterred. I was lying prostrate when they turned my gaze toward the altar. For more than half an hour, I watched as she covered her hand with the edge of her sleeve and with her free hand pulled the other sleeve over the other hand. I asked my guardian angel why they brought me this vision. He said, *so that you can commend her spirit to God,* which I should do. Even though I felt very afraid, it was not like other occasions when I [det] with God. With this vision I forgot many things. [det] I adore my Lord Jesus Christ. The fears I have [det] and God allows that because of His secret judgments. If they came [det] . . . saw me, it would be the second time . . .

Friday, the feast day of Saint Lucas,[160] they had asked me [det] to commend a matter to God. I took it upon myself, and then . . . [det] . . . do so. After I received communion, I gave thanks and made foolish remarks to Him. One thing I said was that He was a lamb. I then thought, "What did I just say?" He said to me, *Yes, I am a lamb. The night of the Last Supper when I instituted the Most Holy Sacrament.* . . . I do not remember how He joined the lamb to the Most Holy Sacrament, but He said when He instituted it, He received communion first and then gave it to the apostles, just as priests do now. *When I washed their feet and then dried them with a piece of cloth, the stains of their sins remained on the cloth, which signified confession. Knowing well what Judas had planned, I could easily not have washed his feet, nor given him communion as I did for the others. To him, though, I only gave bread, and did this in order to prevent him being dishonored. First and foremost, one must guard the honor of God and say what needs to be remedied. It must be done in such a way that it cannot be understood who said it or where it came from.* This He told me apropos of what had been commended to me.

Saturday, I do not know how to say this, but today I owe ten reales.[161] I had some sleeves and a scapulary, which they asked me to use to pay off the account. I forgot to carry out my duties and slept without asking permission. I went to pray, and the voices said, *How could I give that without asking permission? Is that mine, or am I mine? When I took my vows, what did I promise with so much determination? I always say I only want to do His will and that I am not mine.* I said, "Yes, the enemy can come to me with this." He said, *The enemy makes you forget what your duty is. Nothing should be done without asking permission. Do not give or receive anything, as insignificant as it may seem. Mortify yourself and go ask for permission.*

They told me while I was praying that anguish and tribulation were necessary to reach humility and perfection. I was looking at the Christ with fear; wherever (54r) I turned I saw Him closing the eyes . . . [det] . . . She asked what I had come to pray for. To set an example for us, He had experienced anguish and the agonies of death, and had sweat blood in great agony from head to toe . . . [det] since we no longer have to endure that. It is necessary to endure tribulation and anguish with great humility. That beast can do nothing if God does not allow it to and the beast cannot understand the interior . . .

[entire paragraph deteriorated]

Wednesday, I received the Lord. After more than half an hour of praying, I thanked Him for allowing me to receive Him. They told me to look at the grandeur and authority He had in heaven and on earth. With just one glance, He could do or undo anything. *Mind what you have received.* Those who received Him in grace, received Him as He was in heaven and in the Holy Sacrament. For those who did not, it was just like when an acequia is clogged with mud: the sacrament cannot pass, and that is what happens to those in mortal sin. In order not to commit mortal sin they should always be vigilant. Our Lord told His apostles to be on guard and pray so they would not fall into temptation. I should be thankful for having received Him, love my neighbors, and want for them what I would want for myself. His Majesty told His apostles, "Love your neighbor as yourself." Love Him above all other things and your neighbor above yourself. There should be much silence, and I should be very humble. When they tell me these things it is not without reason. I tend to go into a room. I always find it, which is my misfortune, and I usually say, "This room is an annoyance. Is there no one to clean it?" They tell me to go clean it and to scrub away the filthy vapors, so they do not smell bad. Another time, when I refused to go into this room, they told me I should go where there are thorns.

It happened that a nun suddenly became ill, and I commended her to God. They told me that God sent the illness to remind her that she needed to mend her ways. He implied that if no amends were made, He would cut . . .

(54v) Wednesday afternoon they told me [det] that if the señora abbess ordered me to jump off a wall, I should be willing [det] . . . and more. No one would order this. If they ordered me to do something [det] and then ordered me to do one thing, and then another, I should be so resigned that I have no will whatsoever. Later, I asked our Lord to help calm someone in anguish. I told Him to give her the knowledge to mend her ways herself so she would not be damned and go to hell. Hurriedly, they responded, *Hell, no,* . . . [det] . . . *not to see God forever.*

[entire paragraph deteriorated]

It was very dangerous to neglect what is most important until the hour of death, because by then nothing can be done. If a king did not live as he should and a poor person did, the poor person would live in heaven as a king. Much was said about how important it is to try to develop a friendship with God, and what one heartfelt tear cried in front of Him is worth. Intention is what saves. Obey the Ten Commandments, listing them one by one. They are summed up in two: to love God and my neighbor. Could I do even one of these things that happen to me? If God left me, I would sin more than before. The more gifts one receives, the humbler one should be. I should receive them like the spittle others drool. As for the knowledge I have, when I go to Him, I say, "I come before my master."

Thursday during mass my sins spun around my head. I praised and blessed the Holy Trinity and felt the divine presence with me. They said I should confess all that I had gossiped about others from the time I had the use of reason, and the names I called them. I said that I had already confessed this. They said I should confess a little more. As I was unable to remember how many, I should denounce myself for what I had done from the time I had gained reason. I contradicted them, saying I had already confessed them. They said, *Do you not remember "Round Foot"?*[162] *That one you saw,* they added, *when you made your general confession?* They scratched my heart with that small bone, which remained stuck to it, and I was not totally cleansed because I hesitated[163] to tell these things to the priest.

55r) [first two paragraphs deteriorated]

While in a state of recollection between eight and eleven at night,[164] I . . . [det] of a cleric who had died more than a year ago and is now buried here. I tried . . . [det] what I could and stayed there without entering a state of recollection because God willed it, although I can do no more unless He wills it. Because it was the night of our father Saint Francis, many nuns remained in the choir practicing their devotions. They stayed until almost one. I saw they had left and gone to sleep and I placed myself in front of a column. It must have been around three—it must have been, for that night there was no clock—and while I was recollecting, I heard something call out twice from the grille. Although I was frightened I thought it might be some cat. I was praising God and commending myself to my father Saint Francis, and recollecting with my eyes closed when I saw the clergyman in his earthly form. It looked as if he walked a few steps away from his grave and then returned to it. He said that for the love of God I should pray for him. With the Holy Spirit, I said, "How did you come like that from purgatory?" He said, "If I came the way I really am, you would die from fright. Give many thanks to God so that He will save me." In the morning, while I was prostrate and about to receive communion, he returned and said, "In the name of the entrails of my Lord Jesus Christ, commend me to God." I offered part of my communion for him and everything I did throughout the day. I did not remember who that cleric was.

Friday, the day of our father Saint Francis,[165] I worked hard all day. They told me that this path was full of hard work, one always had to strive hard, and that I was very thin. I should leave things well enough alone because everyone was content, but I was always feeling distressed, even since I started coming to pray, and many other things along these lines. I knew it was the devil.

(55v) [two paragraphs deteriorated]

Saturday afternoon while I was praying the rosary the voices said, *I am God who came down from the heavens to suffer. For my part, I did not need to. My mother, although she was the Mother of God, suffered terribly. All those now in glory traveled the same path. I spent my whole life in terrible travail, anguish, and sorrow. Have you not heard the expression, "the labors of Christ"? Rest assured that whoever seeks Him in earnest will not fail. When someone loves, the more they suffer, they more they love.*

Later, while in the choir I saw a crucified Christ in front of the ciborium. They told me to look at Him, see what He had suffered, what pain He must have felt while hanging from those nails for three hours. Those sinews were so contracted, and He was unable to move or feel relief in any way. If He wanted to lift up His head the thorns pushed deeper into His head. *Look at those hands, how they tore bearing all the weight of His body. Look at how one foot was over the other, also bearing the weight of that body. What pain that must have been, what anguish, what sweat, what agony that must have been. Look, if any man here stood for an hour with one foot over the other, would he be able to stand it? He would fall here and there.* What did I feel when I placed my body in a crosslike position? His Majesty spent three full hours in that terrible condition.

(56r) [three paragraphs deteriorated]

This flesh, this is what it meant to dig up the well.[166] Look at how they carved one [det] below. Everything is like that. There always had to be temptations. Did I not know that . . . [det] . . . the devil had wanted me and had gone to try to tempt Him. To be free [det] during the work period, later, when he distributed the water from the well, leading me to understand that it would be something else. On this occasion, God said a great deal about imitating His Son, about poverty, obedience, humility, meekness, and all the other virtues, and how I should imitate Him, thanking Him for all the benefits.

Sunday, as soon as I prostrated myself they told me He wanted to be my teacher. I said, "I believe in God the Father. I know nothing about a teacher. I come to praise God."

On Sunday, the first day of Advent, while in a state of recollection I saw a horrible stairway with four faces. They led me to understand that those are the four parts of the world. The stairway was so high it reached heaven. It was very wide at the bottom. The stairs were wide and solid but became increasingly narrow at the top. There, much higher than the stairway, at the very top, I do not know exactly how to describe it, I caught a glimpse of the Lord watching over everything. They told me to prostrate myself at the feet of my Lord Jesus Christ. From there, that Lord could hear what I told Him with my heart. What king, or lord of the world, could hear me from such a distance or from a city so far away? I said, "I believe in God, the Father almighty." He said, *I am almighty, everything is manifest to me, everything is done by my will, I see everything. When someone dies suddenly, I see it, and it is my will.* They said a lot about this. Then, I saw, at the foot of the stairway, there, at all four parts, a great multitude of people of all nations and another great multitude surrounding them . . . It is.

(56v) [first paragraph deteriorated]

I see a crucified Christ where the Most Holy Sacrament is. I said, "If you are the true God, I adore you." Then they told me that my Lord Jesus Christ had been naked when He went to the cross. He always went with His head uncovered and His garment was only a poor tunic. I should imitate Him. He had given me understanding so that I would know Him, memory to remember Him, and free will to love Him. I had nothing to fear, so long as these faculties were occupied with God.

Tuesday, they told me that I would work in the kitchen next year. I had looked around for the book about Christ's travails so they could read it to me, but realizing I would have little time for it, I told the Lord I wanted to return it to its owner. While I was in a state of recollection later they asked why I wanted a book. Had they not taught me about Christ's travails when I saw Him tied to the column, and with a crown of thorns and nailed to the cross? These were Christ's travails. Did I not feel great compassion when I saw Him that way? In the ciborium I could see Him from head to toe with His hands tied behind His back. He was naked, but for that piece of white cloth, which is how they tend to paint Him. They said that when His Father sent Him, He obeyed at once. Why did He need to do that? He only did it to redeem us and set an example for us. I dreaded one year of work when He had had thirty-three years of infinite travail. They said a lot here. Then they said what they had said the day before about the faculties of the soul. With memory I should remember Him, His Passion, and His gifts. With understanding I should know Him and know His gifts. With free will I should love Him, for without it, how could I? Here they spoke a great deal about these faculties, and that . . .

(57r) [det] One should perceive that. Did they not teach me or give it to me, with no effort on my part? After I had received communion, I spent an hour giving thanks. I asked my Lord for permission to prepare food for a sick woman. They said when I went, I should think about what I had received and thank Him. The body should work, for He always worked. Whenever I work standing up, I should think about when they had Him standing and how much He suffered. When I work sitting down, I should think about when they sat Him on that little bench. I do not know what this is, but God does. I do not know why, but when I was eating later I started thinking about whoever was in hell and whether they made sure to feed them. I threw myself to the floor and thanked God. They quickly said to me that this is what it means to speak with God, and I did not have my eyes closed. I told God a lot of foolish things, that here was my head, my hands, my shoulders for Him to burden as He wished.

Friday, in anguish over the fears I tend to feel, I said, "Lord, if I am yours, who comes to me? Why do I feel such affliction?" The voices said, *Because you are, and because you did not believe that it was He.* I said, "Because I am such a sinner I deserve nothing but hell." He asked me whether I believe in the creed. I said, "Yes." He said, *Does it not say, "I believe in God, the Father almighty"?* Then he repeated the whole creed. When the creed says, "I believe in the living God, to whom the Virgin gave birth," that was He. Did I not realize that just by looking, He could pardon many . . .

(57v) [paragraph deteriorated]

That I doubt that His Majesty communicated with His creatures and would pardon sins. One drop of His blood is enough for everyone . . . [det] . . . Who, but He, could get me away from that love? When the mass had ended, I said, "My Lord, when can I be rid of this lost, and annoying love?"[167] I know it is the truth. When I was looking at them, and when I saw them, I would say to myself, "What do I want with these unfeeling people?"[168] I could not free myself from this, and it seemed impossible to me. I also referred to the other two benefits, which had also seemed impossible to go without and that He should give them to me. Who could get me away from these things, if not His almighty hand? That beast will carry me from ravine to ravine and cast me off the cliff. Even though I went about so absentmindedly, His hand never let go of me. Even though sinners offend Him, they know who will return to a state of grace, or will be helped by His mother's intercession. He never abandons them, just those who know they will not return. Who makes me feel fearful to receive communion when the community goes? I said that I could not receive communion now but would prepare myself. What the priest asked me when I made my general confession was whether I had hidden any sins in the other confessions I had made. Who would have freed me, had it not been for Him? It was the first time I had heard such a thing being said. I did not even know sins could be concealed. I had always sought out the strictest confessor before. I should be very thankful to Him, because I always commended myself to Him and His mother. That is why he comes and helps me remember that when I was a child, I was always looking at the images of our Lady. I would say, "Would that I could be the little black servant of the Mother of God." Later, when I was working around the con[vent] . . . [det]

(58r) [deteriorated]

[det] because I had provided all the means necessary to save them and someone who would teach them, and still they refused to mend their ways. I said, "If you are God, and I come in search of God, why do you let me feel such affliction?" He said, *There always has to be temptation.* I asked if it was His will for me to spend this year in the kitchen. He said that there I would see what the enemy had in store for me. Since the day of the Transfiguration, they told me that God would separate Himself from me.[169] He said, *This is what they told you then.* I said, "The enemy must have told me that." He said, *He does not know what will be, save what God wants him to know.* I wanted to think about one stage of the Passion. Twice He answered no. I should think of Him as a shepherd of souls who had cost Him a lot. I am not recounting this exactly the way it happened, but only telling it in little bits that I recalled long afterward. Later in the afternoon I saw Him again, in the same way, with a flock of the whitest little sheep. He held a staff in His right hand and tended them. They told me to look at how He was a shepherd.

They called me to the door to show me a young girl who seeks shelter in this house. She has been requesting this for several days, but I did not find anyone to discuss the matter with. I then went to pray, and the voices asked why I needed to go out and speak with anyone when I had Him to speak with. Whoever had Him to talk with did not need to deal with children. What did I need them for? Had he not provided me with all that I needed? I should only speak with my guardian angel, nothing more.

Sunday morning I went to the choir, and when I prostrated myself I saw a stairway that reached to heaven. They told me it was extremely difficult to climb up. I saw that two people . . .

(58v) [paragraph deteriorated]

. . . Sunday, in the evening while I was . . . [det] . . . to the Lord. He told me that He wanted me to see those nuns in order [det] . . . how it was purifying. The nuns were being purified so that when they finally go to heaven they will then go fully cleansed. Once there, there is nothing but enjoyment. On behalf of these souls, I should offer to their eternal Father what He suffered when they placed that crown of thorns on Him: what He felt when they stripped Him naked to whip His body in front of the entire village in shame; what He suffered after being flogged, when He carried that cross on His shoulders through those streets of Jerusalem; and the falls He had taken with it; and the terrible weariness with which He bore all this. On behalf of those souls, I should offer all this to His eternal Father, for that is what the souls had asked me.

Tuesday I adored my Lord Jesus Christ, while lying prostrate at His feet. I saw Him there from head to foot. I said, "How can I see all this when I am lying prostrate?" He said, *Lying at my feet you can see everything through me, even hell.* I do not know how it happened, but after He said this they shifted the image and carried me through some pitch-dark ravines, and placed me in a profound darkness. There I saw an enormous pillory[170] and a great throng of condemned souls held by their throats, some face up, others face down. They explained that they were there because they had not aided the dying with every kindness.[171] On the other side were innumerable souls, chained in gangs with iron chains through the fleshy part of their limbs, all twisting and turning in great confusion. First these, and then the others, were viciously flogged. They said that these were the lovers of a luxurious life who did not fear God's judgment. Others were lying on the floor and were . . .

(59r-v and 60r) [deteriorated]

(60r) [last paragraph] He says, *This is how you should receive me.* On this occasion, I felt very afraid, [det] a very large figure, in such a sorry state with His hair falling out. I said, [det] "be the Most Holy Sacrament. On the other hand, you are my God. Here are the [det] of my heart, to stanch the wounds and my heart, so that you might rest in it."

I leave much unwritten because I can do no more. Fifty-seven folios are written.

Notes

1. "Each creed said was the equivalent to an instant, each moment, each step, each hour, each day," in other words, all the time (*Diccionario de autoridades* [henceforth *DA*], 2:653).

2. The terms *recogerse* and *recoger* have a variety of meanings, but here Ursula refers to the act of spiritual contemplation or meditation. The term recollection is the closest English equivalent because it shares the same Latin root. For a fuller explanation, see van Deusen, *Between*, 9.

3. 6 January.

4. This is a reference to Satan and is used throughout the text.

5. The alb is the vestment priests wore to say mass (*DA*, 1:161).

6. "So-and-so" is a translation of the term *fulana*, often used to avoid naming someone.

7. San Cristóbal Mountain is visible from the Convent of Santa Clara.

8. Viceroy Luis Enríquez de Guzman, the Count of Alba de Aliste (1655–61) reported that in November 1655, Lima experienced a number of serious tremors (Hanke, *Los Virreyes españoles*, IV:90).

9. *Generación* can also mean "progeny" or the word "generation" as we know it.

10. Ana de San Joseph was elected interim *vicaria* (assistant abbess) in 1650, while the conventual election was pending. See "Auto Arzobispal," 1650, AAL, SC, 9:6. The word *caridad* can be translated as "love," "compassion," or "charity" (*DA*, 2:309).

11. Doña Apolonia de Moya appears in two documents related to a dispute over the sale of her cell. It is probably the same person (see "Autos que sigue Francisca de Aliaga . . . contra Apolonia de Moya," 1639–44, AAL, SC, 6:41; and "Autos que sigue Francisca de Aliaga," 1642–44, AAL, SC, 7:20).

12. Another reference to the devil.

13. Mariana de Machuca spent thirty years as a nun in Santa Clara and died on 8 September 1630 (Córdova y Salinas, *Crónica*, 904).

14. I was unable to understand what *la sid* referred to in the document.

15. 16 January.

16. The rosary was divided into three groups of ten beads each.

17. Francisco de Saldaña was a wealthy Portuguese man who donated his estate to the foundation of the Convent of Santa Clara. The four foundresses were Justina de Guevara, Ana de Illescas, Barbola (or Bartola) de la Vega, and Isabel de la Fuente.

18. In 1620, Ana Delgado (in the convent, called Ana de Jesús), an aristocratic married woman, decided, along with two of her daughters to become nuns. Popular among the community, she was known for her humility, ecstatic raptures, and rigorous disciplines. After fifteen years as a clarisa, she died on 29 November 1635 (Córdova y Salinas, *Crónica*, 900).

19. 20 January.

20. Literally, the room where the Last Supper took place, but it is understood to represent the scene of the Last Supper (*DA*, 2:262).

21. When a novice took her vows and became a nun, she became a bride of Christ.

22. Support for the belief in Mary's immaculate conception (without original sin) was strong among the Lima population in general, and among the Franciscans in particular. In December 1662, colorful celebrations and processions were held (Muguburu, *Chronicle*, 40, 74–76).

23. Another reference to the devil.

24. This could mean that the altar had been moved or restored at some point during the convent's expansion.

25. It is not clear whether her "mother" is her biological mother or a mother figure.

26. Although a more common translation of *buena voluntad* is "willingly," Ursula may also mean, "those who profess in the true Religion celebrate festivities, not in an indecorous or lascivious manner, but in true *consciousness*" (*DA*, 2:474).

27. This painting, in a deteriorated condition, is still in the convent.

28. This third-person reference is confusing. It may be a reference to the Trinity or the two thieves who died on the cross at Calvary with Christ.

29. *Ceñirse* means to moderate or reform one's behavior, to cut back on household expenditures, games, and other prodigality (*DA*, 2:273). In the modern sense, it signifies to wear a girdle. She could have meant both.

30. This implies an untoward relation with a nun, but the sentence is incomplete.

31. The first Sunday after Easter.

32. A part of the rosary.

33. 4 May.

34. A bronze trumpet.

35. *Licenciate* refers to a title of someone who has received a degree from a Spanish university.

36. Pedro Urraca of the Mercedarian order died on Tuesday, 7 August 1657 (Muguburu, *Chronicle*, 44).

37. Serrano was an Augustinian and, until his death, one of her confessors.

38. *Pelotero* has various connotations. It can mean a disturbance or commotion, or someone who makes a ball out of skin. It can also be someone who presides over a game, a referee (*DA*, 5:198). "*Traher al pelotero*" is a phrase that means to delude people relentlessly into having false hopes, without leaving them in peace.

39. Her biographer reports that this occurred in 1659 (AFL, "Vida," 594v).

40. I believe that by saying "a" lord, rather than "the" Lord, Ursula is hesitant to suggest that it is actually Christ.

41. 4 May.

42. The word *custodia* can be the monstrance, as well as the care and vigilance one exercises toward something important (*DA*, 2:712).

43. 3 May.

44. 24 June.

45. The nuns were interested in adding adornments to their habits.

46. The term *perseverancia* can mean "perseverance" or maintaining a state of grace until death or glory is reached (*DA*, 5:233–34).

47. Here they refer to the nuns' alterations to their garments.

48. It is unclear whether Ursula's companion was a cell-mate, or someone she worked with, but she was most likely a nun.

49. *Alforjas* were large bags made of coarse woolen cloth that were carried over one shoulder. One part hung down the front of the body, the other over the back (*DA*, 1:200).

50. I use the word "bound" here because it repeats the usage of the term *remachar* used earlier in the paragraph. It can also mean to render stationary, to keep, hold, or freeze in place.

51. 28 December.

52. Every three years the Convent of Santa Clara elected or reelected an abbess. The election of 1656 was particularly contentious and may be the one Ursula refers to in her diary. In 1656, Magdalena de Vélez Roldán was chosen and began her tenure the following year (see AAL, SC, 9:149, 1656).

53. The terms *prelada* and *abadesa* were synonymous.

54. 20 January.

55. By committing mortal sin, he "condemned" himself to hell.

56. 1 November.

57. By "behaving as though he were married," the priest broke his vows of celibacy.

58. 23 January.

59. Her biographer's account says, "*Hincarnatus est de Spiritu Santo, ex Maria Virgine*" (AFL, "Vida," 591r).

60. His saint's day was 29 January.

61. The eight-day period following a religious festivity.

62. The ascension is 15 August.

63. This might have been in 1615 when the Dutch attacked the port of Callao.

64. A reading with the names and stories of saints martyred during the Roman period who pertain to that given day.

65. This refers to Christ taking on human form. Only the body (the flesh) died, not Christ.

66. There is an abrupt transition from folio 25r to 25v, which does not flow.

67. The *presidenta* (president) served until elections were held.

68. She was either older or more senior.

69. *Aturdida* can also refer to someone who has received a blow to the head and is now confused or mentally impaired (Covarrubias, *Tesoro*, 166–67).

70. A deferential way of addressing any important person; though here, Ursula is speaking to God.

71. The day of Saint Martin (of Tours) was 11 November.

72. 13 November.

73. Saint Catherine of Alexandria, 25 November.

74. The convent was dedicated to the Immaculate Virgin of the Rock of France (La Inmaculada de la Peña de Francia) and maintained a chapel to her in the convent.

75. 30 November.

76. María de Santo Domingo talked about the Eucharist as a winepress of the blood of Christ (Giles, *Book*, 105).

77. I have interpreted *soldados* as "soldiers of Christ" or fellow Christians (*DA*, 6:139).

78. The scribe is writing and switches voices in the sentence.

79. The nuns were making one chapel a site of special devotions.

80. Vestment worn over the alb, which covers the front and back of the body, and has wide, open sleeves.

81. The biographical account says his name was Juan Valero, rector of the third order and censor of the Inquisition. He had died suddenly in the Colegio de Nuestra Señora de Guadalupe (AFL, "Vida," 594r). See also Córdova y Salinas, *Crónica*, 1013, which cites him as a preacher.

82. Magdalena Vélez Roldán served as abbess a number of times, including from 1645 to 1650; as interim president in 1650; and again from 1656 to 1658. Ursula is probably referring to the contentious election of 1656.

83. The Feast of the Visitation was 31 May.

84. This phrase appears as marginalia in the text. The designated scribe, a nun, begins writing and the handwriting clearly changes.

85. This nun provided funds to help purchase Ursula's freedom.

86. This vision corresponds to the three crosses in the background of the two portraits of Ursula.

87. Her biographer claimed that the friar was her guardian angel (AFL, "Vida," 589v).

88. Many individuals were buried in the habit of a member of a regular order. Male and female religious were often "envisioned" wearing religious habits in heaven.

89. The bed had a curtain around it. This was probably a real incident, but what motivated the woman to behave like this is not made clear.

90. The scribe switches pronoun referents in this sentence.

91. The phrase literally means, "if someone had to take a ring."

92. A chapel in the convent.

93. Ten days before don Luis Enríquez de Guzmán, the Count of Alba de Aliste y Villaflor (1655–61) assumed his post as Viceroy in Peru, Araucanian natives in Chile revolted on 14 February, 1655, causing considerable damage. On the revolt, see Vargas Ugarte, *Historia del Perú: Virreinato (Siglo XVII)*, 295–96; Hanke, *Los Virreyes españoles*, 4:98–99. See also Mugaburu, *Chronicle*, 37, which mentions that on 26 November 1655, the new governor, Pedro Porter de Casanare, and troops left for Chile.

94. 1 and 2 August.

95. Literally, the grapes left behind because they are too small.

96. 7 August.

97. Here the voice switches from the third to first person.

98. This is probably a reference to her guardian angel.

99. 13 June.

100. 25 July.

101. By encouraging her to take confession.

102. 26 July.

103. A rochet is a vestment, like a closed surplice with tight-fitting sleeves.

104. Ursula is referring to the 1655 Araucanian uprising.

105. Ursula's biographer refers to a fire in one chapel that occurred sometime between 1645 and 1647, before she decided to take her vows as a donada. Ursula interpreted it as a sign of divine disapproval. It is unclear whether the two fires were one and the same.

106. Here the voice switches to the first person.

107. This is a reference to the nine rays of light, which in groups of three form a crown in pictures of the Christ child. They represent the universal power over creation.

108. Isabel of Bourbon (1602–44), queen of Spain.

109. The standard definition is "godmother," but it can also refer to a protectress, or sponsor, which is more likely in Ursula's case (*DA*, 4:451).

110. 9 August.

111. 10 August.

112. (Vespers) 10 August.

113. 11 August.

114. (Vespers) 14 August.

115. 15 August.

116. 17 August.

117. Here the handwriting changes. Perhaps yet another scribe is writing for her.

118. 20 August.

119. Here Ursula's voice changes to the third person.

120. Here Ursula has reverted to the first-person voice.

121. The second person in charge, just below the abbess. She also is in charge of the choir.

122. *Mortificación* can mean the restraint of desires and passions by means of physical discipline; it may also mean that the abbess came to chastise them (*DA*, 4:612).

123. *Desengaños* also means the recognition of errors committed and an end to delusion (*DA*, 3:162).

124. Here the handwriting changes again and resembles the script of folios 8r–29v.

125. 24 August.

126. The first canonical hour at 6 AM.

127. Apparently, the newly elected abbess was crowned during an inaugural ceremony.

128. *Dar pena*, means to heed, have strong feelings, anguish, or feel great affliction (*DA*, 3:199).

129. As a metonym, the color purple refers to "royal dignity" reserved for kings and cardinals. Because the color purple came from the dye of a rare type of mollusk and was difficult to obtain, it was reserved for the robes of kings and emperors (*DA*, 5:442). I would like to thank Meredith Dodge for pointing this out to me.

130. The voice probably refers to the Bethlehem Chapel in the convent. Ballanos was where the slaves washed clothes.

131. Here again she refers to the scribe or secretary.

132. 28 August.

133. *Llaga*: an open wound, an ulcer; something that causes pain. Metaphorically it signifies any harm or misfortune that causes pain, suffering and affliction (*DA*, 4:418).

134. Nuns in charge of supplies.

135. A *patacon* is a coin made out of one ounce of silver.

136. Although Christ does not have a specific feast day in the Western Catholic tradition, this translation makes sense within the narrative context. However, another possible translation might be, "given to a nun for her feast day." I leave it to the reader to decide.

137. The Franciscan Rule regulated the religious life of each member of the order, including the Clares. The Rule included the observance of the vows of obedience, chastity, and poverty and was divided into twelve chapters with twenty-four precepts. I thank Meredith Dodge for clarifying this point for me.

138. 8 September.

139. This may have been Rafaela de Esquivel, whose name appears on a report issued by the abbess, doña Justina de Guevara, in 1616 ("Autos seguidos," AAL, SC, 1:1). Rafaela, however, does not appear on a 1633 list of the nuns ("Relación de religiosas y donadas," 1633, AAL, SC, 4:42).

140. 8 December, the feast of the Immaculate Conception.

141. *Ensalmar* literally means to cure by repeating verses from the Psalms or prayers (*DA*, 3:489).

142. 4 October.

143. The girl probably waited at the *torno*, or revolving door, where goods were received by and sent from the convent.

144. She promised all that she did in the name of the suffering of Christ while He wore the crown of thorns.

145. This is similar to a passage in Teresa of Avila (*Vida*, ch. 15).

146. *Voladora*: that which flies, or vanishes swiftly, or someone who is unsettled, distracted, or crazy (*DA*, 6:513).

147. *Lugar* can mean "motive, cause or reason for something" (*DA*, 4:437).

148. Covarrubias, *Tesoro*, 897, says it is a headdress or hood that covers the face and when wrapped around, the mouth. It could also be a figurative way of saying they were trying to cover something up. See also RAE, *Diccionario*, 2:1736; *DA*, 3:393.

149. Ursula is referring to a foolish and insufferable person (*DA*, 1:656).

150. A bed with a hurtle made out of sticks. She is probably making a play on the two meanings of the word: barbecue and bed. See the painting in Vovelle, *Les âmes*.

151. Either they were lazy and slept a lot or they fell prey to their lascivious natures.

152. Here Ursula is comparing herself to saliva, something exceedingly minimal.

153. It is hard to get the true sense because of the incomplete text.

154. Here they refer to Isabel of Bourbon.

155. 23 July.

156. *Garrapata* means both "tick," and "useless horse." The first definition seems more likely. *DA*, 4:28, also used the term to describe someone with a very small body, a homunculus.

157. Metaphorically, *blanco* signifies the object toward which we direct our affections, or the end toward which a person directs his actions or thoughts (*DA*, 1:615).

158. Ursula may be implying that some donadas took their vows involuntarily or that they did not take them seriously and subsequently left the convent.

159. A *corral* is usually the place at the back of the house (and in this case, probably the cell) where chickens or wood are kept.

160. 18 October.

161. A real is one-eighth of a peso.

162. This was probably a mean name Ursula called someone.

163. *Escrupulear* is the same as *escrupulizar*, to have doubts about something, and as a result, to feel restless, hesitant, and dispirited (*DA*, 2:575).

164. *Prima de noche* refers to this period of time (*DA*, 5:376).

165. 4 October.

166. *Poso*: the liquid that remains at the bottom of a vessel. It also means quietude, repose, and tranquility (*DA*, 5:334).

167. Here, Ursula may be alluding to an unrequited love for a woman.

168. Literally, "wooden bodies."

169. The Transfiguration is 6 August.

170. An instrument meant to hold prisoners by the throat or leg. Metaphorically this term signifies torment, vexation, and the imprisonment of the soul, senses, and faculties. It can also mean a trap or net that ensnares someone (*DA*, 2:275–76). Ursula's vision may be similar to the structure that appears in the painting of hell, attributed to the artist Tadeo Escalante, located in Huaro. See Mesa and Gisbert, *Historia de la pintura cuzqueña*. I would like to extend my gratitude to Javier Flores for drawing my attention to this.

171. To say "Jesus" many times helps someone to die a good death (*el buen morir*) (*DA*, 4:320).

PART III
Selections from Ursula's Diary

(8r) en nombre de la santisima trinidad no se si es alguna cosa de aquel engañador/ desde el año nuebo que fue el biernes pasado asta oy que es bispera de rreyes todas las mas/ Beses que boy a la orasion biene a mi un frayle fransisco que jamas conosi que es aquel que se echo/ de la pared dios sabe si es berdad lo que es biene pidiendo que le encomiende mucho a dios que esta en/ grandisimas penas que le ofresca al eterno padre por el aquellas terribles agonias que padesio/ nuestro señor jesuchristo aquellas tres oras que estubo pendiente de la crus asta que espiro eso di-/ je entre mi dios tubo tantas agonias dijo en cuanto honbre las tubo terriBles el para si/ no lo abia menester mas por nuestro Remedio y cuando se encomendo en manos del padre/ tanbien lo yso por enseñarnos y darnos exenplo que el por si no lo abia menester que era/ dios entre otras cosas que digo fue que muchos Relijiosos y Religiosas estaban en las Reli-/ jiones como estatuas solamente con el cuerpo que si estaban en el ofisio dibino era sin/ considerasion ni debosion ni atension si en la misa dibertidos y sin la prepa-/ rasion que se Requiere y no lo se desir como alli paso finalmente dijo que por esto/ se pasaban terriBles penas y que el desde el instante que cayo abia echo muchos/ actos de contrision y que no abia echo aquello con mala yntension y que el padesia las/ mesmas penas del infierno y me enseñaba un paredonsillo que me llegaria a mi/ al pecho y desia que solo aquello estaba de por medio entre el y el infierno mas que las/ llamas de alla eran las que le atormentaban yo le dije a dios que si aquello era suyo/ yo ofresia por el todo todo cuanto podia y todas las estasiones y ynduljensias que ga-/ nase - bolbio oy bispera de los Reyes a darme las grasias disiendo que dios me lo pa-/ gase y me diese los descansos que yo le abia dado/ dije que si dios a Resebido aquello poquito/ Dijo que si que dios Resebia lo que se asia por bibos y muertos y que yo continuase el enco-/ mendarle y ganarle ynduljensias porque padesia de pies a cabesa y que en la corona tenia/ particular tormento porque no la traya como lo ordeno nuestro padre san francisco/ esto ba a pedasitos como se acordado tanbien dijo que los credos se asian años/ en aquellas penas como no tengo por siertas estas cosas no las digo luego que me suseden/ asta que persebera tanto mas a de dies dias que me persigue este flayre [sic] todas las beses/ que me rrecojo y sienpre lo e bisto en pie las manos puestas y de pies a cabesa en lla-/ mas de fuego como me pedia con tanto aynco dije que que era yo y que balia para aquello/ dijo que en cualquiera que dios ponia sus dones que muchos Reyes y monarcas enpera-/ dores y potentados estaban en el ynfierno y Relijiosos y Relijiosas/ como lo estubiera el sino fuera por la gran misericordia de dios y otras cosas/ que se me an olbidado - - -

dia de los Reyes estando rrecogida despues de aber comulgado no se si son en-

/ bustes de paton o de mi cabesa se me bino a la memoria maria bran que era una/ negra del conbento que a mas de catorse años que murio supita [*sic*] - una de las cosas/ mas olbidadas que abia para mi en este mundo y juntamente la bi bestida/ de una alba albisima señida con un singulo corto con unas Riquisimas/ borlas tanbien el alva estaba mui bien guarnesida una corona de flores/ en la cabesa tan bien se me yso que bi de palma aunque tenia su cara/ estaba mui linda y un negro lustrosisimo dije yo que como una negra tan/ buena que no era ladrona ni enbustera abia estado tanto tienpo dijo que a-/ bia estado por su condision y que alli se penaba el sueño fuera de tienpo y la co-/ mida y que aunque abia estado tanto tienpo abian sido lebes las penas y que daba/ muchas gracias a dios que con su dibina probidensia la abia sacado de su tieRa/ y traydo la por caminos tan dificultosos y barrancosos para que fuese cristiana/ y se salbase dije que si las negras yban asi al cielo dijo que como fuesen agradesidas (8v) y tubieson atension a los benefisios y le diesen grasias por ellos las salbaba/ por su gran misericordia yo cuando ago estas preguntas no las ago porque/ quiero sino que asi como beo y me ablan sin que quiera asi me asen ablar sin/ querer yo e menester que me encomienden mucho a dios todo esto me sirbe de tormen-/ to tanbien me dijo que yo diese grasias a dios por los benefisios que le abia echo aunque/ me paresio que se yba al cielo no lo supe de sierto - -

yo traygo una tentasion terrible y es que cuando topo a las monjas me quisie-/ ra enterrar porque no me bieran — biniendo al coro estaba en el camino una/ Rueda de monjas y entre ellas estaba fulana y pasando yo dijo que ay en casa quien/ aga milagros penseme caer muerta fuime a dios tan aflijida como el sabe/ como permitis esto señor — que ay en mi para que digan estas cosas aflijime mu/ chisimo que no me cabia el corason en el cuerpo= no agas caso deso dejalo todo a/ mi a mi me llamaron enbaydor enbustero y no me creyan y todabia mi a-/ flic-sion y alla al cabo disenme mas dificultoso es eso que pides que si dusientos/ onbres quisiesen con sus fuersas mover un monte de una parte a otra sin mi bo-/ luntad despues se me ofresio subir a una selda alta y bi un monte y ofresioseme/ lo que me abian dicho y aca ynteriormente que aunque fueran mil y muchos mas/ buelbo a mirar a otro lado y beo el monte de san cristobal y como si me di-/ jeran ynteriormente que aunque fueran muchisimos mas sin la boluntad/ de dios no arian nada se me olbido que me dijo que no temiese a ese enbaydor/ que no tenia mas poder del que le querian dar - - -

Juebes un dia despues de pascua de Reyes estando con el señor tenblo yo me a-/ suste tanto que no supe que aserme y corriendo alli me olbide de dios bolbi lue-/ go y yse alli lo que dios me enseño y ofresi aquello a dios en union de lo que su dibina/ majestad yso por nocotras y particularmente por las que estamos en pecado/ mortal en esta casa y pedile perdon de aberle dejado sin acordarme ni aun/ de mis pecados para pedir perdon disenme que eso se a de aser con tienpo y sien/ pre por que cuando biene la tribulasion nada se puede aser desto era para ala/ bar a dios lo que me desian yo daba grasias a dios de que no abiamos peresido —/ todas con aquel tenblor desianme que la sangre de mi señor jesuchristo clama/ ba delante de su eterno padre por las ofensas que se le asian que sino abia yo bisto/ cuando agrabiaban aun yjo de la suerte que su padre queria bengar aquella ynjuria/ que asi el padre queria acabar con todo asta que el yjo bolbiera aplacar al padre que se/ cometen muchos pecados y de muchos generos unos ocultas otros

tan sin/ Rienda ni temor y que en las casas de rreligion donde no abia de aber
mas/ que amarle y serbirle es donde mas le ofenden que el infierno esta lleno de
los/ que pasan la bida en triscas y pasatienpos y disen que es esto que es aquello
dios es/ bueno de nada asen caso ni piden perdon de sus pecados ni se acuerdan
que ay dios/ a quien temer cuantas lagrimas derramo nuestro señor jesuchristo
en a-/ quel jerusalen por estos pecados y cuanto padesio y todo por salbarnos y su
san-/ tisima madre toda su bida lloro desde que encarno su yjo que aunque por
enton-/ ses tubo aquel goso los mas eran amarguras y llorar lo que alli paso no lo
se desir/ ni entender como fue aunque entonses mui bien lo entendia dios sabe/
(9r) y le digo que mui bien sabe que no busco mas que agradarle - - -

(Excerpt [E] from 9r) domingo ynfraoctaba de rreyes tube terrible aflicsion
queriendo rrecoger-/ me estando olbidada de que abia ynfierno bi una profundidad tan edion-/ disima mas que muchisimos posos tantos mas profundo me paresio que ay de alto [det]/ aqui al sielo y alli grandisima multitud de jente que
paresian ormigas/ y desian desdichado de mi para sienpre e de estar aqui dije
jesus sea conmigo/ tanta jente ay aqui dijeronme cada dia cae tanta como bes ay
porque de todas las/ partes del mundo de ynfieles moros y judios dijo muchas
generasiones y de/ los cristianos que eran pocos los que se salbaban porque abia
muchos descuidados/ yngratos y que se daban a los bisios y desian que la sangre
de dios lo aria bueno/ yo desia creo en dios padre todo poderoso — criador del
sielo y de la tierra/ y en jesuchristo - y desian desdichados dellos que no creyeren
en jesuchristo/ subian aquellas llamas por ensima de las cabesas y abian ensima/
una cosa a manera de rred - por donde subian aquellas llamas y desian/ que aquello de arriba era purgatorio y que aunque aquellas penas eran tan/ terribles eran
nada en conparasion a la pena de no ber a dios y tanbien/ me paresio que bi de alli
monjas - yo me afliji terriblemente y le pedi/ a dios me librase de bisiones - y me
Respondieron que era mui probechosa/ la considerasion del ynfierno - lo que alli
paso ni lo se desir ni entender/ dios sea conmigo y me de su lus y me tenga de su
mano tanbien dijeron/ que dios tenia las manos bajas que cuando las lebantaba era
para castigar/ y echar alli que tanto como era misericordioso era justisiero - - -

Lunes asi que bine al coro y me postre al señor beo benir por debaxo/ de
tierra dos negras - llegandose en un probiso mui junto a mi la una/ de ellas me
dijo yo soy lusia la que era de señora ana de san joseph - que a/ tanto que estoy en
el purgatorio por la gran misericordia de dios que me yso/ esta caridad — no abido
quien se acuerde de mi mui despasio se puso a/ desir de la bondad de dios de su
poder y misericordia de lo que debemos/ amarle y serbirle y que ella abia serbido
esta comunidad con mui bue-/ na boluntad mas que algunas beses le abia aplicado
algunas cosillas/ della y que penaba a tienpos en aquella parte que solia aser cosina
que por a-/ mor de dios la encomendase mucho a dios - y que ella antes que
muriese/ abia tenido grandisimos trabaxos y que por ellos le abian discontado/
mucho de las penas todo esta boca a baxo como me acuerdo — ella ablo/ mucho y
mui consertado la bia a ella en la mesma figura que era — la otra/ no conosi — otro
dia por la mañana bolbio con la mesma demanda/ y pedido por doña polonia de
moya lo mismo que padesia terribles penas/ i que no abia quien se acordase della
y se me asia que la bia yo alli yo le dije a dios/ que si el enbiaba aquello yo se las
encomendaba y que le ofresia todo cuanto/ ysiere por ellas y por aquel frayle que

casi sienpre lo traya delante - / un dia destos me desia que era gran cosa lo que asia una comunidad (9v) junta por un alma mas que cuando era por muchos cabia a/ poco a cada una yo le beo que no le saben llamas de la cabesa como/ de antes mas asta la mitad de la frente no se si son enbelecos de aquel/ enbustero - - -

    otra bes bolbia la morena con la monja pidiendo que le pida al padre/ por la encarnasion de su yjo por ellas - yo dije por la encarnasion/ dijo la angola que si por la encarnasion que si no encarnara ni nasiera/ ni padesiera ni muriera que tomo este medio para nuestro Remedio - a la/ monja la bia yo con aquel ojo que tenia - que paresia que se le queria Rebentar - - -

    Juebes algunas beses e tenido deseo de saber de doña mariana machuca/ y en sintiendo esta tentasion le digo a mi señor jesus que me la guia que no se aga/ sino lo que el quisiere - estando oy donde suelo - binome este deseo yo le Resis-/ ti lo mas que pude no se si fue ynbensiones de aquel yo la bide de la misma/ manera que estaba aca sentada en su silla con su bordon aRimado/ a ella en purgatorio desia yo que como una persona tan santa – desian - / que alli estaba purificando que estos cuerpos bibos es menester mortificar-/ los en muchas cosas que andu- biesen como si no andubiesen que oyesen y mirasen/ como si no oyesen ni mirasen deste modo muchas cosas que fuesen como si no/ fuesen que aca desian que por no pecar dejaban algunas cosas como no castigar/ cuando era menester o se dejaban otras cosas de obligasion - que esto era engaño/ del demonio que las cosas de obligasion no se an de dejar por ninguna cosa/ que no se an de dejar las criaturas de dios sin la correcsion nesesaria porque se-/ ria causa de su perdision que son Redemidas con la sangre de nuestro señor/ jesuchristo no se desir lo que alli paso que no era mucha la pena que tenia/ y que los niños tanbien pasaban por fuego y que el dia de la encarnasion/ yria al sielo esto ba como se acordado a peda- sitos dios sabe lo que es/ yo no ago caso dello - - -

    (E from 9v) despues a la noche estando en mi cama encomendando a dios con los ojos se-/ rrados poneseme delante sisilia diome grandisimo pabor que me yso ten-/ blar como un asogado y a cualquiera parte que bolbia el rrostro se me ponia/ delante de la misma suerte y traje que andaba aca esta era una yndia/ donada que algunos años que murio - - -

    el sabado por la tarde dia de san marselo que estube Resando el Rosario en-/ tero disenme que piense como desenclabaron a mi señor jesus de la crus y en/ los yntolerables dolores y agonias que alli abia padesido y que mirara yo que a-/ quel señor abia padesido todo lo que padesio desde que entro en este mundo/ por solo nuestro Remedio y salbasion y que en todo abia echo la boluntad// (10r) de su eterno padre - que si quiso que nasiese desia agase tu boluntad si que/ padesiese agase tu boluntad si que muriese agase tu boluntad/ de suerte que en todo asia la boluntad de dios que yo desia no quiero/ ber ni oyr nada ya me quiero lebantar y yrme de aqui que mi señor/ jesus era nuestro maestro que del abiamos de deprender a ser obedi-/ entes y umildes y todas las demas birtudes que yo conosiera de mi/ que era una nada un gusano y que no meresia sino el ynfierno y que por/ sola la bondad y caridad de dios se me asian estos benefisios -/ y que le de muchisimas grasias por ellos que adore yo a mi señor - con la Re-/ berensia y amor que le adoraron los ange- les en el pesebre y en la crus/ y en el sepulcro que tan bien pensara como con la boluntad de dios/ se abia alsado aquella gran losa del sepulcro a mi me dio aca ynte-

/ riormente deseo de saber como abian llebado a mi señor al sepul-/ cro y disenme
que de la mesma manera que le bia yo llebar cuando se a-/ sia la prosesion el biernes
santo que asi yban con el santisimo cuerpo/ aquellos benerables barones [det] aquel
cantico juntamente/ con los anjeles – no se desir lo que alli paso despues ofresi mi
Rosario/ Repartiendo cada tres dieses por cada anima y las mas eran de/ fuera - por
clerigos y frayles y disenme con un modo de Repreension/ que teniendo en casa
tantas por quien ofreser o Rogar - porque estoy/ buscando los de fuera a fulano
nonbrando a una que yo abia nonbra-/ do en disiendo lo Referido enpesaba a salir
i una maquina de mon-/ jas como de debajo de la tierra que por aquel de profundis
grande por/ la parte de la cosina benian de dos en dos y la primera de todas era/
doña teresa de mui buena cara con su tocado bajo la toca mui/ blanca conosi algunas que a mas de beynticuatro años que murieron/ todas benian con sus belos echa-
dos sola doña teresa lo traya descubier-/ to conosi una beatris dos joanas una mensia
admireme de que es-/ tubiesen tanto tienpo en purgatorio y disenme deso te espan-
tas desde/ el tienpo del saldaña estan ay pregunte por algunas - y en parti-/ cular
por doña ana delgado dijeronme que estaba en el sielo pregun-/ te por otra que no
dire y me Respondieron que desde el punto que murio/ con grandisimo peso abia
desendido a los ynfiernos - que alla le aguar-/ daban con terribles calderones
[d]onde estaria para sienpre alli di-/ jeron los pecados por que se abia condenado y
que nunca abia pedido/ perdon - que aunque abia tenido males en ellos sienpre se
estaba deley-/ tando en sus bisios y que siquiera cuando se estaba muriendo le ubie-
/ ra pedido es dios tan bueno que le ubiera perdonado mas que no lo yco/ que bea
yo el daño que causa bibir sin atension y dejarse llebar de sus apetitos/ desto ubo
gran dotrina y de lo mucho que ynportan los ejersisios ynterio-/ res que en esta casa
le desagrada a dios un pecado grandemente/ y a nuestro padre - san francisco y a
nuestra madre santa clara que es el de las amis-/ tades lo que alli paso no ay poderlo
desir que de atonita de todo aquello/ que paso y de aber preguntado por aquella
que estaba tan fuera de mi (10v) memoria y es que me ase preguntar sin que
[testado: me] yo tenga boluntad porque/ yo no se quien me abla y tengo miedo de
que me Responda quien no quisie-/ ra - si yo preguntara por mi gusto preguntara
por otras mui diferentes/ tanbien bi benir en aquella prosesion a un lado a la negra
lusia y pre-/ gunte si las negras estaban alli tan bien Respondieronme que asi que a
un la-/ do estaban apartadas que alla pasaban las cosas con gran consierto. el
domingo estando suspensa pensando en lo que abia pasado bi a doña/ teresa en un
lugar mui claro - ella con senblante alegre y mui bien tocado con/ una toca mui
blanca y el tocado baxo que parese que no tiene mas pena/ que de no ber a dios y
entre mi pense si en el purgatorio abia senos disen que/ si - que conforme eran las
culpas eran las penas - que los penaban/ en los senos eran atormentados con las
mesmas penas del ynfierno/ que aquel poso en que yo bi alfonsa era seno que
cuando se cometian pecados/ mortales aunque pedian perdon y se confesaban se les
perdonaba la culpa/ y yban alli a purgar y [det] que para yr al sielo abian destar mas/
que mil cristales que los que bibian deseosos de agradar a dios y le temen/ y andan
con cuidado de no ofenderle y le piden perdon estos estan/ como doña teresa que si
como miserables y flacos cayeren en culpas/ grabes que pidan a dios perdon con tal
que les pese de beras de aberle ofendi-/ do - y pueden llegar con gran confiansa que
para eso esta la sangre de nuestro señor/ jesuchristo que se la ofrescan al eterno

padre con todo lo que padesio ubo gran/ dotrina - no se puede desir lo que alli pasa
dios sea conmigo y me libre/ de todo mal todo me sirbe de tormento - - -

el martes estando en mi ejersisio beo alla debajo de mil onduras/ aquella des-/
dichada que me dijeron el otro dia - estaba en aquel des-/ dichado lugar tendida de
espaldas en una como barbacoa y alRe-/ dedor muchisimos demonios y todos ator-
mentandola de la boca/ y ojos oydos le salia un fuego como cuando pegan fuego a
un coete bola-/ dor y no le dejan bolar con aquel Ruido en la cabesa estaban tocan-
dose-/ la con mil jeneros de tormentos - los pies llegaban otros y se los calsaban/ con
terribles yeRos y me desian beys ay desta manera pasan los Re-/ galados los osiosos
los que todo lo echan a las espaldas de nada asen/ caso no temen a dios cunplen todo
lo que les pide el apetito todo el/ tienpo gastan en burlas y triscas dios les da los
ausilios nesesarios/ y ablando de la que estaba alli dijo que aquella le abia dado
memoria/ entendimiento y boluntad para que escojiese lo que le conbenia que ella/
abia escojido aquello que daba los confesores los predicadores las/ ynspirasiones
libros que nuestro señor jesuchristo abia dicho belad y orad porque no entrasen en
la tentasion que aquello era aber caydo/ en la tentasion y lo que abia escojido todo
ba a pedasitos como/ me acuerdo mas alli es lo que se abla con tanto consierto (11r)
tan derecho y tanto que admira yo salgo de alli tan confusa/ y de pensar para que
me bendran a mi con esas cosas una pobre-/ sita que no bale nada de que probecho
soy yo algunas beses me/ quiero lebantar yrme de alli corriendo - ya le digo a dios
que bien/ sabe que no quiero otra cosa mas que agradarle que yo no bengo a que
me/ esten ablando y lo de mas de bistas tanbien me dijeron que cuando/ biera
alguna de aquella manera la aconsejara con blandura por/ bien - - -

(E from 12r) esta mañana estube linpiando la asequia de la enfermeria de
prin-/ sipio a fin y de en cuando en cuando me salpicada [sic] y me ensusiaba -/ y
alli me estaban disiendo que te enpuercas que te tornas para que ases eso desiale/
yo quien te mete en eso mas que me enpuerque peor soy yo y otras muchas/ cosas
que me cansan y asi las dejo - a la tarde boy al coro y enpiesan a desirme [det] se
yo el consuelo que an de dar en el fin aquellas cosas que se asen por dios -/ ablando
por lo que abia pasado por la mañana - en aquel tienpo dise/ tan apretado y de tan
grandisimos trabajos todo lo que se a echo por dios en-/ tonses se bera de cuanto
probecho nos es — es tan agradesido que aunque sea cual-/ quier cosa la gratifica
digamos aora si a un Rey cualquier onbre le ysiese/ un presente de un millon
siempre estaria agradesido a este onbre y cada/ año le a aria [sic] alguna merced
y le [det] devia lo que le pidiese que asi asia dios con sus/ sierbos - - -

otro dia por la noche bine al coro y fue tan grande el sueño que me dio que/
no me podia baler y dijele a mi señor ya yo me boy porque no puedo mas/ y debio
de ser probidensia suya porque alle a una enferma mui mala y llamo-/ me y
mandome ensender bela y carbon y otras cosas y que le llamase a u-/ na ermana
que la curase que lo suele aser ella me Respondio con tan mala/ grasia disiendo
que estaba cansada y que la enferma lo era mucho que ya/ abia echo su obligasion
bolbi disiendo que ya la abia llamado como se tar-/ do bolbio aquella llamase otra
bes dijome que no queria yr dijele a la enferma/ que aquella no benia que me
mandase lo que queria que mal o bien yo lo aria mandome/ todo lo que ubo
menester y mui tarde pasada la noche diseme aquella erma-/ na en toda la noche
e podido sosegar de escrupulo de no aber ydo a soco-/ rrer aquella enferma boy al

coro y enpiesa no se quien a ablar que de su gloria/ estaba gosando y la dejo por nosotros y bino a padeser grandisimos traba-/ jos toda su bida por Remediarnos y darnos ejenplo que para si no lo abia/ menester que nos olbidamos de sus bene- fisios que nos crio que nos Redimio -/ con tan grandisimos trabajos y desta manera Refirien-/ do los benefisios que nos a echo y nos esta asiendo despues desto me disen/ que diga yo grasias te doy señor porque me ysiste cristiana - sien mil millones/ de grasias os doy porque me trujisteys a buestra casa sien mil millones/ de grasias os doy por los santos sacramentos que ordenasteys para nuestro — rre-/ medio sien mil millones de grasias os doy porque quisisteys que os Resibiera oy/ y por este modo se Refirieron muchos benefisios y como se an de dar gra-/ sias por ello y a cada cosa destas me disen a mi de cuantos males me an sacado/ por cuantas cosas meresia estar en los ynfiernos y como debo dar grasias/ a dios por esto// - - -

(12v) otro dia despues de aber comulgado disenme que encomiende a dios una/ negra que abia estado en el conbento y la sacaron mui mala a curar y a po-/ cos dias murio ya casi treynta años no me acordaba mas della/ que si no ubiera sido yo me espante y entre mi pense que tanto tienpo/ y Respondenme que aquellas cosas en que ella andaba - y aca dabanme a/ entender que era un amor desorde- nado que tenia a una monga to-/ da la casa lo sabia que mi padre san fransisco y mi madre santa clara se abi-/ an yncado de Rodillas a nuestra señora porque alcansase de su yjo/ la salvasion de aquella alma porque abia serbido a esta casa suya/ con mui buena Boluntad - luego bi que pendiente de un sinta baja-/ ba de arriba una corona de unas espinas grandes casi delante me/ e numero no se si fueron sesenta y tantas - dentro de dos dias/ buelbo a ber la morena en un rrincon mui apartada como la pri-/ mera bes que tanbien la bi alli y me dijeron entonses que penaba en el/ dormitorio biejo aora la bi en su propia figura con un faldellin/ berde y paño de cabesa y desiame que la grandisima misericordia de/ dios la tenia alli que nuestros padres san francisco y clara se abian yncado/ de Rodillas por ella yo le pregunte sin querermelo asen preguntar/ y estoy [y]nteriormente que como o porque tanto tienpo de purgatorio — dise/ me — ama dios tanto a sus esposas que cuando las be que faltan a sus obliga-/ siones lo siente mucho si los onbres sien- ten tanto cuando no les guar-/ dan fidelidad dios que crio y Redimio y nos ase tantos benefisios tan-/ to ubo alli que no ay cabesa para persebirlo - - -

(E from 13r) otro dia apenas me puse delante de dios cuando me enpesaron ablar/ y sienpre es esto dije jesus sea conmigo quien es este que me abla disenme/ tan apriesa el anjel del señor es el que te abla que desde que nasiste te fue dado// (13v) para tu guarda tan bien te dieron otro anjel malo el bueno te asiste/ al lado derecho - y el malo al isquierdo el bueno te libra de males/ y el malo te mete en ellos/ [tachado: estabase muriendo la madre de una monja y enbiole a pedir-] no te acuerdas cuando te saco de tal occasion/ y dijome una cosa que aunque estubiera un año escarbando no me acorda-/ ra y cuando me aparto de otra cosa que conosi ser berdad tres cosas/ me dijo desta manera y otras que aquel feo me abia echo caer todo berdad/ paso una maquina de cosas - yo desia entre mi si seria esto enbustes de/ aquel o si seria mi cabesa y disenme quien puede blasonar de si aun-/ que mas os quebrarays la cabesa pudierays formar nada que lo que aqui/ os an dicho despues que paso esto disenme que mire yo aquel señor que tanto a-/ bia padesido en este tienpo por nosotros yo desia creo en dios padre [det] asi ase/ que

le bia yo con las manos atadas angustiadisimo - con sudores y desianme/ que
considerara yo que sentiria aquel señor por aberse encargado de todos los peca-/
dos del mundo desia yo que los mios bastaban para tenerle asi enpese-/me aflijir
muchisimo [det] tubiera mucha confiansa que quien/ le deseaba agradar y amar
y yba a sus pies no tenia que temer engaños del/ demonio — algunos dias antes
desto en otra ocasion que estaba con este temor/ me dijeron que si yo tubiese dos
personas delante y a la una amase mucho/ y a la otra aborresiese y estubiese yo
ablando con la que amaba que caso aria/ de la que aborresia aunque mas chufle-
tas me ysiese que asi era esto que yo yba/ derechamente a dios que aunque mas
dilijensias ysiese el enemigo no ysie-/ se caso dellas yo desia entre mi que no tenia
quien lo biese si era bueno o malo/ disenme que dios es el berdadero maestro que
me podia enseñar el padre - ni los/ libros que fuese como lo que aqui me enseñan
mas yo digo que aunque sea quien/ fuere a mi me ase probecho - - -

    el miercoles santo por la madrugada desperte a las tres con un pabor/ tan
grande que tenblaba yo y la cama terriblemente que me yso dios grandes/
mercedes — en que no undiese a gritos aquel cuarto este miedo desde el dia antes/
lo abia enpesado a tener de una negra que se abia muerto sin con-/ fesion que era
del conbento y la abian llebado a la chacara por enferma/ para ber si mudando
tenple sanaria - murio como e dicho y aquella/ ora me dijo que estaba con tan
grandes trabajos porque cuando era cosinera/ y panadera sacaba mucho y que la
señora abadessa podia rremediar aquello/ despues me bine al coro mientras se
asia ora de yr a la cosina y luego que me/ postre beo un christo crusificado y que
de la llaga del costado le salia un a-/ royo de sangre finisima y se juntaba con otro
que salia de los pies y se asia/ todo un aRoyo grueso y salia con mucha fuersa y se
yban llegando/ algunos y les caya ensima y quitados unos llegaban otros y desian
que aquello/ era un mar que nunca se a de acabar asta la fin del mundo que
mirase que yo/ si aunque todos cuantos ay en el mundo sacaran agua del mar si
se pudiera/ agotar que asi esto no se agotaria jamas quien puede desir lo que alli
paso/ yo estaba atonita asiendome cruses - - -//

    (E from 14v) el terser dia de pascua entro una mulata en la cosina mui afliji-
/ da disiendo que todas las beses que benia la madre de su ama la mal quista-/ ban
con ella disiendole muchas mentiras asiendo ella cuanto podia/ por dar [por dar
sic] gusto - boy a la siesta al coro y digole a mi señor dios no/ soys bos señor padre
de misericordias como esta aquella pobre tan descon-/ solada y no la socorreys
disenme yo me agrado de unos sufran/ a otros y otros a otros y otros a otros con
esta Respuesta lo deje despues de/ un Rato digole señor yo no estaba por ay
descuidada sin saber desto/ ni pasarme por el pensamiento y bos me abeys traydo
y por buestra or-/ den bino aquel padre y nunca tiene lugar para mi - no os de pena
el padre que yo soy padre - de misericordia como bos desiys buen maestro y entre/
muchas enseñansas y [det] confiansa que debia tener del/ me dijo que si no bi yo
como me abia librado cuando el padre abia llebado/ aquella papelera que otras
abian padesido mucho yo no se desir lo que aqui/ paso aunque me lo daban a
entender mui bien yo dije entre mi si tu eres/ dios como ases caso deste basurero
deste estropajo¹ que aunque mas lo linpien/ sienpre se queda susio diseme - que
soys - bolbi a Repetir disen cuando yo es-/ taba en jerusalen en el tienpo de mi
pasion todas las preguntas que me a-/ sian eran con los pies enpiesa a desir lo que

abia echo por nosotros y los sacra-/ mentos que ordeno para nuestro - Remedio
que alla los judios le abian muerto/ Refiriendo todo lo demas - no conosiendolo/
mas aora conosiendo le los onbres asotan - coronan y crusifican - de nuebo con sus
pecados/ yo no se desir lo que Refirio — benefisios que abia echo - a los onbres -/
asta que los animales yrrasionales los abia criado para bien del onbre/ yo me estaba
encojiendo y pensando que que era yo para que me dieran cuenta/ de aquellas
cosas disenme que aquella debosion que yo tenia con nuestra señora y aquello/ que
le estaba pidiendo sienpre me lo abian Resebido y que aquel deseo que yo/ traya
de saber leer para saber los misterios de su bida y pasion que aquello/ es lo que me
enseñan aora y aunque mas leyera los libros no deprendie-/ ra en ellos nada de lo
que aqui me enseñan yo ando llena de temores/ no quisiera que estos fueran
engaños de aquel estos dias sienpre/ se esta asiendo dios el que me abla tantas cosas
tan derechas tan con-/ sertadas tan bien dichas y luego los deseos que quedan y con
esto temo-/ res no lo entiendo dios lo sabe y que yo no deseo otra cosa mas de agra-
/ darle y amarle y serbirle algunas me disen de que estas flaca no sa-/ ben ellas las
congojas y agonias de mi corason encomiendenme a dios/ mucho que bien lo e
menester - el biernes santo en la noche fui/ a conpañar a nuestra santa a monserrate y enpesele a desir/ disparates que me paresia mas ermosa y mas linda que el
sol/—(15r) y la luna y las estrellas y disenme tan apriesa si bos bierays como es/ y
despues [y despues] que me Recoji biene aquel obrero de la yglesia que a mas/ de
un año que murio a pedir que lo encomendase a dios yo con muchos mie-/ dos uno
de lo que ello se trae consigo si son enbustes del paton - - -

(E from 15r) el dia del pascua digole a mi anjel que baya de mi parte a dios
padre y le/ de el para bien de la ResuResion de mi señor jesuchristo su yjo diseme/
que no rresusito aora sino que quiere dios que todos los años sega memoria/ de lo
que paso dije entre mi este anjel lleba los rrecaudos que yo le doy/ diseme tan
sierto es que los llevo como es sierto que Resusito si yo pudiera/ Retener - en la
memoria lo que alli me pasa fuera nunca acabar no di-/ go de todo mas que unos
pedasitos - boca abaxo - si estoy trabajando/ alli me ablan si boy de aqui alli me
ablan - y me enseñan - lo que e de pen-/ sar como me e de mortificar si me
descuido tantito la Repreension/ la enseñansa - una noche destas estando yo dando
de senar al Refitorio/ enbiome un plato de ensalada y puselo junto a mi y cuando
acabe/ no lo alle y estaba una muchacha junto a mi - teniendo malisia/ de que lo
abia tomado dijeselo y al punto disenme que porque le abia/ dicho por malisia
aquello - aquella muchacha que aunque era cosa po-/ ca lo abia sentido - y que yo
no sufriera que lo dijeran por mi - que maria/ de pineda me lo abia puesto en tal
parte — (E from within same paragraph from 15v) despues que paso esto y otras/
muchas cosas — disenme de como se agradaba dios de los pequeñitos –/ y umildes
y que en esta casa le agrada florensia bravo y antonia/ de christo — que son
desechadas y nadie ase caso dellas la primera/ es una mulata chabacana y la otra
una negra siega -/ despues estando pensatiba con temores y desconfiansa disenme/
que por que desconfio — que sino e oydo desir fulano es onbre de mucha/ Berdad
y de mucho credito no ay mas que temer fiaysteys de los/ onbres y poneys buestra
confiansa — y de mi no la teneys que no puedo fal-/ tar a los que se fian de mi — no
me acorde desir de cuando Sali/ del locutorio de con mi madre — bineme luego a
la cosina y pen-/ sando en las misericordias de dios y como por todos caminos me

so-/ coRe – y dando le grasias porque asi a mi madre disenme que se las de/ por el
benefisio que me abia echo en que entrara yo deste talle en el locuto-/ rio que
cuando entrara yo en otro tienpo menos de yr mui ador-/ nada y eserticimo que
me aliñaba de pies a cabesa de manera/ que si el calsado estaba algo Rosado no
entraba = despues en el coro// (16r) cuando me dijeron como se abia de confesar
rrepitieron que si no era/ benefisio que yo entrara en las comunidades con este
traje y es sierto que/ para solo contonearme me solia engalanar y dar una buelta
por/ el coro – y disenme que pues gaste tanto tienpo en adornarme para/
conplaserme a mi que aora me siña para agradarlo a el/ no se que sera esto - - -

(E from 16r) sabado despues de pascua no se que es esto no se si son enbustes
de el enemigo dios lo/ sabe y sea conmigo que no se como librarme destas cosas -
entrando oy en la siesta a los/ confesionarios en llegando al arco donde estaba la
yglesia o la rreja me dio/ un grandisimo pabor - mas fiada de dios - lo bensi y pase
adelante y luego que me/ puse en los pies del señor - Recojida - me paresio que
sentia pasar por donde yo estaba/ asia la rreja que solia ser y con el espiritu - quise
uir de alli - y fue ynposible -/ y luego me enpeso ablar - aquel saserdote de que se
a echo memoria estos dias/ disiendome que no abia palabras para desir la
teRibilidad de las penas que/ padesia y que estaba condenado a ellas - por muchos
años y que por la birjen/ santisima se abia librado que el estaba penando en aquel
lugar de la/ rreja porque gastaba mucho tienpo alli en osiosidades - y que cuando
yba/ la comunidad al refitorio el se benia a parlar - y que cuando benia// (16v) jente
se escondia en la sacristia y me parese que dijo que se estaba es-/ condido todas las
oras o bisperas – y que ella era Relijiosa - y el mistro de dios/ que no lo debia aser
de aquella manera porque le corrian mui diferentes obli-/ gasiones - y que yo le
encomiende a dios y beo le parado en el mismo lugar - / que estaba la rreja de la
misma figura y Rostro que era tan tiesesito -/ y con sus canas y el manteo cojido por
de baxo del braso ysquierdo – como/ el solia ponerse – un atamo de lo que el me
dijo es esto - jamas oy desir/ semejantes - cosas - deste clerigo - por eso tengo yo
tanto miedo - no benga/ aquel engañador a aser estos enbustes - yo creo - en solo
dios – merced/ - me encomiende - mucho a el que estoy mui aflijida - quedo [det]
en estas/ cosas que quisiera meterme debaxo de la tieRra Bestirme de pellejos no/
Ber ni oyr - ni ablar - con nadie no se que me quisiera aser Dios lo Remedie - -

(E from 17r) miercoles por la mañana enbiame señora doña antonia de
serantes - que le cosine/ dije le a la negra beos con dios buestra ama no se acuerda
de mi sino para mandarme/ y bolbila a llamar para aser lo que me desia - bengo
a la siesta a la orasion/ y disenme - si abeys dejado el mundo - porque os quejays
- no fuera mejor tomar a-/ quello sin enfado y aserlo con caridad por amor de
dios - y otras cosas a este modo - - -

Juebes - algunos dias tengo apurado el corason y me cansa todo bineme de-/
lante de dios a pedirle su grasia y beo una escalera desde la tieRa al sielo/ y un
camino asia mi lado derecho - y otro al isquierdo desianme que aquella/ escalera
era el camino de los que llevan la crus - y el camino derecho era – los/ que yban al
purgatorio – el del yzquierdo de los condenados – de los que no te-/ men a dios –
y no guardan sus santos mandamientos que estos cuando caen/ en este tremendo
lugar – ban despeñandose por terribles barrancos – y bia/ yo unas tinieblas escurisi-
mas- mas desian que aunque estos dos caminos/ se juntaban y los del purgatorio –

padesian de las mismas penas - de los/ condenados - con la esperansa de que se an de acabar estan consolados -/ mas los que an de subir por esta escalera son los que lleban la crus que nuestro señor/ jesuchristo la llebo primero – y solos los que le siguieren yran por este camino/ yo no se desir lo que alli paso - sabado estaba apare-jandome para comul-/ gar y disenme que los cuerpos eran custodias de su sacra-mento – y alla de/ delante que nos mostraba su gran caridad despues de lo que tenia echo en su en-/ carnasion - bida - pasion y muerte y de los sacramentos que nos abia de-/ jado - mentandolos cada uno de por si - en sufrirnos y aguardarnos/ tanto tienpo - muchas cosas a este proposito - pasaron alli - luego me de-/ sian - que yo e de dar cuenta de los benefisios - una multitud de cosas me/ dijeron de que abia de dar cuenta - un dia destos aora poquito a - me de-/ sian que aqui los mundanos - asian mucho caso de los Reyes de los birreyes/ que todo era un poquito de tierra - que el era señor unibersal de sielos y tieRa/ y que por su mano pasaban todas cuan-tas cosas ay criadas - y de todas tenia/ particular probidensia - y aqui en mi cabesa me numeravan tan gran/ multitud de jente que paresia ynfinito - yo no se desir lo que alli pasa si yo/ supiera escrebir y tubiera lisensia del padre - fuera cosa admirable mas todo/ se me olbida - cuando estoy trabajando y Recojida se me biene a la memo-/ ria - y alli bienen otras – todo se pasa como no ay ocasion de desirlas – luego/ un dia destos estaba en los confisionarios cansada y flojeando y enpese/ ablar con dios y desia entre mi - si me oyra dios esto que le digo - disenme todo/ lo oygo todo lo beo – y todo lo que el pobresito ase por mi - lo agradesco – como/ abello menester - no se que palabra me desia - no se si era trino y uno//

(E from 17v, middle of paragraph) martes - fueron tantos los aogos que me binieron/ de que me enbiaron unas y otras que les guisara que les ysiera estoy aquello y lue-/ go del conbento que basta para ocuparlo todo - y como yo ando con ansias/ de yr donde esta el señor = y con estas cosas me quitan el poco tienpo que me queda/ fue un dia trabajosisimo para mi de suerte que asi como di de comer/ al Refitorio sin comer yo me fui a postrar al señor - y por el camino/ (18r) le yba disiendo señor tu gastas destos aogos si yo se que no es tu boluntad no e/ de añadir mas de lo que mandan asi que me postre disenme en treynta y tres años/ que estube en este mundo todos los pase con grandisimos trabajos y aogos y al salir/ del me pusieron en un palo - como si fuera un bil esclabo y ladron con es-/ tas palabras se me quitaron cuantos aogos y cansansios tenia - bine alegre/ grasias a dios que abia algunos dias que paresia que queria espirar – miercoles/ ubo los mismos cosinados y aogos - fui donde esta el señor dijele que si aquello/ de aquel clerigo era suyo yo le ofresia por el todo lo que asia y estubele encomen-/ dando mucho - aquella monja de la pendensia y disenme que cuando estaba/ en su casa la libro de muchos peligros - y que si aca no se enmendaba dando/ a entender que beria el castigo - juebes enbiame una monja un poco de/ carne para que se la asara y considerando que si esta bes lo asia sienpre abia/ de querer lo mismo y no lo yse despues estube con pesadunbre y le enbie una es-/ cudilla de caldo - el dia de san felipe y santiago desde la noche antes estube/ deseando prepararme para la comunion y sino era pensar que le abia de Rese-/ bir no pude aser otra cosa y despues de la comunion paso de la misma manera/ despues de comer boy al coro y alle que abia clarin y caja que abia traydo la que asis-/ tia al santisimo sacramento y encomendela a dios y disenme que en el corason/ se sele-

braba y festejaba dios que aquello era banidad y para que dijesen que do-/ ña
fulana nonbrandola por su nonbre asia el dia – y luego diseme que por que/ abia
dejado de asar aquella carne que me pedia aquella monja que si no era projimi-
dad/ que yo digo bengan cruses cargad señor sobre estos onbros - y cuando biene
un poquito/ los desecho - que el no bolbio el Rostro al trabajo que que era amar
sino se pasaban/ trabajos por el - abia sobrado arto carbon ensendido - cuando
acabaron/ de comer y bi que andaba fulana por alli y dijeles a las cosineras que lo
apagaran/ y como no lo ysieron tan presto tome agua y lo apague - diseme - que
asi abia sido/ buena yntension aquella que si quisiera yo que ysieran aquello
conmigo si quisiera/ cosinar - que aquello me abia ynsistido el demonio – y es
berdad que lo abia echo/ con rregaño y no abia caydo en ello asta que me lo
dijeron lo que oy ubo de Repreen-/ sion yo no lo se desir mas destos pedasitos -
abia un dia destos pasados quemado-/ se un pie una conpañera quitando una olla
yrbiendo de la candela y de-/ jose caer con el dolor quejandose mucho yo le tube
gran lastima/ y tome una poca de agua -echesela en nombre del padre y del yjo y
del espiri-/ tu santo - y no se quejo mas – y a estado trabajando sin faltar aunque
tiene una/ mancha parda donde se quemo no lebanto enpollas -diseme oy con los
demas/ que yo me asia desentendida de los benefisios y que por eso no le daba
grasias mire/ vuestra merced - si abia yo de pensar que por mi la abian sanado -
asi que amanesio me dije-/ ron que pensara en los terribles dolores que padesio
la santisima birjen biendo a/ su santisimo yjo colgado de aquellos tres garfios en
la crus y en los que el pade-/ sio - con este ynconparable tormento - - -

(E from 19r) dia de los ynosentes a 28 de disienbre del 59 estado Recojida
delante/ del señor - bi una lus mui grande clarisima y dentro desta lus una bidrie-
/ ra mas clara que los cristales y dentro della a mi padre fray pedro urraco lleno/
de toda esta lus – y esto bi por espasio de medio cuarto de ora – y disiendo yo/ entre
mi - como a mi padre jose garsia serrano no biene esta lus sino e-/ n otra menos -
clara al modo de luna me dijeron por que este trabaxo/ mas que el otro – y antes
de ber esta lus bia las beses que me Recojia a cristo nuestro señor/ crusificado y a
sus lados dos personas a estas no le dibisaba Rostro ni cuer-/ po - mas bia claramente estaban alli y aca ynteriormente me pare-/ sia era la santisima trinidad desiame este señor crusificado quien/ me adora a mi adora a mi padre – y al espiritu
santo esto me desia allando-/ me yo confusa y temerosa [det] no ber nada mas de
aser en todo/ la boluntad de dios desde que bi esta lus no la aparto de la memoria/
y sienpre lo mas del tienpo estoy rrecojida teniendo presente a este/ gran señor =
que obra estas misericordias con esta pobresita que no bale nada - - -

un dia estando rrecojida bi alla en el sentro de la tierra una concabidad grande
y en e-/ lla muchos enemigos aguardando las almas que cayan las cuales despedasa-
ban/ y trayan al pelotero como cuando un perro despedasa a un pedaso de carne o
co-/ mo cuando despedasa un trapo biejo y lo arrastra - y trae al pelotero -/ aflijiame
mucho - y desiale al señor - que para que bia yo esto que no queria ber nada/ mas de
asertar amarle y asertar a serbirle - desianme que pues yo tenia en-/ tregada mi
boluntad mis potensias y sentidos al señor - el me gobernaba,/ como era serbido - que
aquellos enemigos que atormentaban y despedasaban/ estas almas desian a cada una
los bisios y los pecados porque les daban -/ aquellos tormentos = dios lo sabe todo su
dibina majestad me tenga de su ma-/ no y me libre de mal - - -

estando una negra para morir en este mes de marco - fia a berla y le y-/ se
aser un acto de contrision – y solo mui de beras - con muchas lagrimas/ y dandose
muchos golpes en los pechos - yo fi consolada de aberla bisto/ a encomendarla a
dios y bi un santo christo - y a sus pies a esta morena amor-/ tajada con que biera
sierta su muerte y que por la misericordia de dios se abia/ de salvar y le di muchas
grasias - no se si es mi cabesa dios lo sabe todo a quien/ pido me tenga de su
mano—una rrelijiosa que tubo mui gran contrision a la/ ora de su muerte y mui
gran confiansa en dios se me aparese continuamente/ desde el dia que murio
como una niña Resien nasida y dandome a entender/ que es alma del señor.

(E from 21v) estando una Relijiosa para morir y aflijidisima de no poderse
confor-/ mar con la boluntad de dios - y con esto le davan unas ansias como deses-/
perasiones y pedia a todas que la encomendasen a dios - yo tube lastima/ della y
encomendela a dios - y disenme que como nos ama tanto - a cada/ uno le da lo que
le conbenia - que a su tienpo le daria la conformidad que agora/ aquel trabaxo le
estaba mejor - porque con la tribulasion se purifican/ esto - ba a pedasitos - no se
desir - lo que alli pasa = boy a nuestro señor = pidole/ que me de pasiensia y me
enseñe como e de sufrir - al proximo y que me/ de grasia - para que no mormure yo
del - en mi corason que como soy -/ mala negra - algunas beses me da no se que con
mi conpañera porque/ de todo rregaña - no se como llevarla – si le pregunto malo
si/ no le pregunto peor – no ay modo - para ella otras beses me dise/ que porque no
tomo mis alforjas - y boy a pedir limosna para las/ enfermas - otras que por que no
las sano - y otras cosas a esta talle/ yo me rrio - dios sabe como - y disenme que sufra
todo lo que se ofre-/ siere sin queja ni mormurasion ni dar a entender que lo siento/
como si fuera una piedra que si no lo beo yo que si pisan un ladrillo/ por un lado que
se esta sin menear - por el otro tendidos los que es-/ tan tuertos//

(E from 22v) esto fue por tienpo de elecsion el juebes abia abido una gran
pesadunbre en que le/ perdieron el Respeto a la señora abbadesa - estando delante
de dios le dije - que como aquellas/ que le querian agradar las abia dejado de su
mano disen no me quieren agra-/ dar - y aunque tienen boluntad - no es con afecto
no es con beras estan llenas/ de propia boluntad - yo no rreuse la crus - nunca le
bolbia el rrost[r]o manda-/ la perlada - dentrese dentro - y desirle no quiero - y no
querer umillarse/ asi como caen almas - al infierno - asi ubo enemigos = para
tentar-/ las y animarlas - y aser lo que ysieron anoche - como sentiria yo esto
cuando - es una mu-/ jer casada no se ase otra cosa en casa mas de lo que quiere el
señor della/ cuando me prendieron - y dieron bofetadas - en mi rrostro - mui bien
pu-/ diera yo confundirlos - a los ynfiernos -y cuando me llebaban a en pe-/ llones
- yo los sufri - por daros exenplo - y en la crus Rogue por los que alli// (23r) me
pusieron y blasfemaban de mi y toda mi bida pase con grandisimos trabaxos por
buestro/ rremedio - y por dar los exenplo que yse en aquel desierto si no pedir al
padre - por bosotros -/ y que os enseñase - aser su boluntad - que es la causa - pasar
tanto tiempo - con tan poca medra/ sino falta de umildad - y la propia boluntad -
mientras uno no se umilla - poniendose a los/ pies - de todos - humillandose de
todo corason - y con berdadera Resignasion - con esto se me-/ dra se pasa - adelante
- quando una se pone delante de mi - y luego me muestro a ella es por-/ que - lo a
menester - porque si yo no me mostrara - no bolbiera mas quando una ba mucho -
/ tienpo con perseberansia - yo no me muestro - eso es lo que le conbiene a cada uno

le doy lo/ que mas le conbiene - tanbien le conbiene a cada uno llebar - la crus que
le dieren - tanbien dixo/ que queria que la que aora gobierna llebe su crus todo esto
es una tilde salpicado y sin orden lo que puedo rrecojer - - - /

(E from 23v) dia de san yldefonso despues de aber comulgado estando rrecojida - en un ynprobiso haseseme/ que bia al licenciado colonia y disenme que por
aquella caridad con que nuestro señor jesuchristo bino del sielo a la tie-/ rra le
encomendara a dios - y le pidiese por esa mesma caridad - tubiese misericordia del
- encaresio grandemente quan grandes son los trabaxos que se pasan alla que ya a
el le paresia/ que abia mil años que estaba alla y que abia padesido mucho por
francisca - su negra que la traya arRas-/ trando - con mal tratamiento - y no
cuidando - de lo que abia menester = yo preguntele que no se quien/ me ase aser
estas preguntas - que son contra mi boluntad - en fin le pregunte por aquel clerigo/
y dijome que ya ese se abia perdido - que se abia condenado - por aquello - que ya
me abian dicho/ no me lo dijo asi si no rrefirio lo mismo - en que gastaba - las
noches y los dias - dijele que como lo/ sabia y dijo que en dios lo bian todo y dijele
- que si los que estaban en el purgatorio bian/ a dios dijo - que como eran almas
que estaban en grasia y no abian de bolber mas aca/ en dios sabian estas cosas - mas
dijo que a el le abia balido la yntersesion de nuestra señora/ y de la santa Rosa que
rrogaron mucho por el y tanbien le balio quando cantaba misa en esta/ casa la
cantaba con particular debosion y atension que cuando desia el credo le desia//
(24r) con particular atension y particularmente cuando llegaba aquellas palabras
(quin a tres/ es de maria birjine) se gosaba grandemente con estas palabras - y se
rratificaBa en es-/ ta fe - y en todo lo demas del credo - que como yo me acordaba
- de encomendar a otros me a-/ cordava de el - y es verdad que abia algun tienpo
- que no me acordaba de encomendarle a/ dios - y a otros si - y eso me señalo - yo
le dije a nuestro señor = que si aquello - era berdad y suyo yo/ le pedia por lo
mismo que el me abia pedido - por el amor con que abia benido del sielo -/ a la
tierra tubiese misericordia del - y le librase de aquellas penas - y que yo le ofresia/
por el - la comunion - y todo lo que ysiera aquel dia y a nuestra señora le pedi -
que por aquellos pa-/ sos que dio buscando a su yjo - cuando le perdio - todo esto
es una miaja - boca abaxo/ lo primero el todo que se me abia olbidado - y fue que
bi pasar una y otra bes un animalejo/ como un perrillo - desollado - lleno de lepra
asquerosisimo - encojido mala cosa/ entre mi pense - que seria aquello y disenme
- que asi paresian delante de dios los pecado-/ res - dije que con que se quitaba
aquello - y disenme que con la sangre de nuestro señor jesuchristo/ y llorando sus
pecados - postrarse a sus pies y pidiendole perdon - - -

sabado dia de san pedro nolasco digo la bispera vino a mi una cosa que estaba
tan olbidada della/ como si nunca hubiera sido estando asi rrecojida llegose una
cosa dios sabe que es quisa/ sera paton que es amigo de marañas y diseme yo soy
marucha - la ermana de juana de esco-/ bar - por amor de dios te pido que me
encomiendes a dios - que con aberme criado en esta casa/ no ay quien se acuerde de
mi - yo quede con pesadunbre pensando - quien soy - para que bengan/ a mi con
estas cosas - y pidiendole a dios que asi aquello era berdad y es suyo - tenga miseri-
cordia/ de aquella - el dia del santo - comulgue por ella y por otros difuntos - y por
otras nesesidades/ y despues por la tarde aconpañando a las enfermas alli sentada
me rrecoji - y luego/ haseseme que beo a marucha con el rrostro mui

Resplandesiente y me dijo que por la con-/ fiansa que abia tenido - en la misericordia de dios se abia salvado que ella abia estado en/ pecado mortal hasta que le
dio la enfermedad - de que murio -mas que como conosio que era/ tan grave: luego
se conpuso - y se arrojo a los pies - de nuestro señor jesuchristo — pidiendole/ misericordia - con gran confiansa de que la abia de salvar - yo preguntele por su a-/ ma -
alfonsa - dijo que estaba - en el purgatorio - que abia tenido grandes penas que alla/
abia gran consierto que cada uno tenia su lugar conforme a su estado - que las mon-
/ jas a una parte - los rrelijiosos a otra - los seglares - saserdotes yndios negros todas/
las jenerasiones y estados de cada uno y las obligasiones que tenian se les daban/ las
penas - que ella - por la bondad de dios no abia sido enbustera ni rreboltosa/ ni
ladrona que solo aquella flaquesa tenia que la encomendara a dios - dijele -/pues
era yo una pobresita - para que me benga con estas cosas - dijo que le diera/ muchas
grasias a dios por aquel conosimiento que me daba de lo nada que era y que/ sienpre le pidiese a dios me le diese - que era mui agradable a su dibina majestad/ y que
a ella le abia acortado pasos - esto es una tilde de lo que alli paso todo me/ sirbe de
congojas - algunas beses tengo tentasion de no yr - ni tener - ///(24v) orasion mas
porque esto no sea de el enemigo boy disiendole a dios que bien/ sabe mi ynterior
que es de aser su boluntad y alavarle y amarle sin estas/ cosas -mas si el quiere - que
padesca yo estas cosas que se aga su boluntad y sea/ por su amor - - - /

    a 4 de julio - biernes - ynfraoctava de corpus ysose una solemne/ fiesta - y entre
los aparatos della - ubo unas camaretas - y despues de/ aberse selebrado todo el dia
con gran aplauso y gusto de todo - a la ultima/ prosesion que se yso - para - enserrar
el santisimo - disparando las camaretas/ una dellas Rebento - y un gran pedaso della
fue a dar en la cabesa de un/ negrillo - del doctor Retes - llevole - un pedaso del casco
y algo de los sesos/ yo dolime grandemente de la falta que abia de aser a su amo y
bolbime a dios/ disiendole - que tubiese misericordia de aquel saserdote enfermo y
pobre y di-/ senme - que si por el probecho del amo han de quitar - al criado lo que
le conbiene/ que este se abia de perder - si bibiera que ya enpesaba abrir los ojos al
mundo/ que cuando dormiamos aca - en el sielo se desbelan mirando lo que nos
conbie-/ ne a cada uno - para salbarnos que le costamos mucho y enpiesa a rreferir/
asotes - corona - espinas - crus en fin cuanto yso - desde que encarno que bien pu-/
diera dar - aquel golpe - en fulanito y sutanito - en fin en aquellos que abia alli/ y
que solo aquel - solo - le conbenia - y que mirara yo - las fiestas deste mundo/ cuan
aguadas eran - entre muchas cosas que pasaron - se me acuerdan estas/ y se asia mi
señor jesuchristo = bibio - el negrito - asta las dies de la noche — del/ dia siguiente -
sabado - cuando lo supe - por la mañana - bolbia encomen-/ darle a dios - y disenme
- que mire yo - cuan bien - le abian pagado la debosion/ que tenia con la Birjen nuestra señora con ser tan cortos los serbisios que le asia/ era tan agradesida - y tan buena
pagadora que todos los que la tenian debo-/ sion y se encomiendan a ella - les
faborese — y ayuda y que yo aconseje a todos/ la debosion desta señora - que este era
birjen - y que ya enpesaba a lebantar/ los ojos - para su perdision y asi le conbino -
cortarle los pasos - sea dios bendi-/ to por sienpre - - -

    Bispera de la asunsion de nuestra señora - por la madrugada bi en la sala
donde/ pusieron el santisimo - un biejo bestido - de negro y de rrodillas entre/ mi
dije que sera esto disenme - este es fulano - yo espanteme - de que es-/ tubiese
tanto tienpo que fue cuando se perdio aquel nabio pelean-/ do con los

pechilingues dije pues no murio este defendiendo la/ causa de dios - disenme si - pero este estaba en pecado mortal -/ y se le yso mucha carida[d] en darle contrision que el cuando cayo/ en el mar estaba a braso partido con el enemigo encomiendalo// (25r) y comulga por el y di que le encomienden a dios dije mi padre me a mandado que no diga/ yo estas cosas - disen por fuersa an de desir quien es - sino poner un papelito que en-/ comienden a dios a un padre de unas monjas dijele a dios que si era suyo que yo lo toma-/ ba a mi cargo para encomendarle = quando se llego la ora de comulgar con una/ fuersa - por fulano - por fulano - sea por el y muchos dias adelante si yba a la orasion/ por fulano - si comulgaba - de la misma manera - yo e menester - que encomienden-/ mucho a dios - ase pasado mucho sin asentar - - -

(E from 26v) a dies y nuebe de nobienbre - asi que me postre delante del señor = me la arrebataron/ y luego me bino a la memoria doña joana de ynojosa - y sin berla me abla - va no se quien asiendose ella - yo conosia su abla pidiome - que por amor/ de dios - la encomendara a su dibina majestad y le ysiese desir a su madre/ catalina ximenes que le ysiese desir cuatro misas una a san juan baptista/ otra al enbajelista otra a san joseph - y otra a nuestra señora de la encarnasion/ dijele que yo no me abia de meter en eso que mi padre me lo tenia mandado/ (27r) disenme aslo por la virjen del carmen que tenia mucha nesesidad pregunte-/ le si con aquellas misas - saldria dijo que no - mas que le serian de mucho probecho -/ preguntele – si abia alla jente de aca desta casa - dijo que mucha que ella abia seys años/ cunplidos - y andaba en siete -que se pagaba mui por menudo - todo lo que se faltaba a la o-/ Bligasion - de la rrelijion - que si era poco - estar en el coro - con parlas y Risas - y faltando/ a las benias – y a las demas seremonias - y el traje - no conforme a la rregla - y tañer/ a silensio - y no guardarlo - y despues de aber pasado - la bisita bolberse a lebantar y a-/ ndar discurriendo - de unas partes en otras - hablando -mormurando – quebrantando/ silensio de las rrisas - banas - y el amor desordenado - a las criaturas - tanto dijo/ desto que no ay cabesa - para ello - y que no ay trabajo - ni palabras - con que se pueda de-/ sir - lo que se pasa - en el arrancarse el alma -de el cuerpo - y que con ser tan teRribles los/ tormentos del purgatorio - de ninguna manera = las que estan alla - querrian bolber/ aca - aunque los ysiesen señores de todo el mundo - por el peligro que aca ay - de perder a/ dios - que esto solo se a de temer - y de cuanta - ynportansia es tener santos - por debotos/ y cuan solos se allan - los que pasan -alla sin ellos - trujo una conparasion - que si aca un on-/ bre ysiese a un Rey - un presente de un millon todo - cuanto le pidiese este honbre - se lo consede-/ ria - que asi los santos alcansan de dios- lo que le piden - y por tres beses me pidio que por la birjen del/ carmen le pidiese estas misas - y que ella me encomendaria a dios - y le pediria que me diese la pasien-/ sia que yo le andaba pidiendo - yo estoy atonita de lo que alli paso - tanbien que el padre eterno – conse-/ dia todo lo que le pedian - con confiansa - por la encarnasion de su yjo - la caridad que le dio con nos – para/ nuestra Redenpsion - de sus mismas entrañas - y que lo que permite - en nosotros - adberso - lo ase su caridad/ porque nos conbiene - que asi le debemos - dar continuamente grasias y que tanbien la virjen maria/ alcansa de dios todo lo que le pidieremos por aquel grandisimo goso que tubo cuando encarno el ver-/ bo en sus entrañas todo ba lo de abaxo arriba a pedasitos - - -

dia de santa catalina martin - despues de aber Resebido a nuestro señor = me postre y estube tanto/ tienpo sin desir jesus - y alla al fin disenme - que nosotros - somos cruses unos de otros - que maria/ flores me exersita a mi - y marisa anjeles a felisiana que cada rrato – esta desde su cama/ disiendo –fo - fo - y ella tiene todo el sircuita de la suya tan escupido que pone horror – dijele/ yo estando – con estos aseos ella - que sufriera al proximo - que todos teniamos - que nos sufrieran/ desto quedo - tan ynquieta que por que le abia yo de desir aquello - yo estaba atonita - que lo que yo no abia/ echado por la boca - antes abia estado examinando si lo abia dicho - con algun enfado/ para rreconsiliarme - uno - asi comulgue - y disenme que hagan que buelban yo no aga/ mas de conformarme - con la boluntad de dios - que si me ago aquello y es otro me are sensible/ que no me conbiene - que mire en la bida de los santos que en todo se conformaban con la dibina/ boluntad que yo a todo diga - hagase la boluntad de dios que esta era una orasion que le agrada-/ ba mucho - - -

sabado adelante - se me asia que bia una sala mui grande y con mucha jente en e-/ lla con gran consierto como que estaban por sus antiguedades y al cabo de la sala //(27v) al padre fulano bestido con sotana puestas las manos y abaxo alla mui hondo/ muchas llamaradas de suerte que aunque estaba - mui alto partisipaba de aquel/ fuego y desian que aquel abia sido buen saserdote y mui casto y deboto - y particu-/ larmente de nuestra señora que salio al encuentro - en su fabor - y que cuando desia misa/ en el altar - de nuestra señora de la peña de fransia - era con particular debosion que era/ temeroso de dios dije pobre de mi con todo eso esta de aquella manera disenme para ir/ a gosar de una eternidad - de dios abian de yr mui purificados - que este padre - le a-/ bian dado lugar en su enfermedad para que dispusiese de su asienda y que tanbien/ dado - muchos consejos -sobre eso - y no creyendo que se moria no lo abia echo yo mira-/ ba aquellas llamaradas - y desianme - que aquello era seno del ynfierno y que las mas de/ las animas de las que yban al purgatorio - las tenian en aquellos senos pediame que le/ encomendara a dios y que le dijesen una misa - a nuestra señora - yo digo que si es de dios comul-/ gare mañana -por el - -

dia de san andres daba el [l]abatorio la señora abbadesa y yo dudaba si le besaria la mano/ por no dar en que entender - y disenme - que aga mi obligasion y no aga caso de nadie -/ despues de la comunion Recojime un poco y asenseme tantas fabulas que no se que sera esto/ haseseme - que beo un rrio grandisimo que mientras mas mirava mas grande paresia/ vialo tan claro que las piedras estaban patentes y a las orillas del abia gran numero/ de monos con unas colas mui largas unas manos con unas uñas mui largas -/ con unas caras como de leones dando muchos brincos y a un lado deste rrio estaba/ un christo crusificado yo hasia la señal de la crus y desia (gloria patri) -/ si grande era el rrio mucho mas lo era un orno que estaba junto a el con teRribles/ llamas - y desian que aquello era la tibiesa con que serbimos a dios que alli se castigaban/ y que de aquellos yelos yban aquel horno que era su rrefrijerio y del orno al rrio - y luego/ desian que aquella era la caridad de dios - librarnos de aquello - y que la begninidad/ de dios es lebantar a los que estan en pecado y traerlos a penitensia que se confiesan/ y bayan quitando sus bisios que aquella caridad que le trujo del sielo a la tieRra// (28r) y padeser tantos trabaxos y tormentos y quedarse en el santisimo sacramento = del altar esa/ le ase estarnos llamando dandonos ynspirasiones que sola su piedad le muebe -/ a esto que que

nesesidad tiene de nosotros o para que nos a menester que que se le diera sino fuera/
por esta caridad - que nos tiene y que gusta mucho de que con atension miremos
sus llagas/ y lo que a echo por nosotros y que asi como en sus entrañas de la birjen
entran en los que le/ Resiben en el santisimo sacramento = que todo esto hase su
begninidad - que sino bi yo quando vio me/ mostraron como bañaban en su sangre
- a los pecadores y esto fue que a mucho tienpo/ que bi un christo - que de las sinco
llagas salian sinco aRoyos de sangre y cayan en un/ lagar - y alrrededor del abia
mucha jente — y a lado derecho estaban dos anjeles/ de cuando en cuando - estos
anjeles tomaban a uno de aquellos que estaban alRededor/ de llagar - y los anpus-
aban alli y desta manera yban tomando - no por orden sino sal-/ picando - esto me
acordaron alli - y que cuando bautisaban tanbien los bañaban/ en la sangre de
nuestro señor = jesuchristo - que le demos muchas grasias por tantos benefisios/
contandolos cada uno de por si a el padre eterno - que nos dio su yjo unijenito - y
cuando dije-/ ron que abia entrado en las entrañas de la virjen que le rresibio con
gran umildad agra-/ desimiento que sienpre l[e] estaba dando grasias con gran
atension y debosion a lo que tenia/ en sus entrañas - y que sienpre estaba dentro de
si - alabando - con su yjo — que en esto emos de y-/ mitar a esta señora cuando le
rresebimos de la piedad - ubo gran dotrina que cuando se/ nos ofresian - ocasiones
de pecar - tenemos temor de no ofender a dios que quien ase esto/ sino su piedad -
que cuando estamos asiendo - plegarias a dios señor = sacame desto -/ señor -
sacame de este otro - no me dejes de tu mano - para que te ofenda - quien ase esto/
sino la piedad de dios - que cuando pedimos señor perdoname mis pecados asedme/
humilde - y las de mas virtudes - quien ase esto sino su pi[e]dad - olbidoseme desir/
de aquel ynfierno de dos que asian conoser no en el Rio ni el horno - sino en aquel/
lugar que yo las e bisto otras beses —particularmente - la una estaba sentada como/
en un banquito no bia yo en que mas estaba - algo en alto - en medio de terribles
lla-/ maradas - que la cubrian toda - y con estar asi - bia yo mui claro su rrostro y
de lo que es-/ taba bestida que era de un faldellin berdegay - y camisa de pecho mui
labrado/ de blanco -y sus cuerpesitos - tenia un pie - sobre una rrodilla contrario y
la/ mano derecha en la mejilla el senblante tristisimo - maldisiendo desia/ mala y a
mis pecados porque poquito - perdi - un bien ynfinito - desta suerte/ s[e] estaba
lamentando - algunas beses lo quisiera dejar todo porque estas/ cosas me sirben de
confusion y le pido a dios me las quite porque si boy alabar-/ le luego bienen - estas
ynquietudes - si estoy asiendo - lo que tengo a mi cargo - alli me es-/ tan disiendo
lo que pasa aca y a culla - para que quiero yo - esto tan bien me desian de/ mi - que
en aquello de la piedad de dios - que mirara yo de cuantas cosas me abia sacado/ y
que cotejara yo aquella bida con esta de agora que si no abia sido gran piedad esta
que me/ resiendo estar en los ynfiernos mucho mas de muchos de los que estaban
alla — porque/ muchos estan por solo un pecado ya digo que meresco nuebos ynfiernos y que aun-/ que no soy la que debo conosco que me a sacado de muchisimos
males sea bendito// (28v) por sienpre - y me de grasia para que yo le sepa agradeser
y serbirle y agradarle en/ todo y alabarle por todos los siglos de los siglos amen - - -

    (E from 28v) domingo tersero de adbiento despues de aber comulgado
encomende a dios a fulana difunta/ y hase mi cabesa unos fabulones que cuando esa
yba a la orasion se ponia en el trafago de la/ jente que entraba y salia en el coro -
que alli estaba biendo — y oyendo lo que pasaba que si aca cuan-/ do se abla con

alguna persona de rrespeto cosas de ynportansia si no se apartaban a so-/ las para tratarlas y que para estar con el era asi y que en el ofisio dibino no estaba con aten-/ sion - y que ablaba ynterrunpiendolo - que a cada uno le pedian cuenta conforme/ al talento que se le a dado - que al donado - como a donado que al negro como a negro se le/ pide quenta de los dies mandamientos mas que al Relijioso le corrian muchas/ mas obligasiones - y un dia destos me dijeron a este proposito que si eran sinples o ygno-/ rantes -que por eso abia sermones y consejos y libros - y que si no querian correjir -dando a/ entender que pagarian - otro que nos ama tanto que como nosotros nos olbidamos del y/ de sus benefisios de lo que padesio por nosotros nos enbia enfermedades para que nos conosca-/ mos - para que le llamemos que si no beo yo cuando estan fatigados - como le llaman dios mio/ dios mio que nos enbia las enfermedades para que le pidamos perdon de los pecados/ y misericordia - - -

(E from 29v) vispera de la elecsion comi bi - de esta casa tan alborotada y estos bandos tan/ encontrados - alla a las cuatro de la mañana encomende a dios estas cosas/ pidiendo le el asierto y la pas desta casa - y en un ynprobiso por detras de la ca-/ ma me desian ursula - mañana - con la bendision de la santisima trinidad/ sera la Roldan - abbadesa - dejaronme asustadisima grandemente estas pala-/ bras mas despues - con gran sosiego y seguridad -de que seria asi lo que me abian di-/ cho - -

la vispera de la bisitasion de nuestra señora = por la madrugada encomende a dios-/ ana de san joseph - y luego se me puso delante yo de ynprobiso le pregunte por/ doña fulana - y me señalo con el dedo - y me dijo - que aqui abajo - dando a enten-/ der que estaba en algun profundisimo seno del purgatorio lo que a este proposito me/ dijo - no ay palabras - del benefisio que [det] dios en aRa[n]carlas de aqui porque no/ se perdiesen - benia la ana de san joseph - con un senblante mui apasi-/ ble y alegre y me dijo - que la gran confiansa que abia tenido en dios y la buena yn-/ tension y llana la abia aprobechado mucho - con todo esto traya un poco de/ fuego - en los pies - luego yo pregunte por antonia de salinas - y me dio a enten-/ der que ella no abia tenido tan buena yntension - como ella nunca abia tenido/ segunda yntension que dios le abia echo esa caridad - y que esto le abia aprobecha-/ do mucho [tachado: estaba adorando al señor cual pesebre – boca abaxo]

[In the margin: prosigue una monja que le escrebia.]

(E from 30r) otra bes vio una grandiçima y ferosiçima boca de un dragon/ y munchas almas como cuando ierbe una olla a borbollones açi/ subian y bajaban - mas cuando bajaban era con un terible gol-/ pe y las llamaradas sobrepujaban y le digueron que aquel cast-/ igo era para los que comulgaban mal - - -

(E from 33r) cuando traguieron las nuebas de la desolaçion de chile pusose a lame[n]-/ tar al señor y entre otras cosas le dijo como señor a çido esto. mostro-/ se sentidisimo. y disiendo que los hombres no açian caso del que/ al birey temian como si fuera algo porque les puede quitar la vida// (33v) sabeys quien es el birey echa una poca de tiera en agua y despues/ de desecha mira si pueden coguer alguna cosa esto memo/ es el birey un olbido tan grande un pecar tan çin rienda dijo/ señor asta los montes dijo asta los montes ay algun Rey ni/ nayde que pueda aser lo que alli pasa no deçir en el credo creo en dios/ padre todo poderoso eso es y no me temen los honbres que no echo por/ ellos. que no me an costado. desde el de su creaçion me an costado/ trabajo con mis propias manos almase el baro y lo forme todo -/ con mucho trabajo y para ynfundirle el alma solo con un alien-/ to de mi boca. se la di todas las mas cosas solo con desir aganse fueron/ echas. ael siempre açiendole benefiçios y el çin conoserlos tan-/ to olbido. siempre pecar y mas pecar sin reparo tan çin temor/ que no pase por ellos desde que naçi que me perçiguio aquel erodes querien-/ dome matar que pase en ejito que en el diçierto. y en todo el res-/ tante de la vida. munchiçimo paso aqui de quejas sentidi-/ simas de tanta yngratitud. y al prinçipio desto leyose un/ papel en el coro en que refería lo que abia pasado y todo aquello/ y muncho mas me tenian dicho dije al senor como de noche/ de noche. ago io mis castigos. no bistis cuando se queme [sic] la capilla/ de mis ymaguenes entonses lo quise destruir todo sino que por/ ruegos de mi madre la virgen de la conse[p]çion y del padre san/ francisco y santa clara no lo yse. mas como ya estaba difinido exe-/ cute. en mis mismas ymaguenes el castigo no bistis cuando/ la virguen se puso negra y cuando lloro dijo no lo vi de oy lo dijo/ pues eso mas aunque no fui yo a donde estaba la ymaguen estando/ en el coro vi todo lo que alla paso de concurso de jente mas no vi la/ ymaguen mas dijo no bistis como no paço adelante aquel fuego/ mas que a quemar la capilla con estar tan pegada a las seldas si es-/ te castigo se ejecutara quien se escapara durmiendo. y dio a en-/ tender que si aca no se enmendaban seria lo mesmo - - -

(E from 34r) algunos dias duraron las quejas del olbido y poco temor con que vi-/ ben los hombres de su divina maguestad el poco agradeçimiento a/ sus benefiçios y particular de su vida y paçion y mas de las reli-/ guiosas diçiendo que ni bian con el mismo descuydo y olbido y que los/ mayores pecados que se açian en esta casa era por las malas comu-/ niones tan çin co[n]cideraçion. de lo que reçivian antes y despues/ con el pensamiento en otras cosas y que apenas le abian reçivi-/ do cuando se salian del coro y que abia muncha guente en esta/ casa y que de las cuatro partes no se disponian las tres y que todas/ comulgaban y que era su boluntad que este proposito. se ysiesen/ dos sedulas que la una se puçiese en el coro y la otra en el claustro/ quien escribe esto. lo tomo a su cargo ya ablo a la señora abade-/ sa. en secreto. y me mando que yo ysiese las sedulas era por la pro-/ sincula y el domingo. antes abiendo reçivido a nuestro señor/ me postre a sus pies pidiendole que si era su boluntad a que me en-/ señase que y como aria las sedulas alli se me ofreçieron- / unas palabras mui a proposito de lo propuesto. y diferen-/ tes de otras que io abia pensado açiendo [pre]guntar a la pi [det] lo la santa abbadesa le ablo con gran eficaçia proponiendoles la/ obligaçion y cuidado con que se abian de preparar para re-/ çivir este santo sacramento. y las faltas con que lo açian y/ yso leer la sedula diciendo que aquello era de parte de dios mui/ enojado y con mucho afeto. les digo munchas cosas aeste pro-/ posito. y con ser cer que de cu[a]lquier palabrita suelen lebantar/ un murmollo y despues mil guiçios sobre quien fue o de don-/ de salio este enbuste. no se a oydo una palabra sobre el caso/ si no es a una monja que leyendola al cabo de algunos dias dijo/ que la queria trasladar para traerla conçigo. y açido desde que paso/ esto mui frecuentes las comuniones y parese que se ase con mas/ cuydado tanbien abido confesiones jenerales y se ban con-/ tinuando graçias a dios esto es de la cecretaria bolbiendo// (34v) a nuestro negoçio dije al señor que me daban unos deseos de yr de ro-/ dillas a reçivirle si no que tenia [sic] el que diran respondio nada es tu-/ yo y mando que saliese del rincon donde estaba y me pusiese en me-/ dio del estrado al prinçipio del io reusarlo. muncho porque aun en el/ rincon. me estoi desaçiendo de berguensa yso tanta ystançia que me/ ube de poner y diseme lo que os doi no os lo doi para vos solo quiero que me/ traygais pecadores yo no sabia que aserme. dijele que çi queria que se escribie-/ se dijo que si yo pregunte que çi lo diria a una monja con quien estado/ çiempre y desde los prinçipios que me binieron estas cosas asta que ella/ me dijo que no lo anduviera diçiendo a todas que entraban en ondo/ y que era menester tratarlo con quien lo entendiera dijome que fue-/ ra a la que lo esta açiendo nonbrando por su propio nonbre porque/ avia leydo mas esta hermana tiene muncho miedo de estas cosas/ dise que si nuestro señor avia de ber [det] a un gusarapo con estas cosas/

otro dia çiguiente a un rato que estaba alabando al señor bi dentro/ del mismo sagrario a nuestro señor jesucristo cruçificado tan grande co-/ mo lo debia de ser. tan al bibo que pareçia de carne con los pechos/ llenos de leche que pareçia que ya queria salir y dijo esto tengo para/ los pecadores umildes y arepentidos era de linda figura y blanco/

murio en casa una negrita algo mas de dose años seria las ocho de la/ noche io estaba sola. en nuestro dormitorio apenas espiro cuando vi/ un bulto blanco que me causo gran espanto. de que estube mala de un do-/ lor que me suele dar estube en la cama y alli la encomende a dios deje-/ ronme que en el conçistorio de dios se abia decretado que muriese por-/ que çi vivia no se avia de salbar estube alabando al señor y encomen-/ dandome al alcanguel san miguel disenme que el alcanguel/ san miguel era gran prinsipe en el çielo y que era mui querido de/ dios y que era alferes de su hijo y aministrador de las almas en-/ piesame a deçir otra bes de la encarnaçion muchas cosas lo que me/ acuerdo es que açi que bino el anguel y la virguen dado su consen-/ timiento. abia tomado carne en el berbo y al punto avia/ la virguen y al niño en sus entrañas con el mundo. en las ma-/ nos: mui lindo en cada cosa de estas no lo pude apersevir lo que/ alli paso luego ablo de la paçion y al punto vi alla bajo de tie-/ ra un sepulcro con un sol y en el un cuerpo mui grande/ todo moreteado y de la cabesa cayendo gotas de sangre sobre// (35r) una almoada y dijo que cuando su hijo padeçio abia enbiado mu-/ chos angueles para que recoguiesen la sangre estava a la cabecera/ de este sepul-cro el arcanguel san miguel. con su estandar-/ te blanco y moltitud de guente que subia y bajaba y luego vide a/ nuestro señor como resuçitado; con tres como potençias en la cabesa/ y deçian me que çi no creya yo que abia subido al çielo y que se le abia/ dado potestad sobre todas las cosas. luego disenme del juiçio/ final io digue que balgo io para estas cosas no es porque tu ni nay-/ de lo merese. quien io quiero bien no podia yr a los potentados/ a los Reyes como dellos tengo en el ynfierno. a los Reyes que/ viben - conforme a mi ley y tratan a los suditos con caridad. y a-/ sen justiçia con misericordia aestos cuando mueren lleboles/ a mi purgatorio como tengo agora a la reyna de españa pasome/ por el pensamiento. como se llamaria diseme doña ysabel lo/ que este dia paso no se puede decir. io quede atonita encomendado/ a dios a la Reyna. y comulgue por ella - - -

dos dias despues de esto vi alla en una profundidad unos pare-/ dones de cuatro baras en alto. algo mas o menos por debajo/ de ellos unas manos mui grandes. con unos cucharones de yero cale-/ do muncha candela. y apartado desto. estaban - unos

palos en-/ çima de estos paredones. a modo de barbacoas y ençima estaba/ una
señora. mui autoricada. dese saber quien era diseme la [det]/ Reyna de españa estaba
sentada. y con muchos libros delante/ no tenia muncho purgatorio - - -

(E from 36v) dia de san Lorenzo despues de haver estado media/ ora de
oraçion dandole muchas graçias al señor/ me digeron que para que las diese mejor
mirase/ aquello y bi un abujero grande oscurissimo y con/ estarlo tanto bia yo claramente que estava/ lleno de perbersas sabandijas entre me dezia/ yo alabado sea el
santissimo sacramento porque/ estava. muy espantada sin ber quien me ha-/ blava.
me dezian como crio el cielo y la tierra/ y los angeles para que sirbiesen a todo
genero de/ criaturas assi quiero que beas esso y saved que esas/ sabandijas son
leones que despedazan a los que/ bienen aqui esto es para los que no guardan los/
mandamientos y se dan a plazeres huyen del tra-/ bajo y de la penitenzia no se
aquerdan de lo que/ Padezi por ellos. yo lloraba mucho deziame que/ el padre
eterno tenia su çielo para los que guar-/ daban sus mandamientos y todas las orde-
nanzas/ de la yglesia y bibian onesta y santamente mas/ me dezia que mirase yo
muy bien todo aquello/ y que supiese que por solo un pecado mortal esta-/ ban alli
que mirase quantos abia cometido y diese/ muchas grazias a dios por los benefiçios
que me/ hazia en esto dio la ora yo atendi al ave maria/ que suelo Rezar dejeronme
que siempre que la/ Reçase me acordase de aquellos desdichados que/ yban alli ultimamente me digeron que Dios te-/ nia su zielo para los que si sabian dejar - - - //

(E from 40v) a la tarde me llamo una monga para que la oyese leer despues/
en la oraçion disenme que sacatis de la letura. estube como un leño/ deçianme aca
dentro eso es tuyo perseberando ora y media la ora se fue/ en grandes ynquietudes porque pareçia que cuantas pulgas abia en/ los muladares estaban sobre
mi y açia el lado ysquierdo me de-/ çian pensaras que as comulgado como judas
que el no comulgo porque/ a el no le dieron mas de la forma porque no yba en
ella el jesus// (41r) maestro. y se lo dieron porque estaba delante de los otros ançias
comul-/ gado ya te quieres acer. mui bestida de sayal. y poniendote delante de
todas/ para que la miren de esto ubo muncho asta que paso la ora despues me
dijeron/ mañana que es miercoles poneos una ora çiliçio y otra benia al coro con
las ma-/ nos atadas y açi pensareys. cuando me tubieren açi que sentiria con/ aquellos cordeles que se me entraban por las manos. Otra ora yreys a la en-/ fermeria
como lo soliais aser. porque lo abeys degado y lo que soliais aser/ los viernes digui
que por que se yba alli una monja. lo abia degado diseme/ pues ya se fue. pregun-
tole la secretaria que era lo que solia aser au[n]que lo/ reuso açiendole ystançia me
digo que los viernes echaba unos frijoles/ en el sielo y açi los comia los miercoles
yba a la enfermeria diçien-/ do ynteriormente. y a una monja. con quien estaba se
lo desia/ boy a ser la cama de mi señora la virguen maria y aunque abia mun-/ chas
camas esto era a la guente de serviçio en cada una deçia esta/ es la cama de mi
señora bolbiendo el colchon este es de mi señora/ esta sabana o fresada de mis
señora los sabados. bengo a barer la ca-/ sa de mi señora la virguen maria en fin
dise que lo digo porque se espan-/ to un dia que vi yo una cosa. que se quedo
atonita que estando con la ropa de/ una cama en las manos no pudo pasar adelante
y que todas le desian/ que tienes mas que ella se fue y no bolbio mas a aser aquello yse le ystan-/ çia. que me diguese que avia visto y dise. que bio salir a nuestra
señora de en-/ tre las camas. bestida be blanco. y unos cabellos tendidos asta las/

rodillas. que ella temiendo no fuera alguna trasa del enemigo lo dego –

miercoles al amaneser. ofreçime a nuestro señor como çiempre diçien-/ dole que alli estaba. que ysiese al punto me dijeron que pensase. en el ece/ omo yo puse el pensamiento en el çielo y alla le bi con la corona/ de espinas mui encajada. y una caña en la mano ysquierda con/ una como manta colorada con nudo por los onbros como lo pin-/ tan sentado. y lastimadiçimo bia io que estaban dos personas/ a sus lados. no las debisaba bien que açi lo abia sacado el jues/ a una bentana de su casa enseñandole al pueblo ece/ omo que es lo mismo que deçir. bes aqui al hombre digo io que esto ya me/ vienen con otras cosas no me bengan a engañar aqui con latines que en-/ tiendo io de eso. buelbo a deçir lo mismo. que hece omo es beys aqui al/ hombre. alli me açian mil escarnios y me adoraban asiendo burla/ como a Rey finguido me llegaban al rostro diçiendo munchos bituperios/ y no abri mi boca y me defendi que vi en pudiera mas era la bolun-/ tad// (41v) de mi padre. autualmente estaba asiendo beneficios llego bituperan-/ dome llamandome de enbustero de encantador y otros nombres yn-/ iominiosos abia entrado la señora vicaria y dicho algunas palabras/ de mortificaçion y aunque no le digue palabra referidos beses lo que avia/ pasado y diseme que çi cuando lo llamaron a la coluna hablo pala-/ bra o cuando lo llebaron a la cruz que aquellas cosas no se abian de re-/ ferir ni retener un punto çi no que cuando se ofreçiesen deçir di-/ jo quiere agase su boluntad todo el dia tube mui ocupado de suer-/ te que no pude aser las camas de la enfermeria aunque lo desee mu-/ cho me cojio la noche sin poder digue al señor aunque sea/ una e de aser diseme no bayas que con la boluntad as cunplido/ cuando pudieres lo aras - - -

juebes estando mui ocupada y eche de ber que la ocupaçion me açia/ olbidar de dios y tanbien tube un enfadillo con una negra dije/ al señor que es esto señor que Reçiviendo tantos benefiçios de ti vi bajo/ tan çin atençion cayga en estas miserias diseme esas son las/ dificultades çi por estar ocupada tubierais algunos olbidos/ y a tu buena boluntad. se a reçevido dige señor oy no e podido/ oyr misa. diseme los domingos y fiestas por ninguna cosa se an de/ dejar que son presetos de la ygleçia. los demas dias a deja a dios por dios/ y en alabando con lo que tienes que aser vien puedes yr a tu ora jamas/ dejes de yr a donde te llamaren y trabaja que io no tube ora de descan-/ so. y estar con cuidado de dejarse por momentos aqui ubo muncho/ de esto - Luego vi dentro de mi una cosa nueba que açia guarda a un peda-/ cito de carne que via io que dentro que no se deçir. como era. mene-andose mu-/ cho y palpitando luego vi que era coraçon y alli serca dos ojos gran-/ des y mui abiertos queriame yr de alli de mi[e]do y desianme estos/ son los ojos. ynteriores con estos se conose dios y se conose aci/ con esto se be el berdadero desengaño en fin me dijo todo aque-/ llo de que estos ojos servian y que lo esteri-oreses [*sic*] eran de ninguna/ ynportançia y que mientras estan estos abiertos los otros es-/ tan serados y al rebes cuando los ynteriores estan abier-/ tos los esteriores estan serados y desdichados de los que mueren/ sin aber avierto estos ojos. digue al señor dadme graçia/ para que mire con estos ojos no mas y luego me enceñaran/ alla en una profundidad unas parillas de yero y un des-/ dichado encima boca bajo y rodeado de demonios que ati-/ saben aquel fuego que estaba abajo teriblemente alli serca estaba //(42r) en una tina grande - la cual destapaban estos malditos a gran/ priesa y sacaban de alli como brea - y se la echaban por la boca/ y desianme

que pensays quien son estos - los que en su bida abrieron/ estos ojos los bagamun-
dos que pasaron su bida en plaseres los men-/ tirosos - glotones - los que nunca se
superion dejar - los bengatibos deso-/ nestos y que no temian a dios - - -

    dia de san bartolome me bino la señora abbadesa al coro y como allase po-/ cas
monjas para prima saliose del mui enojada en busca dellas y tru-/ jo una maquina
dellas - y a un rrato disenme oy an coronada a la a-/ badesa por esto que a echo dije
yo yo no quiero saber de coronasion ni de na-/ da - sino conoser a mi dios y alabarle
disenme pues no crees que eso puede/ ser creeys en la comunion de sus santos – dije
si creo - creys la Remision de los pecados si creo – dijo [det] rremision de los pecados pensan-/ do como le rresponderian – dijome rremision de los pecados es
cuando/ uno biene a mi contrito con dolor de los pecados y se confiesa y yo le per-/
dono esa es - dijo luego creys que el padre y el ijo y [e]l espiritu santo - que es un
solo/ dios berdadero - dise creis que son tres personas si creo dise pues la mesma/
berdad tiene lo uno que lo otro - luego disenme que desde que entro por la/ puerta
del coro la madre abbadesa la estaban aguardando dos anjeles/ que enbio dios para
que con los dos que ella tiene la coronasen - y que la abian a-/ conpañado asta su
lugar donde le pusieron la corona - pasome por el pen-/ samiento preguntar si a las
monjas que estaban en el coro - se les abia/ dado premio dise a todas se les dios
corona - y a las que binieron esas como/ forsadas - y luego a profundanme esta bista
con tanta fuersa que por/ mucha que yo me asia no me pude Resistir - y mues-
tranme alla en lo -/ profundisimo - muchisimas monjas no tenian mas bestidura
que/ unas toquitas blancas en señal de que eran monjas – y otras dos beses/ que las
e bisto de la mesma manera - dise entre mi todas son de santa clara/ dise jeron de
todas partes - estas son las forsadas - despues que paso esto bi/ entrar a la yglesia un
mestiso que abia yo conosido en abito de donado/ dije aca como me enfada este
cuando yo lo bia con el abito de mi padre/ san francisco - me paresia un rrey
disenme este ynquietaba la rreli-/ jion y asi mejor esta fuera - - -

    despues dije a mi señora la birgen maria ya señora - mañana entro en la/
cosina aser mi mes todo lo que alla ysiere es buestro yo boy algo mala/ como
sabeys si mi dios quiere lo podre aser echadme buestra bendi-/ sion dise cuando
fuistis la otra bes tanbien y bais mala y salis-/ tes buena asi sera aora -yo os asis-
tire y mi yjo y el anjel de// (42v) buestra guarda dije no señora a mi y mi señor -
abia de yr a la cosina dise/ si - y estara contigo y luego dijo el enemigo no pu[e]de
tomar mi figura que no/ a dado mi yjo facultad para ello el ase mil aparatos mas
no los ase sin li-/ sencia de mi yjo porque sin ella no tiene facultad para ello - y
cuando se/ la da es por pecados - y otra cosa que me dijo se me a olbidado mas
dijo-/ yr a prima y al Refitorio y a las demas obediensias de buena gana es pe-/
nitensia y lo paga mi yjo mui bien - poneos a sus pies y umilde caminar - - -

    (E from 44r) Biernes estube mui apurada de muchas cosas juntas - estube
sufriendo/ toda la mañana despues al medio dia cargo tanta jente al Rededor de mi/
para cobrar la comida que con rrabia dije apartaos de mi - luego cayen lo/ que abia
echo y dije a mi señor - que me perdonase y al punto diseme bien podias/ desir que
se apartasen sin aquel enojo mas cuando acontesiere - no aya se-/ gunda yntension
no quede nada en el corason dejar que pase luego dije quie-/ n es este que me abla
tan a priesa puede ser dios dise no pediste perdon dije/ señor - cada dia estoy peor
- la otra bes que estube en la cosina mestaba desasien-/ do por ir al coro - y cuando

enpesaba a caminar me yba desasiendo en/ lagrimas y aora estoy tan tibia tan miserable y ynpasiente y tan/ sin memoria con cualquier cuidadito me ocupo y me olbido de dios/ dise esa es buestra ynconstancia que nunca estays de un ser dijele señor/ quitame esta mala condision que tengo dise que me as de ofreser si te la/ quito yo abia dicho por la mañana que en pudiendo urtaria unos/ Ratitos por la puertesita del coro que cae serca de la cosina a la no-/ che fui al coro un Ratito antes de yrme a Recojer y diseme como/ no beniste por la puertesita - - -

estos dias adelante abido tanto que aser que apenas tengo un rratito - / de lo cual anda mi alma arto aflijida mas tomando un Rato para yr a misa = y reco-jerme un poco estube alli que no me conosia //(44v) ni me podia Recojer nada es tuyo me dijeron y luego si sentia/ mucho no poder comulgar - como lo asia antes dije que si que si me/ tenia ocupada la obediensia - que abia de aser dise comulga espirit-/ ualmente -postrate al eterno padre - y di la confesion y asi lo podras/ aser - sienpre andas disiendo no quiero esto si quiero el otro quitame/ esto y un poquito que te a faltado lo sientes - - -

(E from 45r) despues serca de la orasion me puse delante de una ymajen del desen-/ dimiento que esta en un claustro y bi de alla en una altura grandisima/ en un trono - las tres dibinas personas aunque no las bia claramente/ a la birjen que estaba alli mui serca la bia mui claro y desian que mirase/ aquellos nuebe coros de angeles que desde alli desendia y a todos los demas coros/ y que todos cuantos estan en el sielo endando la orasion se postraban y que/ nuestra señora - les asia cortesia abajando la cabesa y que luego se bol-/ bian a sentar dije yo delante de dios se sientan en sillas disenme si/ que dios les ase esa mersed porque ellos lo trabajaron y ganaron - - -

diseme en este mesmo dia no fue benefisio el del abito que tanto bos Reusas-/ teys y queriays señal para aber lo de tomar ya tubisteys señal cuando/ mi capilla se quemo y no quise yo que lo Resibierays antes porque no os abiais/ de aprobechar no a sido benefisio la perseberansia que abeys tenido// (45v) siete años que a que benis a mi puede aser esto el demonio meteras/ en cuantos males ay si - - -

(E from 45v) despues en la siesta fuime al coro alli me ynquieto un temor grandisi-/ mo y aunque no bi nada mui bien eche de ber que era una señora monja/ que a algun tienpo que murio por entonses quiteme de alli a la ora de o-/ rasion bolbi y al punto la bi - en una ondura profundisima onde/ la e bisto otras beses y con esto [det] la bi claramente senta-/ da y un pie sobre otro como se solia sentar aca con un pedasito de to-/ ca en la cabesa y el Rostro mui negro alli la e bisto sienpre - yo estaba/ ofresiendo los trabajos del dia llamandome por mi nombre me di-/ jo como te olbidas de mi - y andas asiendo por unos y por otros dije/ yo sienpre te encomiendo a dios si mas no con el afecto que pide mi ne-/ sesidad aunque ayas ofresido el dia tanbien puedes ofreser por mi/ que dios no es Ratero por amor de dios te pido que con mucho cuidado/ y afecto te acuerdes de mi no nos criamos juntas y que me apligues/ sinco dias de tu trabajo ofresidos a las sinco llagas mira que padesco/ mucho y por sola la misericordia de dios me salbe y estube e-/ n un aprieto mui grande y a punto de condenarme yo nunca/ cunpli con mis obligasiones y aunque tube aquella enfermedad/ tan larga nunca entendi que me moria y asi no cuidaba mas/ que de mi mal y el deseo destar buena y asi no asia actos de/ contrision – si no en lo ultimo en esto enpeso la disiplina/ de la comunidad y ella descubrio sus espaldas y juntamente/ se asoto - yo estaba admirada de ber aquello y dise pues no los debo/ despues en la cosina la bolbia a ber alla en aquel lugar/ profundo que dije que le abian señalado asi todas las beses que la e/ bisto asido alli tanbien me dijo que poco nos llebamos yo y gra-/ sia que era una negra de una ermana suya que a uno a tres sema-/ nas que murio despues me dijo el señor que mirase el braso derecho/ con mucha atension y que con esta meditasion se me avian// (46r) fasiles los trabajos y bi solo el braso y mano con la llaga lastimadisima/ y todo el braso lo estaba mucho - - -

(E from 47r) domingo disenme entre otras cosas yo no quiero nada de bos sino que sea-/ ys agradesida abra tres meses algo mas o menos que me enbio a lla -// (47v) mar una monja que abia mucho tienpo que estaba mala de gota arte-/ tica y otros males que le abian echo muchos Remedios y tomado dos o tres/ beses jaRillos y nada le asia probecho enbiome a llamar esta enferma/ que sienpre se triscaba conmigo yo pense que era para algo desto y aunque lo/ abia Reusado ube de yr y pideme que por amor de dios le diga unos cre-/ dos en la parte enferma yo le dije que no sabia aser aquello que una mon-/ ja que sabia de aquello la traeria para que lo ysiera y esto por ecsimirme/ mas ella - porfio tanto algunos dias que me estube escusando mas como/ lo pedia por amor de dios no me pude reusar ysele unas cruses e[n] non-/ bre de la santisima trinidad - y no se si abe maria o paternoster/ no e cuidado mas desto que si no fuera [det] tube por tenta-sion la/ desta monja o que me tentaba a mi [det] pues disenme a mi que si no/ fue benefisio aber sanado [det] que con tantos Remedios como/ le abian echo nada le abia aprobechado - y que esta Relijiosa non-/ brandola por su nonbre lo abia dicho a sus parientas abia estado u-/ na dellas mui mala y no asia sino enbiarme a llamar y yo como/ entendi para que era no quise yr — yo y entrando en la puerta una er-/ mana desta que emos dicho diseme ensalbame esta si en que me duele/ yo dijele que no sabia aser aquello y fuime de alli - despues mui descui-/ dada de todo esto - cuando fui a la orasion sacanme todo esto tan-/ bien me dijo que a no aber sido esto estubiera [a]tendida como las demas/ olbideme de desir el prinsi-pio que asi que me Recoji dentro de mi me a-/ Rancaron con tanta fuersa que fue ynposible Resistirme y ponen-/ me en otra parte de lo que yo llebaba - - -

(E from 48r) juebes un rratito que tubeme entre en un confisonario y como estaba tan/ cansada senteme aRincando las espaldas a la pared frontera y luego bi a-/ ca delante al señor dije como esto si esta aca detras esto fue ynterior que sien-/ pre mis preguntas y Repuestas son asi - diseme no se quien solo dios se be asi/ porque esta aqui y en potosi y en españa y enpiesame a encarnar todo el/ mundo y ultimamente que esta en el purgatorio y en el ynfierno que lo estaba/ mirando que si pudiera yo ber de la otra parte de la pared lo que pasaba - / aunque ubiera jente.//

(48v) biernes a medio dia Repartiendo una pitansa que me cupo llego una/ muchacha a cobrar de comer y tomando su olla misma se de-/ bio de deRamar lo que llebaba y dijo que yo la abia quemado y sobre esto dijo/ cuanto quiso - y con la grasia de dios no le dije palabra mas de que no le a-/ bia echo nada ni me abia pasado por el pensamiento aserle ni a un gato/ base de alli y biene su madre - con la demanda asiendo un gran caramillo/ yse lo mismo que con su yja despues que paso esta batalla bolbime a dios y dije/ le bien sabeys señor que no fue mi intension

aser mal a nadie dise a mi/ me pisaron la Ropa y los pies y la cabesa no Respondi
palabra y si tru-/ jerays presente mi pasion todo se [det] fasil y no os apurarays
tan-/ to - como estaban tantas juntas [det] me pisando y gotando sobre/ mi el
locro yo me estaba apurando [det] ales o pasa por aqui delan-/ te pensad - la caridad con que buestro padre san francisco serbia a todos o a/ buestra madre santa
clara yo mui [det] beo como lo asyes bos con bues-/ tros ermanos y mis yjos dije
entre mi por onde beo por el techo dise no es-/ toy yo en toda parte no me bisteys
antaño con cuatro caras mira a-/ qui alli y a todas partes no ay cosa que yo no bea
por pequeña que sea y por es-/ condida que este a la tarde Reprentaseme con la
crus a cuestas bes-/ tido de morado dije no es menester ber crus para aser buestra
bolun-/ tad dadme lus para conoserla y grasia y fuersas para poner la por o-/ bra
- aqui no ablo mas abia dicho antes que era menester armarse/ de mucha fort-
alesa para las ocasiones - - -

(E from 53r) estando adorando al señor que tenia en frente y postrada -
llebanme la bista a un lado/ del coro - donde bi sentada en un banco una monja
que a mas de quinse años que murio/ yo espanteme - y pregunte que era aquello
abiendo tanto tienpo disenme que como la cojio/ la muerte sin aber echo penitensia -sino la cojio en sus entretenimientos que pa-/ ra yr al sielo se purificaban
como el oro y que abian destar como un christal - // (53v) que aca si les mandan
quitar aquello o es otro no disiendo deste modo cuantos defectos/ ay en esta
comunidad y que desian a cada cosa que es esto y nada enmendaban -/ ni
obedesian ni quedaron puntas ni camas [det] ni nada todo lo Refirieron uno por
uno/ y que con los seglares no abia tanto - que aser – que estaba esta difunta
sentada en un escaño/ junto a la puerta del coro - y con una lusesita delante tenia
su propio Rostro el tocado/ bajo como las entierran - los ojos bajos - las manos
como de la muerte de solos gue/sos el abito como desenteRado - y estando
postrada asia laltal me llebaron la/ bista por mas de media ora que las tube
mirando - tomo el canto de una man-/ ga y se cubrio la una mano – y con la mano
abierta tiro la otra manga y se cu-/ brio la otra – y dije al anjel de mi guarda
porque me trayan a mi aquello y dijo/ que para que la encomendara a dios y la
[det] e dar aunque tube mucho te-/ mor no fue como otras beses- que me [det] ba
con dios con esta/ bision me olbide de muchas cosas [det] yo adoro a mi señor/ –
jesuchristo – que los temores que yo tengo [det] y que aquello lo permite/ dios
por sus secretos juisios – que si binieran [det] que me biesen seria/ segunda - - -

Notes

1.Planta trepadora y enredadera.
2."Porque los professores de Religión verdadera celebran sus fiestas, no con lascivias
torpes, sino con *conciencia* pura" (*DA*, 2:474).

Glossary of Terms

abbess: The female superior of a convent of nuns in certain orders.

Advent: The season immediately preceding Christmas and lasting four weeks.

alb: A full-length vestment worn by a priest. Has close-fitting sleeves and can be confined by a girdle.

ama/o: Female or male master of a slave.

ánima sola: Literally, lost soul. A soul without family connections in purgatory.

aposento: A room or small apartment in a building.

arrobamiento: A state of ecstasy.

Audiencia: A high court of the Spanish colonial state; also the territorial jurisdiction served by that court and within the viceroyalty.

auto-de-fé: Literally, an act of faith. A public procession where the Inquisition proclaims the punishments of transgressors. Often the condemned are paraded through the streets.

beata: A lay pious woman who took informal religious vows.

beaterio: Community or house of women living under informal religious vows.

beatification: A papal decree that declares the candidate to be "Blessed" and honors that individual's public cult. The formal process involves gathering testimonies after the death of that person showing their virtues and miracles.

bozal: A recently arrived African slave, who presumably is unbaptized and unfamiliar with the Spanish language and customs.

calenda: The part of the martyrology that treats the lives of the saints of that day. Also, from Roman times, the first day of each month.

calidad: Individual's social standing or rank based on religion, race, ethnicity, gender, legitimacy, personal virtue, occupation, wealth, and relationship to others (for example, as father or mother).

capellanías: (chaplaincies). Capital and its interest invested in a pious work and in the custody of a priest. An example would be a certain number of masses to be said on behalf of a deceased family member.

carta de libertad: A letter of freedom drawn up to legitimate the manumission of the slave.

casta: Person of non-European ancestry; especially a person of mixed Indian, African, and European ancestry.

celadora: A female warden in the convent.

chaplain: A priest assigned to say masses on behalf of the deceased and in charge of a chaplaincy (*capellanía*).

chasuble: The outermost ecclesiastical garment in the form of a wide sleeveless cloak worn by a priest.

choir: An enclosed or screened-off area, usually with two levels (upper and lower choir), adjacent to the church of a convent, from which enclosed nuns could attend mass without being seen by others.

ciborium [sagrario]: A covered goblet-shaped ecclesiastical vessel that holds the consecrated wafers of the Eucharist (the *host*).

clarisas: Nuns of the Franciscan Order of Saint Clare.

cofradía: Religious sodality or confraternity established to promote a particular devotion among the lay populace. A member was a *cofrade*.

colegios: Schools for daughters of the elite. In some instances, used interchangeably with *recogimientos*.

conventos grandes: Colloquial term for the largest, most populous colonial convents in Lima (for example, La Concepción, La Encarnación, and Santa Clara), as distinct from the relatively small, observant ones (for example, El Prado or Santa Ana).

conventos recoletos: Convents with a small population, strict vows of obedience and poverty, and only minimal contact with people in secular society. Also called observant convents.

Corpus Christi: A Catholic festival to honor the Eucharist. A movable feast, usually in June.

criada: A servant.

criollo/a: American-born person of Spanish or African descent.

crónicas conventuales: Chronicles or histories written by members of a *regular order.*

cuarterona: A woman of one-quarter non-Spanish blood.

dalmatic: An outer vestment worn by a priest.

definidora: An advisor who may have served previously as abbess, who accompanied the current abbess on her duties and discussed internal administrative matters with her in council. The Convent of Santa Clara had four at any given time.

Divine Majesty: A formal term for God.

Divine Office: The daily canonical hours of prayer.

donada/o: A female or male convent servant who professed simple vows. Females usually brought a small dowry. Nearly always a person of color.

educandas: Girls educated in convent schools.

encomienda: A grant of authority over a group (ethnicity) of native Andeans. The *encomendero* (the holder of this grant) had the responsibility to Christianize and provide military protection for the Indians, in exchange for their labor and services.

enfermera: A nun who administered or assisted in the convent infirmary.

ensalmadora: Literally, those who cured with psalms and assisted in the healing process of the infirm.

Epiphany: Held on January 6 and also known as "The Day of the Kings," when the three Magi arrived to venerate the newborn Christ.

escuchas: Those nuns charged with listening to conversations in the public spaces of the convent, particularly the parlors or *locutorios.*

Eucharist: The central act of worship and sacrament of the Christian church, in which communicants receive the consecrated wafer (the *host*).

Franciscan: A male or female member of the regular Order of Saint Francis of Assisi.

friar: A male member of the *regular clergy*, who went through training and a novitiate (probationary period) and then professed solemn vows of poverty, chastity, and obedience.

general confession: A private confession to a priest of all the sins committed throughout one's life.

hair shirt [cilicio]: A strap, woven of horsehair or other coarse material, sometimes bearing thorns or metal barbs; it was wound tightly around a part of the body under clothing and used for the practice of *mortification* of the body.

Holy Commandments: The Ten Commandments.

Holy Spirit: The third member of the *Holy Trinity*, also known as the Holy Ghost.

Holy Trinity: The union of the Father (God), Son (Jesus Christ), and Holy Ghost (Spirit).

Holy Week: The week before Easter and part of the Passion of Jesus Christ commemorated by Catholics.

Host: A round wafer made from unleavened bread, which symbolically represents the body of Christ.

Immaculate Conception: The belief that the offspring conceived is free of original sin through divine grace. In the seventeenth century, a cult venerated by the members of the Franciscan Order.

india: Native Andean female. Term created by Spaniards to encompass people of pure Andean ancestry.

indulgence: A granting of remission of punishment, especially of purgatorial atonement.

infraoctave: The eight-day period following a religious festival.

jornalero: An individual who earns a daily wage.

Last Judgment: The final judgment of mankind (both living and dead) before God at the end of the world.

Last Supper: A supper partaken by Christ and his disciples on the night of his betrayal by Judas to the Roman authorities.

locutorio: Visitors' parlor in the convent.

madrina: A godmother by baptism. Also used as a term of affection among women.

matins: A liturgical office, which together with the *lauds* forms the first, and chief of the canonical hours. It includes the recitation of psalms and other scriptural and patristic readings, hymns, and prayers.

mestizo: Usually a person of mixed Spanish and Indian ancestry.

monstrance [custodia]: A receptacle in which the consecrated *host* is held and displayed, either at the altar or in a religious procession.

moradas: Deepening levels of mystical experience as defined by Saint Teresa of Avila.

morena: A casta woman of predominantly African descent.

mortification: The practice of disciplining the physical appetites and submitting the body to rigorous and often painful procedures, as a way to achieve detachment from earthly desires, to imitate the sufferings of Christ's Passion, and to attain spiritual perfection.

mulato/a: A man or woman of mixed African and European ancestry; like Indians, subject to the tribute tax.

negra criolla: An American-born woman of African descent.

novitiate: The period of training required of a novice; also, the part of the convent where novices live.

oidor: A judge on the high court (*Audiencia*).

Palm Sunday: The Sunday before Easter, and the second Sunday of the *Passion* of Christ.

parda: A woman of African and Spanish descent, usually darker than a *mulata*.

Passion: The redemptive suffering of Christ from the agony in the garden of Gesthemane until his death by crucifixion at Calvary. Strictly speaking, any receptive experience of suffering felt in Christ's body, soul, external or internal faculties.

paten: A plate used in the Eucharistic service on which the consecrated *host* is placed for the Offertory.

pena de daño: The suffering experienced by a soul in purgatory that is unable to reach God.

pena de sentido: The physical suffering experienced by a soul in purgatory.

Porciuncula: A Franciscan holiday at the beginning of August when food and goods are distributed to the poor.

portera (portress): The nun in charge of guarding the main entrances to the convent.

prelada: A term used synonymously with the abbess.

provisora: The nun in charge of purchasing and dispensing provisions.

refitolera: The nun in charge of the kitchen and refectory.

regular clergy: One of two divisions within the Catholic Church (the other being the *secular clergy*). It consisted of priests, friars, and monks who were members of a religious order. Specific orders, such as the Franciscan, required its members to follow special rules of life, or *regula*, hence the origin of the term "regulars."

retablo: An altar screen.

rosary: A series of Hail Marys, Our Fathers, and Glory be to the Father prayers said on a series of strung beads. In addition to the prayers, fifteen mysteries (three sets of five: Joyful, Sorrowful, Glorious) are meditations on different aspects of the lives of Jesus and Mary.

sacraments: Catholic doctrine has seven: Baptism, Confirmation, Penance, Eucharist, Holy Orders, Marriage, and Extreme Unction.

sacristana: A nun or donada in charge of making preparations to celebrate the Divine Office. This included preparing the candles, flowers, laundering and ironing the linens and religious objects that the priest officiating the mass would need.

scapular: A sleeveless outer garment of a friar's habit that falls over the shoulders. It may have been a badge of membership that consisted of two cloth squares connected by strings and worn over the shoulders and under the clothing.

secular clergy: One of two divisions within the Catholic Church (the other being the *regular clergy*). It consisted of clerics and priests who lived "in the world," *seculum* (from Latin), from which the term "secular" derives. They fell under the jurisdiction of the Spanish Crown.

seglares: Lay women and girls in convents, akin to the term *recogida*.

senos: Cavities, or levels thought to exist in purgatory.

siglo: Nuns used the term, derived from the Latin *seculum*, to refer to the secular world beyond their cloisters.

Society of Jesus (Jesuits): A religious order of active clerics, founded in 1540 by St. Ignatius of Loyola and dedicated to the promotion of the Catholic faith through education and missionary work.

spiritual exercises: Practices of contemplation, prayer, penance, and mortification used in religious retreats to train the soul in the way of perfection; the sixteenth-century *Spiritual Exercises* of St. Ignatius of Loyola were both representative of and a model for similar guides to specific procedures for such training.

suffrage: An intercessory prayer.

surplice: An outer vestment made of white linen worn by a priest.

tertiary: A member of a third order of the regular clergy. They take more informal vows and are not required to be cloistered. In Peru the term was synonymous with *beata*.

torno: A revolving window akin to a large, cylindrical lazy susan, where goods were received into the convent.

velo blanco: Literally, "white veil," the term for a half-dowry nun. Women in this category were second to the nuns of the black veil in their convent's hierarchy and ranked above donadas, servants, and slaves.

velo negro: Literally, "black veil," the term for a full-dowry nun (also known as a *monja de coro*, or "choir nun").

vespers: The evening before a feast day; the sixth and next to the last of the canonical hours; an evening service that is often musical in nature.

vestment: Liturgical ecclesiastical garment.

via purgativa (the purgative life): The purification and cleanliness of a soul while living. An extremely high level of spiritual development.

viaticum: The Eucharist, administered to a person about to die, to provide him or her with grace and strength (from the Latin for "provisions for a journey").

vicaria: The assistant abbess who also stands in for the abbess if she is away or indisposed; the vicaress in charge of ensuring the nuns follow the Constitutions and Rules of the Order. There is also a *vicaria del coro,* who was a senior nun in charge of the choir.

vice royalty: Until the eighteenth century in Spanish America, two main jurisdictional units in Mexico and Peru that were administered by a crown-appointed viceroy who served six-year terms.

Glossary of Important Individuals

Ana de los Angeles Monteagudo (Arequipa, 1602–86), Dominican nun of the Convent of Santa Catalina, who helped save souls in purgatory. Attempts to promote her beatification were not successful.

Ana de San Bartolomé (El Almendral, 1549–Antwerp, 1626), Carmelite nun and companion and nurse to Teresa de Ávila. After Teresa's death, she moved to France to found Carmelite orders there.

Angela of Foligno (1248–1309), Italian Franciscan tertiary, mystic, wrote Memorial and Instructions (dictated).

Birgitta of Sweden (1303–73), founder of Birgittine Order, wrote Revelations; a prophet and visionary.

Catherine of Genoa (Caterina Fieschi Adorno) (1447–1510), wrote Treatise on Purgatory and Spiritual Dialogue (posthumously recorded by disciples); hospital sister, teacher, mystic.

Catherine of Siena (1347–80), Italian Dominican tertiary and mystic, wrote the Dialogue and more than four hundred letters. During the summer of 1370 she entered a prolonged trance known as a mystical death, in which she had a vision of hell, purgatory, and heaven. A Divine command ordered her to leave her cell and enter the public life of the world.

Christina the Astonishing (Mirabilis) (1150–1224), an orphaned, peasant girl, at age twenty-one she had a severe seizure and was thought to have died. During her funeral Mass, she suddenly recovered and levitated to the roof of the church. She then landed on the altar and stated that she had traveled to hell, purgatory, and heaven, and had been returned to earth with a ministry to pray for souls in purgatory. Her amazing life was recorded by Thomas de Cantimpré.

Clare of Assisi (1194–1253), companion of St. Francis and leader of Franciscan sisters at San Damiano; founder of the Poor Clares; author of Testament and letters (Latin); vita by Thomas of Celano; canonized in 1255.

Estephanía de San Joseph (d. 1645), native to Cuzco and daughter of a Portuguese slave. Although Estephanía was freed, she had to defend her case before the Royal Audiencia. In Lima, she became a Franciscan tertiary and was well known for her piety and literacy.

Francisca del Santíssimo Sacramento (Pamplona, Spain, 1561–1629), originally from Soria, she took the Carmelite habit and then lived an isolated life in Pamplona. She wrote a number of revelations of saints and souls in purgatory.

Gertrude of Helfta (1256–c.1302), Benedictine nun and mystic. Author of The Herald of Divine Love and Spiritual Exercises (in Latin). An anonymous nun wrote her vita.

Hildegard of Bingen (1098–1179), Benedictine abbess and founder of St.-Ruper; visionary, prophet, theologian, preacher, composer. Author of numerous important theological works in Latin, including a treatise on purgatory.

Juana de la Cruz (Azaña, 1481–Cubas, 1534), Franciscan abbess, visionary, and mystic. Author of unpublished El libro del conorte. Antonio Daza wrote her biography (1610).

Luisa de Melgarejo Sotomayor (1578–1651), heralded as one of the foremost mystics of seventeenth-century Lima. A tertiary who was profoundly influenced by the Jesuits, wrote numerous notebooks on theology, and was tried and acquitted by the Inquisition (1622–25).

Lutgarde of Aywières (1182–1246), at age twenty she became a Benedictine nun, but the order was not strict enough. At age twenty-four she joined the Cistercians at Aywières where she lived for her remaining thirty years. She displayed the gifts of healing, prophecy, spiritual wisdom, and was an inspired teacher on the Gospels. Thomas of Cantimpré wrote her biography.

Margaret of Cortona (Italy, c. 1247–97), peasant, mother of an illegitimate son, later became an important Franciscan tertiary (1277). She developed a deep and intense prayer life, and in her ecstasies received messages from heaven.

María de la Antigua (Spain, 1566–1617), born in 1566 near Seville, took the Clarisa habit at thirteen years, in the Monastery of Clarisas of Marchena. Said to have written more than thirteen hundred notebooks of doctrine, dictated to her by God.

Martín de Porras (Lima, 1579–1639), a mulato saint. Apprenticed to a surgeon, he then entered a Dominican convent as a donado. He is renowned for his healing powers and visions. Was beatified in 1837 and canonized in 1962.

Rose of Lima (Lima, 1586–1617), Dominican tertiary and the first American saint. She modeled her life on Catherine of Siena and, during her lifetime, reached a high degree of mystical union with God. She was beatified in 1668 and canonized in 1671.

Virgin of Carmen: A Virgin that appeared at Mount Carmel, and who is known for helping to save souls in purgatory.

Works Consulted

Archival Sources
Peru
Archivo Arzobispal de Lima (AAL)

Causas de Negros, Leg. XII: 24.
Cofradías, Leg. XXXVI: 6.
Convent of Santa Clara (SC), Leg. I: 1, 33; III: 23; IV: 25, 42; V: 2, 20, 42; VI: 24, 32, 35, 37, 42; IX: 52, 70, 134, 149, 157; X: 16, 35, 72; XI: 25, 71; XII: 24, 27, 96, 99, 120, 181.
Visitas, Leg. 25, s.f.

Archivo Franciscano del Perú (AFP)

Registro 17.
 s.n. Marceliana de Caravajal, 357r–65v.
 no. 35. "Escritas de la Venerable Soror Gerónima de San Dionosio," 433r–36r.
 no. 38. "Sor Gerónima de San Francisco, Descalzas, 1635," 449r–78v.
 no. 41. Isabel de Porras Marmolejo, 1638, 506r–11v.
 no. 43. Estephania de San Joseph, 1645, 569r–73v.
 no. 45. "Vida de la Venerable Ursula de Jesús," 585r–607v.
Vega, Ana María. "Catálogo del Registro de Bienes Muebles del Monasterio de Santa Clara de Lima," unpublished manuscript.

Archivo General de la Nación (AGNP)

Protocolos
 Francisco Ramiro Bote, 230 (1602–4).
 Lopé de Valencia, 1927 (1615).
Real Audiencia, Causas Civiles, Leg. 42, cuad. 158 (1617).

Biblioteca Nacional del Perú (BNP)

C1313. Fernando Rodríguez Tena. "Origen de la Santa Provincia de los Doce Apóstoles," 1773.

Convento de Santa Clara de Lima (ASCL)

"Vida de la Hermana Ursula," Libro 5, 1928.

Spain
Archivo del Ministerio de Asuntos Exteriores (AMAE)

Santa Sede, Leg. 152.

Archivo General de Indias (AGI)

Lima 40.
Lima 94.

Archivo Histórico Nacional: Madrid (AHNM)

Inquisición, Lima.
 Leg. 1028, 1030, 1031, 1032.
 Leg. 1647, exp. 5.
Inquisición, Toledo.
 Leg. 104, exp. 5, 1564–65.

Leg. 114, exp. 9, 1636.
Leg. 115, exp. 1, 1627.
Inquisicíon, Valencia.
Libro 937.
Inquisición, Censuras.
Leg. 4432, no. 19.
Leg. 4440, no. 18.
Leg. 4467, no. 11, no. 19.

Biblioteca del Escorial
Juana de la Cruz. *El Libro del Conorte.* 1509. Ms. J-II-18.
Vida y fin de la bienabenturada virgen sancta Juana de la Cruz. Ms. K-III-13.

Biblioteca Nacional de Madrid, Sala Cervantes (BNM)
Agreda, María de Jesús. "De la redondez de la tierra y de los abitadores deella." and "Describase la luz infussa." Ms. 9346.
Catherine of Genoa. *El tratado del purgatorio.* Ms. 21716.
Juana de la Cruz. "Autos y representaciones que se hacían en este convento de esta Santa y mercedes que por su intercesión hacia Dios a las monjas de él." Ms. 9.661.
Juana Bautista, embustera, llamada beata. Auto de Fé. Ms. 2031, 18728, no. 9.
Manuela de Jesús. "Confesión de Manuela de Jesús [hecha ante el Tribunal de la Inquisición, 1674]." Ms. 718, fs. 405ff. See also, Ms. 8180, 24–29.
María de la Trinidad. "Escritos de la Venerable Sor María de la Trinidad, 1630–1701, monja mercedaria de Sevilla." Ms. 2714, ff. 56–71v.
María de San José. "Carta de fray Félix de Jesús a fray Francisco de Santa María, remitiendo la información siguiente, sobre la vida de la Madre María de San José." Lisbon, 20 agosto 1627. Ms. 2711, fol. 5.
María de San José. "Mercedes y favores que Dios hizo a la madre María de San José." BNM, Ms. 2711, fol. 23.
Memoria de las misas que en sus testamentos y por las animas de Purgatorio y por negocios grandissimos a devociones particulares se dicen. Recopilados por el Ldo. Juan Garcia de Polanco. Madrid, 1625. Ms. 18728, no. 9.
Paredes, Manuel de. "Vida de la Venerable Madre Mariana de Antequera, Congreganta Professa, del orden de Nra. Sra. Del Carmen de la antigua observancia de Toledo." Ms. 10520.
Pazzi, María Magdalena. "Breve relación de la vida, muerte y milagros de la seraphica virgen y esposa de Christo . . ." Sevilla, D. Pérez, 1627. Ms. 2711, fol. 300.
Romero, Gregorio. "Exemplar primoroso de la perfección christiana, en la vida de la fiel sierva de Dios, Francisca María de la Hara, natural de la Ciudad de Huescar del Reyno de Granada." s.f. Ms. 7474.
Teresa de Jesús María. "Tratado de una breve relación de su vida que quenta una monja descalça carmelita." 1636. Ms. 8482.

United States
Nettie Lee Benson Latin American Collection (BLAC).
María Magdalena (de Lorravaquio Muñoz [1576–1636]). "Libro en que se contiene la vida de la Madre María Magdalena; monja profesa del convento del Sr. S. Gerónimo de la ciudad de México hija de Domingo de Lorravaquio, y de Ysabel Muñoz, su legítima muger." Ms. G94.

PRIMARY PRINTED SOURCES

Ahumada, Juan Bernardino. *Libro de la vida de la Venerable Madre Soror Leonor de Ahumada, Religiosa del Convento de Nuestra Señora de las Nieves de la ciudad de Córdova.* Seville: Juan de Ossuna, 1674.

Andrade, Alonso. *Órden de la vida para la eterna vida y nuevo arte de servir a Dios.* Madrid, 1600.

_____. *Vida de la Gloriosa Señora Santa Gertrudis la Magna.* Madrid: Colegio Imperial de la Compañía de Jesús, 1663.

Angela of Foligno. *The Complete Works.* New York: Paulist Press, 1993.

_____. *Vida de la bienaventurada Santa Angela de Fulgino.* Translated from Latin to Spanish by doña Francisca de los Rios. Madrid: Juan de la Cuesta, 1618.

Antigua, María de la. *Desengaño de religiosos, y de almas que tratan de virtud.* Seville: Juan Cabeças, 1678.

Antonio de Santa María, Francisco Xavier. *Vida prodigiosa de la Venerable Virgen Juana de Jesús, de la tercera órden de penitencia . . . en el Monasterio de Santa Clara de Quito.* Lima: Francisco Sobrino y Bados, 1756.

Arriaga, Pablo José. *Directorio espiritual, para ejercicio y provecho del Colegio del San Martín en Lima en el Pirú.* Lima, 1608.

Astorch, Maria Angela. *Mi camino interior.* Edited by Lázaro Iriarte. Madrid: Hermanos Menores Capuchinos, 1985.

Avila, Teresa of. *Escritos de Santa Teresa.* Biblioteca de Autores Españoles, v. 53. Madrid: Real Academia Española, 1952.

Bautista y Lanuza, Miguel. *Vida de la bendita Madre Isabel de Santo Domingo compañera de Santa Teresa de Jesús, coadjutora de la Santa. . .* Madrid: Imp. Del Reino, 1638.

_____. *Vida de la Sierva de Dios Francisca del Santíssimo Sacramento, carmelita descalza del convento de San Joseph de Pamplona, y motivos para exortar que se hagan sufragios por las almas de Purgatorio, hallados en los santos exercicios desta religiosa.* Zaragoza, 1659.

_____. *Vida de la Venerable Madre Catalina de Christo Carmelita Descalza, compañera de la Santa Madre Teresa de Jesús.* Zaragoza: Joseph Lanaja, 1659.

Boneta y Laplana, José. *Gritos del purgatorio y medios para acallarlos.* Zaragoza: Gaspar Thomás Martínez, 1699.

Bridget, of Sweden, Saint. *Saint Bride and her Book: Birgitta of Sweden's Revelations.* Introduction and translation by Julia Bolton Holloway. Newburyport, MA: Focus Texts, 1992.

Cantimpré, Thomas de. *The Life of Lutgard of Aywières.* Translated by Margot H. King. Saskatoon, Sask.: Peregrina Publishing Co., 1987.

Carrillo, Martín. *Explicación de la Bula de los difuntos en el qual se trata de las penas y lugar del Purgatorio; y como puedan ser ayudadas las Animas de los difuntos con las oraciones y sufragios de los vivos.* Zaragoza: Juan Pérez de Valdiviesso, 1601.

Cartagena, Teresa de. *The Writings of Teresa de Cartagena.* Translated and edited by Dayle Seidenspinner-Nuñez. Cambridge: D. S. Brewer, 1998.

Castillo, Francisca Josefa de la Concepción. *Obras completas.* 2 vols. Edited by Dario Achury Valenzuela. Bogotá: Talleres Gráficos del Banco de la República, 1968.

Castillo, Francisco del. *Un místico del siglo XVII: Autobiografía del Venerable Padre Francisco del Castillo de la Compañía de Jesús.* Lima: Imprenta Gil, 1960.

Castillo Grajeda, Joseph. *Compendio de la vida y virtudes de la venerable Catarina de San Juan.* 1692; reprint, Mexico: Ediciones Xochitl, 1946.

Catherine of Genoa. *Purgation and Purgatory, The Spiritual Dialogue.* Translated by Serge Hughes. New York: Paulist Press, 1979.

Ciruelo, Pedro. *Reprobación de las supersticiones y hechicerías.* Salamanca: Pedro de Castro, 1538.

_____. *Tratado en el qual se repruevan todas las supersticiones y Hechiceras.* Barcelona: Sebastián Cormellas, 1628.

Cobo, Bernabé. *Obras.* Preliminary study by Francisco Mateos. 2 vols. Madrid: Atlas, 1956–64.

Constituciones generales para todas las monjas, y religiosas, sujetas a la obediencia de la Órden de nuestro Padre San Francisco, en toda la Familia Cismontana (1639). Madrid: Imprenta Real, 1748.

Córdova y Salinas, Diego de. *Crónica franciscana de las provincias del Perú.* 1651. Reprint, edited by Lino G. Canedo, Washington DC: Academy of American Franciscan History, 1957.

Cruz, Francisco de la. *Tesoro de la Iglesia: En que se trata de indulgencias: Jubileos: Purgatorio: Bula de difuntos, ultimas voluntades i cuarta funeral.* Madrid: Diego Flamenco, 1631.

Daza, Antonio. *Historia, vida y milagros, éxtasis y revelaciones de la bienaventurada virgen Santa Juana de la Cruz de la Tercera Orden de Nuestra Seráfico Padre San Francisco.* Madrid: Juan Godínez de Millis, 1611.

Díaz, Nicolás. *Tratado del Juyzio Final . . . se hallarán cosas muy provechosas y curiosas.* Valladolid, 1588.

Difiniciones, y constituciones, que han de guardar la Abadesa, y Monjas de el Monasterio de la Sanctissima Trinidad, de esta Ciudad de los Reyes. Lima: Antonio Ricard, 1604; reprinted, Lima: Casa de los Niños Expósitos, 1759.

Echave y Assu, Francisco. *La estrella de Lima convertida en sol sobre sus tres coronas.* Antwerp: Juan Baptista Verdussen, 1688.

Félix de Jesús, María. *Vida, virtudes y dones sobrenaturales de la venerable sierva de Dios la madre sor María de Jesús.* Rome: Imp. Joseph y Phelipe de Rossi, 1756.

Ferrazzi, Cecilia. *Autobiography of an Aspiring Saint.* Translated and edited by Anne Jacobsen Schutte. Chicago: University of Chicago Press, 1996.

Gama, Leonarda Gil de. *Astro brillante en el Nuevo Mundo.* Translated from Portuguese to Spanish by Antonio del Riego. Manila: Thomas Adriano, [1755].

Gertrude, Saint. *Libro intitulado insinuación de la divina piedad.* Translated from Latin to Spanish by Leandro de Granada. Salamanca: Antonia Ramírez, 1605.

———. *Oraciones y exercicios espirituales, con la practica de los quales Sancta Gertrudis subio a la alteza de la Gloria: que possee oy en los Cielos.* Salamanca: Antonia Ramírez, 1604.

Gómez de la Parra, José. *Fundación y primer siglo: Crónica del primer convento de carmelitas descalzas en Puebla, 1604–1704.* Introduction by Manuel Ramos Medina. Mexico: Universidad Iberoamericana, Departamento de Historia, 1992.

González de Acuña, Antonio. *Rosa mística, vida y muerte de Santa Rosa de Santa María, virgen de la tercera Orden de S. Domingo.* Rome: Nicolás Angel Tinassio, 1671.

Granada, Luis de. *Libro de la oración y meditación en el qual se trata de la consideración de los principales mysterios de nuestra Fé.* Barcelona: Sebastián Cormellas, 1612.

Hansen, Leonard. *La bienaventurada Rosa peruana de Santa María de la tercera órden de Santo Domingo.* 2nd edition. Madrid: Francisco Nieto, 1669.

———. *Vida admirable de Santa Rosa de Lima.* 1664. Translated by Jacinto Parra. Lima: "El Santísima Rosario," 1929.

Hildegard of Bingen. *The Book of the Rewards of Life (Liber Vitae Meritorum).* Translated by Bruce W. Hozeski. New York and London: Garland Publishing, 1994.

Horozco y Covarrubias, Juan de. *Tratado de la verdadera y falsa prophecia.* Segovia: Juan de la Cuesta, 1588.

Ignatius of Loyola, Saint. *Exercicios espirituales.* Madrid: Imprenta de Tejado, 1858.

———. *Exercicios espirituales del glorioso patriarca San Ignacio de Loyola.* n.p., 1686.

Instrucción para remediar, y assegurar, quanto con la divina gracia fuere posible, que ninguno de los Negros . . . carezca del sagrado Baptismo, ordered by Señor D. Pedro de Castro y Quiñones, Arzbpo. de Sevilla, del Consejo del Rey. Lima: Geronymo de Contreras, 1628.

Jesús, Isabel de. *Vida de la Venerable Madre Isabel de Jesús, recoleta agustina, en el Convento de San Juan Bautista de la Villa de Arenas.* Madrid: Francisco Sanz, 1671.

Jiménez de Cisneros, Francisco. *Obra de las epístolas y oraciones de la bien aventurada virgen sancta Catalina de Sena de la órden de los predicadores.* Toledo, 1512.

Jiménez Salas, Hernán, ed. *Primer proceso ordinario para la canonización de Santa Rosa de Lima.* Lima: Monasterio de Santa Rosa de Santa María de Lima, 2002.

Juan de Ribera (or Jaime Sanchiz). *Relacion breve de la vida, virtudes y milagros de la humilde sierva del Señor y Virgen Sor Margarita Agulló, natural de la ciudad de Xativa, Beata professa de la Orden de San Francisco.* Valencia: Juan Crisóstomo Garriz, 1607.

Leandro de Granada. *Luz de las maravillas. [Segunda y ultima parte de las admirables y regalada Reuelaciones de la Gloriosa S. Gertrudis].* Valladolid: Juan de Bostillo, 1607.

Leite, Serafim, ed. *As primeiras cartas dos jesuítas do Brasil para o conhecimento da América.* Genova: Civico Instituto Colombiano, 1951.

Lewin, Boleslao, ed. *Descripción del Virreinato del Perú: Crónica inédita de comienzos del siglo XVII.* Rosario: Universidad Nacional del Litoral, Facultad de Filosofia, Letras y Ciencias de la Educación, 1958.

Lorea, Antonio de. *La Venerable Madre Sor María de la Santíssima Trinidad, religiosa de la tercera Orden de Santo Domingo, natural de la Villa de Aracena en el Arçobispado de Sevilla.* Madrid: Francisco Sanz, 1671.

Losa, Andrés de la. *Verdadero entretenimiento del christiano: En el qual se trata de las quatro postrimerias del hombre, que son muerte, juycio, infierno, gloria.* Seville: Casa de Alonso de la Barrera, 1584.

Manescal, Honofre. *Miscellanea de tres tratados: de las apariciones de los espiritus el uno: donde se trata como Dios habla à los hombres, y si las almas del purgatorio bueluen . . .* Barcelona: Geronymo Genoves, 1611.

María de San José. *A Wild Country out in the Garden: The Spiritual Journals of a Colonial Mexican Nun.* Edited by Kathleen A. Myers and Amanda Powell. Bloomington and Indianapolis: Indiana University Press, 1999.

Meléndez, Juan. *Tesoros verdaderos de las Indias: Historia de la Provincia de S. Juan Baptista del Perú, del Órden de Predicadores.* 3 vols. Rome: Nicolás Tinassio,1681.

Montalvo, Francisco Antonio. *El sol del Nuevo Mundo, ideado y compuesto en las esclarecidas operaciones del bienaventurado Toribio Arçobispo de Lima.* Rome: Imp. Angel Bernavò, 1683.

Morán de Butrán, Jacinto. *La azucena de Quito. . . La Venerable Virgen, Mariana de Jesús Flores y Paredes, admirable en virtudes, milagros y profecías.* Lima: Joseph de Contreras, 1702.

Navarro, Gaspar. *Tribunal de superstición ladina. Explorador del saber, astucia y poder del demonio.* Huesca: Pedro Blusón, 1631.

Oré, Gerónimo de. *Relación de la vida y milagros de San Francisco de Solano.* Edited by Noble David Cook. Lima: Pontificia Universidad Católica del Perú, 1998.

Ortíz de Moncada, Pedro de. *Declamación católica por las benditas almas del purgatorio, regulada por la doctrina de los concilios, y Padres, y de la más fundada Theología.* Madrid: Juan García Infanzón, 1692.

Palafox y Mendoza, Juan de. *Luz a los vivos y escarmiento en los muertos.* Madrid: María de Quiñones, 1661.

Pardo, Francisco. *Vida y virtudes heróicas de la Madre María de Jesús.* Mexico: Imp. Bernardo Calderón, 1676.

Pérez de Montalván, Juan (1602–38). *Vida e purgatorio de S. Patricio.* Pisa: Universitá, 1972.

Pérez de Moya, Juan. *Varia historia de sanctas e illustres mugeres en todo genero de virtudes: Recopilado de varios autores.* Madrid: Francisco Sánchez, 1583.

Pinelli, Luca (1542–1607). *Noticias de la otra vida y del estado de las almas en el otro mundo.* Translated from Latin to Spanish by Alonso López de Rubiños. Madrid: Oficina de Manuel Martín, 1757.

Proceso de beatificación de fray Martín de Porres. Vol 1. Proceso diocesano, años 1660, 1664, 1671. Palencia: Secretariado "Martín de Porres," 1960.

Pudenziana, Sister. *La chiave del cielo: Lettere di suor Pudenziana Zagnoni, mistica e visionario bolognese del XVII secolo.* Edited by Valerio Dehò. [Bologna]: Re Enzo Editrice, [1996].

Puente, Luis de la. *Vida maravillosa de la Venerable Virgen Doña Marina de Escobar, natural de Valladolid, sacada de los que ella misma escrivio de órden de sus Padres Espírituales. Valladolid: Francisco Nieto, 1665.*

Quiroga, Domingo de. *Compendio breve de la vida y virtudes de la V. Francisca de Carrasco del Tercer Orden de Sto. Domingo.* Mexico: Imp. Joseph Bernardo de Hogal, 1729.

Raymond, of Capua. *La vida de la bien aventurada sancta Catarina de Sena trasladada de latin en castellano.* Translated by Antonio de la Peña. n.p.: 1511.

Relación verdadera del Auto de la Fé, que se celebró en la villa de Madrid, a catorze días del mes de Julio deste presente año de 1624. Madrid: Diego Flamenco, 1624.

Riants de Villerey, Susanne de (1639–1724). *Vinte e cinco apariçoes de almas do purgatório.* Translated from French to Portuguese by María de Jesús. Lisbon: Gráfica Leira, 1949.

Rivadeneyra, Pedro de. *Flos Sanctorum, o libro de las vidas de los santos.* 2 vols. Madrid: Luis Sánchez, 1601.

Roa, Martín de. *Estado de las almas de purgatorio. Correspondencia que hazen a sus bienhechores. Meditaciones, y varios exemplos a este propósito.* Barcelona: Pedro Lacavalleria, 1630.

_____. *Estado de los bienaventurados en el cielo, de los niños en el limbo, de los condenados en el infierno, y de todo este universo despúes de la resurrección, y juyzio universal.* Barcelona, 1630.

Ruíz de Montoya, Antonio. *Silex del divino amor.* Edited by José Luis Rouillon Arróspide. Lima: Pontificia Universidad Católica del Perú, 1991.

Salinas y Córdova, Buenaventura de. *Memorial de las historias del Nuevo Mundo.* Lima: Gerónymo de Contreras, 1630.

Salmerón, Pedro. *Vida de la venerable madre Isabel de la Encarnación, carmelita descalça, natural de la Ciudad de los Angeles.* Mexico: Imp. Francisco Rodríguez Lupercio, 1675.

Santoro, Juan Basilio. *Discurso de los cinco lugares a donde han ydo y van las almas después que parten de esta vida.* Pamplona: Thomas Porralis, 1586.

Serpi, Dimas. *Tratado de purgatorio contra Luthero y otros hereges.* Barcelona: Hieronymo Margarit, 1611.

Siría, Antonio de. *Vida de Doña Ana Guerra de Jesús.* [1716]. Santiago de Chile: Imp. Universitaria, 1925.

Suardo, Juan Antonio. *Diario de Lima.* Edited by Rubén Vargas Ugarte. Lima: Imp. Vásquez, 1935.

Teresa de Jesús María. *Las obras de la sublime escritora del amor divino Sor Teresa de Jesús María, Carmelita Descalza del siglo XVII.* Critical edition by Manuel Serrano y Sanz. Madrid: Gil Blas, 1921.

Valdes, Joseph Eugenio. *Vida admirable y penitente de la V.M. Sor Sebastiana Josepha de la S.S. Trinidad.* Mexico: Imp. de la Bibliotheca Mexicana, 1765.

Venegas, Alejo. *Agonía del tránsito de la muerte, con los avisos y consuelos que cerca della son provechosos.* Toledo: Juan de Ayala, 1553.

Villegas, Alonso de. *Flos sanctorum. Tercera parte. Vidas de sanctos.* Toledo: Juan Pedro Rodríguez, 1588.

REFERENCE SOURCES

Barbeito Carneiro, María Isabel. *Escritoras madrileñas del siglo XVII: Estudio bibliográfico-crítico.* 2 vols. Madrid: Universidad Complutense, 1986.

Covarrubias Horozco, Sebastián de. *Tesoro de la lengua castellana o española según la impresión de 1611.* Edited by Martín de Riquer. Barcelona: S. A. Horta, 1943.

García-Villoslada, Ricardo. *Historia de la Iglesia en España.* 5 vols. Madrid: Biblioteca de Autores Cristianos, 1980.

Hanke, Lewis, and Celso Rodríguez, eds. *Los Virreyes españoles en América durante el gobierno de la casa de Austria: Perú.* 7 vols. Madrid: Atlas, 1978–80.

La Iglesia de España en el Perú: Documentos para la historia de la Iglesia en el Perú. Edited by Emilio Lissón Chaves. Vol. V, no. 23 (1619–29). Seville, 1947.

Mendiburu, Manuel de. *Diccionario histórico-biográfico del Perú.* 2nd edition. 11 vols. Lima: Imp. "Enrique Palacios," 1931–35.

Porras Barrenechea, Raúl. *Fuentes históricas peruanas: (Apuntes de un curso universitario).* Lima: Instituto Raúl Porras Barrenechea, 1963.

Real Academia Española. *Diccionario de autoridades.* Facsimile edition. 6 vols. Madrid: Editorial Gredos, 1963.

_____. *Diccionario de la lengua española.* 2 vols. Madrid: Espasa Calpe, 1992.

Serrano y Sanz, Manuel. *Apuntes para una biblioteca de escritoras españolas desde el año 1401 al 1833.* 2 vols. Madrid: Sucesores de Rivadeneyra, 1903–5.

SECONDARY SOURCES: BOOKS

L'autobiographie dans le monde hispanique: Actes du colloque international de Baume-lès-Aix, 11–12–13 mai 1979. Aix-en-Provence: Publications Université de Provence, 1980.

Alberro, Solange. *Inquisición y sociedad en México, 1571–1700.* Mexico: Fondo de Cultura Económica, 1988.

Antonazzi, Giovanni. *Catarina Paluzzi e la sua autobiografia (1573–1645): Una mistica popolana tra san Filippo Neri e Federico Borromeo.* Rome: Edizioni di Storia e Letteratura, 1980.

Araújo, Ana Cristina. *A morte em Lisboa: Atitudes e representações 1700–1830.* Lisbon: Editorial Notícias, 1998.

Arenal, Electa, and Stacey Schlau, eds. *Untold Sisters: Hispanic Nuns in their Own Works.* Translations by Amanda Powell. Albuquerque: University of New Mexico Press, 1989.

Ariès, Philippe. *The Hour of Our Death.* Translated by Helen Weaver. New York: Alfred A. Knopf, 1981.

Bernales Ballesteros, Jorge. *Lima: La ciudad y sus monumentos.* Seville: Consejo Superior de Investigaciones Científicas, 1972.

Blumenfeld-Kosinski, Renate, and Timea Szell, eds. *Images of Sainthood in Medieval Europe.* Ithaca, NY: Cornell University Press, 1991.

Bobo, Jacqueline, ed. *Black Feminist Cultural Criticism.* Malden, MA: Blackwell Publishers, 2001.

Bornstein, Daniel, and Roberto Rusconi, eds. *Women and Religion in Medieval and Renaissance Italy.* Translated by Margery J. Schneider. Chicago: University of Chicago Press, 1996.

Bowser, Frederick P. *The African Slave in Colonial Peru, 1524–1650.* Stanford, CA: Stanford University Press, 1974.

Braxton, Joanne M. *Black Women Writing Autobiography: A Tradition Within a Tradition.* Philadelphia, PA: Temple University Press, 1989.

Bromley, Juan, and José Barbacelata. *Evolución urbana de la ciudad de Lima.* Lima: Concejo Provincial de Lima, 1945.

Brownley, Martine Watson, and Allison B. Kimmich, eds. *Women and Autobiography.* Wilmington, DE: Scholarly Resources, 1999.

Burdick, John. *Blessed Anastácia: Women, Race, and Popular Christianity in Brazil.* New York: Routledge, 1998.

Bynum, Caroline Walker. *Fragmentation and Redemption: Essays on Gender and the Body in Medieval Religion.* New York: Zone Press, 1991.

———. *Holy Feast and Holy Fast: The Religious Significance of Food to Medieval Women.* Berkeley: University of California Press, 1987.

———. *The Resurrection of the Body in Western Christianity, 200–1336.* New York: Columbia University Press, 1995.

Cabibbo, Sara, and Marilena Modica. *La Santa dei Tomasi: Storia di suor Maria Crocifissa (1645–1699).* Turin: Enaudi, 1989.

Carmen Passarell, Elias del. *Vida de la Venerable Madre Sor Ana de los Angeles Monteagudo que florecio en el Monasterio de Santa Catalina de la ciudad de Arequipa.* Barcelona: Imp. de la Librería Religiosa, 1879.

Caro Baroja, Julio. *Las formas complejas de la vida religiosa: religión, sociedad y carácter en la Espana de los siglos XVI y XVII.* 2 vols. [Valencia]: Galaxia Gutenberg: Círculo de lectores, 1995.

Christian, William A. *Apparitions in Late Medieval and Renaissance Spain.* Princeton, NJ: Princeton University Press, 1981.

Cirac Estopañán, Sebastián. *Los procesos de hechicerías en la Inquisición de Castilla la Nueva (tribunales de Toledo y Cuenca).* Madrid: "Diana," Artes Gráficas, 1942.

Collins, Patricia Hill. *Black Feminist Thought: Knowledge, Consciousness, and the Politics of Empowerment.* 2nd edition. New York: Routledge, 2000.

Cope, R. Douglas. *The Limits of Racial Domination: Plebeian Society in Colonial Mexico City, 1660–1720.* Madison: University of Wisconsin Press, 1994.

del Busto Duthurburu, José Antonio. *San Martín de Porras (Martín de Porras Velásquez)*. Lima: Pontificia Universidad Católica del Perú, 1992.

Díaz y Díaz, Manuel C. *Visiones del más allá en Galicia durante la alta edad media*. Santiago de Compostela: Biblioteca de Galicia, 1985.

Dronke, Peter. *Women Writers of the Middle Ages: A Critical Study of Texts from Perpetua (†203) to Marguerite Porete (†1310)*. Cambridge: Cambridge University Press, 1992.

Eguiguren, Luis Antonio. *Diccionario histórico cronológico de la real y pontificia Universidad de San Marcos y sus colegios: crónica é investigación*. 2 vols. Lima: Imp. Torres Aguirre, 1940.

Eire, Carlos M. N. *From Madrid to Purgatory: The Art and Craft of Dying in Sixteenth-Century Spain*. Cambridge: Cambridge University Press, 1995.

Escandell Bonet, Bartolomé, and Joaquin Pérez Villanueva, eds. *Historia de la Inquisición en España y América*. Vol. 1: *El conocimiento científico y el proceso histórico de la Institución (1478–1834)*. Madrid: Biblioteca de Autores Cristianos, 1984.

Espinosa Polit, Aurelio. *Santa Mariana de Jesús, hija de la Compañía de Jesús; estudio histórico-ascetico de su espiritualidad*. Quito: La Prensa Católica, 1957.

Fernández Fernández, Amaya. *Santa Rosa de Lima*. Lima: Editorial Brasa, 1995.

Fernández Fernández, Amaya, et al. *La mujer en la conquista y la evangelización en el Perú (Lima 1550–1650)*. Lima: Pontificia Universidad Católica del Perú, 1997.

Few, Martha. *Women Who Live Evil Lives: Gender, Religion and the Politics of Power in Colonial Guatemala*. Austin: University of Texas Press, 2002.

García Fernández, Máximo. *Los castellanos y la muerte: Religiosidad y comportamientos colectivos en el Antiguo Régimen*. Valladolid: Junta de Castilla y León, 1996.

Gardiner, Eileen, ed. *Visions of Heaven and Hell Before Dante*. New York: Italica Press, 1989.

Geary, Patrick J. *Living with the Dead in the Middle Ages*. Ithaca, NY, and London: Cornell University Press, 1994.

Gertrude the Great of Helfta. *The Herald of God's Loving-Kindness: Books One and Two*. Translated by Alexandra Barratt. Kalamazoo, MI: Cistercian Publications, 1991.

Giles, Mary E. *The Book of Prayer of Sor María of Santo Domingo: A study and translation*. Albany: State University of New York, 1990.

Giles, Mary E., ed. *Women in the Inquisition: Spain and the New World*. Baltimore, MD: Johns Hopkins University Press, 1998.

Glave, Luis Miguel. *De Rosa y espinas: Economía, sociedad y mentalidades andinas, siglo XVII*. Lima: Instituto de Estudios Peruanos, 1998.

Gómez Nieto, Leonor. *Ritos funerarios en el Madrid medieval*. Madrid: Asociación Cultural Al-Mudayna, 1991.

Gracia Boix, Rafael. *Autos de fe y causas de la Inquisicion de Córdoba*. Cordoba: Excma. Diputación Provincial,1983.

Greenblatt, Steven. *Hamlet in Purgatory*. Princeton, NJ: Princeton University Press, 2001.

Guthke, Karl Siegfried. *The Gender of Death: A Cultural History in Art and Literature*. Cambridge: Cambridge University Press, 1999.

Hamilton, Alastair. *Heresy and Mysticism in Sixteenth-Century Spain*. Toronto and Buffalo, NY: University of Toronto Press, 1992.

Hine, Darlene Clark, Wilma King, and Linda Reed, eds. *"We Specialize in the Wholly Impossible": A Reader in Black Women's History*. New York: Carlson Publishing Inc., 1995.

Huerga Teruelo, Alvaro. *Historia de los alumbrados (1570–1630): Los alumbrados de la alta Andalucia (1575–1590)*. Madrid: Fundación Universitaria Española, Seminario Cisneros, 1978.

_____. *Historia de los alumbrados (1570–1630): Los alumbrados de Extremadura (1570–1582)*. Madrid: Fundación Universitaria Española, Seminario Cisneros, 1978.

_____. *Santa Catalina de Siena en la historia de la espiritualidad hispana*. Rome: n.p., 1969.

Ibsen, Kristine. *Women's Spiritual Autobiography in Colonial Spanish America*. Gainesville: University Press of Florida, 1999.

Imirizaldu, Jesús de. *Monjas y beatas embaucadoras*. Madrid: Editora Nacional, 1977.

Johnson, Lyman L., and Sonya Lipsett-Rivera, eds. *The Faces of Honor: Sex, Shame and Violence in Colonial Latin America*. Albuquerque: University of New Mexico Press, 1998.

Koslofsky, Craig M. *The Reformation of the Dead: Death and Ritual in Early Modern Germany, 1450–1700*. London: MacMillan Press, 2000.

Le Goff, Jacques. *The Birth of Purgatory*. Translated by Arthur Goldhammer. Chicago: University of Chicago Press, 1984.

————. *El órden de la memoria: El tiempo como imaginario*. Barcelona: Ediciones Paídos, 1991.

Lockhart, James. *Spanish Peru, 1532–1560: A Colonial Society*. Madison: University of Wisconsin Press, 1968.

Lorente, Sebastián. *Historia del Perú bajo la dinastia austriaca, 1598–1700*. Paris: Imp. Rochette, 1870.

Lorenzo Pinar, Francisco Javier. *Actitudes religiosas ante la muerte en Zamora en el siglo XVI: Un estudio de mentalidades*. Zamora: Instituto de Estudios Zamaranos "Florian de Ocampo," Diputación de Zamora, 1989.

Louvet, Louis-Eugene. *Le purgatoire d'après les révélations des saints*. Albi: Imprimerie des Appretis-Orphelins, 1899.

Mack, Phyllis. *Visionary Women: Ecstatic Prophecy in Seventeenth-Century England*. Berkeley: University of California Press, 1992.

Maggi, Armando. *Uttering the Word: The Mystical Performances of Maria Maddalena de' Pazzi, a Renaissance Visionary*. Albany: State University of New York Press, 1998.

Mannarelli, María Emma. *Hechiceras, beatas y expósitas: Mujeres y poder inquisitorial en Lima*. Lima: Ediciones del Congreso del Perú, 1998.

Marshall, Sherrin, ed. *Women in Reformation and Counter-Reformation Europe*. Bloomington: Indiana University Press, 1989.

Martín, Luis. *Daughters of the Conquistadores: Women of the Viceroyalty of Peru*. Dallas, TX: Southern Methodist University, 1989.

————. *The Intellectual Conquest of Peru: The Jesuit College of San Pablo, 1568–1767*. New York: Fordham University Press, 1968.

Martínez Arancón, Ana. *Geografía de la eternidad*. Madrid: Ed. Tecnos, 1987.

Martínez Gil, Fernando. *Actitudes ante la muerte en el Toledo de los Austrias*. Toledo: Ayuntamiento de Toledo, 1984.

————. *Muerte y sociedad en la España de los Austrias*. Mexico: Siglo Veintiuno Editores, 1993.

Matter, E. Anne, and John Waylan Coakley, eds. *Creative Women in Medieval and Early Modern Italy: A Religious and Artistic Renaissance*. Philadelphia: University of Pennsylvania Press, 1994.

McKnight, Kathryn Joy. *The Mystic of Tunja: The Writings of Madre Castillo, 1671–1742*. Amherst: University of Massachusetts Press, 1997.

Mesa, José, and Teresa Gisbert. *Historia de la pintura cuzqueña*. Lima: Banco Wiese, 1982.

Mitre Fernández, Emilio. *La muerte vencida: Imágenes e historía en el Occidente Medieval (1200–1348)*. Madrid: Encuentro Ediciones, 1988.

Monson, Craig, ed. *The Crannied Wall: Women, Religion, and the Arts in Early Modern Europe*. Ann Arbor: University of Michigan Press, 1992.

Montoya, Arturo. *Vida de la Venerable Madre Sor Ana de los Angeles Monteagudo, en romance castellano*. Lima: Imp. Seminario, 1939.

Morales, Ambrosio. *La virgen arequipeña, Sor Ana de los Angeles de Monteagudo y Ponce de León*. Arequipa: n.p., 1954.

Morgan, Ronald J. *Spanish American Saints and the Rhetoric of Identity, 1600–1810*. Tucson: University of Arizona Press, 2002.

Mott, Luiz. *Rosa Egipcíaca: Uma santa africana no Brasil*. Rio de Janeiro: Editora Bertran Brasil, 1993.

Mujica Pinilla, Ramón. *Rosa limensis: Mística, política e iconografía en torno a la patrona de América*. Lima: IFEA; Fondo de Cultura Económica; Banco Central de Reserva del Perú, 2001.

Muñoz Fernández, Angela. *Beatas y santas neocastellanas: ambivalencias de la religión y políticas correctoras del poder (ss. xiv–xvi)*. Madrid: Comunidad de Madrid, 1974.

————, ed. *Las Mujeres en el cristianismo medieval: Imágenes teóricas y cauces de actuación religiosa*. Madrid: Asociación Cultural Al-Mudayna, 1989.

Muñoz Fernández, Angela, and María del Mar Graña Cid, eds. *Religiosidad femenina: Expectativas y realidades, ss. VIII-XVIII.* Madrid: Asociación Cultural Al- Mudayna, 1991.

Muriel, Josefina. *Cultura femenina novohispana.* 2nd edition. Mexico: Universidad Nacional Autónoma de México, Instituto de Investigaciones Históricas, 1994.

Patterson, Orlando. *Slavery and Social Death: A Comparative Study.* Cambridge, MA: Harvard University Press, 1982.

Petroff, Elizabeth. *Body and Soul: Essays on Medieval Women and Mysticism.* New York: Oxford University Press, 1990.

———, ed. *Medieval Women's Visionary Literature.* Oxford: Oxford University Press, 1986.

Pons Fuster, Francisco. *Místicos, beatas y alumbrados: Ribera y la espiritualidad valenciana del s. XVII.* Valencia: Edicions Alfons el Magnánim, 1991.

Pou y Martí, José María. *Visionarios, beguinos y fraticelos catalanes.* Madrid: Ed. "Colegio Cardenal Cisneros," 1991.

Poutrin, Isabelle. *Le voile et la plume: Autobiographie et sainteté féminine dans L'Espagne moderne.* Madrid: Casa de Velázquez, 1995.

Ramos Medina, Manuel. *Místicas y descalzas: Fundaciones femeninas carmelitas en la Nueva España.* Mexico: Centro de Estudios de Historia de México, Condumex, 1997.

Redondo, Augustín, ed. *Images de la femme en Espagne aux XVIe et XVIIe siècles: Des traditions aux renouvellements et à l'émergence d'images nouvelles.* Paris: Presses de la Sorbonne Nouvelle, 1994.

———, ed. *Le corps dans la société espagnole des XVI et XVII siècles.* Sorbonne: Université de la Sorbonne Nouvelle–Paris, 1990.

———, ed. *Le peur de la mort en Espagne au siècle d'or: Littérature et iconographie (analyse de quelques exemples).* Paris: Presses de la Sorbonne Nouvelle, 1993.

Rodríguez Valencia, Vicente. *Santo Toribio de Mogrovejo: organizador y apóstol de Sur- América.* 2 vols. Madrid: Consejo Superior de Investigaciones Científicas, 1956–57.

San Cristóbal Sebastián, Antonio. *Lima: Estudios de la arquitectura virreinal.* Lima: Epígrafe Editores, 1992.

Sánchez Lora, José Luis. *Mujeres, conventos y formas de la religiosidad barroca.* Madrid: Fundación Universitaria Española, 1988.

Scaraffia, Lucetta, and Gabriella Zarri, eds. *Women and Faith: Catholic Religious Life in Italy from Late Antiquity to the Present.* Cambridge, MA: Harvard University Press, 1999.

Schmitt, Jean-Claude. *Ghosts in the Middle Ages: The Living and the Dead in Medieval Society.* Translated by Teresa Lavender Fagan. Chicago: University of Chicago Press, 1998.

Sebastián, Santiago. *Contrarreforma y barroco: Lecturas iconográficas e iconológicas.* Madrid: Alianza Editorial, 1981.

Segura Graiño, Cristina. *Los espacios femeninas en el Madrid medieval.* Madrid: Horas y Horas, 1992.

Silverblatt, Irene. *Moon, Sun and Witches: Gender Ideologies and Class in Inca and Colonial Peru.* Princeton, NJ: Princeton University Press, 1987.

Smith, Sidonie. *A Poetics of Women's Autobiography: Marginality and the Fictions of Self-Representation.* Bloomington: Indiana University Press, 1987.

Smith, Sidonie, and Julia Watson, eds. *Women, Autobiography, Theory: A Reader.* Madison: University of Wisconsin Press, 1998.

St. Jean, Yanick, and Joe R. Feagin. *Double Burden: Black Women and Everyday Racism.* New York: M. E. Sharpe, 1998.

Surtz, Ronald. *The Guitar of God: Gender, Power and Authority in the Visionary World of Mother Juana de la Cruz (1481–1534).* Philadelphia: University of Pennsylvania Press, 1990.

———. *Writing Women in Late Medieval and Early Modern Spain: The Mothers of Saint Teresa of Avila.* Philadelphia: University of Pennsylvania Press, 1995.

Tardieu, Jean Pierre. *Los negros y la Iglesia en el Perú, siglos XVI–XVII.* 2 vols. Quito: Centro Cultural Afroecuatoriano, 1997.

Thornton, John K. *Africa and Africans in the Making of the Atlantic World, 1400–1800.* 2nd edition. Cambridge: Cambridge University Press, 1998.

_____. *The Kongolese Saint Anthony: Doña Beatriz Kimpa Vita and the Antonian Movement, 1684–1706.* Cambridge: Cambridge University Press, 1998.

Tollo, Roberto and Elena Bisacci. *San Nicola da Tolentino e le Marche: culto e arte.* Tolentino: Centro Studi "Agostino Trapè," Convento San Nicola, 1999.

Torres Saldamando, Enrique. *Los antiguos Jesuitas del Perú: Biografías y apuntes para su historia.* Lima: Imp. Liberal, 1882.

Valerio, Adriana. *Domenica da Paradiso: Profezia e politica in una mistica del Rinascimento.* Spoleto: Centro Italiano di Studi Sull'Alto Medioevo, 1992.

van Deusen, Nancy E. *Between the Sacred and the Worldly: The Institutional and Cultural Practice of Recogimiento in Colonial Lima.* Stanford, CA: Stanford University Press, 2001.

Vargas, Juan Domingo. *Piadoso ejercicio: Para pedir la beatificación de la sierva de Dios, Sor Ana de los Angeles Monteagudo.* Arequipa: Tip. S. Quiroz, 1943.

Vargas Ugarte, Rubén. *Historia de la Compañía de Jesús en el Perú.* 4 vols. Burgos: Imprenta de Aldecoa, 1963.

_____. *Historia de la Iglesia en el Peru.* 5 vols. Spain: Burgos, 1953, 1958, 1959.

_____. *Historia del Perú: Virreinato, siglo XVII.* Buenos Aires: Librería Studium, 1954.

_____. *Historia del Santo Cristo de los Milagros.* Lima: H. Vega Centeno, 1957; 4th edition. Lima: [s.n.], 1984.

_____. *Vida de Santa Rosa de Santa María.* 2nd edition. Lima: [s.p.], 1951.

Vauchez, André. *Sainthood in the Later Middle Ages.* Translated by Jean Birrell. Cambridge: Cambridge University Press, 1997.

Vauchez, André, and Daniel Bornstein, eds. *The Laity in the Middle Ages: Religious Beliefs and Devotional Practices.* Translated by Margery J. Schneider. Notre Dame, IL: University of Notre Dame Press, 1993.

Vera Tudela, Elisa Sampson. *Colonial Angels: Narratives of Gender and Spirituality in Mexico, 1580–1750.* Austin: University of Texas Press, 2000.

Vovelle, Michel. *Les âmes du purgatoire: ou le travail du deuil.* [Paris]: Éditions Gallimard, 1996.

Vovelle, Michel, and Gaby Vovelle. *Vision de la mort et de l'au-delà en Provence d'après les autels des âmes du purgatoire, XVe–XXe siècles.* Paris: Armand Colin, 1970.

Weber, Alison. *Teresa of Avila and the Rhetoric of Femininity.* Princeton, NJ: Princeton University Press, 1990.

Weinstein, Donald, and Rudolph Bell. *Saints and Society: The Worlds of Western Christendom, 1000–1700.* Chicago: University of Chicago Press, 1982.

White, Deborah Gray. *Ar'n't I A Woman? Female Slaves in the Plantation South.* New York: W. W. Norton, 1985.

Wood, Jeryldene M. *Women, Art, and Spirituality: The Poor Clares of Early Modern Italy.* Cambridge: Cambridge University Press, 1996.

Zaleski, Carol. *Otherworld Journeys: Accounts of Near-Death Experience in Medieval and Modern Times.* New York and Oxford: Oxford University Press, 1987.

SECONDARY SOURCES: ARTICLES

Abreu, Laurinda. "Purgatório, misericordias e caridade: Condições estruturantes da asistencia em Portugal (séculos XV–XIX)." *Dynamis 20* (2000): 395–415.

Ahlgren, Gillian T. "Negotiating Sanctity: Holy Women in Sixteenth-Century Spain." *Church History* 64, no. 3 (September 1995): 373–90.

_____. "Francisca de los Apóstoles: A Visionary Voice for Reform in Sixteenth-Century Toledo." In *Women in the Inquisition,* edited by Mary E. Giles, 119–33. Baltimore, MD: Johns Hopkins University Press, 1998.

Alberro, Solange. "La licencia vestida de santidad: Teresa de Jesús, falsa beata del siglo XVII." In *De la santidad a la perversión, o de porqué no se cumplía la ley de Dios,* edited by Sergio Ortega, 219–37. Mexico: Ed. Grijalbo, 1985.

Álvarez Santaló, León Carlos. "El libro de devoción como modelado y modelador de la conducta social: el <<Luz a los vivos>> de Palafox (1668)." *Trocadero: Revista de Historia Moderna y Contemporaneo* 1 (1989): 7–25.

Amelang, James, and Mary Nash. "Los usos de la autobiografía: monjas y beatas en la Cataluña moderna." In *Historia y género: Las mujeres en la Europa moderna y contemporanea*, edited by James Amelang and Mary Nash, 191–214. Valencia: Ediciones Alfonso el Magnànim, 1990.

Arenal, Electa. "The Convent as Catalyst for Autonomy: Two Hispanic Nuns of the Seventeenth Century." In *Women in Hispanic Literature: Icons and Fallen Idols*, edited by Beth Miller, 147–83. Berkeley: University of California Press, 1983.

Arenal, Electa, and Stacey Schlau. "'Leyendo yo y escribiendo ella': The Convent as Intellectual Community." *Journal of Hispanic Philology* 13 (1989): 214–29.

———. "Strategems of the Strong, Strategems of the Weak: Autobiographical Prose of the Seventeenth-Century Hispanic Convent." *Tulsa Studies in Women's Literature* 9 (spring 1990): 25–42.

Atwell, R. R. "From Augustine to Gregory the Great: An Evaluation of the Emergence of the Doctrine of Purgatory." *Journal of Ecclesiastical History* 38, no. 2 (April 1987): 173–86.

Barriga Calle, Irma. "La experiencia de la muerte en Lima: siglo XVII." *Apuntes* 31, no. 2 (1992): 81–102.

Bilinkoff, Jodi. "Confessors, Penitents, and the Construction of Identities in Early Modern Avila." In *Culture and Identity in Early Modern Europe (1500–1800): Essays in Honor of Natalie Zemon Davis*, edited by Barbara Diefendorf and Carla Hesse, 83–100. Ann Arbor: University of Michigan Press, 1993.

Bloch, Maurice. "Death, Women and Power." In *Death and the Regeneration of Life*, edited by Maurice Bloch and Jonathan Parry, 211–30. Cambridge: Cambridge University Press, 1982.

Boyer, Richard. "Caste and Identity in Colonial Mexico: A Proposal and an Example." *Latin American Studies Consortium of New England, Occasional Papers*, no. 7, February 1997.

Brown, David. "No Heaven Without Purgatory." *Religious Studies* 21 (December 1985): 447–56.

Brown, Judith. "Everyday Life, Longevity, and Nuns in Early Modern Florence." In *Renaissance Culture and the Everyday*, edited by Patricia Fumerton and Simon Hunt, 115–38. Philadelphia: University of Pennsylvania Press, 1999.

Brubaker, Rogers and Frederick Cooper. "Beyond 'Identity,'" *Theory and Society* 29, no. 1 (2000): 1–47.

Bynum, Caroline Walker. "The Female Body and Religious Practice in the Later Middle Ages." In *Fragments for a History of the Human Body*, edited by Michel Feher, 1:161–219. New York: Urzone Inc., 1989.

———. "And Woman His Humanity: Female Imagery in the Religious Writing of the Later Middle Ages." In *Gender and Religion: On the Complexity of Symbols*, edited by Caroline Bynum Walker et al., 257–88. Boston: Beacon Press, 1986.

———. "Women Mystics and Eucharistic Devotion in the Thirteenth Century." *Women's Studies* 11 (1984): 179–214.

Cacciola, Nancy. "Through a Glass, Darkly: Recent Work on Sanctity and Society." *Comparative Studies in Society and History* 38, no. 2 (April 1996): 301–9.

Castañeda Delgado, Paulino, and Pilar Hernández Aparicio. "Los delitos de superstición en la Inquisición de Lima durante el siglo XVII." *Revista de la Inquisición* 4 (1995): 9–35.

Courcelles, Dominique de. "Les fictions de la mort ou le prix de la légitimité du discours dans le le Livre de la Vie de Thérèse D'Avila." In *Le peur de la mort*, edited by Augustín Redondo, 69–79. Paris: Presses de la Sorbonne Nouvelle, 1993.

———. "Les corps de hommes et les corps des saints aux prises avec la mort, dans les 'goigs' de Catalogne." In *Le corps*, edited by Augustín Redondo, 209–15. Sorbonne: Université de la Sorbonne Nouvelle–Paris, 1990.

Cussen, Cecilia. "La fe en la historia: Las vidas de Martín de Porras." In *Historia, memoria y ficción*, edited by Moises Lemlij and Luis Millones, 281–301. Lima: Biblioteca Peruana de Psicoanálisis, 1996.

Davis, Natalie Zemon. "Ghosts, Kin, and Progeny: Some Features of Family Life in Early Modern France." *Daedalus* 106, no. 2 (spring 1977): 87–114.

Ditchfield, Simon. "Sanctity in Early Modern Italy." *Journal of Ecclesiastical History* 47, no. 1 (January 1996): 98–112.

Doriani, Beth Maclay. "Black Womanhood in Nineteenth-Century America: Subversion and Self-Construction in Two Women's Autobiographies." *American Quarterly* 43 (June 1991): 199–222.

Durán Montero, María Antonio. "Lima en 1613: Aspectos urbanos." *Anuario de Estudios Americanos* 49 (1992): 171–88.

Edwards, Graham Robert. "Purgatory: 'Birth' or Evolution?" *Journal of Ecclesiastical History* 36, no. 4 (October 1985): 634–46.

Edwards, John. "Religious Faith and Doubt in Late Medieval Spain." *Past and Present* 120 (August 1988): 3–25.

Ehlers, Benjamin A. "La esclava y el patriarca: Las visiones de Catalina Muñoz en la Valencia de Juan de Ribera." *Estudis* 23 (1997): 101–16.

Estenssoro Fuchs, Juan Carlos. "La construcción de un más allá colonial: Hechiceros en Lima, 1630–1710." In *Entre dos mundos: Fronteras culturales y agentes mediadores,* edited by Berta Ares Queija and Serge Gruzinski, 415–39. Seville: Escuela de Estudios Hispano-Americanos, 1997.

Flores Espinoza, Javier. "Hechicería e idolatría en Lima colonial (Siglo XVII)." In *Poder y violencia en los Andes,* compiled by Henrique Urbano, 53–69. Cusco: Centro de Estudios Regionales Andinos Bartolomé de las Casas, 1991.

García Cárcel, Ricardo. "Cuerpo y enfermedad en el antiguo régimen. Algunas reflexiones." In *Le corps,* edited by Augustín Redondo, 131–39. Sorbonne: Université de la Sorbonne Nouvelle–Paris, 1990.

Goldey, Patricia. "The Good Death: Personal Salvation and Community Identity." In *Death in Portugal: Studies in Portuguese Anthropology and Modern History,* edited by Rui Feijó, Herminio Martins, and João de Pina-Cabral, 1–16. Oxford: Journal of the Anthropological Society of Oxford (JASO), 1983.

Gómez Acuña, Luis. "Las cofradías de negros en Lima (siglo XVII): Estado de la cuestión y análisis de caso." *Páginas* 129 (October 1994): 28–39.

Gómez Nieto, Leonor. "Actitudes femeninas ante la muerte en la Edad Media Castellana." In *Religiosidad femenina: Expectativas y realidades, ss.* VIII–XVIII edited by Angela Muñoz Fernández and María del Mar Graña Cid, 61–71. Madrid: Asociación Cultural Al-Mudayna, 1991.

Graziano, Frank. "Santa Rosa de Lima y el cuerpo sacrificial." In *Mujer y cultura en la colonia hispanoamericana,* edited by Mabel Moraña, 195–99. Pittsburgh, PA: University of Pittsburgh, 1996.

Greenspan, Kate. "The Autohagiographical Tradition in Medieval Women's Devotional Writing." *Auto/biography Studies* VI, no. 2 (1991): 157–68.

Greer, Allan. "Colonial Saints: Gender, Race, and Hagiography in New France." *William and Mary Quarterly* 57, no. 2 (April 2000): 323–48.

———. "Savage/Saint: The Lives of Kateri Tekakwitha." In *Habitants et marchands, Vingt ans après: Lectures de l'histoire des XVIIe et XVIIIe siècles,* edited by Sylvie Dépatie et al., 138–59. Montreal and Kingston: McGill-Queen's University Press, 1998.

Guillaume-Alonso, Araceli. "Images de la femme en Espagne." In *Images de la femme,* edited by Augustín Redondo, 319–30. Paris: Presses de la Sorbonne Nouvelle, 1994.

Guilhem, Claire. "La Inquisición y la devaluación del verbo femenino." In *Inquisición española: Poder político y control social,* edited by Bartolomé Bennassar, 171–207. Barcelona: Editorial Crítica, 1981.

Hamburger, Jeffrey M. "The Visual and the Visionary: The Image in Late Medieval Monastic Devotions." *Viator* 29 (1989): 161–82.

Hampe Martínez, Teodoro. "The Diffusion of Books and Ideas in Colonial Peru: A Study of Private Libraries in the Sixteenth and Seventeenth Centuries." *Hispanic American Historical Review* 73 (1993): 211–33.

———. "Universo intelectual de un "extirpador de idolatrías": La biblioteca de Francisco de Ávila (1648)." *Historia y Cultura* 22 (1993): 119–43.

Harley, Sharon. "When Your Work Is Not Who You Are: The Development of a Working-Class Consciousness among Afro-American Women." In *"We Specialize in the Wholly Impossible": A Reader in Black Women's History,* edited by Darlene Clark Hine, et al., 25–37. Brooklyn, NY: Carlson Publishing, Inc., 1995.

Henningsen, Gustav. "El 'Banco de Datos' del Santo Oficio: Las relaciones de causas de la Inquisición española (1550–1700)." *Boletín de la Real Academia de la Historía* (1978): 547–70.

———. "La evangelización negra: Difusión de la magia europea por la América colonial." *Revista de la Inquisición* 3 (1994): 9–27.

Heras, Julián. "El P. Fernando Rodríguez Tena (+1781) historiador franciscano del Perú (siglo XVIII)." *Archivum Franciscanum Historicum* 85 (1992): 581–613.

Herpöel, Sonja. "Bajo la amenaza de la Inquisición: Escritoras españolas en el Siglo de Oro." In *España, teatro y mujeres: Estudios dedicados a Henk Oostendorp,* edited by Martin Gosman and Hub Hermans, 123–31. Atlanta, GA, and Amsterdam: Rodopi, 1989.

Homans, Margaret. "'Racial Composition': Metaphor and the Body in the Writing of Race." In *Female Subjects in Black and White: Race, Psychoanalysis, Feminism,* edited by Elizabeth Abel, Barbara Christian, and Helene Moglen, 77–101. Berkeley: University of California Press, 1997.

Iwasaki Cauti, Fernando. "Fray Martín de Porras: Santo, ensalmador y sacamuelas." *Colonial Latin American Review* 3, nos. 1–2 (1994): 159–84.

———. "Luisa Melgarejo de Soto y la alegria de ser tu testigo, señor." *Histórica* 19, no. 2 (1995): 219–50.

———. "Mujeres al borde de la perfección: Rosa de Santa María y las alumbradas de Lima." *Hispanic American Hispanic Review* LXXIII, no. 4 (1993): 581–613.

———. "Vidas de santos y santas vidas: Hagiografías reales e imaginarias en Lima colonial." *Anuario de Estudios Americanos* LI, no. 1 (1994): 47–64.

Jaffary, Nora. "La percepción de clase y casta en las visiones de los falsos místicos en el México colonial." *Signos Históricos* 8 (July–December 2002): 61–88.

———. "Virtue and Transgression: The Certification of Authentic Mysticism in the Mexican Inquisition." *Catholic Southwest: A Journal of History and Culture* 10 (1999): 9–28.

Kieckhefer, Richard. "Holiness and the Culture of Devotion: Remarks on Some Late Medieval Male Saints." In *Images of Sainthood in Medieval Europe,* edited by Renate Blumenfeld-Kosinski and Timea Szell, 288–305. Ithaca, NY: Cornell University Press, 1991.

———. "The Holy and the Unholy: Sainthood, Witchcraft, and Magic in Late Medieval Europe." *Journal of Medieval and Renaissance Studies* 24, no. 3 (1994): 355–85.

Laplana Gil, José Enrique. "Algunas notas sobre espectros y aparecidos en la literatura del siglo de oro." In *Le peur de la mort,* edited by Augustín Redondo, 81–98. Paris: Presses de la Sorbonne Nouvelle, 1993.

Lavrin, Asunción. "Indian Brides of Christ: Creating New Spaces for Indigenous Women in New Spain." *Mexican Studies/Estudios Mexicanos* 15, no. 2 (summer 1999): 225–60.

———. "La vida femenina como experiencia religiosa: Biografía y hagiografía en Hispanoamérica colonial." *Colonial Latin American Review* 2, nos. 1–2 (1993) : 27–52.

Lohmann Villena, Guillermo. "Libros, libreros y bibliotecas en la época virreinal." *Fenix* 21 (1971): 17–24.

Loreto López, Rosalva. "Familial Religiosity and Images in the Home: Eighteenth-Century Puebla de Los Angeles, Mexico." *Journal of Family History* 22, no. 1 (January 1997): 26–49.

MacKay, Angus. "Mujeres y religiosidad." In *Las Mujeres en el cristianismo medieval: Imágenes teóricas y cauces de actuación religiosa,* edited by Angela Muñoz Fernández, 489–508. Madrid: Asociación Cultural Al-Mudayna, 1989.

Manero Sorolla, María Pilar. "Visionarias reales en la España áurea." In *Images de la femme,* edited by Augustín Redondo, 305–18. Paris: Presses de la Sorbonne Nouvelle, 1994.

Marshall, Peter. "Fear, Purgatory and Polemic in Reformation England." In *Fear in Early Modern Society,* edited by William G. Naphy and Penny Roberts, 150–66. Manchester: Manchester University Press, 1997.

McGuire, Brian Patrick. "Purgatory, the Communion of Saints, and Medieval Change." *Viator* 20 (1989): 61–84.

McNamara, Jo Ann. "The Need to Give: Suffering and Female Sanctity in the Middle Ages." In _Images of Sainthood in Medieval Europe,_ edited by Renate Blumenfeld-Kosinski and Timea Szell, 199–221. Ithaca, NY: Cornell University Press, 1991.

Milhou-Roudié, Anne. "Un _transito espantoso_: la peur de l'agonie dans les préparations a la mort et sermons espagnols des XVI et XVII siècles." In _Le peur de la mort,_ edited by Augustín Redondo, 9–16. Paris: Presses de la Sorbonne Nouvelle, 1993.

Millar Carvacho, René. "Falsa santidad e Inquisición. Los procesos a las visionarias limeñas." _Academia Chilena de la Historia_ 108–9 (2000) : 277–305.

Mitre Fernández, Emilio. "El sentido medieval de la muerte: reflexiones desde el prisma del siglo XX." _Anuario de Estudios Medievales_ 16 (1986): 621–30.

Miura Andrades, José María. "Formas de vida religiosa femenina en la Andalucía medieval: Emparedadas y beatas." In _Religiosidad femenina: Expectativas y realidades, ss. VIII–XVIII,_ edited by Angela Muñoz Fernández and María del Mar Graña Cid, 139–64. Madrid: Asociación Cultural Al-Mudayna, 1991.

Montagut Contreras, Eduardo. "Servicio doméstico y educación en los conventos femeninos del antiguo régimen (siglo XVIII)." _Torre de Los Lujanes_ 15 (1990): 156–66.

Mujica Pinilla, Ramón. "El ancla de Rosa de Lima: Mística y política en torno a la patrona de América." In _Santa Rosa de Lima y su tiempo,_ edited by José Flores Araoz, 53–211. Lima: Banco de Crédito del Perú, 1995.

Muñoz Fernandez, Angela. "Actitudes femeninas ante la muerte en la Edad Media castellana." In _Religiosidad femenina: Expectativas y realidades, ss._ VIII-XVIII, edited by Angela Muñoz Fernández and María del Mar Graña Cid, 61–71. Madrid: Asociación Cultural Al-Mudayna, 1991.

Muriel, Josefina. "Lo que leían las mujeres de la Nueva España." In _La literatura novohispana: Revisión crítica y propuestas metodológicas,_ edited by José Pascual Buxó and Arnulfo Herrera, 159–73. Mexico: Universidad Nacional Autónoma de México, 1994.

Myers, Kathleen A. "The Addressee Determines the Discourse: The Role of the Confessor in the Spiritual Autobiography of Madre María de San Joseph (1656–1719)." _Bulletin of Hispanic Studies_ 69, no. 1 (1992): 39–47.

————. "The Mystic Triad in Colonial Mexican Nuns' Discourse: Divine Author, Visionary Scribe, and Clerical Mediator." _Colonial Latin American Historical Review_ 6, no. 4 (fall 1997): 479–524.

————. "Testimony for Canonization or Proof of Blasphemy?: The New Spanish Inquisition and the Hagiographic Biography of Catarina of San Juan." In _Women in the Inquisition,_ edited by Mary E. Giles, 270–95. Baltimore, MD: Johns Hopkins University Press, 1998.

Newman, Barbara. "Hildegard of Bingen and the 'Birth of Purgatory.'" _Mystics Quarterly_ 19 (1993): 90–97.

Osorio, Alejandra. "'_El callejón de la soledad_': vectors of cultural hybridity in seventeenth-century Lima." In _Spiritual Encounters: Interactions between Christianity and Native Religions in Colonial America,_ edited by Nicholas Griffiths and Fernando Cervantes, 198–229. Lincoln: University of Nebraska Press, 1999.

Paniagua Pérez, Jesús. "Las décadas iniciales del Monasterio de Santa Clara de Quito, reflejo de su medio (1596–1640)." _Archivo Ibero-Americano_ 58, no. 229 (January–April 1998): 127–44.

Perry, Mary Elizabeth. "Beatas and the Inquisition in Early Modern Seville." In _Inquisition and Society in Early Modern Europe,_ edited and translated by Stephen Haliczer, 147–68. Totowa, NJ: Barnes and Noble, 1987.

Petroff, Elizabeth Alvida. "A Medieval Woman's Utopian Vision." In _Elizabeth Petroff, Body and Soul: Essays on Medieval Women and Mysticism,_ 66–79. New York: Oxford University Press, 1990.

Pons Fuster, Francisco. "Mujeres y espiritualidad: Las beatas valencianas del siglo XVII." _Revista de Historia Moderna: Anales de la Universidad de Alicante_ 10 (1991): 71–96.

Poska, Allyson M. "Matters of Life and Death in Galicia." _Mediterranean Studies IV_ (1994): 91–112.

"El Proceso de una seudo Iluminada: 1649." _Boletín del Archivo General de la Nación_ 17, no. 1 (1946): 33–73; 17, no. 3 (1946): 387–442.

Rábade Obradó, María del Pilar. "La religiosidad femenina, según los procesos inquisitoriales de Ciudad Real-Toledo, 1483–1507." In *Las Mujeres en el cristianismo medieval: Imágenes teóricas y cauces de actuación religiosa,* edited by Angela Muñoz Fernández, 435–49. Madrid: Asociación Cultural Al-Mudayna, 1989.

Rio Hijas, María Elena. "La sanidad en los conventos de clarisas de Madrid capital durante los siglos XVII, XVIII y XIX." *Archivo Iberoamericano* 54, nos. 213–14 (1994): 567–97.

Romero, Juan Ramón. "Morir en Madrid a finales del siglo XV. Economía monástica y mentalidades religiosas." *Anuario de Estudios Medievales* 19 (1989): 573–86.

Sánchez, Ana. "Mentalidad popular frente a ideología oficial: El Santo Oficio en Lima y los casos de hechicería (Siglo XVII)." in *Poder y violencia en los Andes,* compiled by Henrique Urbano, 33–52. Cusco: Centro de Estudios Regionales Andinos Bartolomé de las Casas, 1991.

Scully, Sally. "Marriage or a Career? Witchcraft as an Alternative in Seventeenth-Century Venice." *Journal of Social History* 28, no. 4 (1995): 857–75.

Shoemaker, Nancy. "Kateri Tekakwitha's Tortuous Path to Sainthood." In Nancy Shoemaker, *Negotiators of Change: Historical Perspectives on Native American Women,* 49–71. New York: Routledge, 1995.

Simons, Walter. "Reading a Saint's Body: Rapture and Bodily Movement in the Vitae of Thirteenth-Century Beguines." In *Framing Medieval Bodies,* edited by Sarah Kay and Miri Ruben, 10–23. Manchester and New York: Manchester University Press, 1994.

Smith, Sidonie. "Construing Truth in Lying Mouths: Truthtelling in Women's Autobiography." In *Women and Autobiography,* edited by Martine Watson Brownley and Allison B. Kimmich, 33–52. Wilmington, DE: Scholarly Resources, 1999.

Souza, Laura de Mello e. "Entre o êxtase e o combate: Visionárias portuguesas do século XVII." *Inquisicão: Ensaios sobre mentalidade, heresias e arte.* Anita Novinsky and Maria Luiza Tucci Carneiro, organizers. Rio de Janeiro: Expressão e Cultura; São Paulo: EDUSP, 1992.

Tardieu, J. P. "Genio y semblanza del santo varón limeño de origen africano (fray Martín de Porras)." *Hispania Sacra* 15 (1993): 555–74.

Uribe, María Victoria. "Los ochos pasos de la muerte del alma: La Inquisición en Cartagena de India." *Boletín Cultural y Bibliográfico* 24, no. 13 (1987): 29–39.

van Deusen, Nancy E. "The 'Alienated' Body: Slaves and Castas in the Hospital de San Bartolomé of Lima, 1680 to 1700." *The Americas* LVI, no. 1 (July 1999): 1–30.

―――――. "Circuits of Knowledge Among Lay and Religious Women in Early Seventeenth-Century Peru." In *Race, Religion, and Gender in the Colonization of the Americas,* edited by Nora E. Jaffary. Ashgate Press, 2005, forthcoming.

―――――. "Gerónima de San Francisco: Una mística limeña." In *Escritura y espiritualidad femenina: Semejanzas y contrastes en el mundo Iberoamericano. Siglos XVII-XIX,* edited by Asuncíon Lavrin and Rosalva Loreto López. Santiago, Chile: Biblioteca Barros Arana de Chile; Puebla, México: Instituto de Ciencias Sociales y Humanidades de la Universidad Autónoma de Puebla, forthcoming.

Vauchez, André. "Lay People's Sanctity in Western Europe: Evolution of a Pattern (Twelfth and Thirteenth Centuries)." In *Images of Sainthood in Medieval Europe,* edited by Renate Blumenfeld-Kosinski and Timea Szell, 21–32. Ithaca, NY: Cornell University Press, 1991.

Vinyoles, Teresa María, and Elisa Varela. "Religiosidad y moral social en la práctica diaria de las mujeres en los últimos siglos medievales." In *Religiosidad femenina: Expectativas y realidades, ss.* VIII–XVIII, edited by Angela Muñoz Fernández and María del Mar Graña Cid, 41–60. Madrid: Asociación Cultural Al-Mudayna, 1991.

Vitz, Evelyn Birge. "From the Oral to the Written in Medieval and Renaissance Saints' Lives." In *Images of Sainthood in Medieval Europe,* edited by Renate Blumenfeld-Kosinski and Timea Szell, 97–1145. Ithaca, NY: Cornell University Press, 1991.

Vovelle, Michel. "Les attitudes devant la mort: Problèmes de méthode, approches et lectures différentes." *Annales* 31, no. 1 (January–February 1976): 120–32.

Weber, Alison. "Between Ecstasy and Exorcism: Religious Negotiation in Sixteenth-Century Spain." *Journal of Medieval and Renaissance Studies* 23 (spring 1993): 221–34.

―――――. "Following Saint Teresa: Early Modern Women and Religious Authority." *MLN* 117, no. 2 (March 2002): 286–309.

_____. "The Paradoxes of Humility: Santa Teresa's *Libro de la Vida* as Double Bind."
Journal of Hispanic Philology 9 (1985): 211–30.

White, Deborah Gray. "Female Slaves: Sex Roles and Status in the Antebellum Plantation
South." In *Half Sisters of History: Southern Women and the American Past,* edited by
Catherine Clinton, 56–75. Durham, NC, and London: Duke University Press, 1994.

Zarri, Gabriela. "Living Saints: A Typology of Female Sanctity in the Early Sixteenth
Century." In *Women and Religion,* edited by Daniel Bornstein and Roberto Rusconi, translated by Margery J. Schneider, 219–303. Chicago: University of Chicago Press, 1996.

Unpublished Works

Cussen, Celia Langdeau. Fray Martín de Porres and the Religious Imagination of Creole
Lima. PhD, University of Pennsylvania, 1996.

Jordán Arroyo, María. Nacerá un romero en vuestras casas: Retórica e imaginación en los sueños
y profecías de una Madrileña en el Siglo XVI. PhD, University of Minnesota, 1998.

Lavallé, Bernard. Recherches sur l'apparition de la conscience creole dans la Vice-Royaute
du Perou: l'antagonisme hispano-creole dans les ordres religieux (XVIè–XVIIè Siècles).
2 vols. PhD, Universite de Bordeaux III, 1978. Reproduced by Universite de Lille III:
Atelier National de Reproduction des Theses, 1982.

Ramos, Gabriela P. Death, Conversion, and Identity in the Peruvian Andes: Lima and
Cuzco, 1532–1670. PhD, University of Pennsylvania, 2001.

Index

Illustrations are indicated in bold.